GOVERNMENT STATISTICS

FOR BUSINESS USE

GOVERNMENT STATISTICS FOR BUSINESS USE

Edited by

PHILIP M. HAUSER

Bureau of the Census, Department of Commerce

and

WILLIAM R. LEONARD

Acting Director, Statistical Office, United Nations

NEW YORK
JOHN WILEY & SONS, INC.
CHAPMAN & HALL, LTD.
LONDON

FOREWORD

Facts are important to a free enterprise system. They form the basis for many kinds of judgments: for business decisions, for policies deeply affecting the national welfare, for actions of individuals in the conduct of their own affairs. As economic and social affairs become more and more complex in the present-day world, facts become correspondingly more useful. Facts are indispensable and the availability of facts to all persons interested or affected is as characteristic of our democratic institutions as freedom of the press and freedom of assembly. Facts are not missing in totalitarian states—they are merely withheld from common knowledge. The well-known liking of most Americans for facts is probably a reflection of their profound regard for freedom in all its manifestations.

This volume outlines a great many statistical facts assembled by the Federal Government and emphasizes their availability to potential users.

STATISTICS AS FACTS

To understand what statistics is (or are) one must first ascertain which of two meanings is intended. The word may refer, plurally, to statistical *data*, which are summarized items of knowledge; or it may refer, in the singular, to statistical *method*, a particular kind of orderly thinking. Statistical method is not involved in the present discussion; we will talk about statistical data. Perhaps statistics in this sense would assume a more familiar place in thought if the word were replaced by the term *systematized facts* or *systematized information*.

When I must use information supplied me by others in reaching decisions upon matters of importance, the facts are often set down in a written *report* where they may be studied and reexamined. Sometimes I need a single report upon a single fact or related group of facts. This conveys *intelligence*. Perhaps I am concerned with the promotional activities and plans of a single competitor; my intelligence about this is a principal factor in determining my own business operations. To that extent I do not need statistics, nor possibly even written reports. The grapevine may serve adequately my informational needs.

It is much more probable, however, that I have many competitors,

v

in my own and other industries; that I buy and sell in markets which
are subject to innumerable influences making for fluctuations of price,
supply, and demand; that I am subject to problems of labor supply,
wages, financing, obsolescence of equipment, and innumerable other
matters which fill my mind with endless detail. Individual facts may
then become too numerous for me to comprehend them as a whole.
Individual items tend to cancel each other out so that I cannot clearly
see the general tendencies and trends. I then need *summary information* upon which to base my judgments and actions; I need, in other
words, *statistics*.

Statistics, as summary information, are usually based upon reports
that embody a systematic process of collecting and transmitting facts.
Statistics can be justified only by some practical objective, some use in
formulating policy or guiding action by those who receive them.
However, there are limits to their utility in providing information.
Whereas intelligence may contain many facts about a single situation
(a particular market, a governmental policy, a military movement),
statistical method is unable to handle more than a few *kinds* of facts
in a single operation. But even intelligence may require statistical
summarization. Thus a report on its production by a company to a
trade association (this would be intelligence in the hands of a business
competitor) would fail to disclose general industrial trends. It would
not do so until it was brought together with similar reports from other
companies in the form of production statistics for the industry.

Both intelligence and statistics are indispensable types of information
for men of affairs in a complex world. If I wish to know the manpower
potentials of an enemy nation or the production of an industry, my
information must be in the form of summary figures, i.e., statistics.
If I wish to know the strategic plans of an enemy commander or the
prospects of restrictive legislation affecting my business, my information will take the form of intelligence. Both types of information may
be needed simultaneously and may be interrelated in their use; but
neither is ordinarily substitutive for the other, and to depend upon one
to the exclusion of the other would be unrealistic. Both are substitutes
for the "rules of thumb" and "hunches" on which decisions were based
in a more primitive state of social organization.

Because statistical data are essentially *summaries of individual reports* the needs for statistics increase both absolutely and relatively
to other kinds of information as the range of affairs to which they relate
becomes broader and more complex. Government, because of its large
responsibilities for the economic and social life of the nation, and business, because of its increasing scope, complexity, and sensitivity to

economic trends, are the principal users of statistical information. Without summary information, i.e., without statistics, both business and government would incur innumerable risks and many miscalculations.

THE GOVERNMENT AS A PRODUCER OF STATISTICS

The Federal Government is the largest producer of statistics in the world. As shown in detail in the following text many of the government's statistics are by-products of its own operations or of some regulatory function which it has assumed. Other government statistics arise from a specific demand where some organization, individual, or governmental body demonstrates a need for a particular statistical series. Although the government produces a large amount of statistical information upon an almost bewildering variety of subjects it is only one of several statistical collecting agencies. Trade associations, private research organizations, state and local governments, and universities are all important producers of statistical material, much of which is of direct and immediate use for business purposes. Generally speaking, these different mechanisms for the assembly of statistical information do not duplicate each other; for the most part they are complementary so that the whole statistical picture, as far as we know it at all, is loosely coordinated.

Despite this loose coordination there are frequent and sometimes perplexing problems involved in deciding whether the government should collect statistics or whether trade associations or other similar organizations should collect them. These questions involve decisions relative to the amount of responsibility the government should assume for functions that could be discharged by some other organization and decisions as to the responsibility of the government to provide at the taxpayers' expense information in areas of very limited general interest but areas in which a private organization is not equipped to collect the information. These two problems pose questions which are of mutual concern to business and government.

Trade Association Interest in Statistics. The very nature of trade organizations gives them a vital interest in statistics. Trade associations are created to serve the *common* interests of their members. These common interests are "factored out," so to speak, from the private competitive interests of each individual firm. Similarly, statistical data concerning the industry, needed by its members, are factored out from the records of individual concerns to provide pictures of the industry as a whole. It is obvious that statistics of their industries are the breath of life for the trade associations representing them.

However, the statistical needs of their members usually go further. Most industries are consumers of materials, finished components or supplies, or goods for resale, as well as producers of commodities or services. Their members need to know the statistical position of the industries from which they buy, to which they sell, or with which they compete as well as or better than they know the position of the group to which they and their individual competitors belong. Moreover, entire industries are often in a competitive position in relation to each other. Although a single trade association may be able to collect needed information from its own industry, it is usually not in a position to render its members a similar service for their suppliers, customers, or competitors in another industry.

As this is written, a letter just received from a trade association executive states the matter as follows: "The growth of our industry during the past 25 years has been such as to require more detailed information on production. At the present time the Bureau of the Census is obtaining detailed information on practically all of the industries with which we are competitive and, consequently, it is necessary that similar information is gathered so that statistics covering our industry may be compared with statistics now available for these other industries. We very much desire to have the Bureau of the Census undertake the gathering of statistics on a monthly basis in the same manner as the Bureau of the Census is providing data on competitive industries."

Again, the association is not always in a position to secure the data which are sought for its own industry. It may lack sufficient personnel or funds to undertake the task adequately. The membership may not be sufficiently inclusive to provide necessary coverage, or important firms may decline to cooperate. Some members may fear the disclosure of their own affairs to competitors. The association may then turn to the government to render the service which it cannot itself provide.

An industrial economist for a Federal Reserve Bank comments in a letter as follows: "Here in _____, we have had numerous opportunities to observe that private organizations frequently cannot, or will not, collect needed statistical information themselves because of a fear of the disclosure of individual firm data. This is particularly true in the case of industrial statistics relating in any way to financial considerations. Government, or quasi-government, organizations may have to collect some information on current operations because other avenues for the collection of such mutually desired information are not available."

The Government's Role in Collecting Statistics. Thus there are many reasons why business statistics are collected by the government even though (and sometimes because) there is an active trade association interest in seeing that the figures are available. The government frequently acts as a collector of information that cannot otherwise be satisfactorily obtained, even though this information may not be needed for the exercise of its own administrative responsibilities. Government statistics may serve the broadest public purposes, by the provision of periodic counts of the population or index numbers of the cost of living; or they may serve the needs of special groups whose welfare is in turn of public importance.

In relation to the range of governmental responsibilities and the variety of public interests exerting pressure on the government for data, its statistical activities seem fairly modest. By these standards there is no "avalanche" of published government statistics, nor an antecedent "deluge" of government questionnaires. The almost universal opinion to the contrary results from a familiar fallacy. The "useless" statistics in such conspicuous abundance are those wanted by other people; there are seldom enough of the "important" statistics which *we ourselves* desire. If means could be found to ensure that statistical tables were never seen except by those who use them, the complaints of superabundance would be strikingly reduced, although the number of series might diminish scarcely at all.

As a matter of fact there is vigorous competition for a limited supply of governmental attention to the statistical interests and needs of the public. The activities of the Federal Government cover an enormous range and its own needs for information must come first in its statistical programs. Public demands for the collection of statistics are dealt with sympathetically, in an effort to serve the greatest good to the greatest number, but these demands are never fully satisfied. The fifty questions on the population schedule in the 1940 Census (16 of them addressed to a 5 percent sample of the people) were a highly culled remainder from among thousands of separate questions urged for inclusion by business concerns, civic organizations, other government agencies, and individuals.

The government, however, quite properly may and does compile and publish data which serve the general public interest chiefly by contributing informational tools to these same groups. Statistics are compiled to assist farmers in gauging their markets; to assist business in planning production, purchasing materials, and finding markets; to assist management and labor in negotiating wage contracts. Whenever a *sufficiently large number* of people will benefit, a plausible case may be established for the collection at public expense of statistics designed primarily for private use. If public and private needs for the data are simultaneously present the case will obviously be strengthened.

GOOD STATISTICS REQUIRE COOPERATION

Essentially government statistics are the result of cooperation in the fullest sense between business and government. Cooperation needs to begin at the point where government and business sit down together to decide what statistics are needed and useful and how they can be collected with a minimum burden upon those who supply the statistics. Fortunately there are mechanisms for this purpose. Several government agencies have established committees of leaders in business to advise the agencies as to what statistical programs would be most fruitful. Several trade associations have established statistical committees which work with the government in strengthening the whole statistical structure. These various mechanisms promise a greatly improved national statistical program comprised of segments of information collected by various government agencies, by trade associations, and by other agencies.

In the meantime, business will find it profitable to make all possible use of the statistics which governmental agencies are able and generally eager to supply to them. There need be no reticence by business in the matter. If in doubt whether information of a particular kind is available it often pays to inquire.

The Bureau of the Census, the Bureau of Foreign and Domestic Commerce, and the Bureau of Labor Statistics, among other federal agencies, are empowered by law to make special tabulations of unpublished information at the expense of the citizen who requests them, "expense" in this case meaning the *incremental cost* of compiling data. The original cost of collection has already been met by the Federal Government.

The principal criticism which may be levied against the current business statistics collected by agencies of the Federal Government is their lack of conformity to any single plan or program. Since most projects were established at the behest of business, the data collected generally reflect the needs of a particular business group for information; but they often cannot be related, each to the other or to any general summary of business data like that contained in the periodic *Census of Manufactures*. To the extent that these inquiries pertain to the minutiae of business activity, they must necessarily conform to the suggestions and desires of the business interests concerned since the government cannot ordinarily be staffed adequately with specialists in the many particular fields involved.

The data collected by individual business organizations also fail to show relationship with each other. What is principally lacking therefore is such a uniformity of scope and standards among the individual inquiries as would permit them to be summed up into coherent totals, useful for analysis of the national economy as a whole.

The attainment of a unified program will need the full cooperation of organized business and government. If this is achieved, we may confidently expect a growing integration of the statistical activities of the nation and a continuing adequate flow of data concerning the national economy.

STUART A. RICE
Bureau of the Budget
Executive Office of the President

PREFACE

This volume had its origin in an idea which occurred to Dr. Walter A. Shewhart at a meeting of the Committee on Applied Mathematical Statistics of the National Research Council in January 1944. During the course of the meeting of this Committee, which was also attended by one of us, it became evident that even the leaders of market research activities were unaware of the mine of statistical information available in the Federal Government for business use. On the basis of this experience, Dr. Shewhart concluded that a volume addressed to the business community indicating the major types of data available in the Federal Government for management, production, and marketing needs would serve a useful purpose. The transmission of this idea to us was responsible for the preparation of this volume.

The war produced great changes in the nature and volume of statistics available from the Federal Government. The war's aftermath will undoubtedly also bring about many changes. The general pattern of the statistics originating in the Government which business can use, however, will not change materially; and this volume will for some time serve as a useful guide to the Federal Government's statistical output.

As this volume goes to press there is pending a modification of the statistical program of the Bureau of the Census which will be of interest to the business community. The proposed new Census program may be briefly summarized as follows:

In the immediate future, if Congressional approval is obtained, the Census program will provide business for the calendar year 1946 with a complete Census of Manufactures, a Census of Mineral Industries, and a Census of Business (including retail trade, wholesale trade, and the service trades). It will also include a Sample Census of Population in the fall of 1946 or the spring of 1947 and possibly a Survey of Consumer Income which will report family income by size distribution.

In the longer run, the Census program, if approved by the Congress, will result in quinquennial censuses of manufactures, mineral industries, business, population (including the labor force and housing), as well as agriculture, in lieu of the present series of censuses which are taken at various intervals ranging from biennial to decennial. Moreover, the current statistical program of the Census Bureau, especially in the fields of manufacturing and business (retail, wholesale, and the service trades) will be greatly strengthened.

In addition, several other agencies are planning improvements in their statistical programs for the fiscal year beginning with July 1946. The Bureau of Labor Statistics is seeking to improve its information on labor productivity, labor requirements for construction materials, export and import prices, and on foreign costs of living and labor conditions. The Bureau of Mines is planning to improve its monthly, quarterly, and annual reports on light metals and to develop additional background information on basic trends in mineral economics. The Bureau of Agricultural Economics is expected to improve its reports on prices received and paid by farmers. The Securities and Exchange Commission and the Federal Trade Commission are cooperating in developing a financial statistics program to resume the pattern of financial reports which existed before the war.

In view of the importance of these pending changes it will be well worth the trouble of the readers of this volume to follow closely the results of pending legislation and appropriation measures.

We wish to express our appreciation to the various contributors for their excellent cooperation in the preparation of these materials under trying conditions. All of them had important official posts during the writing of the chapters and, because of the arduous nature of their wartime work, were able to complete their assignments only at the price of considerable personal hardship.

We also wish to acknowledge gratefully the cooperation and counsel in the preparation of this volume of Dr. Stuart A. Rice, Assistant Director in Charge of Statistical Standards of the Bureau of the Budget, and Mr. J. C. Capt, Director of the Bureau of the Census. Moreover, we wish to acknowledge with appreciation the substantial contribution of A. W. von Struve, who assisted in the editing of the materials; M. B. Ullman, who supervised the preparation of the index by Edna Munn; and Mrs. Ingrid L. Millison, Mrs. Helen P. Ballentine, and Mrs. Virginia T. Venneman, whose efficient services contributed materially to the completion of this volume.

P. M. H.

W. R. L.

March 1946
Washington, D. C.

CONTENTS

CONTRIBUTORS

FRANK L. BARTON, *Bureau of the Budget*

HOWARD G. BRUNSMAN, *Bureau of the Census, Department of Commerce*

MAXWELL R. CONKLIN, *Bureau of the Census, Department of Commerce*

WILLIAM W. COOPER, *Bureau of the Budget*

EDWARD T. CROWDER, *Bureau of the Budget*

WALTER F. CROWDER, *Bureau of Foreign and Domestic Commerce, Department of Commerce*

J. EDWARD ELY, *Bureau of the Census, Department of Commerce*

MILTON GILBERT, *Bureau of Foreign and Domestic Commerce, Department of Commerce*

FRANK HANNA, *Bureau of the Census, Department of Commerce*

PHILIP M. HAUSER, *Bureau of the Census, Department of Commerce*

LESTER S. KELLOGG, *Bureau of Labor Statistics, Department of Labor*

WILLIAM R. LEONARD, *Bureau of the Budget*

Y. S. LEONG, *Bureau of the Budget*

AUGUST MAFFRY, *Bureau of Foreign and Domestic Commerce, Department of Commerce*

H. B. McCOY, *Bureau of Foreign and Domestic Commerce, Department of Commerce*

LOUIS PARADISO, *Bureau of Foreign and Domestic Commerce, Department of Commerce*

STUART A. RICE, *Bureau of the Budget*

CHARLES D. STEWART, *Bureau of Labor Statistics, Department of Labor*

CONRAD TAEUBER, *Bureau of Agricultural Economics, Department of Agriculture*

PATRICIA VAN DERAA, *Bureau of the Budget*

CHAPTER 1

INTRODUCTION

PHILIP M. HAUSER

Bureau of the Census, Department of Commerce

AND

WILLIAM R. LEONARD

Bureau of the Budget

"If American business has been able to get along for one hundred and fifty years without statistics why does it need them now?" This was a question recently asked of the statisticians of a federal statistical agency by a prominent public official. Does American business need statistics? If so, why? The answers to these questions are to be found in the history of American business.

THE NEED FOR STATISTICS

Interdependence. The individual farmers and small businessmen who made up the bulk of the population of this nation in colonial times and in the postrevolutionary decades did not do too badly without, or with very little, statistics. They were the pioneers who cleared the land, tilled the soil, initiated domestic and foreign commerce, founded our industries, and gave birth to our political and social, as well as to our economic, institutions. These men, to whom we owe our heritage, accomplished much without statistics, without telephones, without electric generators, without railroads, without accounting machines, and without combustion engines. Can the modern American business-man do the same?

A negative answer to this question is no reflection on the modern businessman. This is merely another way of saying that the world has changed—changed in significant ways that have profoundly affected economic activities including the management of business and indus-trial enterprises.

Perhaps the most important single way in which our economy today differs from that of early America is in the degree of interdependence

1

of its units. The early average American was considerably more independent than his modern counterpart, in the sense that he was less dependent on other elements of the economy in the conduct of his own affairs. Early American society was relatively simple in its structure, comprising predominantly rural or village communities which were comparatively self-sufficient and which enjoyed relatively autonomous existence. In contrast, contemporary America is complex in its organization, is made up predominantly of cities, and is characterized economically by its minute division of labor and interdependence, not only within a national but also within an international framework. It does not require great elaboration to demonstrate that the supply of rubber originating in the Southwest Pacific and controlled in London may greatly affect the affairs of manufacturers in Detroit, Pittsburgh, Akron, and Toledo; of assemblers in Chicago, and of dealers in Dallas.

In the complex world in which we live today, the destiny of the individual entrepreneur hinges on many forces beyond his immediate control. The high degree of specialization in our economy has resulted in a large number of steps between the availability of raw materials and the final consumption of the finished product, in a complex flow of basic materials, components, and finished products through the extractive and manufacturing industries and distributive channels. This long chain of supply has greatly increased the interdependence of the various elements of our economy and created real needs for factual information about the operations of each of the various elements in relation to the others. Such information is sorely needed in our type of a free enterprise system in which efficiency and progress are dependent on the exercise of intelligent decisions of individual entrepreneurs motivated by profit incentives.

Depression. The businessman is periodically plagued by that modern scourge, economic depression. Although the free enterprise system has produced for us the highest standard of living ever achieved by any nation, experience shows that it is subject to periodic deflationary shocks of depressed markets, shutdown plants, idle savings, and mass unemployment. It is in the interest of individual enterprise as well as the public interest that private business operate as efficiently as possible and in a manner that will provide for the greatest economic stability consistent with continued growth. Business and industry cannot make intelligent decisions in the absence of facts relating to their own operations and to the operations which precede and follow them in the chain of supply. For example, business can avoid the accumulation of excessive inventories or the development of excess productive capacity only if it has at its disposal basic information relating to production, consumption, sales, new orders and backlogs, inventories, and productive capacity. Businessmen desire and should be provided with information on the statistics and outlook of the market for their goods and the supply situation for the products which they purchase. Such knowledge will enable business more efficiently to make its products available in the place and in the quantity to satisfy domestic and foreign demand. There are many explanations of the business cycle, but none that would deny that a better factual basis for policy formulation and action by both business and the government would help to cushion at least some of the shock of depression.

Business-Government Relations. As a result of the increasing complexity of our society government functions have been greatly expanded and have tended more narrowly to define areas of free competition. As a result, business and government have a common need for better information as a basis for policy formulation and action. No information or poor information may result in costly decisions on matters of vital concern to both. This is evidenced by merely listing such matters as come within the government purview—the tariff, utility rates, interest rates, loans, monopoly, agricultural production, fair trade practices, international trade agreements, patents, minimum wages, and taxes. These problem areas of private and public interest increase the need for reliable facts to assure sound thought and action on the part of individual businessmen and of the legislative and administrative officials of government.

The Problem of Distribution. During the nineteenth century the major problem confronting the businessman was that of production. In contrast, the major problem today may be described as that of distribution.

During the nineteenth century the industrialist, faced with the problem of utilizing the nation's resources, with an improving but inferior technology, and with expanding but limited facilities, could not keep up with the rapidly growing domestic market which increased population-wise by more than one third each decade. Today, with highly developed resources, tremendous facilities, and an advanced technology adding up to a productive capacity which has amazed the world, our most difficult problem is that of distribution, of achieving and maintaining high levels of effective demand. The stimulation provided to markets by the rapid population growth of the nineteenth century seems now to be permanently gone. The problem of the present and the future seems to be one of increasing effective demand through more intensive cultivation of the mass market and through greater emphasis on and recognition of the function of distribution.

Maintenance of the high levels of production achieved during the war will depend on the maintenance of high levels of consumption. More emphasis may therefore be expected on development of the art and science of distribution and on maintaining high levels of sales. These goals create additional needs for accurate facts to guide business activity.

The problem of distribution involves foreign as well as domestic markets. Experience has demonstrated that the only successful type of foreign trade is reciprocal trade—trade in both directions. Sustained high levels of effective foreign demand, as of effective domestic demand, is dependent on sustained purchasing power and efficient marketing practices. Although postwar reconstruction and reconversion needs point to a large foreign demand for American products, it is clear that a continuing high volume of foreign trade will depend on sound commercial policy in both government and business as well as on the solution of international political problems. For this purpose, business and the government will require current and accurate information on domestic and foreign markets and on general business conditions at home and abroad.

Facts as a Basis for Action. The combination of these factors, together with invigorating but sometimes rigorous competition in the open market which characterizes our free enterprise system, has slowly but inevitably driven the American businessman to a quest for facts as a basis for action, to a search for statistics from whatever source they might be available. Facts are needed with increasing urgency for dealing with problems of management, finance, investment, production, raw materials and components, labor, transportation, and distribution.

This is no news to American business. What else accounts for the rapid expansion within the business world of commercial research departments, of marketing services, and of statistical studies? It has become increasingly clear to the businessman that knowledge, not only of his own affairs, but also of general economic conditions and the affairs of related enterprises, is an important prerequisite to holding, if not improving, his competitive position. Such knowledge is most effectively obtained through statistics, which after all are organized, systematic, quantitative summaries of the characteristics or attributes of many individual items. When available, statistical facts, soundly interpreted and wisely used, provide the safest basis for intelligent business action.

THE DEVELOPMENT OF FEDERAL GOVERNMENT STATISTICS

Trade, manufacturing, and professional associations devote considerable energy and funds to the preparation of business and industrial statistics for business purposes. But the Federal Government has from its very inception been the most important single producer of statistics of value for business use.

Some of the statistical series initiated with the founding of the Federal Government in 1790 have continued to this day. The early reports of a statistical nature were scattered in a large number of volumes and were ". . . too much diffused to be made the subject of immediate reference . . ." according to an early compendium of available statistical information. This volume, prepared by Adam Seybert, M.D., a member of Congress, and published in 1818, carries the highly descriptive title, "Statistical Annals: embracing views of the population, commerce, navigation, fisheries, public lands, post office establishment, revenues, mint, military and naval establishments, expenditures, public debt and sinking fund, of the United States of America; founded on official documents commencing on the fourth of March seventeen hundred and eighty-nine and ending on the twentieth of April eighteen hundred and eighteen." These statistics with the exception of population and some material on industry were based on the various activities of the Treasury Department.

Even at that early date the statistics available from the Federal Government were not limited to by-products of administration but included also the results of a general statistical survey, the Census of Population, taken first in 1790 and decennially thereafter. Although the constitutional provision for a decennial census of population was intended to provide a population base for the apportionment of representatives in Congress among the various states, it also furnished government officials and businessmen of that day with important information on the number and distribution of the inhabitants, as well as with data on the characteristics of the people of the country. The first census, taken in 1790, not only enumerated the population but also obtained, by families and for each political subdivision, the number of free white males of 16 years and over, free white females, all other free persons, and slaves.

Congress was petitioned immediately after the first census to extend the scope of the information collected, but progress toward the detailed comprehensive censuses that we know today was slow. In 1800, the census was virtually the same as in 1790 except for more detail in the age groupings. In 1810 and in 1820 an additional inquiry, on the "arts and industries" of the country, led to the Census of Manufactures. The 1820 Census also saw the beginning of an occupational inquiry; in 1830 the questions were aimed at obtaining a count of the deaf and dumb and others who might be included in dependent classes. In 1840 the first broad attempt was made to include a general economic survey. The 1850 Census, which obtained population information about individuals instead of families and obtained the economic inquiries on separate schedules according to subject instead of on one schedule, is considered the beginning of modern census taking.

From these humble beginnings, the statistical activities of the Federal Government covering both administrative reports and general-purpose surveys, have grown and expanded. Today the volume of statistics produced by the Government which are available for the use of the people of the United States has grown so huge that no one person is in a position to be thoroughly familiar with all the fields covered, as can be seen from an examination of various chapters of this book. The quantity of information available is so great that only the highlights can be touched upon in the hundreds of pages included between these covers.

THE ORGANIZATION OF THE FEDERAL STATISTICAL SERVICES

Statistics obtained by the Government are collected by many different agencies. This fact sometimes gives rise to the supposition that the statistical responsibilities of federal agencies are haphazard and that there is no logical pattern in the information collected. The present pattern of statistical authorities and responsibilities has been determined by many factors, some of which are controllable and therefore subject to change and some of which are firmly fixed in law. There is nevertheless a fairly understandable pattern of agency responsibility for the collection of statistics, and on analysis the confusion which appears so great at first glance largely disappears.

Administrative Agencies. The factor most responsible for the large number of federal agencies engaged in the collection of statistics is the administrative structure of the Government. In the early days of the republic all the executive functions were contained within a very few executive departments. As the nation developed economically and politically, functions assigned to departments were frequently reshuffled into other departments, and independent agencies were established. This process is still going on and will no doubt continue. Just as the departments or divisions into which a business concern is divided are inevitably regrouped as personnel or products change, or as technological developments occur, the structure of the Government must be fluid enough to allow for adaptation to changing needs. As new functions are added to the Government they are frequently placed in new agencies, either because they do not logically fit in with the functions of existing agencies or because they cut across or conflict with functions in older establishments. This process of change is inherent in the democratic process. When a new need emerges to protect or assist a special group and is recognized in new legislation, it is reasonable to assume that the interest of the group might best be served by an agency devoted exclusively to the interest of that particular group. Whatever the reasons, and whether for better or worse, we do have a very large number of administrative agencies, most of which have been created by act of Congress and generally can be dissolved, consolidated, or reorganized only by act of Congress. Each of these agencies has certain duties to perform. In the performance of these duties the agencies inevitably need information which can be added up; when added up this information becomes "statistics."

It is hard for many of us not to overemphasize the importance of information. The typical business executive will usually require his department heads to keep him fully and systematically posted on what is happening. Certain reports must be on certain desks at 9 o'clock every morning, and the information they contain is used both in the appraisal of results and as an indicator of what must be done to improve results. Obviously no executive can run his business without facts on the operation of that business. The same situation holds in the Government; no administrative agency can perform its duties without using statistics. The agencies not only use but must also assemble the statistical information since it is extremely difficult and not very practical to divorce the collection of operating information from the operation itself. The close and mutually beneficial relationship which exists between statistics and operation generally explains why federal statistics are collected independently by many agencies rather than centrally by a single agency. Actually, administrative agencies collect not "statistics" but operating information.

In view of the large number of administrative agencies, what can be done to clarify the responsibilities for collecting statistics and to develop a single well-knit statistical program for the Government as a whole? As pointed out above, there are definite limitations to what can be achieved in this direction. Inescapable facts are that the administrative functions of the Government are varied and widely scattered, and that the operations of the many agencies must be closely tied to the collection and use of statistics. Nevertheless, there is some flexibility present, enough to make it possible to design statistical systems which are much more rational than those we had before the war. No situation needs to be completely flexible in all its parts before improvements and changes can be made.

Statistical Agencies. In addition to the large number of administrative agencies, there are several important agencies whose functions are primarily to supply statistics for general use, rather than for direct administrative purposes. The data collected are used extensively by business, Congress, the executive agencies, and the general public. These general-purpose statistical agencies have recognized areas of responsibility but, because of the interconnections within present economic processes, these areas of interest frequently touch or coincide at various points. It is at these points that coordination and joint action are required to prevent contradictory or duplicating results. The areas of interest of the statistical agencies also obviously coincide at times with the areas covered by the administrative agencies of the Government, and on these occasions too coordination is necessary.

Although a great deal of information is collected by the administrative agencies, it is as a rule not collected for statistical purposes and is not as likely to be available for general use. This is particularly true of the new war agencies which have had neither the manpower nor the inclination to produce statistical material from their operating reports. Moreover, security regulations have operated to prevent publication of their most important and useful data. The older regulatory commissions, on the other hand, have generally done an excellent job in making their administrative material useful for statistical purposes. The primarily statistical agencies and their general areas of responsibility are listed below. These agencies account for the greater part of the statistical material discussed in this book.

1. DEPARTMENT OF AGRICULTURE: All current statistics on the production of crops and livestock; farm wages and labor; farm management; farm taxation and finance; prices farmers pay and receive, and all other matters related to the economic status of the farm as an industrial enterprise. Several parts of the Department provide statistical information, but the most important are the Bureau of Agricultural Economics and the Production and Marketing Administration, successor to the Office of Marketing Service.

2. DEPARTMENT OF COMMERCE, BUREAU OF THE CENSUS: Statistics on manufacturing production; retail and wholesale trade; services; construction; foreign trade; housing; population and the labor market; production of fats and oils; state and local government finances and

operations; births and deaths; and various other fields related to the foregoing. The most important function of the Bureau of the Census in the past has been the provision of periodic benchmark censuses, such as the Census of Manufactures, the Census of Business, Censuses of Population, and the Census of Agriculture, which supplied detailed information on the basis of complete coverage in a number of the most important economic and social areas. In recent years increasing attention has been given to monthly or quarterly information in a variety of fields.

BUREAU OF FOREIGN AND DOMESTIC COMMERCE: This Bureau, also in the Department of Commerce, provides current information on chain-store sales and on trends in manufacturing activity, as well as very important data on national income, gross national product, and international payments. Of considerable usefulness, also, is this Bureau's monthly discussion of the business situation and periodic analysis of the business outlook.

3. DEPARTMENT OF INTERIOR, BUREAU OF MINES: Current and annual reports on the production, consumption, and stocks of minerals, including mineral fuels.

4. DEPARTMENT OF LABOR, BUREAU OF LABOR STATISTICS: Current statistics on employment, earnings, man-hours, labor turnover, accidents, work stoppage, wage rates, and working conditions in industrial establishments; wholesale prices; retail prices and cost of living indexes.

5. OTHER STATISTICAL AGENCIES: Several other agencies also obtain statistical material related to their functions. Among them is the *United States Tariff Commission*, which collects current information on synthetic organic chemicals and in peacetime makes extensive studies of comparative costs of production. The *Federal Trade Commission* from time to time makes industry-wide studies on profits, but during the war this activity was curtailed so that the Commission might assist the war agencies in special investigations. The *Securities and Exchange Commission* and the *Board of Governors of the Federal Reserve System* prepare a number of statistical reports which are discussed in detail in this book.

The agencies named above are the principal agencies of the Government engaged in the collection of data of general interest to business. There are other agencies, and divisions or sections of agencies, which conduct statistical programs or obtain operating information which may be turned to statistical use of interest to business. For example, statistics on tobacco and alcohol come from the Bureau of Internal Revenue, which keeps a running record of its excise tax stamp sales.

Almost any federal agency may contribute at least a small section to the giant jigsaw of the federal statistical program.

How Coordination Is Achieved. The division of responsibility for the federal statistical program among so many agencies, and along different lines, gives rise to some duplication and creates a need for coordination. Coordination is particularly necessary where many agencies may seek to engage in the collection of statistics without taking into account what similar or related data are already being collected by other agencies.

There is a long history of attempts at statistical coordination in the Federal Government, but not until recently have these attempts been backed by statutory authority. At the beginning of the war it was increasingly apparent that mandatory control must be exercised over the statistical activities of the administrative agencies. The newly created war agencies had no previous system of reports and, for the most part, the kind of information necessary to run the war programs was not available from other agencies. Moreover, large gaps existed in prewar statistical information. Each new agency sought desperately for the facts that would enable it to do its job. As a result many hundreds, if not thousands, of hastily prepared questionnaires were sent out in a frantic effort to get the control programs under way. A more deliberative process, and better statistical planning in previcus years, would have avoided the necessity for many of these reports.

In 1942 members of Congress and administrative officials of the Government were urgently petitioned to do something about a situation that seemed to be out of hand. These demands resulted in the Federal Reports Act of 1942, sponsored by the Senate Special Committee to Study Problems of American Small Business and by its companion committee in the House. The Act, which was approved December 24, 1942, instructed the Bureau of the Budget to examine all forms and questionnaires to be sent by any federal agency (with a few exemptions, mainly of bureaus in the Treasury Department) to ten or more individuals or business concerns, and to determine whether or not the information requested was necessary for the functions of the agency. This review of questionnaires in advance of use was designed to bring order to a chaotic situation, and important results have been achieved by this means of control. Budget Bureau approval indicated on the face of the form assures respondents that the request has been carefully considered, that the information sought is in the public interest and is being requested by the appropriate agency.

Another and more important purpose of the Federal Reports Act was a forward-looking one. The Director of the Budget was instructed to do everything he could to centralize responsibilities for the collection of statistics. This meant that wherever possible arrangements should be made for one agency to collect information in specific fields for other agencies interested in the same material. Many such arrangements have been worked out, covering many fields and many agencies, but it is seldom realistic to disenfranchise an administrative agency from all collecting responsibilities.

The designation of single collecting agencies is not a job which can be completed once and for all, but a continuing process: the problems under consideration change, new agencies come into existence, and old agencies disappear. In each case the responsibility for collecting statistics must be reviewed and some decision made. During the war the permanent agencies of the Government, particularly the Bureau of the Census, the Bureau of Labor Statistics, and the Bureau of Mines, were asked in many instances to serve as statistical compiling agents for the new war agencies in order to prevent the growth of competing statistical services. Similarly, as the war agencies disappear, it is necessary to decide what disposition should be made of the statistical materials they have accumulated and the responsibilities they have assumed.

The Federal Reports Act also stresses the importance of uniformity, simplicity, and comparability in reports. Much has already been done and much more remains to be done in standardizing methods, definitions, format, and all such matters related to the collection and tabulation of information.

In summary, the statistical system of the United States Government, shaped in part by historical accidents and subject to continuous change, is the biggest statistical organization in the world and produces the greatest amount of information. The organization of federal statistical services may be described as decentralized, with strong mandatory controls operating to reduce duplication and to effect coordination. The Bureau of the Budget, with the very active cooperation of the operating agencies, is gradually developing a simplified pattern of statistical responsibilities and improved programs of statistical information.

THE WAR'S EFFECT ON STATISTICS

As the reader will note in many of the chapters, much statistical material of direct use to business was greatly restricted during the war. In the first place, many of the peacetime statistical series were deliberately discontinued during the war so that the statistical facilities of the Federal Government could be devoted exclusively to the war effort. Moreover, it was questionable whether business concerns should be asked for statistical information applicable in general to problems which were not at the time of the first importance to business. For example, normal procedures for selling many kinds of goods were almost completely disrupted since the Government procurement agencies, by virtue of their priority status, were so often the only customers. This condition somewhat reduced the need for statistics of the traditional type. The main consideration, however, in the discontinuance of such inquiries as the biennial Census of Manufactures was the need to use the statistical facilities and personnel of the Government to the utmost for war purposes.

In the second place, publication of many of the series which were retained during the war because of their immediate relevance to war purposes was suspended by Executive Order shortly after Pearl Harbor. It was necessary to restrict the amount of statistical information generally available to prevent it from falling into the hands of the enemy and thus revealing strategic or tactical plans. This "black-out" of statistics, although necessary in the interests of national security, meant the withholding of extremely useful information. Relaxations in security regulations have now been made, and we may expect the full disclosure of data which are of use in business planning in the comparatively near future. In so far as it is feasible, most agencies will attempt to assemble back data so that a minimum interruption will have occurred.

As a result of the discontinuance of many important peacetime statistical series during the war, and of the interruption of normal processes for improving series which have been continued, the statistical services of the Government are seriously behind in supplying the kind of information which business finds useful for its operations. The statistics collected by and for the war agencies for purposes of running the war-control programs were not designed primarily for general use. They applied in a very specialized way to minute parts of the war-control programs and were not usually adapted for summarization and distribution or for general analysis. In order to salvage as much of this information as seems useful, several of the agencies are cooperating in publishing "Facts for Industry," a series of releases summarizing the reports received in connection with various control programs. It should be clear, however, that the type of operating control information required by the Government in a war situation is seldom the type of information which would prove useful in peacetime for business planning purposes.

As a consequence, many agencies of the Government are looking ahead toward the reinstatement of adequate statistical programs as soon as conditions permit. In some cases it is necessary to start almost from scratch because of the long interruption. Adequate "benchmarks" in several areas of economic activity will become increasingly necessary so that business concerns and other groups may know from what situation they start in the reconversion to peacetime production. Particularly urgent, as soon as funds and personnel can become available, are censuses of manufactures, retail and wholesale trade, construction, population, and housing. In addition to these basic benchmarks, some of which may actually be on a sample basis, we shall need to reconstruct monthly or quarterly series on manufacturing production and other phases of economic activity, oriented in terms of peacetime production. Federal agencies hope, therefore, soon to be able to announce definite plans for the restoration and development of the statistical services which business users may reasonably expect of the Government.

There have also been improvements in Government statistics as a result of the war. Many of these developments have been publicized, within security restrictions, in the technical journals. The tremendous gains made during the war in sampling theory and practice will operate after the war to provide better information more quickly and at a much lower cost. We have learned that a complete count of the total population, or of the production of farm machinery, may not be necessary; in fact, there are many situations in which a sample enumeration properly planned and carried out may be even more accurate than a complete count. The greatest advantage of sampling, however, is the speed with which it is possible to obtain results. The new techniques of sampling are much more effective than the old techniques, and it is anticipated that they may find wide application when statistical services of the Government are again devoted to serving normal peacetime needs.

The wartime need to collect a lot of information accurately and quickly sharpened the techniques for collecting information. Agencies now know with some exactness what can be done and what can't be done. They know the need for precise definitions, clear instructions, and well-considered questionnaires. Constant improvements in the collection of unbiased and unambiguous statistics may be anticipated on the basis of the very marked improvements during the last three or four years.

The war saw a great improvement in standards of statistical presentation as well as in standards of collection. It is quite likely that government statistics will not look as dreary as they customarily have in the past. Government statisticians have learned much from business sources concerning presentation of the statistical product in terms that are understandable and useful. They were forced to learn improved techniques of presentation because of the wide use made of statistical material in directing the war effort: statistics had to be presented in a way that made sense to military and civilian authorities who could not be expected to have a working knowledge of statistics and how to use them.

In short, although the war resulted in a serious setback in the current availability of statistics for business and other public use, it has also brought about tremendous improvements in the presentation and collection of statistics. We can confidently expect a greatly improved government statistical program in the next few years. Government agencies, however, will still need the advice and counsel of business organizations and individuals in making further improvements.

SUMMARY VOLUMES OF GOVERNMENT STATISTICS

When only occasional reference to certain types of government statistics is necessary, a number of volumes are available, fortunately, which bring together much information in summary form. Such volumes and periodicals published by the Federal Government include the *Statistical Abstract of the United States;* the monthly *Survey of Current Business* and its biennial supplement; the monthly *Federal Reserve Bulletin* and its base book, *Banking and Monetary Statistics;* the monthly *Labor Review* and the quinquennial *Handbook of Labor Statistics;* the quarterly *Crops and Markets;* the annual *Agricultural Statistics;* the *Minerals Year Book;* and others.

The *Statistical Abstract of the United States*, published annually by the Department of Commerce through the Bureau of the Census, brings together all the important summary statistics produced by the Federal Government and by nongovernment agencies into approximately 1,000 pages, and also serves as a reference volume to more detailed statistical data. Since each table in the volume is annotated as to source, one can discover what agency or agencies are responsible for data on a particular subject by examining the material in the Abstract, and then examining other publications of that agency or obtaining more detail through correspondence. A more general approach is also possible through examination of the bibliography of statistical sources published in the appendix of the *Abstract*.

The Federal Government also issues a number of specialized summary publications to which references are made throughout this volume. For convenience, the principal specialized reports are summarized here so that the candidates for a library of summary statistical information can be brought together.

In the field of business and general economic trends, the Department of Commerce through its Bureau of Foreign and Domestic Commerce publishes a monthly periodical, the *Survey of Current Business*, which contains a great many statistical series covering major economic and industrial activities. Technical articles afford a comprehensive review of business trends covering subjects of timely importance and interest to the business community, and presenting new series in some detail. A weekly supplement sent to all subscribers contains weekly and monthly data, thus providing an up-to-date view of business facts. A biennial supplement to the *Survey of Current Business* presents historical time series and detailed source notes for the information presented monthly. The last such supplement was issued in 1942 and was then discontinued for the duration of the war.

In the field of finance as well as general economic activity, the *Federal Reserve Bulletin* is issued monthly by the Board of Governors of the Federal Reserve System. Statistics of current significance relating to finance and business, government, gold, international transactions of the United States, and financial development abroad, are presented either in analytical articles or in tables repeated monthly. Historical figures together with descriptive text for many of the series presented in the monthly bulletin are included in the base book, *Banking and Monetary Statistics*, also issued by the Board of Governors of the Federal Reserve System. Persons interested in finance and money would also find useful the *Daily Statement* of the United States Treasury, the *Monthly Bulletin* of the Treasury Department, and the *Annual Report of the Secretary of the Treasury*.

Monthly estimates of employment and unemployment, hours and earnings, labor turnover, and related material are presented in the *Monthly Labor Review* published by the Bureau of Labor Statistics of the Department of Labor. Every five years this Bureau also issues the *Handbook of Labor Statistics* which gives the historical series and background for material in this field. The last edition of the *Handbook* was published in 1941; it consisted of two volumes, the first volume covering all topics other than wages, and the second including information on wages and wage regulation.

Among other compilations covering specific subject matter fields, the Department of Agriculture issues an annual volume, *Agricultural Statistics*, bringing together its more important statistical series. On a more current basis the statistics are issued in the quarterly *Crops and Markets*. The *Minerals Yearbook*, published annually by the Bureau of Mines, brings together and presents available material on the production and consumption of minerals.

These volumes are the more important general sources of statistical information in the Federal Government but they by no means are a substitute for the more detailed statistics outlined in the chapters which follow.

SCOPE OF THIS VOLUME

The present book is limited to the areas of Federal Government statistics which were assumed to be of most use and interest to business. Even within these areas it was necessary to leave out many statistical series of direct interest to business and to confine attention to the important series which reveal the general course of business activity and serve as guides to industrial and consumer markets. Many of the chapters contain suggestions as to where more detailed information may be secured, and persons interested may write directly to the agency most concerned for further information bearing on particular problems. Federal agencies are anxious to be of the utmost service in making available their regularly compiled information. In fact most statistical agencies will make special tabulations or analyses on request, at a very moderate charge for direct labor.

Many areas of statistics of some importance to business have been entirely omitted from this book. These would include such subjects as public health and social statistics, statistics on state and local government activities, on taxation, on criminal and judicial matters, and on education. Even this list omits a number of fields where the Government can provide current information, obtained by the administrative agencies in the course of their own operations, which is of the greatest interest and value to many business users. Statistics on the flow of surplus property for disposal and the progress of contract termination and settlement, for example, may be obtained from the Surplus Property Administration and the Office of Contract Settlement. Users of government statistics interested in areas omitted from this book should communicate directly with the appropriate agencies or with the editors of the book, who can put them in touch with the proper agency.

Statistics available from private sources have not been discussed by the authors of the several chapters except where they constitute an important segment of a statistical field. It was considered unnecessary to discuss in detail such sources as Dun and Bradstreet, Standard Statistics, Moodys, the financial and business journals, and the outstanding statistical service provided by various trade associations, since these sources are generally well known to business users.

CHAPTER 2

NATIONAL INCOME AND OTHER BUSINESS INDICATORS

MILTON GILBERT AND LOUIS PARADISO

Bureau of Foreign and Domestic Commerce
Department of Commerce

While the statistical work of the Federal Government is devoted largely to the collection and tabulation of quantitative facts, some effort is expended upon the construction of general business indicators. Of course, some primary statistical data may have significance as indicators of general business activity. For example, the volume of employment, steel output, and freight-car loadings are often used as indicators of the broader movement of business activity since they reflect the state of business in many industries. In this chapter, however, the discussion is confined to business indicators, designed as such, in which the statistical series are not merely tabulated data but rather the result of refined statistical techniques. These indicators include national income and product, the index of industrial production, manufacturers' shipments, inventories and orders, transportation activity, and retail sales.

It may be noted at the outset that the conception of a useful indicator of business and economic activity has undergone considerable change during the past ten years or so. Formerly, the most popular indicators were statistical series, or more frequently, a combination of several statistical series, which were believed to be representative of the movement of business activity in general. For example, department-store sales, freight-car loadings, steel-ingot production, bank debits, and electric-power production might be combined into an index to indicate the direction of the change in general business activity and to give some idea of the magnitude of such change. Or again, it was once popular to follow the movement of less-than-carload freight-car loadings as an indicator of production of general merchandise. As a matter of fact, the term "business indicator" came into use because statistical indexes of this sort indicated the movement of business activity rather than really measured it.

In contrast, the most useful present-day indicators attempt actually to measure the activity in a well-defined area of the economy in terms of either volume or value, the areas selected for measurement being known to be important from the standpoint of business-cycle developments. Three factors account for this change in the character of business indicators. First, there has been an increase in the raw statistical data available, making possible the direct measurement of activities which previously could not be adequately measured. Second, developments in business-cycle theory have clarified ideas about what types of transactions and what areas of activity it is important to measure. Third, it has been found by experience that an indicator of some area of business activity which did not really measure that area often went wrong after a few years because of diverse-trend developments.

NATIONAL INCOME AND NATIONAL PRODUCT

The estimates of the national income by the Bureau of Foreign and Domestic Commerce were initiated in 1932 in response to a Senate resolution, and that bureau's first report on the subject was issued early in 1933.[1] Many years of work by private research organizations, particularly the National Bureau of Economic Research, provided both the conceptual and statistical groundwork for this report. In fact, a member of the National Bureau of Economic Research staff, Professor Simon Kuznets, was loaned to the Bureau of Foreign and Domestic Commerce to supervise the preparation of these first official estimates of the national income.

In view of the immediate and widespread recognition of the utility of the national income estimates, the work was established on a permanent basis and the preparation of current annual estimates was begun. In the course of time many improvements in both the scope and accuracy of this work have been made. Not only have the statistical sources from which the estimates are constructed become more abundant and accurate, but the active interest in the field that has been maintained by such organizations as the National Bureau of Economic Research, the Conference on Research in Income and Wealth, and the National Industrial Conference Board have supplemented the efforts of the Bureau of Foreign and Domestic Commerce to broaden the scope of the statistics.[2]

[1] *National Income, 1929–32*, S. Doc. 124, 73rd Cong., 2nd sess.

[2] For conspicuous examples of the excellent work in the income field by private organizations see: Simon Kuznets, *The National Income and Its Composition* and *Commodity Flow and Capital Formation*, both published by the National Bureau of Economic Research; *National Income*, published by the National Industrial Conference Board; and the volumes issued under the sponsorship of the Conference on Research in Income and Wealth, of which six have been published.

The subsequent developments in national income research have been along two major lines. In the first place, more detailed analysis of the national accounts have been prepared, including income payments to individuals, a distribution of income by states, and classifications by type of product and by disposition of income. In the second place, the preparation of the estimates has been put on a more current basis, with many of the series being made available on a monthly or quarterly basis, both unadjusted and adjusted for seasonal variations so as to make the complex of estimates a much more useful instrument for current economic analysis.

The statistical estimates of national income and national product are conspicuous examples of the newer trend in thinking about business indicators, for what these estimates attempt to provide is a broad statistical record of the functioning of the economic system. They constitute a summary view of the economic system in terms of the types of transactions which we know from experience and from business-cycle theory to be the important determinants of the level of and changes in business activity. As such, national income and product are the broadest and most general indicators of changes in business and economic activity that have been constructed. The usefulness of the estimates, moreover, derives not only from the national income or product totals but from the various components of the totals and the interrelationships among them that can be studied by means of these data.

The estimates, for example, not only show the extent to which the total income of the Nation is increasing or decreasing but how that income is being allocated among wages and salaries, entrepreneurial income, rents, interest, and profits. They show the relative contribution being made to the total income flow by the various industries and, on the other side of the national accounts, the way in which the product is being apportioned among consumers, government, and business capital uses. Similarly, for individuals alone, the estimates show the disposition of consumer income among consumption expenditures, taxes, and savings.

Because of their comprehensive character and because they encompass the broad categories of transactions which determine the level of economic activity, the data on national income and product are indispensable in analyzing many of the basic problems that confront the economic and business system. They are used, for example, in business-cycle analysis and forecasting, not only in dealing with the economy as a whole but also with respect to particular industries and businesses. In connection with wage-rate cases, the data are used by business and labor to analyze the repercussions on the economy of the proposals in question. They are used by marketing specialists, who are trying to follow the ebb and flow of consumer purchasing power and its distribution throughout the country so that they can more adequately plan the marketing end of their business. During the war the data were widely used in estimating the probable effect of the government's war production program on the economy in general and on particular lines of business.

In connection with government economic policy, national income and product statistics provide vital categories of information. They are indispensable in formulating government fiscal policy, as they enable one to gauge the fiscal requirements of the economic situation and they are most useful in estimating the probable yield of various tax proposals. The data are used in such problems as estimating the magnitude of the inflation problem in connection with price control, wage control, and rationing programs; determining fiscal capacity of states in connection with public assistance and public health programs; estimating civilian raw materials and transportation requirements; and estimating parity income in agriculture. An important use of the data at the present time is as a basis for appraising the economic potential in the postwar period.[3]

In order to make use of this body of statistical material it is necessary to have a grasp of precisely what is being measured, that is, of the concepts used in measuring income and product and of the economic relation between them. The essential fact to recognize is that the national income and the national product represent a summarization of the receipts and expenditure sides of the accounts of business, government, and individuals with duplicating transactions eliminated. The estimates are dependent upon accounting theory and practice not only for their conceptual framework but also, in large part, for the values of the various transactions themselves. Of course, in actual practice it is sometimes necessary to adjust the data for differences in accounting methods used as well as for the fact that accounting records may not be kept of all relevant transactions.

We will begin our description of these statistical data with the receipts side of the national accounts, generally known as the national income.

NATIONAL INCOME

The national income is the sum of the incomes accruing to the labor, capital, and enterprise of the Nation for their participation in the cur-

[3] See, for example, "Transition to Peace," *Fortune Magazine*, January 1944, and *Markets after the War*, S. Doc. 40, 78th Cong., 1st sess.

rent productive process. As a total, therefore, the national income measures the extent to which economic resources are being utilized for productive purposes in terms of the incomes derived by those resources. A change in the national income from one period to another is indicative of one of three things occurring in the economic system or some combination thereof: (1) a change in prices, resulting in changed earnings by some or all of the factors of production, (2) a change in the amount of labor and capital being utilized, or (3) a change in the efficiency with which these resources are being utilized. Thus, if the influence of price changes is removed from the national income, the resulting total is an all-inclusive measure of economic activity.

While the definition of national income given above conveys the broad meaning of this concept, it has to be amplified in order to make clear its precise scope. As to geographical coverage, the incomes included are those accruing to residents of the continental United States. This means that investment income received from abroad is part of national income, and that investment income flowing abroad is not included in it. The only exception is that all employees of the Federal Government, including members of the armed forces, are considered to be residents of the United States even if they are not actually located in the United States.

As to the type of incomes included in the national income, they are broadly speaking money incomes from productive activity accruing in the market economy, though including the incomes originating in government units, as well as in private business. This limitation is important in the interpretation of the total national income, as can be seen from the following example. If services are bought in the market, the incomes arising from them form part of the national income. If similar services are rendered within the household they are not so counted. Services rendered by housewives in their own households provide an illustration of useful services which are not a part of the market economy and not included in the national income.

In several respects, however, the national income concept does depart from strict dependence on money incomes arising in the market economy. For example, the value of farm output consumed on the farm is included in the income of farmers, since otherwise the income of farmers would not be at all comparable with the income of nonfarm persons. Similarly, remuneration paid to employees in kind (such as the value of board and lodging) is included in income whenever it is of quantitative importance, even though there is no monetary transaction corresponding to this type of income receipt. This is important in such occupations as merchant seamen.

While some incomes other than money incomes are thus included in national income, not all money receipts are counted. Incomes from illegal occupations are excluded, not only because the amounts of such incomes are unknown, but also because these activities are not considered productive by society at large. Similarly, government transfer payments (social security benefits, relief, pensions, the government's share of allowances to soldiers' dependents, etc.), transfers among individuals (such as gifts), and capital gains and losses are excluded because they do not arise in connection with current productive activity.

Finally, a word of explanation is necessary with regard to the treatment of taxes in the definition of incomes. All personal incomes are measured before taxes, while business incomes are measured after taxes. Thus personal incomes (including net business profits of unincorporated business) are measured gross of individual income tax and other taxes paid by individuals in a nonbusiness capacity, whereas business profits are net of all taxes paid, including indirect taxes as well as corporation income and excess-profits taxes. It should also be mentioned that the employers' share of employment taxes is counted as (imputed) labor income, primarily on the ground that the benefits of the social security schemes which are financed by these taxes accrue to workers.

For a complete description of the sources and methods used by the Bureau of Foreign and Domestic Commerce in estimating the national income the reader is referred to *National Income in the United States, 1929–35*, Government Printing Office, 1936, and to the annual articles on national income published in the *Survey of Current Business*.

The statistics on national income estimated by the Bureau cover the period since 1929 but a continuous series starting with 1919 has been obtained by means of the estimates prepared by Professor Simon Kuznets for the National Bureau of Economic Research. This series is shown in Table 1.

Adjustment for Price and Population Changes. As previously noted, the national income in current dollars is affected by changing prices so that the figures must be put on a constant dollar basis when they are to be used as a measure of the volume of economic activity. This adjustment is also shown in Table 1. It should be kept in mind that during the war, when the types of goods produced changed so drastically, it was particularly difficult to adjust the income flow for price changes. The adjusted series does not have the consistency of meaning for such a period that it does for more normal times.

In using the national income as an indicator of economic well-being over long periods of time it is often desirable to put the figures on a per capita basis so as to remove the influence of population growth. As shown in Table 1, the estimates in constant dollars should be used for this purpose.

TABLE 1. NATIONAL INCOME, 1919–1944

Year	Total National Income (millions of dollars)	National Income in 1939 Dollars (millions of dollars)	Per Capita Income in 1939 Dollars
1919	$68,108	$47,462	$452
1920	69,226	43,078	404
1921	51,857	39,495	365
1922	59,746	48,260	439
1923	69,546	55,371	496
1924	69,247	55,002	486
1925	73,630	57,613	502
1926	76,598	59,609	512
1927	76,105	60,884	515
1928	78,815	62,951	525
1929	83,326	67.036	552
1930	68,858	57.096	464
1931	54,479	50,257	405
1932	39,963	40,988	328
1933	43,322	45,023	359
1934	49,455	49,804	394
1935	55,719	55,222	434
1936	64,924	64,218	501
1937	71,513	67,978	528
1938	64,200	63,189	487
1939	70,829	70,829	541
1940	77,574	76,700	583
1941	96,857	91,400	686
1942	121,568	106,000	787
1943	147,927	125,300	918
1944	160,653	130,300	944

It must be emphasized that while the level of the national income is of basic importance in appraising the economic well-being of the nation, it does not tell the whole story without the use of other information. The national income indicates only the volume of economic activity either in total or per capita. To judge economic welfare, however, it is particularly necessary to consider leisure as well as the character of the goods and services being produced. With reference to leisure, the length of the work-week, the prevalence of paid vacations.

and the percentage of the population in the labor force all have a bearing on welfare.

With regard to the character of production it is necessary that the bulk of productive output be constant if a comparison of national welfare at different times is to have meaning. For example, it is meaningless to draw conclusions about welfare from the data on national income during the period 1939 to 1944, despite the huge increase in national income, because the type of benefit derived from war production is simply not comparable with the type of benefit derived from the peacetime goods that were produced in 1939.

Composition of National Income. The usefulness of national income statistics is considerably enhanced by the subclassifications which are published. The first of these is a classification of national income by distributive shares, which is available on a quarterly basis; the second is one by industrial origin, which is computed annually.

National Income by Distributive Shares. The classification of national income by distributive shares divides the total which has been described above into the following components: Compensation of employees, including salaries, wages, and wage supplements;[4] the incomes of independent proprietors, classified into farm and nonfarm proprietors; interest and net rents, and corporate profits, subdivided into dividends and corporate savings (undistributed profits). These data are available annually before 1939 and quarterly since that date. The series for two years are shown in Table 2.

TABLE 2. NATIONAL INCOME BY DISTRIBUTIVE SHARES

(billions of dollars)

Item	1939 Total	1944 Total
Total national income	70.8	160.7
Total compensation of employees	48.1	116.0
Salaries and wages	44.2	112.8
Supplements	3.8	3.2
Net income of proprietors	11.2	24.1
Agricultural	4.3	11.8
Nonagricultural	6.9	12.3
Interest and net rents	7.4	10.6
Net corporate profits	4.2	9.9
Dividends	3.8	4.5
Undistributed profits	0.4	5.4

[4] Supplements consist of work-relief wages, the employers' share of employment taxes and their contributions to pension schemes, and compensation for industrial injuries.

It is not necessary to outline the interest which attaches to each of these series separately. It is apparent that they provide basic background material for the study of problems of labor, agriculture, and business. The statistics may also be used to gauge the relative shares of income which go to various groups of society, and particularly to observe changes in the relative shares over time.

While tracing comparative changes in the various income shares is one of the most important uses of the national income data, it is necessary to recognize fully the characteristics of the data if erroneous conclusions are to be avoided. In particular it must be noted that the income shares refer to group aggregates and are not indicative of changes in per capita income for the various groups. For example, in a given period of time an increase in wages and salaries might be due to an increase in the volume of employment while a comparable increase in farm income might be divided among the same number of farmers. Furthermore, it is often difficult to assess changes in the size distribution of income from changes in the income shares because many individuals receive more than one type of income and because of the wide differences in the size of individual receipts within every type of distributive share. Finally, the fact that the statistics for all income shares cannot be calculated after deduction of taxes in a comparable manner means that they must be interpreted carefully in drawing conclusions about the real income benefits derived by the various groups, particularly in periods of changing tax rates.

Since the profit component of the national income is taken after deduction of corporate income and excess-profits taxes it is sometimes desirable to add these taxes back in comparisons of the income shares. This procedure is necessary in the analysis of economic problems from the cost standpoint where the various income shares are used to measure components of the sales value of production. Needless to say, corporate taxes should not be included in measuring the income accruals that benefit stockholders.

National Income by Industrial Origin. The receipts side of the national accounts can also be classified according to the industry in which the various income items originate. The Bureau of Foreign and Domestic Commerce presents these data annually for about 27 industry groups. In addition to the annual data there are available for selected years, 1929, 1933, 1939–1944, the distributive shares components for each of these industry groups. The industrial distribution of the national income for the years 1939 and 1943 is shown in Table 3.

TABLE 3. NATIONAL INCOME BY INDUSTRIAL ORIGIN

(millions of dollars)

Industrial Division	1939	1943
Total national income	70,829	147,927
Agriculture	5,230	13,993
Mining, total	1,348	2,460
Anthracite coal	117	199
Bituminous coal	503	1,066
Other	728	1,195
Manufacturing, total	16,965	48,096
Food, beverages, and tobacco	2,379	3,764
Paper, printing, and publishing	1,729	2,468
Textiles and leather	2,711	5,007
Construction materials and furniture	1,531	2,860
Chemicals and petroleum refining	1,482	3,515
Metals, machinery, and transportation equipment	6,292	28,246
Rubber and miscellaneous	841	2,236
Contract construction	1,942	4,326
Transportation, total	4,950	9,548
Steam railroads, Pullman and express	2,830	5,665
Water transportation	479	911
Street railways	348	523
Motor transportation, public warehouses, and other transportation	1,293	2,449
Power and gas	1,459	1,616
Communication	925	1,160
Trade, total	10,956	17,424
Retail	7,135	11,385
Wholesale	3,821	6,039
Finance, total	6,796	9,222
Banking	978	1,469
Insurance	1,193	1,307
Security brokerage and real estate	4,625	6,446
Government, total	9,987	25,126
Federal	5,169	19,895
State, county, local, and public education	4,818	5,231
Service	7,027	10,340
Miscellaneous	3,244	4,616

These statistics measure the contribution which each of the various industries is making to the total national income. They also measure the net product or net receipts from sales for each industry after deduction of purchased materials and services, depreciation charges, and taxes. They are useful in following both the long-run and short-run movements of the various industries and more particularly in analyzing changes in the relative position of an industry in the economy as a whole. The cross-classification by distributive shares allows more detailed analysis of the individual industries.

NATIONAL PRODUCT

Just as the national income represents the receipts side of the national accounts, so the national product is representative of the expenditure side of the national accounts. The fact that the national product, as published by the Bureau of Foreign and Domestic Commerce, is on a "gross" basis—hence the designation gross national product—whereas the national income is published on a net basis should not obscure the essential character of the data as the debit and credit sides of the national accounts.

The gross national product may be defined in a general manner as the total value of currently produced goods and services flowing to consumers and to government. It also includes goods and services flowing to business for gross capital formation. But since it is the counterpart of the national income the specific comments which have been made on the definition of national income respecting geographical coverage and the types of goods and services included have their bearing also on the gross national product.

Classification of Gross National Product. A more precise notion of the contents of gross national product is gained by a review of the components in terms of which it is statistically measured. The three major components are: government expenditures for goods and services, business expenditures on capital account (private gross capital formation), and consumer expenditures for goods and services, as shown in Table 4.

Government expenditures for goods and services fall into two broad groups: purchases of the services of labor and capital resources (measured by salaries and wages, wage supplements, and interest) and government purchases of the products of private enterprise. Expenditures are given separately for the Federal Government and for state and local governments. It should be noted that government outlays other than for goods and services are not included—for example, relief payments or old-age pensions.

Private gross-capital formation includes private construction, residential and nonresidential, private purchases of durable equipment, changes in business inventories, and changes in balances due from abroad.[5] Considerable detailed information is available on both type of construction and type of durable equipment.

[5] Include in these claims changes in the monetary stock of the precious metals.

TABLE 4.   GROSS NATIONAL PRODUCT OR EXPENDITURE

(billions of dollars)

Item	1939 Total	1944 Total
Gross national product or expenditure	88.6	198.7
Government expenditures for goods and services	16.0	99.4
Federal Government	7.9	91.9
War	1.4	86.3
Nonwar	6.5	5.6
State and local government	8.1	7.4
Output available for private use	72.6	99.4
Private gross capital formation	10.9	1.8
Construction	3.6	1.6
Residential	2.0	0.5
Other	1.6	1.1
Producers' durable equipment	5.5	4.0
Net change in business inventories	0.9	−1.7
Net exports of goods and services	0.8	−2.1
Net exports and monetary use of gold and silver	0.2	.....
Consumers' goods and services	61.7	97.6
Durable goods	6.4	6.7
Nondurable goods	32.6	60.0
Services	22.7	30.9

In the statistics available quarterly, consumer expenditures for goods and services are subclassified into expenditures for durable goods, for nondurable goods, and for services.   On an annual basis very detailed information showing the value of 175 separate categories of consumer goods and services is available.[6]

It may be asked how it is possible to measure total national production by adding series which refer largely to purchases and not to current production (government purchases, consumer purchases, business purchases of capital equipment).   The explanation lies in the fact that purchases which are not matched by current production result in an offsetting decline in business inventories or in balances due from abroad, and that accordingly they have no net effect on the total measure of production.   Conversely, production which does not result in domestic sales or purchases leads to an accumulation of inventories (or foreign claims) and hence enters into the total of the national product.

The foregoing picture, given by gross-product statistics, of the manner in which the total production of the nation is utilized is valuable for

[6] William H. Shaw, "Consumption Expenditures, 1929–43," Survey of Current Business, June 1944.

many different purposes. The three broad components—government expenditures, private gross-capital formation, and consumer expenditures—are the major transaction aggregates which jointly determine the level of economic activity, and information on their behavior is indispensable in studying the business cycle, either in a theoretical manner or from the standpoint of remedial action by government or business. The statistics also provide basic data for planning the allocation of national resources, such as the planning of war production. The commodity detail provides information on market trends relevant to market analysis. The statistics also shed light on the welfare of the people, both in their capacity as consumers and as adding to their stocks of useful capital equipment.

Relation of National Income to Gross National Product. National income being the measure of incomes earned in production and gross national product being the measure of the total value of production, there exists a close relation between the two totals, which may be explained as follows. We have seen that gross national product consists of the total production of private business and of the production of the government. The latter, we have noted, is measured by government payments to factors of production (employee compensation and interest). These are exactly the same items by which the government contribution to national income is measured. Accordingly, the government contribution to gross national product and to national income is identical.

This identity does not hold for private business. The total value of business production exceeds the incomes accruing in private business by the amount of business expenses which do not constitute incomes. For the business system taken as a whole these expenses are charges to depreciation, depletion and other business reserves, and business taxes, including indirect taxes as well as corporate income and excess-profits taxes.

TABLE 5. RELATION OF GROSS PRODUCT TO NATIONAL INCOME

(billions of dollars)

Item	1939	1944
National income	70.8	160.7
Business tax and nontax liabilities	10.4	29.3
Depreciation and depletion charges	6.2	8.4
Other business reserves	0.8	0.7
Capital outlay charged to current expense	0.7	0.9
Inventory revaluation adjustment	−0.4	−0.1
Adjustment for discrepancies	0	−1.1
Gross national product or expenditure	88.6	198.7

It follows accordingly that, as an alternative to the direct measurement of gross national product via the flow of goods and services, it is possible to estimate it from the income side of the national accounts by adding business taxes and charges to business reserves to national income. The relation of national income to gross national product is shown statistically in Table 5.

This information is available on a quarterly basis. It is useful not only as a check on the alternative method of measuirng total production, but also for the information it yields on business-tax liabilities and on charges to depreciation and other reserves, important expense items of business.[7]

Income Payments to Individuals. Taken together the national-income and national-product series, described above, comprise the income account for the Nation as a whole with respect to current productive activity. A similar type of account can be set up covering only the income and outlay of individuals. Such an account is useful quite independent of the national income account, particularly with reference to problems involving the flow of consumer purchasing power and the disposition of that purchasing power.

In official terminology the controlling total of the individual income account is known as "income payments to individuals." This total differs from the national income in several important respects. In the first place, since it is restricted to individuals it does not include undistributed corporate earnings. Secondly, it contains all income receipts of individuals regardless of whether they arise out of current productive activity or not. This means that such income receipts as relief payments, old-age pensions, and similar transfer payments are included. Finally, wages and salaries are included in the income-payments total net of social security taxes, the idea being that this net figure is the appropriate one in considering the flow of purchasing power to consumers. It might be mentioned that the concept of income payments now used was set up when social security taxes were the only kind of taxes withheld at the source. If income taxes continue to be

---

[7] It will be found that the table giving this information includes several items in addition to charges to business reserves and business taxes which have not been mentioned so far. These are "capital outlays charged to current expense," "inventory revaluation adjustment," and "adjustment for discrepancies." The first two of these entries are of a rather technical nature and will not be explained in this brief survey. See "Preliminary Estimates of Gross National Product," *Survey of Current Business*, May 1942. The adjustment for discrepancies arises from the fact that the direct and indirect measurement of national product does not yield precisely identical results, owing to the imperfection of the basic statistical material and of the estimating methods.

withheld in the future it may be desirable to reconsider the present treatment of withheld taxes. The relationship between national income and income payments is illustrated in Table 6.

TABLE 6. RELATION BETWEEN NATIONAL INCOME AND INCOME PAYMENTS

(billions of dollars)

Item	1939	1944
National income	70.8	160.7
Add Transfer payments:		
Direct relief	1.1	1.0
Veterans' pensions	0.5	0.6
Social Security benefits	0.6	0.4
Retirement payments to government employees	0.3	0.5
Allowances to dependents of enlisted men	....	2.6
Mustering out pay	....	0.2
Less Corporate savings	0.4	5.4
Contributions to social insurance funds	2.0	3.9
Retroactive pay increase to railroad employees	....	−0.2
Equals Income payments to individuals	70.8	156.8

Income payments to individuals are available monthly both in dollars and in the form of seasonally adjusted indexes. Classifications by distributive shares and by industrial origin are given, though the detail is less than that for national income. The nature of this distributive share subclassification is adequately indicated by the headings under which the series are regularly published, as shown in Table 7.

TABLE 7. INCOME PAYMENTS

Item	July 1944
Indexes, seasonally adjusted (1935–1939 = 100):	
Total income payments	233.2
Salaries and wages	263.0
Total nonagricultural income	232.3
Total income payments (millions of dollars)	12,928
Salaries and wages	9,284
Commodity-producing industries	4,045
Work-relief wages	0
Direct and other relief	78
Dividends and interest	914
Entrepreneurial income and net rents and royalties	2,241
Other income payments	411
Total nonagricultural income	11,681

The following comments may be useful in the interpretation of these items. The industrial classification of wages and salaries includes agriculture, mining, manufacturing, and contract construction in commodity-producing industries; trade, transportation, electric light and power, and manufactured gas in distributive industries; and finance, service proper, communications, and miscellaneous industries in the service industries. Work-relief wages are classified as salaries and wages (and not as supplements as in the national-income series); and the subtotal of nonagricultural incomes excludes agricultural rents, whereas in the national-income series agricultural rents are allocated to nonagricultural industries as originating in the real-estate subdivision of the finance industry.

Disposition of Individual Incomes. On the outlay side of the account of individuals there are three main items which together balance the total on the income side of the account. These are consumer expenditures (for goods and services), taxes, and savings. These data are usually published in the form shown in Table 8.

It may be noted that the item "consumer expenditures" in this account is identical with the same item appearing in the gross national product. Personal taxes include all taxes paid by individuals in a non-business capacity, that is, individual-income taxes, estate and gift taxes, personal-property taxes, automobile registration fees and licenses, and various items of lesser importance. Personal taxes do not include sales taxes or excises which are paid in conjunction with the purchase of commodities or services.

TABLE 8. DISPOSITION OF INCOME PAYMENTS

(*billions of dollars*)

Item	1939	1944
Income payments to individuals	70.8	156.8
Less Personal taxes and nontax payments	3.1	19.3
Federal	1.3	17.2
State and local	1.9	2.0
Equals Disposable income of individuals	67.7	137.5
Less Consumer expenditures	61.7	97.6
Equals Net savings of individuals	6.0	39.9

The estimates of savings, which appear in Table 8, are obtained as a residual by subtracting expenditures and taxes from income payments. As a consequence, any statistical errors in the items can affect the savings estimate. The reader's attention is called to the fact that direct estimates of savings are prepared by the Securities and Exchange Commission and issued quarterly (see Chapter 9). While the concepts used by the Commission differ in some respects from those implicit in the Commerce data, the direct estimates of savings do conform in general pattern to the residual estimates. They have the added advantage of furnishing data on the major components of savings.

State Income Payments. On an annual basis there is available a distribution of income payments by states. State income payments differ from the monthly series only in one respect, by excluding income payments made to persons not actually residing in the United States. The most important item excluded under this heading is offshore payments to members of the armed forces.

State income payments are a useful index of economic activity and purchasing power in the various states and regions of the United States. In addition, the detail provided for each state throws light on economic conditions within states and regions. The type of detail provided for each state includes information on distributive shares and industrial origin of incomes, some cross-classification of the two types of data, series on per capita incomes, and other information. A full account of the detail provided is best obtained by consulting the annual reports dealing with the subject. (See, e.g., *Survey of Current Business,* August 1944.)

INDUSTRIAL PRODUCTION

More than any other measure, the index of industrial production compiled by the Board of Governors of the Federal Reserve System has been widely employed for many years as an indicator of changes in business activity. The extensive use of this index is largely due to three considerations: (1) it is the most comprehensive indicator of monthly changes in the volume of industrial production, (2) it immediately registers changes in business activity as reflected by a relatively sensitive sector of the economy, namely, manufacturing and mining—changes which are influenced or have repercussions in many other fields of activity such as trade and transportation, and (3) it is a composite of the output of numerous specific industries and permits a more adequate analysis of fluctuations in the total index by a study of its component parts.

Composition of the Federal Reserve Board's Index. The Federal Reserve Board's index attempts to measure changes in the volume of the physical units of industrial production, restricted, however, to measurement of the output of manufacturing and mining industries. Despite this limitation, the index when properly used serves as an

important indicator of business conditions. Manufacturing and mining currently account for a very large share of total employment.
Furthermore, changes in manufacturing and mining activity reflect,
and also affect, many other economic activities. For example, a high
degree of association has been found between changes in industrial
production and changes in commodity transportation and electric
power production. Thus while as a business indicator industrial production fails to cover many other important segments of the economy—
it does not measure such important activities as agricultural production, construction, government and other services—it nevertheless reflects current changes in a very important and dynamic sector.

The Federal Reserve index has been available by months since 1919
and for the current months is published in detail in the *Federal Reserve
Bulletin*.[8] Monthly data from 1923 to 1940 were published in the
August 1940 issue of the Bulletin. The index first published in 1927 was
based on 60 series representing actual physical units of output. Because of inability to get adequate production data for several important
manufacturing industries, such as the electrical and other machinery
industries, and because these industries had grown in importance since
that time, the Board revised its index in June 1940 by estimating the
output of the machinery, transportation equipment, furniture, chemicals, and a number of manufactured foods industries through the
utilization of data on man-hours. To allow for the changes in production per man-hour through the years, an efficiency factor was developed
and applied to each of the man-hour series. In addition, other important series were added and some of the series in the old index were
revised.[9] With the growing importance of war production, a further
broadening of the coverage of the index was made in September 1941,
when most of the defense work was included. The chief revisions were
the inclusion of production carried on by the Government in arsenals,
quartermaster depots, and shipyards and the inclusion of output of
electric furnace steel.

With the rapid expansion of the military program after Pearl Harbor,
serious doubts were raised regarding the adequacy of the coverage of
the index, and in October 1943 a further revision was made to include
new data available during the war period. The basic method of computing the index, however, remained unchanged.

[8] For recent months the index is also available in the *Survey of Current Business*,
while back data are published in the 1942 *Biennial Supplement to the Survey of
Current Business*.

[9] For a description of the method and detailed series see *Federal Reserve Bulletin*,
August 1940 and September 1941.

The present index is derived from a combination of 101 industrial series, 20 more than were included in the 1941 revision. These series are distributed among 16 groups of manufacturing industries and 5 groups of mining industries. In addition, the manufacturing groups of industries are combined into a durable-goods group, a nondurable-goods group and a total-manufacturing index. The mining industries are combined into a minerals index. Actually some of the basic series used in the index are themselves combinations of the output of two or

TABLE 9. INDEXES OF INDUSTRIAL PRODUCTION, BY MAJOR INDUSTRIAL GROUPS

(1935–1939 = 100)

	1939	*1944*
	(Monthly average)	
Industrial production, total	109	235
Manufactures, total	109	252
Durable manufactures	109	353
Iron and steel	114	206
Machinery	104	439
Transportation equipment	103	719
Nonferrous metals and products	113	259
Lumber and products	106	125
Stone, clay, and glass products	114	164
Nondurable manufactures	109	171
Textiles and products	112	148
Leather and products	105	113
Manufactured food products	108	152
Alcoholic beverages	98	144
Tobacco products	106	125
Paper and paper products	114	139
Printing and publishing	106	101
Petroleum and coal products	110	247
Chemical products	112	324
Rubber products	113	234
Minerals, total	106	140
Fuels	105	145
Anthracite	101	126
Bituminous coal	99	156
Crude petroleum	108	143
Metals	113	113

Source: Board of Governors of the Federal Reserve System and published in the *Federal Reserve Bulletin.*

Note: Indexes are also available for subgroups of many of the major groups shown above.

more component series. To avoid disclosure of confidential information the publication of the production of 27 component industries was discontinued during the war period, although they are included in the combined index. These series include the output of such important war industries as aircraft, shipbuilding, explosives, and ammunition. Table 9 shows the indexes by major industries for 1939 and 1944.

Problems in Constructing the Index. The problem of combining the 100 or more series into a single measure of industrial production offers very serious difficulties, particularly for the war period. There are five basic problems that must be considered in arriving at the composite index and in interpreting the results.

1. CLASSIFICATION OF INDUSTRIES. As presently constructed the industries in the index are classified according to the Census of Manufactures and this classification was continued during the war period despite the fact that many industries were no longer making their usual peacetime products. Most of the output of the automobile industry, for example, no longer consisted of automobiles and yet it was so classified in the index. This problem of classification must be kept in mind in interpreting the components of the index.

2. THE BASIC DATA. The ideal production index would be based completely on data representing physical units of the output of manufacturing and mining industries. Obviously this ideal cannot be achieved since such output data do not exist for many mined and manufactured products. Even if the data were available the labor of compiling and combining them would be prohibitive.

Two approaches are used to overcome these difficulties. Where the industry produces a principal product which is simple and homogeneous, that product is used to represent the output of the entire industry. Examples of such products are cement, shoes, and plate glass. Most industries, however, produce many products in varying stages of fabrication. The steel industry produces shapes, sheets, plates, bars, nails, rails, and many other products. Since most of these products are made from steel ingots and since the loss in converting the steel ingot to steel products is fairly constant, changes in total output are represented by the movement of steel-ingot production. A similar problem occurs in the cotton textile industry where the types of product are more complex and heterogeneous. In this case cotton consumed at the mills is used to measure the output of the industry.

In some industries, however, the products are so diversified that no physical-output series can be considered representative. Examples of such industries are machinery, transportation equipment, and chemicals. For such industries the Board has utilized man-hour series to represent the output. The use of man-hours as such would introduce a distortion through the years in view of the constant changes which occur in efficiency of labor utilization. A correction is therefore made to the man-hour series to allow for changes in labor productivity. Such changes, however, are difficult to measure and existing information is scanty. Consequently, there is some question as to whether precisely correct allowance can be made for the productivity changes in the measurement of output by the use of man-hour data. These problems were magnified in the war period when changes in labor productivity were frequent. Furthermore, there is a virtually insoluble problem in the fact that a given man-hour series may represent entirely different products from one period to another.

Of course, wherever possible the Board periodically adjusts its level to actual physical-units data. For example, physical units for a large number of chemical products are available annually or quarterly and the monthly man-hour series is adjusted to the annual or quarterly physical totals, thus correcting any bias which may have been introduced in the productivity adjustment.

3. WEIGHTING. The decision on how to weight the component series in order to get a single index of the various measures of output ultimately depends on the purpose for which the index is to be used. In general, the purpose of weighting is to introduce the component series in their relative economic importance to each other. From the point of view of use of resources, for example, the production of an automobile has more economic importance than the production of a cigarette.

Since the basis of weighting depends on the use of the index, the problem becomes that of finding the most useful weighting system from the point of view of broad economic analysis. This is achieved by weighting the quantity series by the base price, since the quantities then are combined in accordance with their economic importance as reflected in the market values. This method is applied to the minerals portion of the index.

In manufacturing, however, a modification must be made to the factory price of the product in order to arrive at the relative importance of the output from the standpoint of the factory's contribution to its production. Since the factory price of the finished product includes the cost of raw materials consumed in the process of manufacture and since there is great variability in the use and in the cost of raw materials among manufacturing industries, a more pertinent weight is the part of the total factory price attributable to the value added by manufacture, i.e., to the value of products less cost of materials, purchased fuels, and containers. This would be the portion of the price attributable primarily to the costs of labor, overhead costs, and profits. This procedure avoids the duplication which would result if the entire price were used as a weight. In the shoe industry, for example, it is necessary to eliminate the cost of leather and other raw materials purchased in producing the shoe since the value of these products would already be covered in the treatment of the leather industry.

The actual procedure used in combining the component series is that of the average relative method, i.e., weighting the individual *indexes* of output according to the relative proportion of the value of products in the minerals industry and value added for the manufacturing industries. The Federal Reserve index has been obtained by weighting the manufacturing production indexes by the proportion of the value added in each industry to the total value added in 1937 as shown in the *Census of Manufactures*. Value of products for 1937 as shown in the *Minerals Yearbook*, Bureau of Mines was used to weight the minerals indexes.[10]

As already indicated, certain series are used to represent the output for the entire industry, even though the series themselves cover only part of the output. In computing the weights for individual series within the groups, therefore, many products included are assigned weights which represent not only their own values but also values for the industry of which they are a part and whose changes in output they are designed to represent. For example, the "value added" (as reported in the *Census of Manufactures*) used to weight the steel-ingot index covers the entire "iron and steel and its products" industry.

4. BASE PERIOD FOR THE INDEX. The present Federal Reserve index is stated in terms of the monthly average of the years 1935 to 1939 as the base period and the output of each industry and of the total is expressed as a percentage of the base period output. This conforms to the uniform practice adopted by Government agencies in compiling index numbers. The same relative changes would be shown if the index were converted to any other period as a base.

5. PROBLEMS OF VARYING WORKING DAYS AND OF SEASONAL ADJUSTMENTS. The Federal Reserve indexes are published both with and without adjustment for seasonal variations. In either case they are corrected so as to allow for the differences in the number of working days in the month. The number of working days used for an industry is based on the standard practice for that industry. Allowance was made during the war period for those industries which adopted the practice of working on holidays.

The more important adjustment, however, is that made for the

---

[10] These weights were used for the period since 1929. From 1923 to 1929 the weights were based on 1923 values.

seasonal pattern of production. In some industries, such as certain food manufacturing industries, cement, and automobiles, the seasonal variations are very pronounced. In order to compare month-to-month changes, it is necessary to eliminate the seasonal factor from the data. During the war years, however, the seasonal adjustment for many industries producing war goods was discontinued since seasonal factors of demand and supply no longer prevailed.[11]

Uses of the Index. The Federal Reserve index provides a useful yardstick for economic analysis—for studying both the cyclical and long-term trend changes in industrial output and for determining shifts in the pattern of production. Because of its general character the index is widely used in forecasting the trend in business activity. It is also used in determining the repercussions of changes in the index upon its component industries or upon related activities such as material requirements, transportation or power demands, and import needs. Another type of use of the index, particularly in peacetime, when there are not such violent shifts in the structure of production, is in measuring changes in the efficiency of labor utilization in manufacturing and mining.

The index has added usefulness since it is built up from so many component series and thus makes possible a more penetrating analysis of production changes. The details also enable the individual firm to compare its own activity with the total for its industry and to follow developments in industries which are its suppliers or customers.

It may be mentioned that some caution will be needed in interpreting the decline in the index which will occur in the transition and postwar years from the high levels established in the wartime period. Wartime needs very greatly increased the output of durable-goods manufacturing industries which usually employ relatively more man-hours per unit of materials input than the nondurable goods industries. A decline in the index as industry shifts back to the production of peacetime products will not necessarily reflect generally depressed conditions throughout the economy but may be due to the shifting character of the input requirements for producing civilian manufacturing goods or to a shift from manufacturing to other types of production.

MANUFACTURERS' SHIPMENTS, INVENTORIES, AND ORDERS

In 1939 the Bureau of Foreign and Domestic Commerce initiated, through a monthly survey, data on manufacturers' shipments, inven-

---

[11] The method used in adjusting for seasonal variations is described fully in the *Federal Reserve Bulletin*, June 1941.

tories, and new and unfilled orders. The development of these series was made possible by the cooperation of many firms in all the major segments of the manufacturing industry. Currently a sample of about 1,200 companies, accounting for 40 percent of the total manufacturing activity, reports these basic monthly data. Summaries in the form of daily average indexes and dollar totals for all manufacturing industries and for the major subgroups are published in the Bureau's monthly *Industry Survey* and in its *Survey of Current Business*.

Shipments. The respondent companies report net sales or billings for the current and preceding months and for the corresponding month of a year before. The returns are classified into 14 major industry groups corresponding to the 1939 Census classification. On the basis of these summaries, indexes of the value of shipments are prepared for each major industry. Dollar estimates of shipments are then estimated monthly for each industry group by applying the indexes to the 1939 Census value of products, adjusted for the change in the value of finished-goods inventories in 1939.[12] In addition, daily average indexes are also derived for all manufacturing industries, the durable goods and nondurable goods groups, and for each of the 14 major industries.

The value of manufacturers' shipments represents the aggregate sales made by all manufacturing firms, including both products destined for the ultimate consumers and sales to other firms for further processing. Thus the figures involve duplication to the extent that the value of materials are counted several times in the aggregate shipments. In peacetime periods the amount of duplication constituted about one-third of the value of total shipments. The series is roughly the counterpart of the index of industrial production of the Federal Reserve Board in value terms.

Current measures of sales of manufacturers are valuable in that they can be analyzed in connection with costs, taxes, and profits. In periods of relative price stability they are also valid indicators of changes in physical output. They represent the only over-all measure of current sales and of the value of products since the 1939 Census of Manufactures.

Manufacturers' Inventories. Inventory expansion and contraction has on many occasions been an important factor in initiating and intensifying fluctuations in manufacturing production. Inventory ac-

---

[12] Theoretically the value of products should also be adjusted for the change in the value of goods in process inventories in order to arrive at the value of shipments. However, in deriving shipments data for the base period, no adjustment was made for work partly completed because the basic data are not available.

cumulation played a prominent part in the sharp increase in production in the latter part of 1933 and in the fall of 1939. Inventory liquidation in the latter part of 1937 and in early 1938 was an important factor in the decline of industrial production in that period. Because of the vital role which inventories perform in the major swings of the business cycle it is important to have current measures of their fluctuations. Manufacturers' inventories, which constitute the largest segment of all business inventories, show particularly wide swings.

TABLE 10.   ESTIMATED VALUE OF MANUFACTURERS' SHIPMENTS AND INVENTORIES

(millions of dollars)

| | Shipments | | Inventories | |
| | | | Dec. 31, | Dec. 31, |
	1939	*1944*	*1939*	*1944*
Total	56,887	156,059	10,659	16,737
Durable goods	23,271	89,219	5,046	8,916
Nondurable goods	33,616	66,840	5,613	7,821
Durable goods industries:				
Iron and steel and their products	6,597	16,525	1,531	1,684
Nonferrous metals and their products	2,598	7,179	443	676
Electrical machinery	1,747	8,794	416	1,182
Other machinery	3,262	13,369	998	1,994
Automobiles and equipment	4,032	12,202	411	769
Transportation equipment (except autos)	880	22,237	215	1,392
Other durable goods	4,155	8,913	1,032	1,219
Nondurable goods industries:				
Food and kindred products	10,606	22,701	1,416	2,216
Textile-mill products	3,945	7,571	888	990
Paper and allied products	2,022	3,574	306	382
Chemicals and allied products	3,761	7,905	721	1,092
Petroleum refining	2,457	4,520	608	690
Rubber products	899	2,740	185	292
Other nondurable goods	9,926	17,829	1,489	2,159

The reports of firms to the *Industry Survey* provide the basis for measuring the change in the inventory holdings of manufacturers. Book values of inventories as of the end of the current month, end of the preceding month, and end of the month of a year ago are reported. Indexes are constructed from the sample of firms in each of 14 major industries and dollar estimates of the inventories are obtained by applying the indexes to the total industry value of inventories as of the end of 1938, reported in the 1939 Census of Manufactures. This estimated book value of inventories is available for each month since the beginning of 1939. Dollar values and indexes are also available for the durable goods and nondurable goods industries and for each of the major industries in these groups.

Besides reporting total inventories, manufacturers also give inventory information by degree of fabrication—into raw materials, goods in process, and finished goods. On the basis of these reports dollar values of these types of inventories are also estimated monthly. In interpreting the changes in the inventories by stage of fabrication it must be kept in mind that the classification of inventories is in accordance with the firm's definition of the type of its inventory holdings. For example, a shoe firm reports its leather inventories as raw materials, although in the economic sense such goods would be classified as semifabricated since they have passed through at least one stage of fabrication. A leather company, on the other hand, would report its leather stocks as finished goods. Despite this crossing of products from one class to the other, the subclassification of inventories is nevertheless useful in indicating the trends of the various types of inventory holdings.

At the beginning of 1939 the value of all manufacturers' inventories amounted to 10 billion dollars. Of this total, 4.1 billion dollars consisted of raw materials, 1.6 billion dollars of goods in process, and 4.4 billion dollars of finished goods inventories. Following the outbreak of war in Europe in September 1939, inventories at the mills increased substantially and by the end of 1940 had reached 12 billion dollars. During 1941 manufacturers added 3.8 billion dollars to the value of their inventories, thus creating the greatest accumulation of inventories on record.

Inventories and shipment data have been important in analyzing the trend of the inventory-sales ratio. While the ratio is valuable in certain types of analyses such as determining the number of months of stocks on hand at current rates, there are a few misconceptions regarding its use which should be clarified. Because inventories are stated in book value, which is usually at cost or market, whichever is lower, while shipments are reported at factory selling price, the two sets of data are not comparable unless inventories are expressed in terms of market prices. Thus the ratio based on the reported data may be misleading, particularly when price shifts occur among the products.

The ratio has also been used as an indication of possible distortion in inventories relative to sales. A study of the ratio alone may be very misleading for this purpose. For example, if sales increase by 10 per cent and inventories likewise increase by 10 per cent, the ratio will be unaltered. It cannot be concluded from this that inventories are necessarily in balance with sales since historically the actual inventory requirements relative to the higher volume of activity might have been only 3 percent greater. Furthermore, the increase in sales may be due entirely to an increase in intrabusiness buying for inventory purposes —for example, in expectation of higher prices. Changes in the ratio are not in themselves indicative of abnormal inventory behavior since historically the ratio is also a function of sales.

The movement of business inventories has frequently contributed significantly to the severity of business fluctuations. The sharp inventory liquidation in the period 1929–1932 was followed by a sizable inventory rise in the subsequent period, with the result that the direction of business activity was greatly accentuated in each of these periods. Indeed, in some years inventory accumulation has been so great that it has matched the total business investment in new plant facilities. Thus the analysis of the volume and direction of the inventory movement has added significance in relation to the problem of the business cycle and together with other information can be used as a guide in forecasting the direction of business activity. Business policy respecting investment in inventories can contribute to a greater degree of stability in business activity or to an intensification of its periodic swings.

New Orders Received by Manufacturers. New orders received reflect changes in demand, and as such they constitute one of the most useful indicators of trends in industrial activity and an essential category of information for business forecasting. For those companies manufacturing standardized products which are conventionally stocked by them or which have a short period of production, sales data provide an adequate measure of demand, since in such cases orders are usually filled promptly on receipt. However, for a large part of manufacturing, particularly the durable goods lines, orders take some time to fill and manufacturers keep records of new and unfilled orders.

The flow of new business as measured by the *Industry Survey* index consists of the net sales for those firms that stated they filled orders promptly upon receipt and of the value of new orders for firms which keep such records. New orders are net, that is, less cancellations during the month. Indexes of new orders have been available monthly since January 1939 for all manufacturing industry and for the durable goods and nondurable goods groups in the various issues of the *Industry Survey* and in the *Survey of Current Business*. Since new orders data are particularly important in the durable goods industries, separate indexes are prepared for the major components of this group—iron and steel and their products, electrical machinery, other machinery, and other durable goods. Table 11 compares the values of new orders received by manufacturers in June 1939 and June 1944.

TABLE 11. INDEXES OF THE VALUE OF NEW ORDERS RECEIVED BY
MANUFACTURERS

(January 1939 = 100)

	June 1939	June 1944
Total, all industries	108	301
Total, durable goods	107	445
Total, nondurable goods	109	208
Durable goods:		
Iron and steel and their products	100	366
Electrical machinery	110	398
Other machinery	114	450
Other durable goods	112	589

Three major industries are not directly represented in the new orders index—automobiles, shipbuilding, and aircraft. Most automobile companies do not maintain a new orders record, and in the shipbuilding and aircraft industries the new orders placed have unusually erratic fluctuations, which would distort any measure of the flow of incoming business.

In peacetime, changes in new orders reflect directly and indirectly fluctuations in demand from producers and consumers. Long before a change in business activity, new orders will reflect the changed demands and will point to coming developments. During the war, however, new orders lost much of their usual significance as indicators of changes in demand. Because of fear of shortages, orders were placed in the early years of the war irrespective of actual current needs, even though there was no assurance of delivery. War orders received priority and these were in such large volume that changes in them did not indicate corresponding changes in prospective activity, since backlogs of many firms were in huge volume. Changes in business activity were being restricted by factors on the supply side rather than by demand.

The wartime increase in the value of new orders may be seen from the fact that the index of new orders received by the durable goods industries increased from 107 in June 1939 (January 1939 = 100) to 445 in June 1944; this index excludes orders received by major war industries—aircraft, shipbuilding, and automobiles.

As the war production levels off or declines, however, and government contracts no longer underwrite production at capacity levels, new orders will once more assume their importance as indicators and forecasters of business activity.

The indexes of manufacturers' shipments, inventories, and new orders and unfilled orders can achieve their full usefulness as tools in analyzing and forecasting business developments only if they are considered together. For example, the likelihood that an upturn in manufacturers' sales will continue can scarcely be determined in the absence of information on new business and inventories. If the upturn is accompanied by a continuing favorable level of new orders and if the increased shipments are not resulting merely in an increase in inventories, a prolonged upswing of activity can be more reasonably anticipated than if new business is declining or stocks are rising abruptly. Similarly, the significance of an increase or decline in new orders depends largely upon the condition of unfilled order backlogs, while the proper interpretation of inventory behavior requires a knowledge of the movement of sales. Thus, in effect, the various indexes provided by the *Industry Survey* are more properly employed as interrelated factors of analysis than as independent business indicators.

INDEX OF TRANSPORTATION VOLUME

The Bureau of Foreign and Domestic Commerce transportation index [13] measures the changes in the physical output of our domestic transportation industry. (See also Chapter 8.) Included in the series are five types of freight transport (rail, truck, domestic waterborne, air, and pipeline) and four types of passenger carriers (rail, bus, air, and local transit). In each type of transportation, except local transit, the volume of traffic is measured in terms of either ton-miles or passenger-miles. The local transit index is based on the number of passengers carried since the average haul in this form of traffic has no real significance. It may be noted that only commercial forms of transportation are included and the index covers only transportation between points in continental United States.

The individual series are combined into five general groups: Total commodity traffic, total passenger traffic, combined commodity and passenger, passenger excluding local transit lines, and combined commodity and passenger excluding local transit lines. The omission

---

[13] For a more detailed description of the index and for the statistical data compiled, see the publication of the Bureau of Foreign and Domestic Commerce the *Survey of Current Business* for September 1942 and May 1943. Current data appear regularly in the statistical section of the above publication.

of local transit lines from some of the series meets the need for indexes that are predominantly intercity in character.

The indexes cover the periods 1929 through 1938 annually and since January 1939 monthly. Seasonally adjusted indexes are also available by months since January 1939. Table 12 shows the average indexes for each type of transport agency for 1939 and 1944.

TABLE 12.   INDEX OF TRANSPORTATION VOLUME 1939 AND 1944

(Daily average 1935–1939 = 100)

	1939	1944
Total, all types	105	223
Total, excluding local transit	106	231
Commodity, all types	107	209
Passenger, all types	102	272
Passenger, excluding local transit	105	388
Railroads:		
Combined index	103	247
Commodity	104	223
Passenger	103	434
Intercity motor:		
Combined index	112	228
"For hire" truck	114	210
Bus	104	292
Air:		
Combined index	142	581
Express and mail	132	786
Passenger	148	445
Oil and gas pipeline	110	251
Waterborne (domestic)	113	68
Local transit	100	179

The separate indexes are combined by weighting each component by the proportions of total operating revenues in the base period 1935–1939.[14] This procedure attempts to aggregate the output of the various transport agencies by giving due weight to the *economic* services they perform. The method of weighting adjusts for many of the advantages and disadvantages inherent in the operation of the different types of carriers, so far as the average revenue per ton-mile or passenger-mile attained its true competitive level in the base period 1935–1939.

[14] This is equivalent to weighting the ton-miles and passenger-miles by the corresponding rates.

It is not necessary to dwell on the importance of the transportation industry in our national economy. Perhaps the importance of its position in the economy may be best exemplified by the fact that the total volume of transportation parallels to an astonishing degree the movement of the national income. The movement of the commodity traffic components is closely associated with changes in industrial activity (after allowing for a lag in the timing between the two types of activity) and as such tends to reflect the fluctuations in the more dynamic sectors of the economy. Passenger traffic, on the other hand, is much more closely related to the consumer purchasing power and reflects, in addition, activities which are relatively more stable than industrial production.

The transportation volume index reflects directly or indirectly the combined effects of practically all phases of our economic activity much more comprehensively than the index of carloadings, which has frequently been used for that purpose. It must be kept in mind, however, that the index is a composite of two factors—the quantity of goods transported or number of persons carried and the average haul. The increase in the index during the war period was due not only to moving a greatly expanded physical volume of goods and to carrying more persons but also to the substantial increase in the average haul. The lengthening of haul was particularly noticeable in commodity transportation as a result of the greatly expanded shipments of war goods from the inland centers to the coasts.

Besides its usefulness as a general business indicator the transportation volume index is of considerable importance to the individual companies engaged in transportation. For example, a railroad company can compare its performance with the rail commodity and rail passenger indexes and thus ascertain whether it is doing better or worse than the industry as a whole. Furthermore, each transport agency can determine from a comparison of the separate indexes whether it is gaining or losing business to the other transport agencies. Many other analyses can also be made by the use of the index, including such problems as the determination of the effect of a change in rates on volume of traffic and the shifts from commercial forms of transportation to private forms.

RETAIL SALES

An economic measure of exceptional importance is one that reveals changes in the volume of consumer expenditures. Sales of retail stores represent, for the most part, consumer purchases of commodities.

Not only do purchases of commodities constitute about two-thirds of all consumer expenditures, but they are also the most volatile segment of consumer expenditure. Monthly data on sales of retail stores provide a current measure of consumer demand that is extremely useful to businessmen, investors, and others who are constantly making decisions based upon activity in retail trade. (See also Chapter 6.)

The Bureau of Foreign and Domestic Commerce prepares estimates of retail sales annually and monthly for 25 kinds of business. Annual estimates for the years 1929, 1933, and 1935–1943 and monthly estimates for the period 1935–1943 covering total retail trade were published in the November 1943 issue of the *Survey of Current Business*. Separate data for chain stores appeared in the February 1944 issue of the *Survey*. Currently, the monthly data for both the total and for chain stores are published in the *Survey of Current Business*.

In addition to the monthly estimates of dollar volume of retail trade, indexes of sales adjusted for the number of trading days and seasonal factors are computed. Adjustments are made for the differences in the total number of days in each month and for the different number of Sundays and holidays in order to eliminate the effect of these calendar variations. Further, in some trades the various days of the week are of varying importance in retail sales, such as the heavy week-end purchases of groceries or the large Saturday sales in all lines of trade in most farm communities. Consequently, in the kinds of business where it is appropriate, varying weights are given to each day of the week in accordance with past experience. Finally, the seasonal influence, such as the heavy Christmas and Easter buying, is eliminated. The adjusted indexes, therefore, reflect only the underlying cyclical and long-term trends of retail sales and the influence of random factors such as rationing or special sales. Table 13 shows the annual sales for 1939 and 1944 by kinds of business.

The estimates of the dollar volume of retail sales reflect not only changes in the quantity of goods purchased but also changes in prices. In order to eliminate the effect of price changes the dollar sales have been deflated by a retail price index. This index is prepared by the Bureau of Foreign and Domestic Commerce by combining various existing retail price data compiled by the U. S. Department of Labor and other agencies. It differs from the cost-of-living index published by the Bureau of Labor Statistics by the omission of rents and other service prices and the inclusion of prices for building materials, farm machinery, and other nonconsumer commodities sold through retail stores. In addition, the component indexes are combined according to weights appropriate to retail store sales rather than weights appropriate to a family budget.

TABLE 13. SALES OF RETAIL STORES, BY KINDS OF BUSINESS

(millions of dollars)

	1939	1944
All retail stores	42,042	69,275
Durable goods stores	10,379	9,931
Automotive group	5,549	2,834
Motor vehicle dealers	5,025	1,983
Parts and accessories	524	851
Building materials and hardware group	2,735	3,588
Building materials	1,761	2,171
Farm implements	345	393
Hardware	629	1,024
Home furnishings group	1,733	2,507
Furniture and housefurnishings	1,200	1,989
Household appliances and radio	533	518
Jewelry stores	362	1,002
Nondurable goods stores	31,663	59,344
Apparel group	3,259	6,814
Men's clothing and furnishings	840	1,602
Women's apparel and accessories	1,323	3,170
Family and other apparel	479	976
Shoes	617	1,066
Drug stores	1,563	2,845
Eating and drinking places	3,520	9,314
Food group	10,165	18,947
Grocery and combination	7,722	14,402
Other food	2,443	4,545
Filling stations	2,822	2,604
General merchandise group	6,475	10,853
Department, including mail order	3,975	6,763
General stores and general merchandise with food	922	1,388
Dry goods and other general merchandise	601	1,208
Variety	977	1,494
Other retail stores	3,859	7,967
Feed and farm supply	779	2,319
Fuel and ice	1,014	1,489
Liquor	586	1,456
Other	1,480	2,703

It should be emphasized that retail sales adjusted for price changes do not measure simply unit quantity of goods sold. The factor of quality is equally important. A shift to higher-priced, and presumably higher-quality, merchandise would result in an increase in retail sales adjusted for price changes even though the number of units sold remained the same. The price index takes account primarily of changes in price of articles of a given specification and quality and does not take into account shifts in quality.[15] This is a particularly important consideration when deflated retail sales are compared with physical production, usually counted on a unit basis.[16]

Probably the most interesting aspect of changes in retail sales is the close relationship with the movement of the disposable income of individuals (their income remaining after payment of personal taxes). Although retailers have long known this fact as a general proposition, the significant feature is the very high degree of correlation. Over the 20-year period, 1922–1941, about 70 percent of any given increase in disposable income went for purchases of goods at retail stores and this relation was practically unchanged through the entire period. This means that the change in consumer income is by far the most important single economic factor that retailers need to consider in determining the outlook for their business. A detailed analysis of this relationship by kind of business and its possible uses by business firms appeared in the *Survey of Current Business* for October 1944.

The total volume of retail sales provides an invaluable guide to business as to the strength of consumer demand. When analyzed in conjunction with sales by kinds of business it throws light on the changing pattern and shifts in the character of this demand. For use in marketing analyses such data are indispensable.

[15] During the war some attempt was made to compensate for forced quality shifts due to the disappearance of low-priced merchandise. However, this is a very difficult problem to solve and the adjustment for forced trading-up was necessarily inadequate.

[16] For a description of the method used in the construction of the retail sales estimates see *Survey of Current Business*, October 1943 and November 1944.

CHAPTER 3

MANUFACTURING

MAXWELL R. CONKLIN AND FRANK HANNA
Bureau of the Census

AND

H. B. McCOY
Bureau of Foreign and Domestic Commerce
Department of Commerce

Of all of the facts gathered on business, none are more fundamental or important than those recording and measuring manufacturing. Processing materials and fashioning them into useful articles is one of the oldest and has become one of the principal activities of man in the pursuit of a livelihood. With the exception of some kinds of food and other materials which can be used or consumed in their original state, the products of the mines, forests, the sea and the land must be submitted to a converting process to make them useful or fit for consumption. This process is one of the principal areas in which free enterprise operates to provide employment and to create capital. Thus the measurement of production is one of the most significant indicators of national economic progress.

The products of manufacturing constitute the bulk of the goods that pass in commerce to the hands of the final consumer. Since the industrial revolution, manufacturing has become an increasingly more important part of the world's economic life. With the passage of each decade the number and complexity of manufacturing products have increased markedly. This has made for greater specialization of manufacturing operations, has expanded manyfold the number of steps between raw materials and finished products, and has required large amounts of capital. Usually, a long period of time is involved in converting basic raw materials to final products. Likewise, the flow of basic materials and semiprocessed products and components through manufacturing channels is generally very complex. Thus iron ore is shipped to the blast furnace, pig iron to the open hearth, steel ingots to the rolling mill, bars or billets to the forge shop, forgings to the engine manufacturer, and engines to the automobile assembly plant.

Most products of factories are consumed in other factories as components of some other finished products, and as a consequence the relationship of facts within manufacturing is exceedingly intricate. The market for factory products, therefore, is very likely to be another factory.

During the 38 years 1899 to 1937 the output of manufactures grew at the average rate of 3.5 percent per year, approximately twice the 1.7 percent rate at which our population grew.[1] During the 15-year period 1929–1943 the contribution of manufacturing industries to national income—a rough measure of the proportion of our total energy devoted to manufacturing processes—averaged slightly more than 25 percent.[2] Of all the goods and services available for consumption or for use as capital equipment by individuals, business enterprises, and government in 1939 approximately 40 percent were manufactured products.

There are literally billions of business decisions to be made in the course of a year. Orders are placed, backlogs are built up, materials or components are received, and inventories are enlarged, maintained, or reduced. Needless to say the decisions are not always good ones and the endless procession of materials and parts is not always evenly balanced. Sometimes the flow of commodities becomes so thoroughly disrupted as to give the appearance of shortages where they do not actually exist. Such developments have resulted in buying waves which in turn caused production and stocking of materials and components at a much higher level than the real demand justified. Reduced output, operating losses, and unemployment have been the usual sequel to such situations.

Available industrial statistics do not begin to provide the businessman with all the information he needs to make decisions and thus to maintain a smoother flow of commodities. However, much information can be obtained from both government and private sources. For some types of manufacturing operations data are relatively complete; for others they are practically nonexistent.

USES OF INDUSTRIAL STATISTICS

The principal uses of industrial statistics fall into two general fields, (1) as a part, and a very important part, of the basic statistics on business activity for evaluating general economic changes; (2) for specific

---

[1] Solomon Fabricant, *The Output of Manufacturing Industries, 1899–1937*, National Bureau of Economic Research, N. Y., 1942, p. 52.

[2] *Survey of Current Business*, April 1944, p. 15.

use by businessmen in current operations and future planning. The use of industrial statistics, with other basic measures of commercial operations, to portray a composite picture of the level of total business activity is set forth in other chapters of this book, particularly Chapter 2. This discussion will be devoted exclusively to the principal value and uses of production figures as applied to practical considerations in the everyday problems of business.

As a practical matter, attention is directed to the distinctions between "current" and "benchmark" industrial statistics. While basically the two types are identical in principle, there is a wide variance in scope and detail. These differences determine the use of each as supplied to particular business problems.

The so-called benchmark industrial statistics are principally found in the biennial *Census of Manufactures*. With only few exceptions in privately collected series, the biennial census contains the most detailed enumeration of production of specific products, by physical quantities and values. Because of the complete coverage of all productive establishments, the census production figures are considered the base or benchmark for practically all other statistics relating to production.

Current industrial statistics are usually monthly, quarterly, or on some other short-period basis; they usually but not always cover only a representative portion of the industry or commodity so that the trends shown are considered reasonably accurate. Moreover, current statistics generally are less detailed than census figures as to individual products, and frequently include some data on such items as new orders, unfilled orders, and inventories, which are primarily of interest on a short-term basis.

The two kinds of industrial statistics are supplementary to each other and form a valuable source of information to businessmen when properly understood and applied.

Management. Business management finds many and varied uses for industrial statistics. They are not only used as an aid to making day-to-day decisions, but also find valuable application in the determination of longer range policies with respect to planning for the future. They provide one of the prime bases for the formulation of business policies and sound corporate management.

One of the first and most obvious uses of production statistics is in the evaluation of the production of a particular industry in relation to the total for all industry. Given an accurate array of production data periodically maintained, management can readily determine at all times its relative position in the total, as well as among other competitive industries.

It is easy now to look back at past Censuses of Manufactures and trace the competitive history of the automotive and carriage industries. It must never be forgotten, however, that the industrial economy is in a continuous state of change and that many competitive situations similar in character if not in degree are today being followed most closely by management. Intensely interesting stories of interindustry competition are still being unfolded with the continued compilation of production data in the silk, rayon, nylon, wool, and cotton industries; in the steel, aluminum, and plastics industries; the metal-, glass-, wood-, and paper-container industries, and many other industrial areas where management's decisions would be largely guesswork if it were not for a valuable backlog of industrial surveys.

Series of industrial statistics with a long continuity have great value even for an industry making a product so unique that it is virtually noncompetitive with other producing groups. For such an industry production statistics are essential to a study of the industry's short-term or long-term movements. It is particularly important that such industries have reliable data available. The very absence of competition from other industries is probably indicative of short-term swings, which are at variance with general business trends. These differences may be in magnitude of fluctuation or in the duration of the cycle. Knowledge of such variations is essential and fundamental to proper planning by the management in these industries.

Reliable statistics for an industry afford a basis on which an individual firm can analyze its competitive position within the industry. The individual firm is able to determine its contribution to the industry's total output and to check its management results. This can be done in terms of the firm's share of the industry's total profits, averages of employment per unit or per dollar output, unit labor costs, value of output per worker, materials costs, and other similar measures of efficiency which production information establish as guideposts. The firm must always be striving to better the averages if it is to prosper and grow. The manager of the firm is sailing a virtually uncharted sea if the statistical buoys and lighthouses are missing.

If the statistics are reasonably current, they afford guideposts not only for longer-range study, but also offer a basis for day-to-day operating decisions. Careful analysis of current series of data on production, inventories, shipments, and orders quickly reveals unbalanced operations. Such fundamental supply and demand analyses in the lumber industry, an industry which for a long time has utilized most effectively an extensive reservoir of statistical information, have been credited with being the primary factor in the industry's ability to moderate its formerly wide fluctuations.

Industry management is not limited to analyses of statistics for its own industry. Study of statistics for those industries from which it buys its supplies and to which it sells its products also furnishes illuminating operational guides without in any way necessitating or even fostering speculation. The firms in an industry can buy and stock their materials, components, fuels, and the like in a much more intelligent manner if it is possible to follow statistically the production and sales trends of the supplying industries. They can take appropriate advantage of the suppliers' seasonal operations better to integrate their own purchasing and production programs. Also, production programs can be properly geared to the seasonal and general trends of those industries to which they sell only if it is possible to analyze statistically the trends and fortunes of the consuming industries.

Industrial Marketing. In formulating plans and methods for marketing industrial goods, it is important to concentrate sales efforts and advertising appeals in the geographical areas where these are most likely to bear fruit, that is, in the places where potential customers are most abundant and active. There is a wealth of information in statistics such as those of the Census of Manufactures, which furnish data by states and by counties within the states on manufacturing activities. To utilize the statistics, one may select the industries which are the principal users of the materials, equipment, supplies, or services that a firm offers, and tabulate the combined production of these consuming industries in each state, taking the data from tables compiled in convenient form for just such purposes. The complexity of this analysis depends a great deal upon the commodity to be sold. A producer of foundry equipment wants to know primarily about the establishments that make castings. The producers of steel or machine tools, on the other hand, need to know about a great many industries that consume steel or are potential customers for machine tools. Sometimes it is desirable to use an outline map to indicate graphically the relative importance of the various areas. Distinctive colors or other devices may be used to denote various characteristics of the areas. A system of this kind becomes very useful if applied on the basis of small areas such as counties. It affords the soundest kind of basis for allotting territories to salesmen, and planning their itineraries so as to make the most effective use of their time and traveling expenses. Above all, it makes available to management, in simple visual form, an index of the areas which must be cultivated and those which offer such meager opportunities as not to be worth expenditure of time and money in extensive marketing efforts. If a tabulation or map of this kind is prepared, it frequently shows up weaknesses in distribution or marketing methods, either by pointing out neglected areas or those to which a disproportionate amount of effort has been devoted in relation to the potential in them.

Information Relating to Specific Industries. A progressive manufacturer usually knows the principal industries which use or consume his particular products, but he may not be aware of conditions in some of these fields unless he utilizes available statistics to keep him up to date as to the trend of production and the consequent increased or decreased output of those goods which are the outlet for the things he makes.

From experience it is possible to determine in numerous instances some relationship between output in the plants of customers and the total quantity of a given material or equipment which they will require. If production statistics show a significant increase in output of selected industries, and the sales of a manufacturer to his customers in those industries are not rising proportionately, there is probably something amiss in his marketing which must be corrected. Or, it may be that the product itself should be redesigned to meet changing requirements of industrial consumers.

Size of Outlets. While many government and other totalized statistical presentations do not give data for individual firms, figures as to number of establishments, total value of products, and number of wage earners employed do afford some basis for determining whether there are a large number of small or moderate-sized concerns to deal with, or whether the industry is composed of a few large units. Such factors may properly influence to a marked degree the distribution and sales methods which are most likely to be effective. The situation in this respect may differ greatly in various parts of the country, and this may be learned by examination of the state and county statistics applying to the field of business under investigation.

Broader Application of Existing Products. It is a common experience to find that devices or materials originally designed for one particular industrial use are readily adopted in entirely different industries when manufacturers learn, perhaps even by accident, that the commodity fills their needs. By a study of the products, in type and quantity, made in the various industrial fields, producers can search out these additional applications and develop broader markets for their existing products.

Introduction of New Products. When a manufacturer is considering the introduction of a new product, the need for estimating the probable size of the market for the new article becomes specially significant. In the postwar period, this situation is apt to be prevalent to an unusual degree. Production statistics can be used in a variety of ways as the key to the problem. Policy-makers, by the use of a bit of constructive imagination, may visualize a multitude of uses for the novel material or machine in industries with which they have had little past experience. It is essential to have some basic facts as to the size and products of these new fields from which to gauge the potential sales of the item they have created and to guide them in changes of marketing procedure which may be necessary to achieve success in selling it.

Industrial Statistics as a Stimulant. Examination of the industrial structure as revealed by details of production statistics is certain to create a broader viewpoint as to the potentials of the vast industrial markets of the United States. All makers of industrial goods can profit by a stimulus toward constructive, yet realistic, thinking in respect to their marketing problems. The basic statistics of industry will bring out the negative, or discouraging, elements as well as the highlights of the optimistic factors. Both are valuable for guidance in sound policy decisions.

Uses and Applications of Production Statistics to Consumer Markets. Most persons constantly engaged in consumer market research have found detailed production statistics of inestimable value in their studies. Such data can be used to prove their findings and to determine a sound sales program in line with current trends. There are numerous ways in which this information can be used advantageously such as gauging changing trends, consumer demands, upgrading, downgrading, extent of market, preference for substitute materials, and consumer acceptance.

Changes in prevailing demand are usually indicated more rapidly by the current production statistics than by any other source. Such knowledge cannot be gleaned from current sales data since the retailers are working with older supplies that they are endeavoring to clear off the shelves while they are still salable. However, these are immediately reflected in the orders placed with the suppliers and then by the production data as this becomes available in detail.

Consumer acceptance of substitute materials is also readily reflected in detailed production data. Naturally, this kind of information is very important in consumer market research. It enables sound buying and profitable selling, so necessary in any business venture. There are many ways in which this information can be used in any study of consumer markets.

Two outstanding examples of use of this type of information have been brought out in recent studies. Competition in the flooring field has been very acute in recent years. Complete data showing the production of the various types of materials used for flooring, such as lumber, tiles, and linoleum, enable the distributors to ascertain consumer preference and to cater to or attempt to modify a possible long-time trend.

In men's jackets there was a trend away from all fabric types toward the part-leather or all-leather variety. The current popularity of these was readily shown in the detailed production data, and by maintaining close contact with this information it was possible to plot this trend for one or two seasons in advance. Similarly, distributors of the non-rationed type of shoes were able to determine the consumer acceptance of these by closely watching the monthly production reports.

Availability of supplies is very important to those distributing direct to consumers. This knowledge enables them to plan their sales' activities and advertising programs, as well as their purchases. No other source of information can furnish these facts as well as the production statistics.

Knowledge of manufacturing activity as reflected in the production data can be very helpful to those merchants catering to the requirements of workers in production centers. Information on the hours worked and average hourly wage is reflected in the amount of wages paid, as now supplied in returns included in production statistics. The value of such information in consumer market research as an index of purchasing power does not require any further elaboration.

Many types of special equipment or work clothing are required by workers in certain kinds of factories. Any index of operation activity in such plants, as indicated by the production statistics, is important to those engaged in supplying the workers. Experienced consumer market researchers and the small businessman can use this information to advantage in gauging the extent of the market for the current season— by communities and by types of materials. The information on the number of workers employed, the wages being paid, and the rate of operations will yield a reasonable estimate on the extent of the market.

The foregoing discussion can only mention a few of the general and specific ways in which industrial statistics can be used. Their applications to day-by-day business problems and future business planning are as varied and innumerable as the matters that daily confront people either in the manufacturing business or dependent upon this branch of business for a livelihood. The management of a manufacturing enterprise cannot afford to be without continuous access to all available industrial statistics on the particular business. Postwar industry will be highly competitive, with more shifts and changes due to new materials, new processes, and new products. Under these conditions the need for information is more vital than ever.

THE CENSUS OF MANUFACTURES

The first attempt to obtain a complete statistical picture of manufacturing activities in the United States was in the decennial Census of 1810. The United States marshals and their deputies, who served as enumerators at that time, were asked to obtain information on the products manufactured in their districts, and Congress asked the Secretary of the Treasury to prepare "a report on the condition of manufactures" based on these data. Manufacturing was again surveyed in 1820 and 1840 (but not in 1830). Printed schedules were used in the Census of 1820 and information was requested on the products manufactured, their value, materials consumed, the number of employees classified by men, women, and boys and girls, a list of the machinery used, and "comments." The 1840 Census followed much the same pattern. These first three censuses of manufactures are generally held to be unsatisfactory because of incomplete coverage, lack of uniformity in reporting, and inadequate review and correction of the data obtained. Nevertheless, they provide an invaluable source of information in the beginnings of American industry.

From 1849 to 1899 the Census of Manufactures was a part of the decennial census and covered neighborhood, hand, and building trades, as well as factory industries. From 1904 to 1919 the Census of Manufactures was taken quinquennially, and it covered the factory system only, i.e., establishments whose products were valued at more than $500; those engaged in the custom trades and in the building trades were excluded. Beginning with 1921 the Census of Manufactures has been taken biennially, has continued to cover only the factory system, but firms with products valued at less than $5,000 have been excluded. The Biennial Censuses for 1941 and 1943 were suspended under the Second War Powers Act by Executive Order in order that the facilities of the Census Bureau could be used fully for more immediate and important war work.

Although changes in the industrial economy have made it necessary to modify the amount of information, and its classification, from one census period to another, the Census of Manufactures has maintained since 1849 reasonably comparable series on the number of establishments, number of wage earners, amount of wages paid, cost of materials, value of products, and value added by manufacture. To provide comparisons for industries and geographic areas when new classifications are adopted, the data obtained in the preceding census are often retabulated according to the new classification. It is not always possible to extract an entirely comparable series covering a long period for a particular industry, but these retabulations of data for the periods marked by definite changes help to make possible the construction of reasonable estimates which bridge these gaps.[3]

Basic Industrial Measures. Since manufacturing activities are carried on in establishments, data gathered from all establishments can be made to blanket the entire manufacturing segment of our economy. For each census year since 1909 there have been between 170,000 and 190,000 manufacturing establishments. It is the establishment which hires employees, consumes materials, and produces products. Many of the characteristics of these establishments cannot be related to more particular activities within the establishment, such as one of the several products which a single establishment may produce. Among the more important measures of an establishment's operations are those long compiled in Census of Manufactures: value of product, cost of materials, value added by manufacture, number of employees, and wages and salaries paid.

VALUE OF PRODUCT. The value of product of an establishment is the sum of the values of each of the products it produced during the year and the receipts for contract or commission work it performed for others. This may differ from the total sales of the establishment, since a part of its sales may be made from inventories or a part of the year's production may be added to the year's inventories; an establishment may also engage in some buying and selling operations which are not included in value of product, since goods purchased and resold in the same form are not included; and the sales of the company may be made either f.o.b. the producing plant or may include the cost of delivering the product to a point designated by the customer, whereas all production is valued f.o.b. the manufacturing establishment. The value of product for a given plant is an important measure of its size. And for a group of plants with similar industrial characteristics or geographic location it may serve as a basis of comparison with labor or materials costs.

[3] For a series of such industry estimates which have been prepared, together with the list of changes in census classifications and the problems imposed by these changes in constructing estimates, see Solomon Fabricant, *The Output of Manufacturing Industries, 1899–1937.* National Bureau of Economic Research, New York 1942.

Quite often the product of one manufacturing establishment is sold to other manufacturing establishments for use in the further processing of materials, e.g., an automobile body which the body maker sells to an establishment assembling and selling completed automobiles. Consequently the total value of product for several plants may contain some double counting. For relatively short periods the proportion of products leaving manufacturing industries which is counted twice is likely to be fairly stable, but over a longer period of time the relative amount of duplication may be seriously affected by changes in industrial organization, either from less integrated to more integrated establishments or by increased specialization among manufacturers. Because of these limitations value of product is primarily useful as a measure relating to individual establishments or to small groups of establishments having similar industrial characteristics.

COST OF MATERIALS AND VALUE ADDED BY MANUFACTURE. The entire value of a manufacturing plant's products cannot be attributed to the plant's activities. The plant works on materials which have been purchased from agricultural, mining, or other manufacturing plants; it uses up mill supplies and packs the finished product in purchased containers. The cost of these materials, supplies, containers, fuel, electrical energy, and contract work performed by other plants are compiled in the Census of Manufactures. When the sum of these costs is subtracted from the value of product the residual is a rough measure of the value added by manufacturing process in the reporting plant. The value which has been added to raw materials by all previous processors is included in these costs, which are subtracted, and the residual, "value added," is free from the duplication, which marks value of product. Containing no duplications, "value added" means the same thing for one or for one thousand plants. Consequently, it is the primary value measure for comparing industries, geographic areas, or other groupings of plants.

Value added by manufacture is not a measure of the profits of a particular plant or industry. It includes the costs of depreciation of capital account, advertising, taxes, insurance, maintenance, and repairs. These are all expenses that a manufacturing concern has to meet before its profits can be computed. Advertising, insurance, and possibly taxes represent services performed by other segments of the economy for manufacturing industries, and since the cost of these services is not deducted, "value added" is only a rough approximation of the contribution of the manufacturing segment to national income. Trading activities, which often add to a plant's profits, are excluded from value of product, cost of materials, and value added.

NUMBER OF EMPLOYEES. Another measure for comparing the relative size or activities of manufacturing plants, classified either by industry or geographic location, is the number of employees engaged in manufacturing activities. The Census of Manufactures in recent years has shown separate figures for employees engaged in production work, those engaged in force-account construction work, and those engaged in managerial, supervisory, sales, and other functions. Typically, at least for one period in the year, employees have been shown by sex. The number of wage earners engaged in manufacturing operations often is shown for each of the 12 months of the year.

Since some industries are experiencing peak production loads during the months when other industries are idle or operating at very low levels, no one month can be taken as representative of all industries. An "average number of wage earners" based on the 12 monthly figures is compiled and used as the basis for classifying plants by size.

Total wages and salaries paid employees throughout the year also are compiled by class of employee. An average annual earnings figure can be computed for wage earners by making use of the "average number of wage earners" and wages and salaries paid this class of worker. Since the number of force-account construction workers and of other employees is reported from only one payroll it is not possible to compute an average annual earnings figure for these groups. Wages and salaries, however, represent payment for a major portion of "value added."

Other Industrial Measures. The Census of Manufactures also includes statistics relating to capacity, man-hour input, and inventories for those industries for which these additional measures are needed and can be compiled. At relatively infrequent intervals data on the amount of power equipment in place and on the amount of electrical energy produced by manufacturing establishments are compiled for all industries. While there is a widespread interest in the capacity of the Nation's manufacturing plant to produce specific items it is often difficult and frequently impossible to measure this capacity without making assumptions which are untenable or which limit the value of the results to one specific and relatively unimportant use. Consequently measures of capacity have been limited to single-purpose equipment with physical capacity measurable in unambiguous terms, e.g., the capacity of an elevator to store wheat. The 1939 Census includes capacity figures for only a few industries.

While the "average number of employees" provides a rough measure of various industries as a source of employment, this measure is affected by differences in the length of both the working day and the work week.

A more precise measure is man-hours worked. Until recent years man-hour figures were not maintained by all industries as a part of their basic records, and the compiling of man-hour input data was limited to industries which had come to accept them as necessary operating statistics. The 1939 Census included data on wage-earner man-hours, by months, for 175 of the 446 industries covered.

Inventories are measured as of a particular time, since additions are continually being made to them and shipments continually draw from them. For most industries, inventory information is limited to two value figures, one covering all finished products, and the other covering the materials, supplies, and work in process. On two schedules—agricultural machinery and clay products and other refractories—used in the 1939 Census, inventory data were collected for individual products.

Data on the power-producing equipment, by type of equipment and by type of power (electrical, steam, mechanical), are compiled at infrequent intervals (usually at the decennial census period) in terms of rated horsepower or kilowatt hours. For 1939, this information was supplemented by the number and rated horsepower of electric motors operated. Detailed data were also obtained during this year on fuels, by type of fuel, and on purchased electric energy used in manufacturing plants. Although these data are not included in every Census of Manufactures, the shift from one type of power equipment to another is a slow, cumulative process.

Commodity Statistics. The Census of Manufactures gives a good deal of emphasis to measures of plant activity, as the plant is a convenient unit which permits a detailed classification of all manufacturing by industry and by location. Covering the entire range of manufacturing activity in commodity terms would be much more difficult, as even a small plant may produce a wide variety of commodities. Problems of marketing, shipping, packaging, and production, however, typically relate to specific commodities. With the increasing importance of these problems, the volume of commodity information in the Census of Manufactures has been increasing. These census data provide a benchmark against which currently compiled commodity data can be compared and evaluated. Two aspects of the benchmark concept as applied to commodity production are worth noting. In the first place, it provides complete coverage, including the incidental production of specific commodities in plants engaged principally in the production of other commodities. Too, the same period of production is covered for all plants, which is not necessarily the case when the data relate to billings, sales, or shipments.

Commodity production can be measured either in physical quantity terms or by its dollar value. There is interest in both measures. The Census of Manufactures consistently measures all commodity production by its value at the producing plant before freight and other delivery charges are added. Physical quantity measurement is also used when it is practicable. But physical quantity measurement is not always practicable. For example, to measure, in physical quantity terms, the production of scientific instruments would require a detailed classification of these instruments by type, sometimes by size, and often by degree of precision if their number was to be meaningful. Such classification might result in categories which were relatively unimportant. Detailed classification leading to meaningful quantity data may often leave only one or two producers of the commodities in a particular category. In such a case the results cannot be published without disclosing data reported by an individual establishment, and such disclosure is prohibited by law. Despite these limitations, the Census of Manufactures for 1939 compiled data for some 9,000 different commodity categories. Some categories, of course, were measured only by their value. For most, however, both physical quantity and value were given, and for these useful unit-value figures could be computed by simple division.

A more serious limitation of census treatment of commodity production is that it reflects only the commercial production; production for consumption in the producing plant often is not compiled. Thus fully integrated plants report only final products which go directly to consumers' hands. However, all plants report their production of component and intermediate products sold to other manufacturing establishments. Castings produced by commercial foundries are shown in the Census of Manufactures, but the large volume of castings produced in foundries integrated with subsequent manufacturing operations are inadequately reflected. Consequently, it is not possible to obtain from the Census of Manufactures the total volume of castings made during the year. Similar treatment is accorded forgings and stampings. Consequently, a comparison of the use of forgings, stampings, and castings cannot be made, although there are many areas in which these three types of processes directly compete.

Some plants perform manufacturing operations on a contract basis for other concerns. Receipts from this work are included in the value of product; and in those industries where contract work is prevalent, such as in the apparel trades, galvanizing establishments, and electroplaters, the type of work and the type of product on which the work is performed are reflected by the Census of Manufactures.

The commodities produced form the basis for classifying a plant by industry. An entire plant is classified in a particular industry according to the value of its principal product. Since many plants produce several commodities, there is some overlapping between commodity and industry classification. Typically, the Census of Manufactures shows commodity production classified by plants within the industry and by plants in other industries, thus giving some notion of the extent to which each commodity is produced by industrial specialization or as a secondary product. For the electrical machinery and other machinery fields, there is an additional classification distribution of production between "other industries in the same major group of industries" and "other industries outside the same major group of industries." While it is doubtful whether more information can be shown without disclosing the operations of individual plants, this limitation could be overcome by showing as much detail as possible on the industrial characteristics of the plants producing a commodity.

Industrial Organization. The Census of Manufactures is our chief source of information on changes in industrial organization. It shows not only the rise and decline in importance of particular commodities, but also areas in which specialization or integration increase in importance. The shifts in the location of particular industries are reflected in a series of censuses. Often the continuity of the Census of Manufactures is more important than the data it provides for a single census period.

Materials Consumed. Manufacturing industries are the chief consumers of materials produced by agriculture, mining, and other manufacturing industries. In part the consumption of these materials can be estimated, more or less satisfactorily, from a knowledge of the production of commodities. However, different manufacturers use different specifications, and materials can be substituted. The 1939 Census compiled information on materials consumed by 164 industries. For some commodities, such as sugar, consumption data were obtained from practically all industrial consumers. For others, consumption figures were obtained from only the consumers in a few selected industries; e.g., data on "iron and steel castings, purchased as such" were compiled for only five heating equipment industries.

"Materials consumed" data are direct information on the market for industrial materials. To some extent the need for this information can be satisfied by the rough estimates based on production data. In response to industry requests, data on materials consumption have been compiled for more materials and more industries during recent censuses.

How the Census of Manufactures Is Taken.   Census information is obtained from plant officials, either by enumerators who call at the plant or by mail questionnaire. Extensive use of field enumerators is usually confined to the decennial census periods, when the Bureau of the Census has a large force of enumerators in the field and is also conducting censuses of population, business, and mineral industries.

The questions asked manufacturers are determined by printed schedules which have been prepared after consulting with businessmen, trade associations, research organizations, and government agencies that depend upon the Census of Manufactures as a primary source of information on the operations of the industrial economy.

Enumeration is started early in January following the year covered by the census and is continued until the required information is obtained from all establishments. The editing and processing of the returns can start as soon as the first schedule is received but a final tabulation of the returns for an industry, city, industrial area, or state cannot be made available until the last return for the group is received and processed.

How the Census of Manufactures Is Published.   To make census data available as early as possible preliminary tabulations are prepared and published as soon as returns from all but a few of the smaller establishments in the industry are received and processed. These preliminary releases provide only a limited amount of information, usually the general statistics (the number of establishments, value of product, wage earners, etc.) and product data. Typically these releases also contain comparative figures from the preceding census. Preliminary releases are also prepared for each industry (or small groups of industries), for each state (with totals for each county and city with 10,000 or more inhabitants), for each city with more than 100,000 population, and for each of 33 industrial areas, i.e., groups of highly industrialized counties drawing upon more or less the same labor market. The first of the 359 preliminary releases covering 1939 data was issued July 9, 1940.

Industry is the basis for organizing the commodity production and consumption information in the Census of Manufactures. Statistics on the production of commodities are published as a part of the statistics for the industry typically producing the commodity. Although plants in several industries may produce a commodity, its entire production is shown in one place, that is, in the report for the industry with which it is principally associated. For example, all butter production is shown in the butter industry, although an appreciable part of total butter output is produced in the cheese industry or in other dairy products industries. Usually the production of commodities is shown for the United States only; when state distributions are made of commodity production they are published in the industry series.

When the canvass of an industry has been completed, final tabulations for the industry are issued in a printed bulletin. These bulletins contain all the basic statistics prepared for the industry; in fact, the published census volumes on industries (for 1939, Vol. II, Parts 1 and 2) consist of reprints of these industry bulletins and summaries for groups of related industries. In the 1939 Census the 446 industries were covered in a series of 64 industry bulletins, which were later gathered into two volumes of *Reports by Industries*.

The 20 major industry groups in the 1939 Census, and the number of industries included in each, follow:

Group 1. Food and Kindred Products—46 industry reports.
2. Tobacco Manufactures.
3. Textile Mill Products and Other Fiber Manufactures—15 industry reports.
4. Apparel and Other Finished Products Made From Fabrics and Similar Materials—19 industry reports.
5. Lumber and Timber Basic Products—4 industry reports.
6. Furniture and Finished Lumber Products—24 industry reports.
7. Paper and Allied Products—12 industry reports.
8. Printing, Publishing, and Allied Industries—14 industry reports.
9. Chemical and Allied Products—36 industry reports.
10. Products of Petroleum and Coal—6 industry reports.
11. Rubber Products—4 industry reports.
12. Leather and Leather Products—9 industry reports.
13. Stone, Clay, and Glass Products—31 industry reports.
14. Iron, Steel and Their Products, except Machinery—39 industry reports.
15. Nonferrous Metal and Their Products—21 industry reports.
16. Electrical Machinery—13 industry reports.
17. Machinery (except electrical)—33 industry reports.
18. Automobiles and Automobile Equipment—2 industry reports.
19. Transportation Equipment except Automobiles—8 industry reports.
20. Miscellaneous Industries—34 industry reports.

Bulletins are also issued for each of the 48 states and for "outlying areas." These final bulletins, bound as Volume III of the *Census of Manufactures: 1939*, include general statistics by industry for the state, for cities in the state with more than 100,000 inhabitants, and for all the industrial areas which are either wholly or partly in the state. Totals (i.e., not classified by industry) are shown for each county and each city with more than 10,000 inhabitants. The number of establishments by major industrial group are also shown by county. For the state as a whole, distributions by size of plant (size measured by number of wage earners and by value of product) are also shown.

In addition to the industry and state bulletins, some 22 bulletins dealing with special subjects were prepared from the 1939 Census of Manufactures data. The contents of these bulletins, most of which are bound as Volume I of the *Census of Manufactures: 1939*, are indicated by their titles, which are:

Changes in Distribution of Manufacturing Wage Earners, 1899–1939.

Consumption of Fuel in Manufacturing Establishments for Census Years 1909, 1919, 1929, and 1939.

Consumption of Fuel by Manufacturing Establishments for the United States, 1939, 1937, 1929, 1925, and 1923, and by Geographic Divisions and States, 1939, 1937, and 1929.

Cost of Materials, Supplies, Fuel, Purchased Electric Energy, and Contract Work Used in Manufacturing Establishments, for All Industry Groups Combined, 1939, 1937, and 1935, and by Industry Groups, Industries, Geographic Divisions and States, 1939.

Maps Showing Distribution of Wage Earners Engaged in Manufacturing in the United States, by Counties Classified by Six Size Groups, Principal Industrial Counties, and Industrial Areas, 1939.

General Statistics, for Industry Groups, for Industries, and for Geographic Divisions and States, 1939.

Industrial Areas—Summary Statistics, 1939, 1937, 1935, and 1929, and Areas Ranked by Number of Wage Earners, 1939.

Inventories in Hands of Manufacturers at the Beginning and End of 1939 and 1937.

Manufacturing Establishments Distributed by Industry Groups, for Geographic Divisions, States, and Counties, 1939.

Materials Consumed in Selected Industries, 1939.

Persons Employed in Manufacturing Establishments, by Industrial Areas, 1939.

Persons Employed in Manufacturing Establishments, by Sex, 1939.

Prime Movers, Generators, and Motors; Electric Energy Consumed—Country as a Whole and 33 Industrial Areas, 1939 and 1929.

Prime Movers, Generators, and Motors; Electric Energy Consumed, by Geographic Divisions and States, 1939, 1929, 1927, and 1925.

Relative Importance of Leading Industries, for the United States, 1939.

Relative Importance of States, Based on Value of Products, 1939 and 1937.

Relative Importance of Cities Having 100,000 or more Inhabitants, Based on the Value of Products as Reported for the Census of Manufactures, 1939.

Summary for Establishments Classified as to Size by Number of Wage Earners, for Industrial Areas, 1939.

Summary Statistics for Establishments Grouped by Size as Measured by Value of Products, 1939.

Type of Organization of Manufacturing Establishments—Summary for the United States, 1939 and 1929; Statistics by Industry Groups, Industries, and Geographic Divisions and States, 1939.

Wage Earners, by Months, for all Industry Groups Combined, 1939, 1937, and 1929, and by Industry Groups, Industries, and Geographic Divisions and States, 1939.

Man-Hour Statistics for 171 Industries, 1939. (Prepared in cooperation with the Bureau of Labor Statistics, Labor Department.)

CURRENT INDUSTRIAL STATISTICS

While the Census of Manufactures provides business with a vast quantity of general and detailed data on the growth and structure of American manufacturing, it does not supply current facts which are of primary interest to industry for its day-to-day operations. Census of Manufactures data may be of real help in deciding whether a new factory should be built and, if so, where and whether salesmen's territories should be redistributed. Data available at much more frequent intervals are needed, however, to help a businessman determine what policy he should follow regarding current inventories or what products or regions deserve special consideration as a result of recent developments. These needs can be met in part from the monthly and quarterly statistics compiled and published by the government. In some respects these data represent a continuation on a sample basis of selected important items from the Census of Manufactures. Their use is likely to be more effective therefore if considered relative to the benchmark provided by the Census of Manufactures in previous years.

Current Statistics of the Department of Commerce and the War Production Board. The statistics of the Bureau of the Census of the Department of Commerce and the War Production Board provide the only data that cover a wide range of products. Many of the current industrial surveys of the Bureau of the Census were inaugurated at the request of business groups; others are required by law. In no case does the Bureau have any administrative responsibility other than the collection of statistics. The current statistics of the War Production Board, however, arose entirely as a by-product of the production control activities of that agency.

The statistics compiled by the Bureau of the Census from current reports prior to the war were formerly issued under the general caption "Current Statistical Service" and are now included in "Facts for Industry." The commodities or industries covered are shown in the listing of titles beginning on page 70. These releases, in addition to a tabular presentation of the data, carry a minimum of descriptive text suitable for newspaper and trade journal use.

The War Production Board, in directing the conversion of the vast American industrial organization to the production of military goods, collected far more facts about manufacturing than were ever before obtained by any government agency. Nearly every type of manufacturing establishment in the country supplied some information to that agency. Most of these data were obtained for very specific tasks and were not of a general statistical character. Many of them dealt with individual transactions of particular companies. Applications for materials and components had to be approved and other minute details of plant operation were watched by the War Production Board in the critical areas of military production. As a result of this intimate examination of industrial operations, a large body of detailed information of great potential value to business as well as to government was assembled. In addition, the War Production Board assembled a considerable volume of information of a more general nature which was used in establishing general control policies.

The War Production Board in cooperation with the Department of Commerce and to a limited extent with other agencies began to release statistics on a wide variety of manufacturing activities early in 1944. By the middle of 1945 an appreciable part of this reservoir of industrial information had been tapped, but there remains a great deal that has not been exploited. Permanent agencies of government, particularly the Bureau of Mines, have worked with the War Production Board to preserve these data for future use. The data that have thus far been released are in the "Facts for Industry" [4] series, which also includes the statistical series prepared by the Department of Commerce. The titles of the releases issued up to the early part of 1945 are shown below.

General Reports:
    Facilities Expansion, July 1940–June 1944.
    Metal Products (Part I, Value of Shipments and Unfilled Orders, by Product, Pre-War Industry, and Claimant Agency, 1st Quarter 1944—Part II, Consumption and Inventories of Controlled Materials and Their Use in Metal-Products Industries, 1st Quarter 1944—Plant Operations, 2nd and 3rd Quarters, 1944).
    Summary of Materials Consumption for New Construction in the United States, Quarterly.
    U. S. War Production, Monthly since July 1940.
    U. S. Production of Selected Combat Items, and Scheduled Production, Monthly.
Processed Foods:
    Wheat and Wheat Flour Stocks (Held by Mills, Quarterly).
    Wheat Ground and Wheat-Milling Products (Production, Monthly).
Textile Mill Products, Apparel, and Leather Products:
    Boots, Shoes and Slippers, Other than Rubber (Production, Monthly). Cotton Broad Woven Goods (Production in the United States by Type of Goods, Quarterly).
    Cotton and Rayon Woven Goods Finished (Production in the United States, Quarterly).
    Cotton and Spun Rayon Sale Yarn, Cotton Cordage and Twine (Production in the United States, Quarterly).
    Gloves and Mittens (Production, Monthly).

   [4] Available from the Bureau of the Census.

Knit Outerwear (Production by Type of Garment, Shipments, Yarn Consumption, and Machines in Place, Monthly).

Materials Used in the Woolen and Worsted and Carpet and Rug Industries (U. S. Consumption by Type of Fiber, Monthly).

Men's, Youths', and Boys' Clothing and Cotton, Leather, and Allied Garments Cut (Production, Civilian and Government, Monthly).

Pyroxylin Coated Fabrics and Paper (Production, Shipments, and Unfilled Orders, Monthly).

Rayon Broad Woven Fabrics (Production in the United States by Type and Quantity, Quarterly).

Underwear and Knit Cloth for Sale (Production, Shipments, Stocks and Orders of Underwear, and Production of Knit Cloth).

Wool Manufactures (Commercial Stocks of Wool and Related Fibers, Quarterly; Fiber Consumption and Yarn Production, Monthly; Wool Machinery Activity; Monthly, Woolen and Worsted Woven Goods, Quarterly Production for the United States by Type of Goods).

Yarn Produced by the Woolen and Worsted and Carpet and Rug Industries (U. S. Production by Type of Yarn and System of Spinning, Monthly).

Lumber and Lumber Products:

Hardwood Veneer and Plywood (Consumption and Stocks of Raw Materials, Production, Shipments, and Consumption and Stocks of Veneer and Production of Plywood, by Species for the United States, Annual).

Hardwood Veneer and Plywood Statistics (Monthly).

Lumber (Distributors' Stocks and Receipts, Quarterly).

Lumber (Mill Stocks, by Regions, States, and Species, Monthly).

Lumber (Production by Regions, States, Mill Size Classes, and Species, Monthly).

Lumber in the War Program (Production, Consumption, and Stocks, Monthly).

Red Cedar Shingles and Shakes (Production, Shipments, and Mill Operations in the United States, and Imports of Shingles from Canada, Monthly).

Softwood Plywood (Production, Consumption, and Stocks of Materials, Annual).

Softwood Plywood (Production, Shipments, and Stocks of, and Consumption and Stocks of Materials, Monthly).

Paper and Allied Products:

Book Publishing Industry in the United States (Annual).

Census of Pulp Mills and of Paper and Paperboard Mills (Annual).

Containerboard (Inventory at Converting Plants, by Type of Board and Zone, Monthly).

Magazine Publishing Industry in the United States (Annual).

Newspaper Publishing in the United States (Annual).

Paper and Paperboard (United States Production by Type, Monthly).

Paper and Paperboard (Production by Type of Paper and Paperboard and Consumption of Fibrous Materials by Type of Material, for the United States for Geographic Areas, and for States, 1942, 1943, 1944).

Shipping Containers (Corrugated and Solid Fibre, Shipments by Rating Pattern, Monthly).

Waste Paper (Receipts and Inventory at Mills, Monthly).

Wood Pulp and Other Fibrous Materials (Production and Consumption in the Manufacture of Paper and Paperboard in the United States, Annual).

Chemicals and Products:

Animal Glue and Gelatin (United States Production, Shipments, and Stocks, Monthly).

Cellulose Plastic Products (Production, Consumption, and Shipments in the United States, Monthly).

Chemicals (United States Production, Consumption, and Stocks of, Annual and Monthly).

Chemicals (United States Production, and Stocks of Synthetic Organic Chemicals, Monthly) (Tariff Commission).

Chemicals (United States Production, Consumption, and Stocks of Selected Products of Mines, Coke Ovens, and Smelters) (Bureau of Mines).

Lacquer (Sales, Quarterly).

Paint, Varnish, Lacquer, and Filler (Sales, Monthly).

Plastic Paints, Cold-Water Paints, and Calcimines (Sales, Monthly).

Superphosphate (Production, Disposition, and Stocks by States, Monthly).

Non-Metallic Minerals and Their Products:

Asphalt and Tar Roofing and Siding Products (Shipments, Monthly).

Glass Containers (Shipments, Production, and Stocks of Glass Containers by Type, Monthly).

Structural Clay Products (Production, Shipments, and Stocks for the United States and for Geographic Areas, Monthly).

Basic Metals:

Aluminum (Primary Production and Secondary Recovery, Monthly).

Aluminum (U. S. Metal Production and Fabricated Product Shipments, Monthly).

Aluminum Castings (Shipments by Type, Monthly).

Brass Mill Production (Monthly).

Brass and Bronze Alloy Ingot (Production by Type of Alloy, Monthly).

Gray Iron Castings (Shipments by Type of Castings, Production, Shipments, New Orders, and Unfilled Orders by Type of Casting, Monthly).

Malleable Iron Castings (Production and Orders Booked, Monthly).

Magnesium (U. S. Metal Production and Fabricated Product Shipments, Monthly).

Magnesium (Primary Production and Secondary Recovery, Monthly).

Magnesium Ingot (Production, Monthly).

Silver (Consumption, Production, and Imports, Quarterly).

Steel Castings (Shipments, Production, Orders, and Rated Monthly Capacity, Monthly).

Steel Forgings (Shipments, Unfilled Orders, and Consumption of Steel, Monthly).

White-Base Antifriction Bearing Metals (Shipments and Consumption, Monthly).

Fabricated Metal Products:

Aluminum Fabricated Products (Shipments, Monthly).

Cooking and Heating Appliances, Domestic Non-Electric (Production, Inventory, and Shipments by Fuel Type, Monthly).

Cutlery (Production and Shipments, Quarterly).

Enameled Ware (Shipments, Quarterly).

Files and Rasps (Shipments and Unfilled Orders, Quarterly).

Flatware (Shipments, Quarterly).

Galvanized Cans (Shipments, Quarterly).

Liquid Fuel Lamps and Lanterns (Shipments by Type, Quarterly).

Magnesium Fabricated Products (Shipments, Monthly).

Marine Fittings Hardware (Manufacturers' Shipments and Unfilled Orders, Monthly).

Mechanics Hand Service Tools (Shipments and New and Unfilled Orders, Monthly).

Metal Cans (Shipments by Manufacturers of All-Metal Cans, by Product to be Packed, Monthly).

Porcelain Enameled Products (Shipments, Monthly).

Pressure Vessels (Shipments, New Orders, Orders Cancelled, and Unfilled Orders, Monthly).

Razor Blades (Production and Shipments, Quarterly).

Steel Boilers (New Orders, Monthly).

Steel Shipping Barrels, Drums, and Pails (Production, Monthly).

Tire Chains (Shipments and Unfilled Orders, Monthly).

Machinery Except Electrical:

Angledozers and Bulldozers (Shipments and Unfilled Orders, Quarterly).

Bituminous Heating Kettles (Shipments, Quarterly).

Blowers, Fans, Unit Heaters, and Accessory Equipment (Value of Orders Booked, Quarterly).

Commercial Refrigeration and Air Conditioning Equipment in 1940.

Compressors (Reciprocating) (Shipments, New Orders, Orders Cancelled, and Unfilled Orders, Monthly).

Concrete and Bituminous Pavers (Shipments, Annual).

Concrete Mix-Agitators, Truck-Mounted (Shipments, Annual, 1937–1941, Quarterly).

Construction Machinery (Shipments and Unfilled Orders for Selected Machines, Quarterly).

Contractors' Concrete Mixers (Shipments, Annual, Shipments and Unfilled Orders, Quarterly).

Contractors' Pumps (Shipments, Annual, Shipments and Unfilled Orders, Quarterly).

Conveying Machinery and Mechanical Power Transmission Equipment (Shipments, New Orders, Orders Cancelled, and Unfilled Orders, Monthly).

Domestic Ice Refrigerators (Production, Shipments, and Inventory, Quarterly).

Domestic Pumps, Water Systems, and Windmills (Shipments, Monthly).

Fans, Blowers, and Exhausters (Monthly Shipments, New Orders, Orders Cancelled, and Unfilled Orders).

Farm Machinery and Equipment (Actual and Scheduled Production, Monthly).

Farm Machines and Equipment (Production and Sales of, Annual).

Foundry Equipment and Electric Metal Melting Furnaces (Shipments and Unfilled Orders, Monthly).

Galvanized Range Boilers and Tanks for Hot Water Heaters (Shipments, Stocks, New Orders, Unfilled Orders, and Production, Monthly).

Graders (Shipments and Unfilled Orders, Annual and Quarterly).

Hauling Scrapers (Shipments, Annual and Quarterly).

Heat Exchangers (Shipments, New Orders, Orders Cancelled, and Unfilled Orders, Monthly).

Heat-Treating Furnaces (Shipments and New and Unfilled Orders, Monthly).

High-Pressure Blowers (Shipments, New Orders, Orders Cancelled, and Unfilled Orders, Monthly).

Industrial Power Trucks (Production, Annual).

Internal Combustion Engines (Manufacturers' Shipments of, 1943 and 1944 Monthly).

Machine Tools (Shipments and New and Unfilled Orders, Monthly).

Machine Tools and Foundry Equipment (Shipments and Unfilled Orders, Monthly).

Mechanical Stokers (Factory Sales, Monthly).

Metal Cutting Tools (Shipments and New and Unfilled Orders, Monthly).

Mining Machinery (Distribution of, Produced in the United States, Monthly).

Oil Burners (Unfilled Orders, New Orders, Stocks, Shipments, and Production, Monthly).

Portable Pneumatic and Electric Tools (Shipments and New and Unfilled Orders, Monthly).

Power Cranes and Shovels (Shipments, Annual, Shipments and Unfilled Orders, Quarterly).

Precision Measuring and Testing Machines, Instruments, and Toolroom Specialties (Shipments and Unfilled Orders, Monthly).

Pumps (Industrial) (Shipments, New Orders, Orders Cancelled, and Unfilled Orders, Monthly).

Resistance Welding Electrodes (Shipments, New Orders (Net), and Unfilled Orders, Monthly).

Resistance Welding Machines (Shipments, New Orders (Net), and Unfilled Orders, Monthly).

Road Rollers (Shipments, Annual, Shipments and Unfilled Orders, Quarterly).

Snow Plows (Shipments, Annual, Shipments and Unfilled Orders, Quarterly).

Street Sweepers (Shipments, Annual, Shipments and Unfilled Orders, Quarterly).

Tractor-Mounted Cranes and Shovels (Shipments, Annual, Shipments and Unfilled Orders, Quarterly).

Trenching Machines (Shipments, Annual, Shipments, Quarterly).

Warm-Air Furnaces, Floor and Wall Furnaces, Unit Heaters, and Blower-Filter Units (Shipments and Production, Monthly).

Electrical Machinery, Equipment, and Supplies:

Dry Cell Batteries (Production and Shipments by Type, Quarterly).

Electrical Connectors (AN, Similar to AN, and Coaxial Types, Only) (Manufacturers' Shipments, Orders, and Inventories, Monthly).

Electric Lamps and Bulbs (Production and Shipments, Quarterly).

Flashlight Cases (Production and Shipments, Quarterly).

Lighting Fixtures (Incandescent and Fluorescent, Shipments, Quarterly).

Storage Batteries (Automotive Replacement Type, Shipments, Quarterly).

Transportation Equipment:

Integral Buses and Bus Bodies (Deliveries of Civilian and Military, Monthly).

Motor Trucks and Truck Tractors (Production of Civilian and Military, Monthly).

Motor Truck Trailers (Production of Civilian and Military, Monthly).

Miscellaneous:

Alarm Clocks (Shipments, Quarterly).

Asbestos Power and Construction Products (Production, Quarterly).

Asbestos Textiles (Allocations by End Use, Quarterly).

Baby Carriages, Strollers, and Walkers (Production and Shipments, Quarterly).

Commercial Canning Supplies (Production of Commercial Closures, Beverage Crowns, and Food Crowns, Quarterly).

Fountain Pens (Production and Shipments, Quarterly).

Ground Talc (Supply, Consumption, and Stocks in the United States, Annual).

Home Canning Supplies (Production of Home Canning Jars, Closures, and Sealing Rings in the United States, Annual).

Indexes, "Facts for Industry."

Industrial Diamonds (Average Imports, Annual, Sales, Quarterly).
Mechanical Pencils (Production and Shipments, Quarterly).
Pen Holders and Pen Nibs (Production and Shipments, Quarterly).
Photographic Film (Production and Shipments, Quarterly).
Safety Equipment (Distribution in 1943 and Requirements in 1944).
Toothbrushes (Shipments from Plants, Quarterly).
Wood-Case Pencils (Production and Shipments, Quarterly).
Umbrella Frames (Production and Shipments, Quarterly).
X-Ray Equipment (Shipments, Quarterly).

Development of Industrial Statistics by Other Agencies. Other agencies of government which collect statistics on manufacturing primarily as a part of their administrative operations are recognizing that the dissemination of information to the public has become increasingly important. None of these agencies deal with the entire manufacturing field except with respect to some specialized area such as taxes or labor.

The Department of Agriculture is concerned primarily with the well-being of the American farmer. To watch over the interests of the farmer, the Department needs to know a great deal about farmers, farms, farming, and farm products. The statistical needs of the Department go farther, however. They include, for example, the markets for farm products, which often are manufacturing plants. Sometimes the Department of Agriculture has been able to get this information from the Department of Commerce or from other sources, such as trade associations. Other times the needed data were not collected by anyone and the Department undertook to collect them. Thus statistics on production and stocks of butter, cheese, canned and condensed milk, and other dairy products have been compiled by the Agricultural Marketing Service of the Department so that departmental officials and farmers could be kept informed about the market for milk. Figures on livestock slaughter, where the Department has had special responsibilities for the inspection of meats, were compiled to show the entrance of livestock into processing channels. The United States Forest Service in the Department of Agriculture cooperates with the Bureau of the Census in gathering information on lumber production and other sawmill operations.

The Department of the Interior has a vital interest in manufacturing statistics. Most mineral products move directly from the mine to the mill or factory. In fact, manufacturing establishments like smelters, coke ovens, lime kilns, refineries of natural salts, and some blast furnaces and petroleum refineries are tied very closely with mining activities. For years the Bureau of Mines has been an important source of information on smelter production of various chemicals and other basic manufactured products of mineral origin (see Chapter 4).

The Bureau of Mines has also made estimates of the consumption of both new metal and scrap metal by manufacturing establishments. The Fish and Wildlife Service in the Department of the Interior compiles current data on fish canning and cooperates with the Bureau of the Census in obtaining data on canned fish products for the Biennial Census of Manufactures.

Many other agencies compile industrial statistics collected as an incident to their administrative activities. The Bureau of Internal Revenue, in the Treasury Department, compiles extensive statistics on distilled liquors and other alcoholic beverages. These data include production by type or kind, withdrawals from bonded warehouses, the quantity bottled, the quantity bottled in bond, the quantity rectified, the materials consumed in manufacture by type of grain or other material, and the amount lost in warehouses through leakage or evaporation. These data are distributed by state and some are by seasons of production. All these data are needed for the proper administration of the excise taxes on alcoholic beverages. The Bureau of Internal Revenue also collects data on tobacco products and on other manufactured articles subject to excise taxes. The Federal Power Commission compiles data on the power used by various manufacturing industries. The Tariff Commission is the source of current information on the production of synthetic organic chemicals. The Labor Department compiles some industrial statistics regularly in connection with the collection of data on employment conditions and has made many special surveys in which detailed production data were obtained for use in productivity studies. The War Food Administration and the Office of Price Administration obtain data on stocks of manufactured foodstuffs. The Federal Trade Commission in conducting inquiries about trade practices has made extensive studies of the competitive position, price structure, and other operations of many industries.

The substantial volume of current industrial statistics now compiled by government agencies represents a gradual accumulation of individual series. Nearly all of these were developed individually and independently around a single industry, commodity, or groups of related commodities. They reflect the varied interests of the agencies or trade groups sponsoring them and the peculiarities of production or trade practices in the industries concerned. Thus some data relate to production, shipments, sales, or some other factors measuring the flow of commodities; others cover inventories of material or finished goods; and others reflect anticipated activity, as unfilled orders. Some series cover all manufactures in a particular industry or the entire production of a single commodity. Others include only a part of the total. Unfortunately, it is not always possible to determine how complete the coverage is or how accurate the statistics are in other respects. About the only way for the consumer of statistics to find out about the value of the current statistics for his own purposes is to ask the compiling agency about the particular series in which he is interested.

Availability of Government Industrial Statistics. Most of the government agencies compiling monthly or quarterly data issue them in the form of press releases or reports. Federal agencies, under economy regulations, may not distribute these releases unless there is a specific request for them. Most of the reports are available, however, without charge upon receipt of a specific written request to the compiling agency; others, such as the Census of Manufactures volumes, may be obtained at a nominal cost from the Superintendent of Documents, Government Printing Office.

Coverage and Gaps in Industrial Statistics. Despite all the statistics published by the government and by trade associations, the businessman more often than not is unable to obtain the facts that he needs. Usually he cannot learn the supply of the materials he uses, or the total output of the industry of which he is a part, or how much of this output is being used up.

There are exceptions. For example, the producer of wood pulp can secure information on the supply of his principal material, pulp wood, on the activity of his own industry, and on the consumption of pulp and competitive fibrous materials in the production of paper. Few other industrialists are in as favorable a position as far as figures on their industries operations are concerned. Ordinarily, some facts can be obtained about part of the raw materials a businessman buys or the products that he sells, but rarely will available statistics show a fully integrated picture of an industry's operations, including both the supply and demand situation.

Monthly or quarterly statistics are entirely missing or grossly inadequate for furniture, converted paper products, chemical products, and many other important commodity areas. Prior to the war, government statistics were decidedly weak in the very important field of machinery, electrical equipment, and other fabricated metal products. Data were also incomplete on production of apparel, basic chemicals and related products, various manufactured foods, fabricated wood products, and many other major groups of commodities. During the war these difficulties and deficiencies were remedied to some extent— more, however, in the collection of statistics for the control programs than in the publication of data for business use.

CHAPTER 4

MINERAL STATISTICS

Y. S. LEONG
Bureau of the Budget

This chapter is intended as a guide to important statistical series on production, sales and shipments, stocks held by producers, distributors and consumers, and consumption of minerals and mineral products. The statistics of mineral foreign trade, prices, costs and other financial items, and labor are covered in other chapters of this volume.

SOURCES OF INFORMATION

Bureau of Mines. The Bureau of Mines of the Department of the Interior has long been the main source of statistical information on minerals. Since 1925, when it took over the collection of mineral data from the U. S. Geological Survey, this agency has gathered and published annual statistics for all minerals of commercial importance; more frequent information is available for a smaller number.

The annual statistics are published in the *Minerals Yearbook*, which covers the calendar year and is usually available for distribution the following October.[1] This volume is composed of a series of chapters, each covering one important mineral and its products and by-products, or several minor minerals and their products and by-products, and each chapter is written by one or more mineral specialists. In general each chapter presents for the United States the statistics of the mineral and its products for the year covered and for a varying number of years back. It shows production by states, districts or other geographical

[1] This annual report has undergone several changes in title since its inception in the early 80's. From 1882 to 1893 it was entitled *Mineral Resources of the United States* and was compiled by the U. S. Geological Survey; from 1894 to 1899 it was published as parts of the 16th to 21st annual reports of the Director of the U. S. Geological Survey; from 1900 to 1931 it was published under the original title (by the Geological Survey from 1900 to 1923, and by the Bureau of Mines from 1924 to 1931); from 1932 to date it has been known as the *Minerals Yearbook*. These volumes may be purchased from the Superintendent of Documents ($2.25). Individual chapters of the *Yearbook* are usually printed beginning in June, and may be obtained from the Bureau of Mines as they become available.

subdivisions; distribution; consumption; producers' stocks; prices; imports and exports by countries; and newly discovered reserves. The statistics of production, consumption, and other categories are analyzed for the year in relation to those for past years. The important factors that affected the supply and demand situation during the year—new discoveries and exploration of reserves, opening of new mines, drilling of additional wells, installation of new capacities, introduction of new and improved technology, discovery and extension of new uses—are surveyed. Finally the production of each mineral in each of the major producing countries is shown along with other available data.

There are, in addition to the minerals chapters, usually two sections —one which reviews the major economic and other factors affecting all the mineral industries and presents a statistical summary showing the production of each mineral in the country as a whole and in each state, and one discussing employment and accidents.

Before 1940 the Bureau of Mines collected and published weekly, monthly, and quarterly statistics on only a limited number of minerals. During the war, the collection of this current information was greatly expanded to cover practically every critical mineral and mineral product, including scrap. In general, two types of current surveys were inaugurated for each critical mineral or mineral product—a producer's report of production, receipts, consumption, shipments, and stocks, and a consumer's report of receipts, consumption, sales, and stocks.[2]

The Bureau of the Census. The Bureau of the Census of the Department of Commerce has collected statistics on minerals for almost a century and a half in connection with each decennial census and two special mineral censuses.[3] In recent censuses, data on the following items were assembled for each mineral industry covered: production in terms of quantity and value; number of enterprises; number of mines, quarries, or wells; persons engaged; salaries; wages; contract work; supplies; materials; fuel used; expenditures for development; number and rated capacity of power equipment. For most of the mineral industries the statistics are classified by states, and for some of them by

[2] Current data have been released under the general title of *Mineral Industry Surveys.* These reports also carry a specific title indicating the mineral and period covered, for example, "Zinc in September 1944." They are distributed free of charge. The reader who wishes to receive any of the reports regularly should have his name placed on the Bureau's mailing list. Lists of the reports available for distribution are given in the Bureau's "List of Publications" issued generally once a year, and in the monthly supplements.

[3] The mineral industries were covered in the decennial censuses since 1810, except those for 1820, 1830, and 1900. There were two special censuses, one for 1902 and the other for 1935.

districts, regions, or counties. The 1939 census, which is perhaps the most comprehensive as to industries and subject matter covered, included for the first time information on man-shifts, man-hours, output per man-hour, and number of power loading machines.[4]

War Production Board. The War Production Board was more a storehouse than a source of information on critical minerals, for of the volumes of statistical data that it collected or had other agencies collect for it only little has been released to the public. Each of the divisions administering the program for mineral materials—steel, copper, aluminum and magnesium, mica-graphite, tin, lead and zinc, miscellaneous minerals, and mining—collected periodic detailed statistics, which for the most part were tabulated for confidential administrative use. If and when available, statistical summaries of these data will be of considerable interest and value to businessmen.[5]

Petroleum Administration for War. Although the Petroleum Administration for War administered one of the most complex war production and distribution programs, it collected very little information directly from the petroleum industry. Nevertheless, it was an important storehouse of data on the operations of the petroleum industry during the war period, assembling from existing public and private statistical agencies current statistics on supply, disposition, and requirements.

Solid Fuels Administration for War. The Solid Fuels Administration for War has been the main source of information on bituminous coal since the latter part of 1943, when it took over from the defunct Bituminous Coal Division the function of collecting all statistics on bituminous coal except cost data. By agreement the Office of Price Administration collects data on cost and realization. The Bureau of Mines releases the *Weekly Coal Report*, which contains weekly statistics on the production of bituminous coal and anthracite separately and monthly statistics on production, industrial consumption, retail sales, industrial consumers' stocks and retail dealers' stocks of bituminous coal and anthracite separately, and the *Distribution of Coal Shipments*, a monthly report, which shows the distribution of both bituminous coal and anthracite shipments from producing to consuming areas.[6]

The Office of Price Administration. The Office of Price Administration collects periodically cost and other financial statistics on minerals and mineral products for use in regulating the prices of these commodi-

---

[4] Sixteenth Census of the United States: 1940, *Mineral Industries*, 1939 (U. S. Department of Commerce, Bureau of the Census, 1944), Vol. I.

[5] Many of these data appeared in *Facts for Industry.*

[6] In May 1944 the statistical functions of the Solid Fuels Administration for War were transferred to the Bureau of Mines.

ties. For the most part the cost information has not been tabulated. An exception is the information on crude petroleum which was collected, tabulated, analyzed, and released to the public by the U. S. Tariff Commission for the Office of Price Administration.[7]

Private Agencies. In the collection of current mineral statistics there is a division of labor between Federal Government agencies and private organizations. Where private groups have been collecting and publishing adequate information Federal agencies have refrained from duplicating. This chapter will, therefore, from subject to subject, mention some of the principal private collecting agencies and some of their more important statistical series.[8]

PRODUCTION

Mineral statistics are collected: (1) to enable businessmen, government officials, and the general public to gauge their activities connected with extracting the mineral and with rendering it ready for the market, (2) to permit analysts to determine the economic contributions of minerals to the Nation, the states, and other geographical subdivisions, and (3) to guide Federal and state officials in developing and administering sound mineral policy regarding taxation, employment, transportation, etc. To attain these objectives, analysts generally trace the movement of each mineral through the productive processes, from the extraction of the raw material to the disappearance or consumption of the refined or merchantable mineral or mineral product in fabricated articles.

For illustration, let us take a few generalized examples. A quantity

[7] U. S. Tariff Commission, *Report on the Cost of Producing Crude Petroleum in the United States,* December 1942; *Supplemental Report on the Cost of Producing Crude Petroleum in California,* May 1943. The Tariff Commission, OPA and WPB are jointly tabulating the current data on operating cost for copper, lead, and zinc mines from monthly reports made to the Joint Committee for copper, lead, and zinc (of the OPA and WPB). The reports are from some 350 high cost mines which have been paid premium prices for copper, lead, and zinc production above established quotas, covering about half of the copper and three-quarters of the lead and zinc output. The tabulated data when available will be released to the public.

[8] The following are among the important private agencies whose statistical series are discussed in this chapter:

Lake Superior Iron Ore Association, 1170 Hanna Building, Cleveland, Ohio. American Iron and Steel Institute, 350 Fifth Avenue, New York City. Copper Institute and U. S. Copper Association, 50 Broadway, New York City. American Bureau of Metal Statistics, 33 Rector Street, New York City. American Zinc Institute, 60 East 42nd Street, New York City. American Petroleum Institute 50 West 50th Street, New York City.

of metal ore is mined. It may be recorded and reported as so many tons of ore of a certain grade of iron, or as so many tons of recoverable metal in copper ore. This is the mine production stage and the data collected here is known as "mine production." At this stage it is possible to trace the ore to its source by states, counties, and mining districts, or to the method of mining it, or to its kind or grade. If the ore is not of a sufficiently high grade it must be sent to a plant or mill for concentration, where records are kept of the contents of the incoming ore and of the outgoing concentrates. The ore or concentrates are shipped to a furnace or smelter, where the material is processed and the output is recorded and reported as so many tons of pig iron or so many tons of "blister" copper or simply "smelter production." The pig iron is sent to an open hearth, Bessemer, or electric furnace, where the output is recorded as a certain tonnage of steel. The blister copper is shipped to a refinery where the product is recorded as so many tons of "refined" copper or "refinery production" of copper. Finally the refined material is reported as sold or shipped to a manufacturing plant, where it may eventually be reported as "consumed," having been fabricated into some finished or semifinished product.

Production of Metals. The Bureau of Mines has compiled annual statistics on the production of metals since 1882.[9] The kind of production statistics collected varies from metal to metal. For some metals data are obtained for three stages of production—mine, smelter, and refinery, or the equivalent—for other metals two, and for still others only one. For practically all metals produced at mines figures on mine production are available at least back to about 1907. The mine production data are given in quantity and dollar value. The quantity figures are in terms of the weight of the ore containing a given percentage of metal, or of the weight of the metal content of the ore. The dollar figures represent the value of the metal content of the ore at the mine. The mine production data are the most detailed. For all metals they are available at least by states; for many, by states and districts, and for a few—gold, silver, copper, lead, and zinc—by states, counties, and mining districts. Smelter production data for some metals, for example, copper, show the state origin of the ore smelted. Refinery production data are presented for the country as a whole only. They are given in terms of quantity and value. The dollar figures represent sale value f.o.b. refinery.

---

[9] The data before 1900 and particularly those in the 80's were sketchy for some of the metals. Beginning in the early 1900's they were greatly improved and by the latter part of that decade all series on important metals represent practically complete coverage.

The metals and metal products for which the Bureau of Mines compiles annual production statistics are listed below. The more important series are listed under each metal. Because the greater part of the supply of certain metals is used either in the production of ferroalloys or of alloy steel, these metals are included under iron and steel.

Aluminum:
  Bauxite (domestic mine shipments).
  Primary aluminum.
  Secondary aluminum.
Antimony:
  Antimony ore and concentrates.
  Primary antimony (domestic and foreign).
  Secondary antimony.
Arsenic:
  Crude.
  Refined.
Bismuth:
  Bismuth metal.
Cadmium:
  Metallic cadmium.
Copper:
  Domestic mine.
  Domestic primary smelter.
  Domestic primary refinery.
  Foreign primary refinery (from foreign ores, concentrates, etc.).
  Secondary.
Gold:
  Domestic mine.
  Domestic refinery (supplied by U. S. Bureau of the Mint).
  Secondary.
Iron and Steel:
  Domestic iron ore.
  Domestic pig iron.
  Steel (supplied by the American Iron and Steel Institute).
  Ferroalloys (ferromanganese, spiegeleisen, ferrosilicon, ferrophosphorus, ferrotungsten, ferrochromium, ferromolybdenum, etc.).
  Chromium ore (shipments from domestic mines).
  Titanium ore (ilmenite and rutile) and concentrates.
  Manganese ore (shipments from domestic mines).

Molybdenum ore and concentrates.
Secondary nickel.
Tungsten ore and concentrates (shipments from domestic mines).
Vanadium ore (shipments from domestic mines).
Lead:
  Domestic mine.
  Domestic primary refinery.
  Foreign primary refinery (from foreign ores and base bullion).
  Antimonial lead (by-product of refinery base bullion).
  Secondary.
  Lead pigments.
Magnesium:
  Domestic primary.
  Secondary.
Mercury:
  Domestic mine.
Platinum and Allied Metals:
  Domestic primary refined platinum, palladium, iridium, osmium, rhodium, and ruthenium.
  Foreign primary refined platinum, palladium, iridium, osmium, rhodium, and ruthenium.
  Secondary platinum, palladium, iridium, osmium, and others.
Silver:
  Domestic mine.
  Domestic primary refinery (supplied by Bureau of the Mint).
  Secondary.
Tin:
  Secondary.
Zinc:
  Domestic mine.
  Domestic primary slab zinc.
  Foreign primary slab zinc.
  Secondary.
  Zinc pigments and salts.

In the latter part of 1939, in response to the request for current information on strategic and critical minerals by the Army and Navy Munitions Board and other defense agencies, the Bureau of Mines started the collection of monthly statistics on a number of metals important for rearmament and by the early part of 1942 gathered monthly information on the output of all critical metals except those on which reliable data were already available from other sources.

The following is a list of the monthly statistical series on the production of the metals now available.[10] Although only the larger producers are included in the monthly canvasses, at least 95 percent of the output of each metal is covered.[11]

Bauxite:
   Domestic mine.
Copper:
   Domestic mine.
Iron and Steel:
   Domestic iron ore.
   Domestic chromium ore and concentrates.
   Titanium ore (ilmenite and rutile) and concentrates.
   Domestic manganese ore and concentrates.
   Domestic molybdenum ore and concentrates.
   Domestic tungsten ore and concentrates.
   Domestic vanadium ore and concentrates.
   Ferrochromium and other chromium products.
   Ferromanganese, spiegeleisen, and other manganese products.
   Ferromolybdenum, molybdenum oxide, and other molybdenum products.
   Ferrosilicon.
   Ferrotungsten and other tungsten products.

Ferrovanadium, vanadium oxide, and other vanadium products.
Gold:
   Domestic mine.
Lead:
   Domestic mine.
   Secondary.
Mercury:
   Domestic mine.
Platinum and Allied Metals:
   Domestic primary refined platinum, palladium and allied metals.
   Secondary platinum and allied metals recovered from scrap.
Silver:
   Domestic mine.
Tin:
   Secondary.
Zinc:
   Domestic mine.
   Smelter (supplied by the American Zinc Institute).
   Zinc oxide.
   Zinc dust.
   Secondary (redistilled slab zinc, remelt spelter, etc., compiled from redistillers who are not members of the American Zinc Institute).

[10] This is not a complete list of the metals on which the Bureau of Mines has been collecting current information. Among the metals left out are beryllium, cobalt, and zirconium, of which this country produces relatively little.

[11] Until recently these data were restricted to the confidential use of war agencies.

The Aluminum and Magnesium Division of the War Production Board tabulated monthly series on the primary and secondary production of aluminum and magnesium.[12] Data on primary aluminum and magnesium represented complete coverage, but those on secondary aluminum and magnesium embraced only that part of the secondary production which could be allocated, differing from the annual series of the Bureau of Mines, which include all secondary aluminum or magnesium recovered from old and new scrap, whether as pure metal or as alloys. The Bureau of Mines is continuing the monthly series.

Monthly data on refined gold produced from ores mined in the United States and the Philippines are estimated by the Board of Governors of the Federal Reserve System and are published monthly in the *Federal Reserve Bulletin*. This series, available from January 1929 to date, is based on the annual data on domestic primary refinery production compiled by the Bureau of the Mint and the Bureau of Mines and the monthly data on gold production of the American Bureau of Metal Statistics.

In addition to these government data there are a number of important current series compiled by private agencies that are widely used in current business analysis. The Copper Institute compiles monthly information on mine or smelter production of copper derived from domestic and duty-free ores and from secondary materials and on production of refined copper. The American Bureau of Metal Statistics collects monthly data on the production of refined lead from domestic ore. The American Zinc Institute collects monthly data on smelter production of slab zinc. The American Bureau of Metal Statistics compiles statistics on the production of refined silver from domestic and Philippine ore. Monthly statistics on the production of pig iron, including ferroalloys, are available from two sources. The *Iron Age* compiled data from 1913 to the early part of 1943, when it discontinued their collection. The American Iron and Steel Institute began its compilation in the latter part of 1941. The two series are approximately comparable and may be spliced to form a continuous series. The Institute also collects monthly statistics on the production of steel, which includes ingot and steel for casting made in open hearth, Bessemer, and electric furnaces, and on the production of iron and steel products for sale.

Production of Mineral Fuels. The following current statistical series on the production of mineral fuels are available at the Bureau of

---

[12] Released monthly by WPB in *Facts for Industry* series under the titles *Aluminum: U. S. Metal Production and Fabricated Products Shipments* and *Magnesium: U. S. Metal Production and Fabricated Products Shipments*.

Mines, for the most part on a comparable basis from the beginning of their collection.[13]

Bituminous coal, weekly and monthly.
Anthracite, weekly and monthly.
Coke:
  Beehive, weekly and monthly.
  By-products, monthly.
Coke-oven by-products, monthly:
  Tar.
  Ammonia.
  Gas.
  Light oil and derivatives.
  Naphthalene.
  Tar derivatives.

Petroleum and petroleum products, monthly:
  Crude Petroleum.
  Natural Gasoline.
  Refined Products:[14]
    Aviation gasoline.
    Motor fuel.
    Kerosene.
    Distillate fuel oil.
    Residual fuel oil.
    Lubricating oil.

The statistics on bituminous coal include data on the production of bituminous coal and lignite, coal used at collieries for power and fuel, coal made into coke at the mines, commercial truck shipments, local sales, and anthracite mined outside of Pennsylvania. Both the weekly and monthly series are estimates based upon railroad carloadings and river shipments of coal and beehive coke, supplemented by direct reports from some mining companies, local coal operators' associations, and monthly production statistics compiled by the state mine departments of a number of states. These estimates are adjusted annually when the results of the annual survey of coal producers become available. The adjustments are usually very small.

The anthracite production series covers Pennsylvania anthracite loaded at mines for shipment, used at collieries for power and heat, and sold to local trade. The anthracite produced outside of Pennsylvania is excluded from the series and included in the bituminous coal series. Both the weekly and monthly series are estimated from carloadings of anthracite. The monthly estimates are adjusted annually on the basis of an annual canvass of mine operators. Like the correction of estimates for bituminous coal, the correction is usually small—within 1 percent.

The weekly and monthly series on beehive coke production are also based on carloadings. Because an important part of beehive coke is consumed by the producers, the estimates based on shipments by rail

---

[13] Monthly production statistics on crude petroleum were begun in 1916, on refined petroleum products and by-product coke in 1917; the weekly production figures on beehive coke appeared in 1917, and on bituminous coal, anthracite, and by-product coke in 1917.

[14] Monthly figures on production of other refined products—wax, coke, asphalt, road oil, still gas, and miscellaneous—are also available.

err to the extent of the amount of coke consumed by the producing plants. During recent years the amount of coke consumed by producers has increased. This together with need for more detailed information on coke production has necessitated a direct monthly canvass. The weekly and monthly estimates are adjusted annually.

The monthly estimates on the production of by-product coke and the various coke-oven by-products are obtained through direct canvasses of nearly all producers. An annual correction is made.

The monthly series on crude petroleum production represents the oil that was transported from producing properties by pipelines, tank cars, barges, and other carriers, plus or minus the difference in the producers' stocks between the beginning and end of that month, plus the amount consumed by producers (on leases).

The monthly data on the production of natural gasoline are gathered directly from producing plants in the oil and gas fields and cover practically the total output of the product.

Statistics on the production of aviation gasoline, motor fuel, kerosene, distillate fuel oil, residual fuel oil, lubricating oil, and other petroleum products are obtained monthly. Two of the series—aviation gasoline and motor fuel—may require further explanation. The series on aviation gasoline shows production by octane ratings—below 87, 87 to 99, and 100 octane and higher—as well as total output. Data on production of aviation gasoline are not issued separately but combined with data on motor fuels in the monthly releases. These data represent the gasoline recovered by the "straight run" and by the "cracking" processes from crude runs to stills, plus benzol and the natural gasoline used for blending at the refineries or sold directly to consumers. Separate series are available for straight run production, cracked production, natural gasoline blended, and benzol.

Production of Other Nonmetals. Annual statistics on the production of the nonmetallic minerals and mineral products listed below are available from the Bureau of Mines from 1916 on a comparable basis, and they represent almost complete coverage.

Abrasive materials.
Barite and barium chemicals.
Cement.
Clays.
Feldspar.
Fluorspar.
Gypsum.
Lime.
Magnesium compounds.

Phosphate rock.
Potash.
Pyrite.
Salt.
Sand and gravel.
Slate.
Stone.
Sulfur.
Talc, pyrophyllite, and soapstone.

These annual series are also available by states in which the minerals are produced, by type of materials, and other details. Thus the production data on stone are classified by type of stone: granite, basalt, marble, limestone, and sandstone; and each type of stone is in turn subclassified by use: building, monumental, flagging, paving, curbing, etc. Dollar values are presented for each series and subseries. It should be noted that the basis of reporting production varies from product to product, depending on the nature of the mineral or on the method of recording production. For example, data for cement and sulfur are reported as the amount produced, for gypsum and phosphate rock as the amount mined, and for sand and gravel, stone and clay, and most of the remaining nonmetallic minerals as the quantity "sold or used" or "shipped." Where the producers do not keep large stocks, the quantity of materials "sold or used" or "shipped" is virtually equivalent to production.

Current production statistics are available only on some of the more important products. The Bureau of Mines collects data monthly on portland cement, sulfur, and fluorspar, quarterly on gypsum, and semi-annually on phosphate rock.

Index of Mineral Production. To measure the over-all output of the mining industries and to compare mining with manufacturing and other economic activities, the Board of Governors of the Federal Reserve System constructs a monthly index of mineral production.[15] Nine monthly series are included in the index: Bureau of Mines production figures on bituminous coal, anthracite, crude petroleum, iron ore, and zinc ores and concentrates (mine production), Copper Institute figures on copper production, Federal Reserve-American Bureau of Metal Statistics figures on gold production, and the American Bureau figures on silver production. The ninth is the American Bureau series on lead content of domestic ore receipts by United States smelters. These series are weighted in accordance with their relative importance in the mineral industries as measured by the value at the mine of the output of the nine minerals in 1937. The index, which is based on the average for the period 1935–1939 as 100, is available from January 1919 to date, with and without seasonal adjustments. Index numbers for each of the nine series are also available for the same period with and without seasonal adjustments.

---

[15] The index has undergone several revisions. The most recent revisions are described in the following articles in the *Federal Reserve Bulletin:* "Revision of Industrial Production Index," October 1943; "New Federal Reserve Index of Industrial Production," August 1940.

SALES, SHIPMENTS, AND DISTRIBUTION

The Bureau of Mines collects annual and current data from mineral producers on their sales and shipments of minerals and mineral products. In general, sale and shipment data are collected in lieu of production data.

Metals. With the start of the war the Bureau of Mines began to collect monthly statistics on shipments of the following metallic mineral and metal products:

Aluminum scrap:
  Dealers' shipments.
Processed bauxite:
  Shipments by mines and processing plants by grades.
Copper and Brass Scrap:
  Dealers' shipments.
Iron and Steel:
  Domestic iron ore.
  Iron and steel scrap:
    Shipment by suppliers (dealers, brokers, automobile wreckers) and producers.
  Ferrochromium and other chromium products.
  Ferromanganese, spiegeleisen, and other manganese products.
  Ferromolybdenum, molybdenum oxides, etc.
  Ferrosilicon.
  Ferrotungsten and other tungsten products.

Ferrovanadium, vanadium oxide, and other vanadium products.
Lead and Tin Scrap:
  Dealers' shipments.
  Producers' shipment of secondary lead and tin products (pig bar or ingot metals, fabricated lead and tin products, etc.).
Zinc:
  Slab zinc:
    Smelters' shipments by members of the American Zinc Institute (supplied by the Institute).
    Secondary smelters' shipments by nonmembers of the American Zinc Institute.
  Zinc oxide:
    Producers' shipments.
  Zinc dust:
    Producers' shipments.
  Zinc scrap:
    Dealers' shipments.

These shipment series represent practically complete coverage and are available at least back to 1942.

Data on monthly shipments of aluminum and magnesium fabricated products were published monthly by the War Production Board in the *Facts for Industry* series.

A number of important current series compiled by private organizations should be mentioned. The Lake Superior Ore Association publishes monthly shipments of Lake Superior iron ore through the upper Lake ports. The American Iron and Steel Institute compiles monthly shipments of steel products by processors who are also primary producers of steel. The Copper Institute publishes monthly data on deliveries of domestic, duty-free, and duty-paid copper for domestic consumption. The American Bureau of Metal Statistics publishes monthly data on shipments of refined lead for domestic consumption compiled from all primary refiners in the United States. The American Zinc Institute publishes monthly shipments of slab zinc reported by its members who include all primary zinc producers.

Nonmetals. Since the latter part of 1931, the Bureau of Mines has compiled monthly data on the distribution of shipments of bituminous coal and anthracite. These are not primary data collected directly from respondents but are assembled from secondary sources, principally from the statistical bureaus maintained by the railroads. The data show movements by methods of transportation—river, lake, tidewater, or all-rail—by major fields of origin, and by principal points of destination. The all-rail figures in turn show shipments from blanket origin areas to blanket destination areas, that is, zones within which the freight rates on coal are the same.

These data are particularly useful for comparative purposes. A railroad may compare its shipments with total shipments from a given origin area to a given destination area, or it may compare its traffic to a given destination area from all the origin areas in the territory which it serves with the movements to the same destination from origin areas in territories which it does not serve—in order to determine whether over a given period of time it has been gaining or losing with respect to competing roads. Similarly a coal operator may compare his shipments with the total shipments to a given destination area or areas in order that he may ascertain where he stands in the various market areas. Since freight represents an important element in the price of coal at destination areas, both the railroads serving a given territory and the operators have a mutual interest in adjusting the freight rate so as to permit the coal to enter into competition in given destination areas with the coal from other areas that are served by other roads. Finally, since coal is the most important industrial fuel in many areas, the statistics on shipments to destination points over a period of time will reflect the relative industrial activity in those areas.

Recently the Bureau of Mines published a new series on the distribution of bituminous shipments starting with the third and fourth quarters of 1943.[16] These data are tabulated from monthly reports of producers, dock operators, and transshippers of coal moving by Lake and tidewater required by the Solid Fuels Administration for War. They show the distribution of "all-rail, river and ex-river coal" from districts of origin (as defined by the Bituminous Coal Act) to states of destination and of "waterborne shipments via Lake and tidewater" by states of destination. They differ from the earlier distribution statis-

[16] "Distribution of Coal Shipments." *Mineral Industry Surveys.*

tics described above mainly in that they show districts of origin and state of destination whereas the earlier distribution data show blanket areas of origin and blanket areas of destination.

The Bureau is also preparing similar series on the distribution of anthracite shipments. These will show shipments of Pennsylvania anthracite to states, cities, and other geographical subdivisions and will be published in a separate report.

Since January 1921 the Bureau of Mines has collected from all producers of portland cement monthly data on shipments of portland cement from mills. Monthly data showing the distribution of these shipments by states of destination are available from July 1924.

The Bureau of Mines collects quarterly data on gypsum products sold with separate statistics for each of the major products, which are classified as uncalcined or calcined, and these categories are in turn subclassified by uses. These data represent practically complete coverage beginning in 1938 and are comparable throughout the period 1938–1945. Those before 1938 are not comparable with those since then because of changes in classification and the fact that in the earlier years some of the small producers were not covered.

STOCKS

Statistics on stocks of minerals are generally collected in connection with periodic surveys of the economic operations of producers and consumers of minerals and mineral products. Data on producers' stocks are usually correlated with two other basic figures—production and shipments—and those on consumers' stocks with consumption and receipts.

Metals. Until recent years the collection of statistics on stocks of metals held by domestic producers or consumers was practically neglected by the Bureau of Mines. The only data compiled regularly up to 1935 were those showing the producers' stocks of iron ore, blister copper, and materials in process of refining, refined copper, and slab zinc held at the beginning and at the end of the year. An annual survey of tin consumers began in 1936 calling for stocks of tin held at the beginning and end of each year. In 1939 two series on metal inventories appeared. Data on stocks of home scrap, purchased scrap, and pig iron on hand at consumers' plants at the beginning and end of the year are available annually as are beginning and ending inventories of aluminum, antimony, copper and brass, nickel, tin, and zinc scrap held by remelters, smelters, refiners, manufacturers, and foundries. This was the extent of data on stocks of metals until the latter part of 1939.

By 1942, however, practically all metals, except those on which accurate statistics were already available from other sources, were obtained currently with practically complete coverage. Listed below are some of the more important metals for which statistics on producers' or consumers' stocks as of the first and last day of each month are available.

Aluminum:
  Producers' stocks of crude and processed bauxite by grades.
  Consumers' (manufacturers of alumina, abrasives, refractory, chemicals, etc.) stocks of crude and processed bauxite.
  Dealers' stocks of aluminum scrap.
Antimony: [17]
  Consumers' (manufacturers of antimonial products) stocks of antimonial raw materials (ore and concentrates, metal, oxide, etc.).
  Producers' stocks of finished antimonial products (antimonial lead, bearing metals, batteries, etc.).
Copper and Brass Scrap:
  Dealers' stocks.
Iron and Steel:
  Pig iron:
    Consumers' stocks.
  Iron and steel scrap:
    Consumers' stocks of home and of purchased scrap, by grades.
    Suppliers' stocks of prepared (by grades) and unprepared scrap.
  Chromium:
    Producers' stocks of chromium ore.
    Consumers' (producers of chromium products) stocks of chromium ore.
    Producers' stocks of chromium products (ferrochromium, chrome briquet, metal, etc.).
    Consumers' (iron and steel producers) stocks of chromium products.
  Ferrosilicon:
    Producers' stocks of silvery pig iron, ferrosilicon, and silicon metal.
    Consumers' stocks of silvery pig iron, ferrosilicon, and silicon metal.
  Manganese:
    Producers' stocks of manganese ore.
    Consumers' stocks of manganese ore.
    Producers' stocks of manganese alloys (ferromanganese, spiegeleisen, etc.).
    Consumers' and brokers' stocks of manganese ore and manganese alloys held at plants and at bonded warehouses.
  Molybdenum:
    Producers' stocks of molybdenum concentrates.
  ⋄ Consumers' stocks of molybdenum concentrates.
    Producers' stocks of molybdenum products (ferromolybdenum, molybdenum oxide, etc.).
    Consumers' stocks of molybdenum products.
  Tungsten:
    Producers' stocks of tungsten ore and concentrates.

[17] These data have been tabulated from a WPB quarterly report. The figures on stocks are therefore for the beginning and end of each calendar quarter.

Consumers' stocks of tungsten ore and concentrates.

Producers' stocks of tungsten products (ferrotungsten, etc.).

Consumers' (tool steel manufacturers, stocks of tungsten products, etc.).

Vanadium:

Producers' stocks of vanadium ore and concentrates.

Consumers' stocks of vanadium ore and concentrates.

Producers' stocks of vanadium oxide.

Consumers' stocks of vanadium oxide.

Producers' stocks of ferrovanadium and other vanadium products.

Lead and Tin Scrap:

Stocks of lead-base scrap, by kinds, at consumers' plants (remelters, smelters, refiners, manufacturers, and foundries).

Stocks of tin-base scrap, by kinds, at consumers' plants.

Stocks of secondary pig bars or ingot metals, fabricated lead and tin products, by kinds, held by remelters, smelters and refiners.

Stocks of lead and tin scrap held by dealers.

Mercury:

Producers' stocks at the mines.

Consumers' and dealers' stocks.

Nickel Scrap:

Dealers' stocks.

Platinum and Allied Metals:

Stocks of platinum, palladium, iridium, osmium, and other platinum metals held by refiners, importers, and dealers in the United States.

Tin:

Producers' stocks of pig tin (domestic brand).

Consumers' stocks of pig tin (foreign and domestic brands separately).

Stocks afloat to United States.

Stocks held elsewhere.

Zinc:

Primary smelters' stocks of zinc ore and concentrates (domestic and foreign, separately).

Smelters' stocks of slab zinc by grades as reported to the American Zinc Institute (supplied by the American Zinc Institute).

Secondary smelters' (redistillers') stocks of the slab zinc, by grades, not reported to the American Zinc Institute.

Consumers' stocks of slab zinc by grades, classified for the following consumer industry groups: galvanizers, zinc alloy producers, brass mills, ingot makers and foundries, rolling mills, oxide plants, and others.

Zinc oxide:

Consumers' stocks of zinc ore and concentrates, domestic and foreign separately, slab zinc and residues.

Producers' stocks of zinc oxide, lead-free and leaded by grades.

Zinc dust:

Producers' stocks.

Zinc scrap:

Consumers' stocks of purchased scrap and residues by kinds.

Producers' stocks of secondary zinc-base products (redistilled slab zinc, remelt spelters, and other secondary zinc products).

Dealers' stocks.

Some of the important gaps in the statistics on stocks compiled by Federal Government agencies may be filled by statistical series available from private sources. The Lake Superior Iron Ore Association compiles monthly data on stocks of iron ores at furnaces and on Lake Erie docks. The Copper Institute and the U. S. Copper Association gather monthly statistics on stocks of copper held by the copper industry and by copper users and nonconsumers. The American Bureau of Metal Statistics publishes monthly statistics on lead stocks held by practically all refiners and smelters. The American Zinc Institute compiles monthly data on stocks of slab zinc held by smelters.

Mineral Fuels. Monthly information on stocks of bituminous coal and anthracite held by industrial consumers, retail dealers, and at upper Lake docks and on stocks of coke held by producers is compiled by the Bureau of Mines. The more important series are listed below.

Bituminous Coal:
   Industrial consumers:
      Electric power utilities.
      By-product coke ovens.
      Steel and rolling mills.
      Cement mills.
      Other industrials.
      Railroads (Class I).
   Retail dealers.
   Upper Lake docks:
      On Lake Superior.
      On Lake Michigan.

Anthracite:
   Industrial consumers:
      Electric power utilities.
      Railroads (Class I).
      Other industrial consumers.
   Retail dealers.
   Upper Lake docks:
      On Lake Superior.
      On Lake Michigan.
   Producers' storage yards.
Coke:
   By-product plants:
      At furnaces.
      At merchant plants.
   Beehive plants.

The series representing stocks of bituminous coal held by all industrial consumers and the component series showing the stocks held by the six industrial groups into which industrial users of bituminous coal are classified date back to 1918. Some of the component data are collected directly from consumers; others are supplied by public and private agencies which gather them directly from particular groups of industrial users. Although monthly data for practically all groups have been assembled by the Bureau from their beginning in 1918 it was not until September 1932 that the monthly stock series for all industrial consumers, for the six industrial groups, and for retail dealers began to be published regularly. Before that time they were published only intermittently, with some months in each year missing.

The series for by-product coke ovens, steel and rolling mills, and cement mills are collected by the Bureau as a part of its monthly canvasses of coal consumption and represent practically complete coverage of these plants. The series for other industries prior to July 1, 1943, were based upon a monthly canvass of about 2,000 manufacturing plants, but in 1943 the Bureau made a complete canvass of coal consumption and stocks of manufacturing plants. Thereafter the sample was increased from 2,000 to 15,000 plants, and since July 1, 1943, the expanded sample data have been chained to the new base. The retail dealer series before July 1, 1943, was based on a sample of about 500; on July 1, 1943, the sample was enlarged to cover 13,000 dealers and chained to a base established by a complete canvass of retail dealers in 1943.

The series on bituminous stocks of electric power plants is compiled by the Federal Power Commission from its monthly surveys of coal consumption by public utilities. This series dates back to 1918 and represents complete coverage. The series for railroads is compiled by the Association of American Railroads and dates back to 1918.

In cooperation with the Maher Coal Bureau, the Bureau of Mines compiles statistics on stocks of bituminous coal at all American commercial docks on Lake Superior and on the west bank of Lake Michigan, as of the end of the month. Data are available back to 1918.

The series showing stocks of anthracite held by electric power utilities are compiled by the Federal Power Commission and furnished to the Bureau for publication with its other stock figures. The railroad series is contributed by the Association of American Railroads, representing complete coverage of anthracite stocks held by Class I railroads. Both the electric utilities and the railroad series date back to 1918. The data on stocks of anthracite held by "other industrial consumers" and retail dealers are not continuous statistical series. They are gathered by sample surveys of consumers and dealers and the number of consumers or dealers reporting varies from month to month, with the result that data for a given month are not comparable with data for the preceding or following months in each series.

Statistics on stocks of anthracite in producers' storage yards as of the end of the month have been compiled by the Anthracite Committee of the Department of Commerce of the Commonwealth of Pennsylvania from 1921 to date.

Monthly statistics on stocks of coke at all by-product plants have been compiled by the Bureau since January 1928. This series covers the stocks held by furnace plants and merchant plants, including public utility plants having coke ovens and coal-gas retorts. Data are separately available for furnace plants and for merchant plants since 1928.

Monthly statistics on stocks of crude petroleum and petroleum products held by producers at the end of each month have been compiled by the Bureau of Mines as a part of its survey of the output of these products since the middle of 1917. The following is an outline of the more important series.

Crude Petroleum:
  Refinable or light crude oil:
    Total in the United States:
      At refineries.
      At tank farms and in pipelines.
      On leases.
    Heavy crude in California.
  Natural Gasoline.
  Refined Petroleum Products:[18]
    Finished gasoline:
      At refineries.
      At bulk terminals and in pipelines.

Aviation gasoline.
Unfinished gasoline.
Kerosene:
  At refineries.
  At bulk terminals and in pipelines.
Distillate fuel oil:
  At refineries.
  At bulk terminals and in pipelines.
Residual fuel oil:
  At refineries.
  At bulk terminals.
Lubricating oil.

Statistics on total stocks of refinable or light crude oil (specific gravity of 20° and above) in the United States, that is, the aggregate amount held at refineries, at tank farms, in pipelines, and on leases (producing properties) are available by months since July 1917. Separate data on stocks at refineries (which include foreign crude held by importers) and on stocks at tank farms and in pipelines are also available since 1917, but those on stocks at producing properties were not compiled before 1922.

Before 1938 data on stocks of heavy crude oil in California (specific gravity of less than 20°) were not available separately but were included in the data for residual fuel oil mentioned above. Beginning in January 1938 the Bureau segregated the data on stocks of heavy crude from the data on stocks of residual fuel oil, showing a separate series on stocks of heavy crude in California.

The various series on crude petroleum stocks are fairly comparable and complete beginning in 1933, covering practically all the stocks of crude at refineries, at tank farms and in pipelines, and on producing properties. The figures for stocks on leases are in part estimated. Monthly data are received only from the larger producers and include about 60 percent of the crude on producing properties. The remainder is estimated on the basis of an annual figure representing complete coverage. Since the total stocks on leases are relatively small any error in the estimate would have but a negligible effect on the figures for crude stocks of the country as a whole.

[18] Monthly stock data are also available on wax, coke, asphalt, road oil, and miscellaneous.

The series on stocks of natural gasoline, which dates back to 1925, is not uniform throughout the period covered. Before 1930 it includes stocks at natural gasoline plants only; beginning in 1930, it also includes those at refineries; and starting in 1935, it also includes those at bulk terminals. This series is fairly comparable beginning in 1935.

The various series on stocks of finished products listed under refined petroleum products represent practically complete coverage. They are not completely comparable, however, throughout the period which they cover. The segment of the series on finished gasoline at refineries from July 1917, when it begins, to May 1923 is not comparable with the segment beginning June 1923, when gasoline stocks held by marketers in California were included for the first time. The series on finished gasoline at bulk terminals, in pipelines, and in water transit is available beginning in 1933. Data on stocks of aviation gasoline by octane ratings have been compiled since the latter part of 1939 for the confidential use of Federal agencies and are included in the series representing total stocks of finished gasoline. Data on unfinished gasoline were not available separately before 1934.

The series on stocks of kerosene at refineries and on stocks of lubricating oil at refineries are available beginning in July 1917. Like the series on finished gasoline, their comparability is affected by the inclusion of marketers' stocks in California beginning in June 1923. Statistics showing stocks of gas oil and distillate fuel oil at refineries separately from those of residual fuel oil at refineries were not available before 1930. Prior to 1930 and back to 1917 stock of gas oil and all fuel oils (distillate and residual) were lumped together in a single series which, beginning in 1924, also included heavy crude in California. The series on residual fuel oil at refineries since its beginning in 1930 and through 1937 includes heavy crude in California. Beginning in 1938, stocks of heavy crude in California were excluded from the residual fuel oil series and reported separately. Stocks of distillate fuel oil at refineries as a separate series began in 1930.

Finally, mention should be made of the American Petroleum Institute weekly data on stocks of finished and unfinished gasoline, kerosene, gas oil, distillate fuel oil, and residual fuel oil.

Other Nonmetals. With the exception of a few commodities, the Bureau of Mines has not collected statistics on stocks of nonmetals other than mineral fuels. This neglect is in part due to the fact that producers and consumers of these products usually keep small and more or less constant inventories. Among the more important nonmetals, of which there might be a sizable stock on hand from time to time, are abrasives, cement, fluorspar, gypsum, lime, phosphate rocks, and sulfur. The Bureau compiles annual figures on stocks (as of the end of the year) of artificial abrasives, metallic abrasives, cement, fluorspar, phosphate rocks, and sulfur, covering the stocks held by practically all producers of these products. These series have been compiled at least since about 1920. Data on stocks of phosphate rocks held by all producers as of the end of June have also been compiled since 1937 in connection with a semiannual survey of phosphate rock production. Monthly stock data on cement, fluorspar, and sulfur are available. The series on stocks of finished portland cement held by all producers as of the end of the month dates back to 1921, and that on stocks of clinker (unground cement) held by all the portland cement producers as of the end of the month dates back to 1923. Monthly figures on stocks of fluospar held by all producers and by practically all consumers are available beginning in 1942, and on stocks of sulfur held by producers beginning in 1942.

CONSUMPTION

Data on the consumption of minerals and mineral products in the initial and intermediate stages are useful particularly to mineral producers. But the widest interest is centered on statistics of the consumption of the refined mineral by end-product manufacturing industries or by end products. Current data showing the consumption of a refined mineral are useful not only to the producers of that product, but also to the producers of competitive mineral products, to the many consumers of these products (manufacturers of end products), to business analysts, to businessmen who buy and sell the end products, and to the general public which consumes the end products. Note, however, that the compilation of statistics at this stage is much more difficult than at the earlier stages. Whereas there are hundreds of mineral producers, there are thousands of end-product manufacturers, and many more thousands of end products.

Metals. Until recent years the collection of consumption statistics on metals was largely neglected by the Federal agencies. The Bureau of Mines made some occasional surveys of the consumption of certain metals by industries or by products. For example, it made a study of the consumption of silver by industries for the years 1928 to 1931, inclusive, showing the quantities used annually by certain groups of manufacturers in fabricating silver products during each of these years.[19]

[19] C. W. Merrill "Consumption of Silver in the Arts and Industries in the United States," *U. S. Bureau of Mines Economic Paper 14* and *Information Circular 6647* (mimeographed), 1932.

A survey of the annual consumption of tin by end products and end-product groups was made for the years 1925, 1927, 1928, and 1930. Beginning in 1936 this survey was continued on a regular annual basis, covering practically all producers of tin-contained products. Two other regular annual surveys of metal consumption were added in 1939: one on the consumption of pig iron and iron and steel scrap by iron and steel furnaces and the other on the consumption of nonferrous metal scrap (aluminum, antimony, copper, lead, magnesium, nickel, tin, and zinc) by remelters, smelters, refiners, and manufacturers and foundries. These represent the complete list of metal consumption canvasses until the advent of the war.

Between the latter part of 1939 and the early part of 1942 the Bureau began a series of current and annual canvasses of the consumption of strategic and critical metals in the several production processes. These canvasses generally call for information on consumers' stocks and receipts, as well as on the consumption of the metal during the period covered. The following is a list of the more important series:

Aluminum:
   Consumption of bauxite, by grades, by producers of alumina, abrasives and refractories, chemicals, and others (monthly).
   Consumption of aluminum scrap by remelters, smelters and refiners, aluminum rolling mills, and foundries and other manufacturers (annual).
Antimony:
   Consumption of ore and concentrates, metal oxides, etc., by manufacturers in the production of intermediate products (metal oxide, sulfide, etc.); and of metal products (antimonial lead, bearing metals, batteries and parts, cable covering, etc.) [20] (quarterly).
   Consumption of antimony bearing scrap by remelters, smelters and refiners, and manufacturers and foundries (annual).
Copper: [21]
   Consumption of copper scrap by remelters, smelters and refiners, by brass mills, and by foundries and other manufacturers (annual).

[20] Compiled in cooperation with Tin, Lead, and Zinc Division, War Production Board.

[21] Since June 1933 the Copper Institute and the U. S. Copper Association have compiled monthly data on the consumption of domestic and duty-free, and duty-paid copper. Since 1919 the American Bureau of Metal Statistics has estimated the annual amount of copper used by the following end-product groups: Electric manufactures telephone and telegraph, light and power lines, wire cloth, other rod and wire, ammunition, automobiles, buildings, castings, clocks and watches, copper-bearing steel, radiators and heating, radio, railway equipment, refrigerators, shipbuilding, washing machines, air-conditioning, other uses and manufactures for exports.

Iron and Steel: [22]

Consumption of pig iron by types of furnaces (annual and monthly).

Consumption of home and of purchased iron and steel scrap: By type of furnaces, by districts, and by states (annual). By type of furnaces and by grade of scrap (monthly).

Chromium:

Consumption of metallurgical ore, refractory ore, and chemical ore by producers of chromium products (monthly).

Consumption of ferrochromium, chromium briquets, and chromium metals by iron and steel producers (monthly).

Ferrosilicon:

Consumption of silvery pig iron, ferrosilicon, and silicon metal by iron and steel producers (monthly).

Manganese:

Consumption of manganese ores and manganese alloys by producers of manganese alloys, steel ingots, steel castings, and other steel products, dry cells, and chemicals (monthly).

Molybdenum:

Consumption of molybdenum concentrates by producers of molybdenum products (monthly).

Consumption of ferromolybdenum, molybdate, molybdenum oxide, and other molybdenum products by iron and steel producers (monthly).

Tungsten:

Consumption of tungsten ore and concentrates by producers of tungsten powder and other tungsten products, by tool steel manufacturers, and by others (monthly).

Vanadium:

Consumption of vanadium ore and concentrates by producers of vanadium products (monthly).

Consumption of vanadium oxide, ferrovanadium, and other vanadium products by manufacturers of tool steel, steel forgings, etc. (monthly).

Lead:

Consumption of refined soft lead, by grades, by manufacturers of lead products, classified by groups of end products (cable covering, foil, pipes, sheet, storage batteries, pigments, chemicals) (annual).

Consumption of lead scrap, by kinds, by remelters, smelters and refiners, and by manufacturers and foundries (monthly and annual).

Magnesium:

Consumption of magnesium scrap by remelters, smelters and refiners, and manufacturers (annual).

Mercury:

Consumption of mercury by manufacturers of mercury products classified by end products and end-product groups (pharmaceuticals, fulminate, catalyst, electrical apparatus, control instruments, etc.) (monthly).

[22] The Lake Superior Iron Ore Association compiles monthly data on the consumption of Lake Superior iron ore by furnaces located in the central and eastern districts and the lake front. The American Iron and Steel Institute compiles annual figures on the consumption of pig iron, ferrous scrap, iron ore and other ferrous materials by open hearth, Bessemer, and electric furnaces, which produce practically all the steel in the United States. Since 1942 the same information is compiled on a monthly basis.

Nickel:
  Consumption of metal scrap by remelters, smelters, and refiners and by manufacturers and foundries (annual).
Platinum and Allied Metals:
  Consumption of platinum, palladium, iridium, osmium, rhodium, and ruthenium by manufacturers of platinum products, classified by end-product groups (gauge catalyst, spinnerets, salts and plating solutions, electrical contacts, electronic tubes, dental and medical supplies, etc.) (monthly and annual).
Tin:
  Consumption of primary and secondary tin by manufacturers of tin-contained products, classified end products, and end-product groups (tin plate, solder, Babbitt, bronze and brass, collapsible tubes, tinning, foil, etc.) (annual).
  Consumption of foreign and domestic pig tin by tin plate plants and by other plants [23] (monthly).
  Consumption of tin scrap, by kinds, by remelters, smelters, and refiners, and by manufacturers and foundries (annual).
Zinc:
  Consumption of domestic and foreign zinc ore and concentrates by zinc oxide plants and by slab zinc plants.[24]
  Consumption of slab zinc by manufacturers of zinc-bearing products, classified by end products and end-product groups (galvanized sheets, tubes and pipes, wire, wire cloth and shapes; brass sheets, tubes and other products; rolled zinc; zinc oxide; zinc-base alloys; etc.) (monthly and annual).[25]
  Consumption of zinc dust by industries (zinc or cadmium production, chemical manufacturing, and sherardizing) (monthly).
  Consumption of zinc scrap by remelters, smelters, and refiners and by manufacturers and foundries (monthly and annual).

The coverage of the current series listed above is at least 95 percent for each of the metals. The coverage of the annual series is practically complete. Where both current and annual data are compiled, the latter represent higher coverage, greater accuracy in reporting, and more details and refinement in tabulations.

The Tin, Lead and Zinc Division of the War Production Board compiled current data on the consumption of lead (primary, secondary, and antimonial) by manufacturers of lead-bearing products classified by end products: storage batteries, cable covering, red lead and litharge, white lead and other pigments, construction materials, ammunition, tetraethyl, solder, Babbitt and bearing metals, type metal, and others. Monthly figures are available from January 1941 to 1943 and quarterly figures beginning in January 1944. Practically all lead-consuming manufacturers are covered. Note the difference between these data,

[23] Compiled in cooperation with the Tin, Lead and Zinc Division, War Production Board.
[24] Consumption data for slab zinc plants are supplied by the American Zinc Institute for confidential use of the Bureau.
[25] The American Bureau of Metal Statistics estimated the annual amount of zinc consumed in the galvanizing, bronze making, etc., for the period 1919–41.

which include all lead, and the Bureau of Mines annual series, which represent the consumption of refined soft lead only.

The Miscellaneous Minerals Division of the War Production Board released monthly statistics on the consumption of primary and secondary silver by manufacturers of silver products, classified by end products (bearings, industrial equipment, silverware, jewelry, photographic goods, contacts, etc.). It also compiled monthly data on the consumption of silver scrap in the production of sterling, solder, other alloys, salts, etc. Both series represented practically complete coverage and date back to October 1942.[26]

The Tin, Lead, and Zinc Division of the War Production Board tabulated from its administrative reports monthly data on the consumption of primary and secondary tin by end-product groups: tin plate and terneplate, brass and bronze, solder, Babbitt, tinning, collapsible tubes, foil, type metal, chemicals, pipe and tube, and others. These data are available from the beginning of 1942 and are fairly comparable with the annual figures of the Bureau of Mines.

This review of the statistics on metal consumption has revealed a serious gap—the absence of information on the actual consumption of copper by uses or by end products.

Mineral Fuels. The Bureau of Mines has been compiling monthly statistics on the consumption of coal since 1918. The following series are available:

Bituminous Coal:
  Industrial consumption:
    Electric power utilities.
    By-product coke ovens.
    Beehive coke ovens.
    Steel and rolling mills.
    Cement mills.
    Other industrials.
    Railroads (Class I).

Retail dealer deliveries.
Coal mine fuel.
Bunker fuel.
Anthracite:
  Industrial consumption:
    Electric power utilities.
    Railroads (Class I).
    Other industrial consumers.
  Retail dealer deliveries.

The seven component series listed under industrial consumption of bituminous coal, together with those on retail dealer deliveries, coal mine fuel, and bunker fuel, represent the total amount of bituminous coal currently consumed in the United States. The series on by-product coke ovens, beehive coke ovens, steel and rolling mills, cement mills, other industrials, coal mine fuel, and retail dealer deliveries are collected directly from these various groups. All series except other

[26] Monthly release entitled "Summary of Silver," by the Miscellaneous Minerals Division, War Production Board.

industrials and deliveries to dealers represent practically complete coverage of the respective groups. The data on other industrials and deliveries to dealers are estimated on the basis of monthly sample surveys. The data on deliveries to retail dealers are included with the consumption series to represent consumption by domestic users, commercial establishments, and small industrials. The series on coal mine fuel is also estimated. The data on bituminous coal consumption of electric power utilities are compiled by the Federal Power Commission and those for railroads by the Association of American Railroads, both series representing practically 100 percent coverage. The data for bunker fuel are compiled by the Bureau of the Census and represent the coal loaded for use on ships that are engaged in foreign trade, excluding the coal taken on for consumption by coastwise ships.

The four series of figures listed under anthracite, representing the consumption of the coal by electric power utilities, railroads, other industrial consumers, and the deliveries to retail dealers, cannot be added to show total consumption as can the several series under bituminous coal. The series for electric power utilities and that for the railroads, representing complete coverage of these groups of anthracite users, are prepared by the Federal Power Commission and the Association of American Railroads, respectively. The data for other industrial consumers and for deliveries to retail dealers are based on sample surveys in which the number of respondents varies from month to month.

Since January 1942 the Bureau has collected monthly data on the amount of by-product and beehive coke consumed by or shipped to blast furnaces, foundries, producers' gas plants, water gas plants, other industrial plants, and domestic users. These series account for practically all the coke consumed.

Since 1917 the Bureau has compiled monthly statistics on "crude runs to still," which represent the consumption of both domestic and foreign crude petroleum in the refinery processes. Apart from the figures on crude runs to stills, no statistics on the actual consumption of petroleum or petroleum products are collected. Monthly demand figures for each of the major refined petroleum products—motor fuel, kerosene, distillate fuel oil, residual fuel oil, lubricating oil, wax, coke, asphalt and road oil—are computed. They are derived by adding to producers' stocks at the beginning of the month the production and imports during the month and subtracting therefrom the exports during the month and producers' stocks at the end of the month. Since the stocks held by dealers and consumers are not taken into account these estimates merely indicate the apparent rather than the actual consumption of each of the products. These derived figures represent the domestic demand for the refined products by the Nation as a whole. Monthly data showing the apparent consumption or domestic demand of gasoline by states are available from other sources.[27]

The Public Roads Administration compiles monthly data on gasoline consumption by states from tax returns of gasoline distributors. These show separately the net amount of gasoline taxed and the amount subject to refund for each state; they are published monthly for some of the states only, the number varying from month to month. When the data for all states and the District of Columbia are available for every month of the year, the Public Roads Administration publishes a series of tables showing the total gasoline consumption by months for each state, the highway use of gasoline by months for each state, and a detailed analysis of the use of gasoline in each state during the year.[28] The analysis tables present annual totals for private and commercial use and for public use (Federal, state, county, and municipal). The two groups of uses are in turn classified into highway use and nonhighway use. The data for highway use and nonhighway use are estimated on the basis of state data on tax exemption and refunds.

Three current series on the consumption of fuel oil (distillate and residual) are available. They are: the Federal Power Commission monthly figures for electric power plants; the Interstate Commerce Commission series on the consumption of fuel oil by locomotives on Class I railroads; and the Bureau of the Census series on bunker fuel, that is, fuel oil loaded for use by vessels engaged in foreign trade. The coverage of each group of consumers is practically complete. The electric power series is available back to 1919, the railroad series to 1921, and the bunker fuel series to 1914.

In 1926 the Bureau of Mines began compiling annual statistics on the sale of fuel oil, classified by principal uses: railroads, ships' bunkers, gas and electric power plants, smelters and mines, manufacturing, heating, range, Army and Navy transports, oil-company fuel, and other uses. The sales figures for railroads, electric power plants, and bunker fuel check closely with those three current series described above. Since 1934 data on sales of distillate fuel oil and residual fuel oil, classified by uses, have been presented separately.

[27] The American Petroleum Institute has been compiling monthly figures on the gallonage sale of gasoline as reported by wholesalers and dealers in accordance with the gasoline tax or inspection laws of each state.

[28] See Tables G-21, G-22, G-23, and G-24 for each year, issued by the Public Roads Administration, Federal Works Agency.

This discussion of the available data on the consumption of petroleum and petroleum products would not be complete without including the monthly forecasts of demand for motor fuel and crude oil. These forecasts were begun by the Federal Oil Conservation Board in 1930, were carried forward by the Petroleum Administrative Board, and are finally continuing under the Bureau of Mines.[29] Before the war these forecasts were used by Federal and state officials and by oil producers in stabilizing the production of crude petroleum and petroleum products. During the war increased demand for petroleum products for war uses and the necessity of substituting a Federal war program to increase production as much as possible without serious injury to our crude oil reserves has led to a material change in the use of the monthly forecasts and the data published. As a matter of fact, the Petroleum Administration for War assumed responsibility for determining the military, civilian, and other requirements for petroleum products and of assigning allowables or quotas to the producing states. Since the end of the war the Bureau of Mines has resumed its prewar forecasting services, publishing regularly forecasts of the monthly demand for motor fuel and crude petroleum for the country as a whole and by states.

Other Nonmetals. Statistics on the actual consumption of other nonmetals are practically nonexistent. The only important series available is that of the Bureau of Mines on the monthly consumption of fluorspar, which began in 1942. Statistics on the consumption of fluorspar in the manufacture of basic open-hearth steel, electric furnace steel, and other products are separately presented.

The Bureau collects quarterly data on the quantity sales of gypsum products classified by uses. These data are available back to 1930 but are comparable only since 1938, when the present classification of products was adopted.

For the other important nonmetals—abrasive materials, clays, feldspar, lime, phosphate rocks, potash, salt, sand and gravel, slate, stone,

---

[29] Neither the Bureau of Mines nor its predecessors has disclosed in detail the precise methods used in making the estimates. A general description of the methods employed may be obtained from the following documents: "Federal Administrators Method of Determining Crude Oil Allocations," a memorandum to the Press, December 24, 1934 (U. S. Dept. Interior, Petroleum Administrative Board); Committee Report on the Bureau of Mines Methods and Practices in Making Forecasts of Demand for Motor Fuel and Crude Petroleum, *Transcript of Proceedings of the Interstate Oil Compact Commission at Colorado Springs, Colorado, July 29, 1938* (E. O. Thompson, Chairman, A. L. Walker, Secretary); Herbert A. Breakey, "Trends and Seasonal Variations in Factors Influencing Domestic Motor-Fuel Demand," *Economic Paper 21 (U. S. Dept. Interior, Bur. Mines, 1940).*

and talc, pyrophyllite, and soapstone—the Bureau compiles an annual series on the quantity sold or consumed by uses. These series are available at least back to about 1920.

Two important mineral products are conspicuously absent from the list—sulfur and cement. For sulfur and also sulfuric acid, the Bureau has relied on the annual estimates of the quantity consumed by uses made by *Chemical Metallurgical Engineering*. The Bureau has made no attempt to collect for cement any information on actual or apparent consumption by uses. Since this is one of the more important mineral products, the complete lack of data on consumption by uses on this commodity and on copper, which we have previously noted, constitutes two serious gaps in an otherwise satisfactory coverage of mineral consumption statistics.

USE OF MINERAL STATISTICS

The uses to which mineral statistics may be put are almost as numerous and varied as the statistical series on minerals included in our discussion in this and other chapters of this volume. In the short space allotted it is, of course, impossible to consider all the uses. Nor does it seem practicable to do so. So far as the larger mineral producers, distributors, and consumers are concerned, they are presumably making substantial use of the available statistics on minerals. These companies generally employ a staff of statisticians and economists to advise the management on current and future operations, on the demand and supply situations in the past, present, and future, on planning investments in mine or plant capacity, and on other economic affairs. These experts analyze not only the available statistics on minerals, but also any other data which might throw light on or aid them in the solution of any or all of these short and long range problems; they also utilize the best statistical techniques in accomplishing these ends. With the large mineral producing, distributing, and consuming concerns the question is not what uses they are to make of the data, but what data are available to them for making such statistical and economic analyses as will enable them to operate more effectively.

The small concerns, whether they are mineral producers, distributors, or consumers, are unlikely to use the available mineral data to the same extent as larger concerns. It certainly would not pay them to do so. Nevertheless they may make some simple but practical use of much of the available statistics on minerals without too great an expenditure of time and money.

Thus a mineral producer may compare his output with that of the combined total of his competitors' output in a given state or district from time to time to determine the relative efficiency of his operations; he may compare his sales or shipments with those of the entire industry, or his sales or shipments to any consuming industry with those of his industry to the same group of consumers to find out where he stands in relation to his competitors; he may compare his stocks with those of his industry, or with those in the hands of consumers to check his inventory position; or he may compare his own price realization with the weighted average prices for the mineral commodity as computed annually by the Bureau of Mines. These comparisons of the statistics on his own operations with those of his competitors or his customers may direct attention to certain shortcomings, which, when discovered and obviated, will put his company in a better competitive position. Producers both large and small can study trends in use over long periods of years, and may then orient their activities to conform with changes in the use pattern.

Others too may profit by making some simple use of the mineral data. A study of the production data by county, district, or other geographical subdivision may reveal some new mining developments, the opening of a new production area, or the expansion of the capacity of an existing mine. It may indicate to mineral consumers or distributors where to go to buy a particular mineral and to sellers of mining equipment and supplies where to go to sell their wares. Mineral consumers or distributors may determine the time to buy or sell from a study of the supply and demand situation of a particular mineral product, that is, from an analysis of the current data on production, sales, shipments, consumption, producers' stocks, consumers' stocks, and other pertinent factors.

Since economic activities of one mineral industry are generally related to those of other mineral industries, and those in the mineral industries are in turn related to those in the manufacturing, agricultural, and other industries, the mineral producers, distributors, consumers, and others involved should keep a watchful eye on barometers indicative of the supply-demand situations in other industries, as well as in the mineral industry with which they are immediately concerned. It will probably not pay small concerns to expend the time and effort to analyze the mass of current statistics in order to obtain these necessary barometric measurements, nor is it necessary, since the results of such analyses are currently available from public and private sources.

The Board of Governors of the Federal Reserve System publishes in the *Federal Reserve Bulletin* the findings of its current analyses of the statistics on production, distribution, inventory, consumption, foreign trade, prices, finances, transportation, labor, and other factors affecting the demand for and supply of principal mineral, agricultural, manufacturing, and other products. The Bureau of Foreign and Domestic Commerce also makes current studies and publishes the results in the *Survey of Current Business*. Several trade journals, among them the *Wall Street Journal* and the *New York Journal of Commerce*, publish analyses and interpretations of current data on mineral, manufacturing, agricultural, and other products. Other journals, such as the *American Metal Market*, restrict their analyses to the data on metals. By following one or more of these periodicals regularly one should be able to observe the trend of current business conditions in the United States.

It should be noted, however, that these public agencies and private organizations endeavor to interpret what has occurred in the immediate past rather than to project into the near and distant future. Since the mineral producers must develop their properties for production months in advance, and the consumers and distributors must also place their orders for mineral products in advance, it is necessary for them to foretell the future of business conditions either by guess or by some more scientific method. The more progressive mineral producing and consuming concerns are utilizing their statistical experts to make periodic forecasts of the demand for some of the principal mineral products. Because of the lack of current over-all information on consumers' stocks and on the consumption of these mineral products by end products or by mineral-using industries, these prognostications, based as they must be on such fragmentary data as are available, are subject to a substantial but uncertain element of error. At best, therefore, these forecasts are largely intelligent guesses.

Statistics and statistical methods should be utilized to guide the major mineral industries in stabilizing their production and the principal mineral-consuming industries in stabilizing their purchases. The major mineral industries—coal, petroleum, iron, copper, lead, and zinc—have been plagued periodically by overproduction in relation to demand, resulting in intermittent waste of irreplaceable resources, loss of capital, and irregular employment. The unprecedented expansion in mining capacity and facilities during the war, the rapid improvement in mining and refining technology, and the enormous supplies of metals that may be expected to emerge after the war from stocks at mills, smelters, refineries, foundries, fabricating plants, warehouses, and other storage facilities and from scrap derived from war plants, war equipment, and the battlefield—all these factors are likely to exert a disturbing influence on the mining industries for many years to come.

There is an urgent need for both short- and long-term forecasting so far as businessmen are concerned—short-term to aid producers in balancing current output with market requirements, and dealers and consumers in scheduling their purchases; and long-term to guide industrialists in planning investments in mining and plant facilities. Up to now, petroleum is the only mineral for which such forecasting has been attempted by a government agency. The experiment which was begun in 1930 and has been continued to the present (1945) demonstrates that, with accurate current data and proper statistical methods, reliable forecasts can be made and utilized to aid in bringing production in balance with consumption of a mineral which has had a tendency to be wastefully overproduced.

The lack of current information, particularly on consumption and consumers' stocks, is the main reason why forecasts are not attempted for other mineral commodities. But with the continuation of the excellent compilations of current statistics on minerals developed in connection with the war production program, fairly accurate demand forecasts for all the major minerals should be possible. These forecasts should be useful to guide efforts to stabilize the mineral industries in the United States in the difficult postwar years.

CHAPTER 5

AGRICULTURE

CONRAD TAEUBER
Bureau of Agricultural Economics
Department of Agriculture

The first Commissioner of Agriculture in the United States wrote in his first annual report in 1863:

> Ignorance of the state of our crops invariably leads to speculation, in which oftentimes, the farmer does not obtain just prices and by which the consumer is not benefited ... The relation between agriculture, manufactures, and commerce demand that something should be done to obtain, and publish at brief intervals during the crop season, reliable information of the amount and conditions of these crops. The connexion between the industrial pursuits creates mutual interests.

The present nation-wide crop-reporting system in the development of which he played so large a part has not lost sight of his purposes. It has grown to be an extensive operation in which the government continually swaps information with the farmer. Today, possibly more than in 1863, there is a close relationship between farming and many parts of the business world. The information that is of use to the farmer is also of use to those agencies and individuals who serve the farmer, and having it made generally available helps both. Although the system of collecting and publishing information was developed and is maintained primarily to help the farmers of the Nation, the resulting information is often of direct and immediate value to the business community.

At present, in peacetime and in war, reports are issued publicly throughout the year. Some are daily, some weekly, some monthly, and some are less frequent. Some involve much formality in the release, like the *Crop Reports*, about which the utmost precautions are taken to assure secrecy prior to release, and equal access to the information by all interested parties after release. Others that reach a more restricted audience are released with little fanfare. Not a working day goes by without the issuance of some report which contains agricultural statistics of some kind; and on most days there are several. Some of the data are of so much interest that private estimating services try to anticipate the reports of the Federal Government; for some other types of data, the trade looks to the Federal Government as the only source of the needed information.

Production Statistics. To say that the year for agricultural production statistics begins at any one time or season is to use a convenient fiction. It closely follows the farmer's seasons, and, like the farmer's work, it never ends. The crop year begins with the December wheat report. Early in March there is the report on *Farmers' Intentions to Plant.* It summarizes the reports of farmers in all parts of the country as to their intentions to plant the specified crops and is an advance indication of what farmers intend to do with their land available for crops. It includes the major crops, except winter wheat and rye, which were planted during the preceding fall, and cotton, which is specifically exempted by Congressional Act. Later in the year, at regular intervals, there are reports on the volume of actual planting and on the condition of the crops, with forecasts of yields, which are kept current in response to changing weather and growing conditions. Finally, at the end of the year there is a summary showing the quantity actually produced.

For milk, eggs, and other livestock and poultry products, the reports show inventories and production and the extent to which production is increasing or decreasing, as compared with the preceding season or some longer period. Reports on condition of pasture and the production of feed grains and forage crops are useful because of the light which they throw on prospective production of livestock and livestock products.

Distribution Statistics. The person who analyzes market prices and supplies needs to know not only how a season's production compares with that of an earlier season or with some "normal," but he needs to know also through what channels and at what rate the goods are moving to market and through the various marketing stages. A given proportion of a crop remaining in the hands of the farmers or not moving to terminal markets is often an indication of significant developments in the market for that commodity. Changes in inventories in all positions from time to time and the carry-over from one season to another are items of information of major importance and are collected regularly. Reports on inventories are obtained periodically from farmers, warehouses, and other storage facilities and, for some commodities, from processors who normally store a considerable proportion of the crop. Cold storage reports cover the volume of holdings in cooled or freezer space in public warehouses.

Some agricultural products, such as fresh fruit and vegetables, move directly into retail channels and the hands of the ultimate consumers

For these, the major distribution information concerns rate of flow into the primary markets. For many commodities, daily reports are issued at the central markets, showing volume of movement and prices and commenting on matters of interest and significance to the trade.

For most commodities, processing is necessary before the goods reach the ultimate consumer. Consequently, there is considerable interest in statistics which show the volume of processing and the rate of movement of the processed goods. Some raw products may be used for the production of a number of end products; for example, milk is used as fluid milk, evaporated, condensed, or dried milk, butter, ice cream, cheese, etc. Here it is necessary not only to know the volume that flows into processing, but the volume of production of the important end products, as well as the changes in the proportion of the raw product that is going into the several uses. Many primary producers of milk can sell to alternative markets and many of the original purchasers can move the product into that end product or combination of end products which at the time will yield the highest returns. In such instances it is not sufficient to know the volume of the product that goes to market, but it becomes necessary to develop sensitive measuring devices to keep informed of the changing pattern of use of the product.

The information relating to milk and dairy products illustrates the variety of information that is obtained as to the flow of a commodity from the original producer to the ultimate consumer. Current estimates of production and of the number of cows being milked are prepared monthly throughout the year. Average production per cow, the average butterfat test, and the quantity of butter produced on farms are reported regularly. Processors of dairy products report the volume of milk or butterfat they use and the products they produce, whether cheese, butter, ice cream or ice cream mix, evaporated or condensed milk, powdered whole milk or milk products, powdered skim milk, or the other products for which milk or a derivative is used.

Because dairy products are generally a matter of local and/or state regulation it is possible to develop a considerable volume of information through the cooperation of the appropriate regulatory agencies. In some of the major milk markets, especially the largest cities, information as to the total volume of milk used as fluid milk is obtained through the cooperation of local, state, and Federal agencies. Weekly estimates of production of butter and cheese are now being issued, monthly estimates of production of most of the other major dairy products have been issued for many years, and annual reports ordinarily provide a more detailed résumé of the year's operations. Receipts of butter at principal markets by rail and by truck, receipts by state of origin, the amount of butter and cheese graded, and wholesale prices and manufacturers' selling prices are reported regularly.

As agricultural production becomes more and more specialized, there is greater need for transportation, often across state lines, if the products are to be moved from the areas in which they can be produced most efficiently to the areas of consumption. *Market News* reporters at the major terminal markets collect and disseminate information about movements of many commodities, and during the peak of the season for a given commodity the information is made available daily or several times during the day. Data as to total shipments of major fruits and vegetables are obtained through the cooperation of the railroad and steamship lines.

The nature of the channels through which a commodity reaches the market ordinarily determines the source and character of the information about the marketing which is available. If a commodity is grown by a specialized and localized group of producers their volume of shipments may provide the desired information; if the commodity must pass through some "bottle neck" operation, such as slaughter of livestock, the volume of movement can usually be indicated best by watching the points of concentration. Receipts at terminal markets are a good indicator of the movement of hogs to market; but for fresh carrots, shipments from the major producing area are a good index of the volume of movement.

Wartime programs often made necessary the development of information on the rate of movement from wholesalers' and retailers' stocks for some items. For a few commodities it was found necessary to develop data showing the rate of movement and the adequacy of that movement in relation to the needs of a locality.

Marketing charges, and the difference between prices received by farmers and prices paid by consumers, are reported regularly for a standard list of items. From these figures the share of the consumer's dollar received by the farmer is computed. Differences among the commodities included in this list are readily apparent. An index number shows how the combined total varies in prosperity and depression.

Prices and Incomes. Prices and incomes have been in the forefront of those agricultural topics which have received much public attention in recent years. Prices of farm products are important not only to agriculture, but also to other sectors of the national economy. At the present time they form the basis for many control programs, including support prices, ceilings, subsidies, and parity. Farm parity legislation has relied upon the relation of prices received by farmers to prices paid by farmers and provides in general that the relationship shall be maintained at approximately the same level as in the base period.

Two series of prices are collected—farm prices of commodities sold by farmers and prices of articles bought by farmers. Prices received by farmers for crops and livestock have been estimated since 1910 (see Chapter 11).

The index of prices paid for commodities, when combined with interest and taxes payable per acre, is used in calculating parity prices. The index of prices paid by farmers for commodities measures the over-all changes that occur in the level of prices charged to farmers and their families for the commodities they use in living and farm production. These indexes are based on prices for 86 items used in family living and 94 items used in farm production.

In addition to prices received by farmers, current prices at important markets are secured regularly. These include detailed prices of feedstuffs and prices of grain by grades. For dairy products, they include also dealer buying prices per hundred pounds for standard grade milk and prices to producers at condenseries per hundred pounds for milk, the wholesale price of dried milk, wholesale and retail prices per quart of fluid milk in large cities, wholesale prices for evaporated and condensed milk, and wholesale prices per pound for butter and cheese. Other prices reported include those of wool by grades, the average price and weight of hogs and cattle purchased by packers and shippers, and the prices by grade and staple length of cotton by months in the major cotton markets.

Income for the individual farmer, as well as for agriculture as a whole, depends upon the amount of products sold, the prices received, and the expenses connected with farm operations. Estimates of income include cash farm income, gross farm income, and net farm income. Cash farm income consists of cash receipts from farm marketings of crops, livestock, and livestock products plus government payments. Cash farm income is estimated currently and the figures are published monthly. Gross farm income, estimated annually, includes cash farm income plus the value of products consumed on the farms where produced and the imputed rental value of farm dwellings.

Operating expenses of production must be taken into account in determining the significance of any level of gross farm income and changes in that income. Current operating expenses are estimated for such items as feed bought, livestock bought, fertilizer and lime, the operation of motor vehicles, the purchase of horses and mules, insecticides, containers, twine, ginning, seeds, nursery stock, electricity for production, grazing fees, veterinary services, insurance, tolls, short-term interest, and other items calling for cash outlays to further farm production. Other items of operating expense include maintenance or depreciation of buildings, machinery, and equipment, wages of hired farm labor paid in cash or in kind, farm property taxes levied, farm-mortgage interest, and net payments to nonfarm landlords.

The net income from agriculture to persons on farms is derived by adjusting the net income of farm operators from current operations to take into account changes in inventory, both of crops and of livestock, and by adding the farm wages paid to laborers living on farms. The figures are usually presented in dollars and also as averages per farm and per capita of the farm population. "Agriculture's contribution to the national income" includes the income of persons on farms plus certain items paid out by agriculture to the nonfarm population, in-

TABLE 1. AGRICULTURE'S CONTRIBUTION TO THE NATIONAL INCOME:
1943 AND 1933

(millions of dollars)

Item	1943 *	1933
Cash received:		
From sale of		
Wheat	825	304
Feed grains and hay	1,114	302
Soybeans	296	6
Peanuts	167	15
Cotton, lint, and seed	1,412	577
Tobacco	557	157
Vegetables	1,530	446
Fruits	1,092	333
Cattle and calves	2,560	600
Hogs	2,953	524
Sheep, lambs, and wool	504	181
Dairy products	2,804	1,004
Eggs	1,423	309
Chickens and broilers	840	161
All crops †	7,903	2,473
All livestock and livestock products †	11,349	2,841
All crops, livestock and livestock products	19,252	5,314
From government payments	672	131
Value of products consumed on farms where produced	2,027	1,023
Estimated rental value of farm dwellings of farm operators	787	587
Gross farm income	22,738	7,055
Net income to persons on farms from farming ‡	13,665	2,993

* Preliminary.
† Includes items in addition to those shown separately above.
‡ Including government payments.

cluding farm wages to laborers not living on farms, farm-mortgage interest, and net payments of rent to nonfarm landlords.

How these figures reflect the situation in agriculture may be illustrated by comparing those for 1943 and 1933, a record high and a near-record low year.

Estimates of cash receipts from farm marketings, government payments, and value of home consumption are available by states for each year back to 1924. Available estimates provide a measure of the

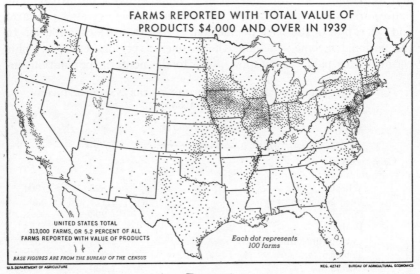

FARMS REPORTED WITH TOTAL VALUE OF
PRODUCTS $4,000 AND OVER IN 1939

UNITED STATES TOTAL
313,000 FARMS, OR 5.2 PERCENT OF ALL
FARMS REPORTED WITH VALUE OF PRODUCTS

Each dot represents
100 farms

BASE FIGURES ARE FROM THE BUREAU OF THE CENSUS

U.S. DEPARTMENT OF AGRICULTURE   NEG. 42747   BUREAU OF AGRICULTURAL ECONOMICS

FIGURE 1

changes in total and average incomes. In addition, businessmen frequently need figures on the distribution of incomes, showing the proportion of farms and farm operators in the several income groups, and the distribution of incomes within smaller areas, such as counties. The Censuses of 1930 and 1940 provided such information through the collection of figures showing the value of all products sold, traded, or used by farm operators and their households. (See Figs. 1 and 2.) These figures have been widely used to show the relative productivity of agriculture of various areas and to locate areas of high productivity and relatively high purchasing power and those of low productivity and low purchasing power of farm families.

These figures, in relation to the amount of part-time farming, the type of farming, and the age of operators, provide a basis for a description of our farmers: Those who produce primarily for their own consumption at home and those who produce primarily for the market;

the family-size farms, the large-scale farms, or other groupings.   They also show the areas in which large-scale commercial farms are the most common type, as well as those areas in which relatively little is produced for the market.

In 1939 one-third of all the farms for which gross value of product sold, traded, or used was reported showed a total of less than $400, and these 2 million farms accounted for only about 3 percent of the total value of the products which went to market.   The top third of the

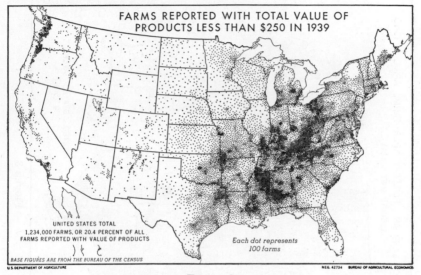

FARMS REPORTED WITH TOTAL VALUE OF PRODUCTS LESS THAN $250 IN 1939

UNITED STATES TOTAL
1,234,000 FARMS, OR 20.4 PERCENT OF ALL
FARMS REPORTED WITH VALUE OF PRODUCTS

Each dot represents
100 farms

BASE FIGURES ARE FROM THE BUREAU OF THE CENSUS
U.S. DEPARTMENT OF AGRICULTURE   NEG. 42734   BUREAU OF AGRICULTURAL ECONOMICS

FIGURE 2

farms, those with gross value of product of $1,000 and over, accounted for 84 percent of all crops which went to market; the top 1 percent, with more than $10,000 worth of products, alone accounted for 20 percent of the product which went to market.   The middle third, those with gross value of product between $400 and $1,000 accounted for 13 percent of the marketed crops.   Obviously, agriculture includes many small units, some part-time, some units which provide an outlet for retired or handicapped persons, and some units on which much hard work is expended in a futile effort to secure a satisfactory livelihood.

The total value of product is a figure that is often used.   In addition, there are many needs for information about the source of the reported income.   Figures showing the value of products provided by farms of various sizes are available for each county for the years covered by the Census and annually in a few states.

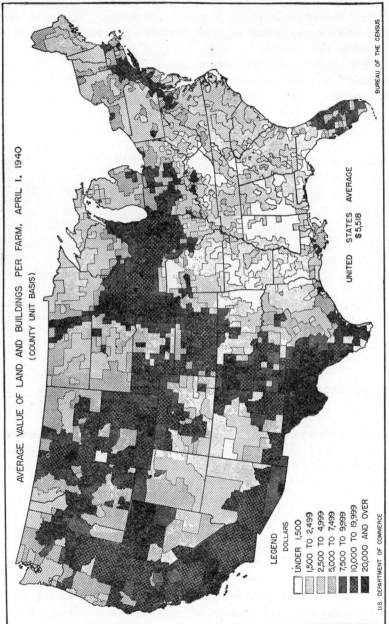

AVERAGE VALUE OF LAND AND BUILDINGS PER FARM, APRIL 1, 1940
(COUNTY UNIT BASIS)

LEGEND

DOLLARS

UNDER 1,500
1,500 TO 2,499
2,500 TO 4,999
5,000 TO 7,499
7,500 TO 9,999
10,000 TO 19,999
20,000 AND OVER

UNITED STATES AVERAGE
$5,518

U.S. DEPARTMENT OF COMMERCE

BUREAU OF THE CENSUS

FIGURE 3

Values and Credit. At the time of each census figures are compiled showing total and average values of real estate per farm for each county, and the number of farms which report farm property of stated value. (See Fig. 3.) There is also an annual estimate of the value of farm real estate and other farm property by geographic divisions. Increasing farm land prices are often regarded as one of the best indexes of inflationary trends in rural areas. Consequently, the current monthly reports which show the prices at which land is being sold and the volume of voluntary real estate transfers are followed with unusual interest.

Farmers are important borrowers of short-term and long-term funds —short-term funds primarily to finance operations before the season's products can be taken to market and long-term funds to purchase farm land or to finance improvements. Reports of the operations of Federal lending agencies, such as the Farm Credit Administration, the Commodity Credit Corporation, the Farm Security Administration, and the Rural Electrification Administration, are readily available. Figures are obtained from other sources as well. Annual estimates show the total farm-mortgage debt to the Federal Land Banks or the Land Bank Commissioner, life insurance companies, Joint Stock Land Banks, the Farm Security Administration, commercial banks, individual lenders, and others.

Lending operations, interest rates, and the amount of payments on account of interest are reported regularly. The volume of mortgage indebtedness in relation to the value of farm real estate held by owner operators is available for census years by counties. In conjunction with the rate of tenancy, these figures indicate the equity which farm operators have in the farms they operate. An annual estimate shows also the amount of farm real estate held outright by such lenders as the Federal agencies, life insurance companies, commercial banks, and state credit agencies in the three states which have such agencies.

Personal and real estate taxes levied against farm property are estimated annually. Taxes per acre and taxes per $100 of value are available by states.

Economic Indicators. One of the recent monthly price reports shows the price of wheat at $1.47 per bushel; corn at $1.15 per bushel; oats at 79 cents per bushel; hay at $16.20 per ton; tobacco at 23.8 cents per pound; apples at $3.17 per bushel; grapefruit at $1.36 a box; hogs at $113 per hundredweight; eggs at 27 cents per dozen; milk cows at $113 per head. Each of these prices is in itself an average of the prices reported in a number of markets. Combining them literally raises the familiar problem of adding horses and apples, with many other farm commodities added for good measure. The most convenient means of combining them is to compute index numbers relating them to an appropriate "base" period. For many of the current figures, the average for 1935–1939 is taken as the base period and changes are measured from that time. The 5 years preceding World War I, 1910–1914, or August 1909 to July 1914, are also frequently used.

Through this device of index numbers it is possible to show rates of change in the price level as a whole for those items which farmers sell as well as those items which they buy. In practice, index numbers are frequently computed for individual commodities and for groups of commodities and are combined as needed. The resulting numbers, if properly combined, can become highly useful and sensitive indicators of general business conditions as they affect agriculture. One of the most widely used index numbers is the ratio of prices received to prices paid. This index shows the ups and downs which agriculture has encountered since 1910. In 1919, the index rose to 109, considering 1909–1914 as 100. By 1932 it fell to 55, and in 1943 it had risen again to 117. This ratio of prices received to prices paid is the basis for the computation of farm parity.

In addition to the general parity ratio, parity prices are computed for individual commodities. As defined by law, the parity price for any agricultural commodity is that price for the commodity which will give it a purchasing power with respect to articles that farmers buy equivalent to the purchasing power of that commodity in the base period. For those commodities whose base period is 1909–1914, the parity price also reflects the relationship of current interest payments per acre on farm indebtedness secured by real estate, tax payments per acre on farm real estate, and freight rates as contrasted with similar items in the base period.

The computation of parity price for an individual agricultural commodity consists in adjusting the price of that commodity in the base period by the index of prices paid, including interest and taxes. For example, if in 1943 the index of prices paid was 164, the parity price for cotton would be 1.64 times 12.4 cents, which was the average price of cotton in the base period. The result is 20.3 cents. Similarly in 1943 the parity price for corn, which had a base price of 64.2 cents in 1909–1914, was $1.05.

Numerous other index numbers and ratios, which summarize a wide variety of information about agriculture, are published, such as indexes of acreage harvested, production indexes, and consumption indexes.

One of the more widely used ratios is the hog-corn ratio that is published monthly for the United States and separately for the North

Central States, which include the bulk of the corn-hog area. The corn-hog ratio shows the number of bushels of corn equal in value to 100 pounds of live hog based on average prices of corn and hogs for the month. When this ratio is high, farmers get more return by feeding corn; when it is low, it is more profitable to sell the corn rather than to feed it. Fluctuations in the ratio have proved to be a useful tool to economic analysts in predicting changes in the number of hogs. The ratio has also proved to be a useful tool for feeders in indicating the relative profit of selling corn or feeding it. The utility of this ratio has suggested the computation of other similar ratios which are now currently available: egg-feed, chicken-feed, turkey-feed, milk-feed.

Population and Employment. Recent manpower shortages have focused attention on one of the great resources of farms in this country, their manpower. The farm population normally produces more than enough young men and women to provide for its own labor needs or to maintain its own numbers. During the 1920's some 6 million persons net moved from farms to towns and cities. During the 1930's the number was only about 3.5 million persons, a number just about balanced by the excess of births over deaths during the period. Since 1940 the migration from farms has broken all earlier records. Some 6 million persons have moved from farms since 1940, which is 4 million more than would have been expected if migration had been at the same rate as during the last five prewar years. About 1.5 million of the 6 million have gone into the armed forces. Annual estimates of farm population and movement to and from farms provide a picture of the changes in farm population which are taking place currently. A comprehensive description of the numbers and characteristics of farm residents is provided once every 10 years by the Census of Population (see Chapter 12).

Agriculture is a highly seasonal industry. In recent years the total volume of agricultural employment ranged from about 8.5 million at the low point to about 12 million at the peak. In 1943 some 14.5 million different persons worked on farms at some time. Monthly estimates of farm employment report changes in the numbers of persons working on farms, both hired workers and members of the farmer's family working without pay. In addition, the age composition of the farm working force and the length of the workday are reported intermittently, and wages paid with and without board are reported quarterly. The reported wage rates include an average rate which records changes in the general wage level from time to time. Rates for specific operations, such as bunching carrots and picking cotton, are also collected.

Consumption. Consumption is the end purpose of production, and, except for tobacco and certain fiber crops, virtually all agricultural production results directly in consumption as food or feed. The measurement of the volume of consumption is much more difficult than the measurement of production, but some measures of total food consumption have been developed. Wartime food management problems have greatly increased the need for such data, and wartime food regulation has, in turn, provided some information not available before. Figures that show total and per capita consumption of each of the major foods are published quarterly, and an index of per capita food consumption is published regularly.

Trends in consumption of various food products clearly reflect changing tastes and food habits. Compared with the years immediately preceding World War I, the average American was eating about the same amount of food in 1935–1939. But it was not the same kind of food that his parents ate, for he was using more dairy products, including butter, less meat, about the same quantity of eggs, a third less potatoes, a third less flour, more sugar, half again as many beans, peas, and nuts, about the same amount of fats and oils other than butter, more fresh fruit, about four times as much canned fruit, one-fourth more fresh vegetables, almost twice as many canned vegetables, and about one-third more of the group including coffee, tea, cocoa, and spices.

Despite wartime shortages the average civilian American had about 6 percent more food in 1943 than in 1935–1939, less of some things but more of others. It is generally believed that in 1943 there was less difference in the amounts of food available to high-income and low-income consumers than in 1935–1939. The figures on average per capita consumption give no clue to that, however, and data are not available as to the distribution of food by income classes in 1943.

Feed. A large proportion of the production of corn, oats, barley, and grain sorghums is normally fed to livestock. During the five years 1937–1938 to 1941–1942 average annual production of corn amounted to 2,582 million bushels, and, of this, 2,225 million bushels was fed to livestock. The production of oats during that period averaged 1,130 million bushels and the average quantity fed to livestock amounted to 985 million bushels. During some years considerable wheat is fed to livestock, and in recent years wheat has been imported for use as feed. Production and consumption of feed grains are estimated currently, and early in the calendar year computations are made to arrive at the livestock-feed balance for the succeeding feeding year. In addition to figures showing the production and consumption of feed grains, the feed estimates include figures for the production of oilseed meal, particularly soybean cake and meal and cottonseed cake and meal; animal proteins, including tankage and meat scraps and fish meal; and an estimate of the dry equivalent of skim milk, buttermilk, whey, and whole milk fed on farms. Estimates of the production and supply of hay, as well as the quantity of hay fed, are made quarterly. In estimating the prospective livestock-feed balance, it is necessary to take into account the number of feed-consuming animal units and prospective changes in the numbers of these units, along with figures showing the rate of feeding and the uses of feed grains for processing, for seed, and for other purposes, as well as imports and exports. In order to arrive at regional totals, it is necessary also to estimate the supply of grain locally grown and the net volume of shipments to and from regions. To help meet wartime feed problems, information as to interstate shipments of some of the major concentrate feeds has also been secured recently.

Farm and Home Equipment. Businessmen interested in the farmer as a market have long wanted information as to the incomes and the buying habits of farmers, the amount of equipment of various kinds which farmers have on hand, and their prospective purchases. A long list of machines is included in the list of items for which annual estimates of farmers' inventories are prepared, including motortrucks, automobiles, tractors, corn pickers, plows, cultivators, milking machines, combines, peanut pickers, drills, mowers, and balers. For some of the major machines the estimates include size, age, and distribution by regions and states. Estimates of the amount of time a machine is used have been made for a number of major machines in order to arrive at replacement needs. The Census in 1940 asked each farmer to report whether he had an automobile, truck, and tractor, and for each of these it asked also for the year of latest model.

In 1920, 31 percent of all farms reported an automobile; by 1940 this was 58 percent. In 1940 half the automobiles on farms were 1934 models or older. These figures, which are available by states, suggest clearly some of the marked possibilities in the automobile field. Farms with trucks increased from 2 percent of the farms in 1920 to 16 percent in 1940. In some states, the figure is considerably larger; for example, in Montana, 44 percent of all farms reported a truck. Trucks tended to be of more recent makes than automobiles. In 1940 about half the trucks reported were 1935 models or older.

The facilities available in farm homes are an important part of farm equipment. The Censuses of 1920, 1930, and 1940 reflect the rapid increase in electricity in the farm home. In 1920 only 7 percent of the

farms had electricity in the home; by 1940 this had been increased to
33 percent; and current estimates place the number in 1944 at approximately 40 percent. In 1940, 46 percent of the farms were within a
quarter of a mile of an electric power line.

Although the proportion of farm homes with electricity increased,
the proportion of farm homes having telephones decreased between
1930 and 1940 in all parts of the country except New England. The
proportion of farm homes with radios increased rapidly between 1930
and 1940. The number of farm homes having running water was also
reported in 1930 and 1940. As part of the Housing Census of 1940, a
great deal of other detailed information as to the size, age, type of
structure, heating, and other facilities of farm homes was obtained.

Since farmsteads are ordinarily some distance apart, considerable
interest attaches to the kind of road on which the farm is located. In
1925 only 7 percent of the farms reported that they were on hard-
surfaced roads, and by 1940 this had been increased to nearly 20 percent. The number living on unimproved dirt roads at the same time
decreased from 43 percent to 24 percent.

Administrative Statistics. The lending program and other programs
of the Farm Credit Administration, the Commodity Credit Corporation, the Farm Security Administration, and the Rural Electrification
Administration are in themselves of interest to some elements in the
business community. The volume of new loans, the rates of interest
charged, repayments, volume of outstanding loans, extent of refinancing—all these furnish information as to the operations of the major
governmental lending agencies in the agricultural field, and, as such,
they are important to other lending agencies. These agencies submit
annual reports and release other information on their operations as well.
Some of the major items made available by the Farm Credit Administration, besides the purely fiscal statements, include figures showing
how borrowers in the several states used the proceeds of their loans:
How much went for the refinancing of indebtedness; the purchase of
land and redemption from foreclosure; general agricultural uses, including buildings and improvements; the purchase of National Farm
Loan Association stock, which is required of every borrower; and loan
fees. The rapid decrease in recent years in the number of Land Bank
and Land Bank Commissioner Loans "delinquent and/or extended"
is the subject of a table which reports the status of these two classes
of loans by states for the first of each year. Short-term production
credit is provided through the Production Credit Associations, which
report regularly on the volume of loans made and the amounts of
loans outstanding. The Emergency Crop and Feed Loan programs,

which are designed to meet emergency situations, also report by states on the volume of loans made and the amounts outstanding. Federal Intermediate Credit Banks report on the loans made to Production Credit Associations, the Regional Agricultural Credit Corporations, the Banks for Cooperatives, direct loans to cooperative associations, and other lending operations.

The lending, debt adjustment and appraisal policies and programs, and the related activities of the Farm Credit Administration influence the extent of all borrowing to finance farm land purchases. Farm ownership loans, made by the Farm Security Administration to enable farm tenants to become owners, are less numerous and considerably circumscribed, but in some states the volume of such loans is one of the factors affecting the farm real estate situation.

Rural Rehabilitation loans, made available by the Farm Security Administration to farm families unable to borrow from other established credit agencies, are ordinarily quickly translated into purchases of workstock, livestock, farming equipment, seed, fertilizer, and other needs. The volume of activity of this program bears directly on the plans of manufacturers and dealers who can or do reach low-income farmers.

The lending and purchasing activities of the Commodity Credit Corporation cover a variety of agricultural products, and reports on the activities of this organization are important to business groups which follow trends in prices and marketing of the commodities affected. Wartime programs have considerably increased the extent of their activities, including price support and subsidy operations.

The Rural Electrification Administration makes loans for the provision or extension of electrical facilities to local consumers, organized into cooperative associations, and provides some management and advisory services to the local associations. Working primarily through nearly 800 local cooperative associations, its activities have stimulated the use of electricity in farm homes and operations. Up to the end of March 1944 a total of 482 million dollars had been allotted to cooperative associations, public bodies, such as municipalities, public power districts and state authorities, and private utilities. The number of consumers had grown to 1.4 million, and 434,000 miles of line had been built. Its policies and activities in many areas have had an appreciable effect on the policies and rates of public utility companies which serve rural areas.

The activities of the Agricultural Adjustment Administration reach into every agricultural county in the country, and in most areas they affect a large proportion of all farmers. The volume of payments by commodities by states has been reported regularly, the coverage varying with the provisions of the Act for the year in question. In addition to amounts paid out, the figures include also the number of payees, the percentage of the cropland of the state that is covered by applications, and the number of payments of specified size. In recent years much of the activity of AAA has been centered on soil-building and range-building practices. These are reported in detail, including the extent of the use of seed and of limestone, superphosphate, and other fertilizers for this purpose.

Purchases of products for shipment under the Lend-Lease Act and for domestic distribution were reported daily. They were shown by commodities, origin, grade, packaging, quantity, and price. These were also assembled in a *Monthly Summary of Purchases*. A *Monthly Report of Deliveries* showed shipments to various agencies and other receivers, and a *Monthly Sales Report* listed sales of government-owned stocks of food and related agricultural products no longer needed by United States military forces or for war agencies.

The Department is responsible for administering regulatory acts relating to agricultural warehouses, commodity exchanges, cotton, cotton futures, dairy exports, exports of apples and pears, grain standards, insecticides, marketing agreements, meat inspection, naval stores, packers and stockyards, perishable agricultural commodities, peanuts, produce agencies, seed, standard containers, sugar, tobacco, and wool standards. Reports on activities under these acts and regulations are issued regularly.

The Crop Reports. The crop reporting service goes back officially to 1839, when Congress made an appropriation to the Patent Office for the distribution of seeds and the collection of agricultural statistics. Development was relatively slow for some years. In 1862 the Department of Agriculture was established and the agricultural statistics work was taken over from the Patent Office. By 1863 monthly or bimonthly statistics on condition of crops were published, based on voluntary reports from crop correspondents selected to represent each county in the Northern States.

The Crop Reporting Service is now operated in cooperation with 40 state governmental agencies for the collection, collation, and publication of data relating to acreage, condition, and production of crops; number and production of livestock; prices of farm products; and related information. Each year, on an average, about 600,000 farmers and 175,000 other persons make reports to the Service. About 70,000 of these are the farmers who report monthly on crops and livestock. The primary purpose is to provide adequate, accurate, and timely information concerning crops and livestock for crop and livestock producers. All of the farmers who report are doing so voluntarily, and many families have reported for two generations or longer.

Speed, accuracy, and equal access to the data on release are essentials of the procedure for handling these materials. Many of the crop reports are forecasts of production and future supply and if known in advance of publication could be used unfairly for speculative purposes. Therefore, the preparation and publication of the crop reports are surrounded with every possible safeguard to prevent advance information from being obtained or utilized by unauthorized persons. The work is so arranged that no individual who handles the returns, whether a member of the Crop Reporting Board, a clerk making the computations, or the Secretary of Agriculture himself, has any means of knowing what the United States total or average for any crop will be until the final computations are made and approved behind locked and guarded doors a short time before the report is released to the public.

Statistics and War. Wartime Federal regulations relating to food, feed, and agricultural machinery and equipment called for a variety of reports and a great deal of information, if the regulations were to be administered effectively and equitably. Some entirely new procedures were necessary for collecting information, especially in those fields in which no reports were previously secured. This was particularly true for some of the commodities which account for only a small volume of total agricultural production but which, because of shortages, assumed considerable importance during the war; e.g., dehydrated onions. Some of the war needs for information were met by building on the reports which were already collected regularly. For meat and livestock statistics prewar information was built largely on the reports from those firms which were under Federal Meat Inspection. As a result much information began to be available about the operations of groups of slaughterers and butchers who before the war had not been represented in the statistics.

Single-Time Surveys. Most of the statistical information about agriculture which is published results from information collected annually, quarterly, monthly, weekly, daily, or at some other time intervals, or it results from a Census of Agriculture taken in the years ending in 0 or 5. But occasionally special needs arise which call for the assembly of a large body of statistical information through a one-time survey. There are, of course, many smaller research studies which require the single-time collection of information in order to have at hand the specific information needed to answer the question which led to the study. The coverage in such studies tends to be

limited and the major interest is in the conclusions which the analyst
reached rather than in the statistics as such. There are other studies
in which a single-time survey is undertaken to provide information of
wide general use. Some of the new wartime programs necessitated
such single-time surveys to establish operations during a specified base
period, to provide information on the structure of an industry, and to
determine the relationships among the several parts of the industry,
or the relative contributions of large and small or independent and
captive operators. One of the most extensive of these single-time
surveys in recent years was the Consumer Purchases Survey, undertaken jointly by the Bureau of Home Economics and the Bureau of
Labor Statistics with the cooperation of the National Resources Committee and the Works Progress Administration (see Chapter 11).

The Census of Agriculture. The publications available from the
Bureau of the Census are illustrated by the materials which resulted
from the Census of Agriculture, taken as of April 1, 1940, in connection
with the Census of Population and the Census of Housing for the
United States and its Territories and Possessions. A Census of Irrigation and Drainage was taken at the same time. Within continental
United States information was secured from each of the 6,096,799
farms.

The schedule on which the information was recorded included 232
numbered inquiries, some of which had several subdivisions. Despite
this number of questions, it was impossible to secure more than a fraction of the information needed by public and private agencies who had
expressed their needs for such information. A number of the questions
were "catch-all" questions which provided for reporting separately
miscellaneous items for which reports would be too infrequent to justify
separate inquiries on the schedule. The questions included information
as to the age and color of the operator, whether he lived on the farm he
operated, the number of acres in the farm, and whether he owned all,
part, or none of the land in the farm; and for tenants the method of
rental and the items furnished by the landlord as his share of the
operations of the farm. The total number of acres in the farm was
called for, and this was divided into that portion used for crops, pasture, woodland, and other uses. Total value of land and buildings
was also reported. Farm-mortgage debt and interest rates, farm taxes,
acres irrigated, and the amount of land owned by the operator other
than in this farm concluded the general questions about the farm.
Questions concerning the extent to which the farmer worked off the
farm and the kind of work he did during 1939 provided some information as to the extent of part-time farming. Because farmers' coopera-

tives occupy an important position in marketing and purchasing, several questions were asked to show whether the farmer did any buying or selling through cooperatives. The number of persons working on the farm, whether unpaid members of the farmer's family or hired workers, and the amount paid out in wages were recorded.

Among other expenditures included were those for hay and feed, farm implements, fuel for farm machines, building materials, fertilizer, and lime. The number and age of automobiles, tractors, and trucks, nearness to an electric distribution line, whether the house was lighted by electricity from a power line or a home plant, whether there was a telephone, and the kind of road were also recorded. Detailed information was obtained as to the acreage and yield of crops, vegetables harvested for sale, acreage and production of small fruits, orchard fruits, nuts and citrus fruits, and the production of livestock and livestock products. The value of products sold or traded from the farm and of those used by the operator's family was reported.

Questions relating to crops included not only such staples as wheat, corn, oats, barley, rye, and cotton, but also clover and grass seeds, annual legumes, potatoes, sugar beets, broomcorn, mint harvested, and many others. Likewise, the reports on inventory and production of livestock and livestock products provided information not only about the dairy and poultry enterprises, but also on hives of bees and honey produced, fur animals in captivity, livestock purchases and sales, mohair clipped, and goats milked during any part of 1939.

In order to permit the use of the large number of questions for which needs had been found and to lighten the burden on the farmer and the enumerator in so far as possible, the schedule was regionalized. Nine different regional schedules were prepared, differing only in that separate inquiries for crops not grown or grown only infrequently in a region were omitted in the schedules for that region and more detail was secured for the important crops of the region. For example, cotton was not called for in the schedules used in the North; there was considerable detail on fruits, nuts, and vegetables in the schedules used in California and Arizona; and questions on irrigated acreages were more detailed in those parts of the country where irrigation was a common practice.

All this information is summarized in 21 volumes of the Census of Agriculture of 1940, which provide some 26,000 pages of statistics. The bulk of the information presented there is given for United States totals, by geographic divisions and by states and counties.

Volumes I and II include statistics by counties; these are also available in paper-bound separates for each of the states. Volume I includes

the statistics concerning farms and farm property, with related information for farms and farm operators, livestock and livestock products,
and crops. Volume II gives statistics for value of farm products, farms
classified by major source of income, and farms classified by total
value of products.

The reader who is primarily interested in state, regional, and national
figures and who wants to study general relationships or to see what
kinds of materials are available will find Volume III particularly helpful. The information is presented in ten chapters:

1. Farms and farm property.
2. Size of farm.
3. Color, tenure, and race of farm operator.
4. Farm mortgages and farm taxes.
5. Work off farm, age (of operator) and years on farm.
6. Cooperation, labor, expenditures, machinery, facilities and residence (whether
   living on the farm he operates).
7. Livestock and livestock products.
8. Field crops and vegetables.
9. Fruits and nuts and horticultural specialties.
10. Value of farm products.

For the information about the Territories and Possessions there is a
separate volume, and there are also separate bulletins for each of the
following: Alaska, Hawaii, American Samoa, Guam, Puerto Rico, and
the Virgin Islands of the United States.

A separate volume is devoted to irrigation of agricultural lands,
showing data by drainage basins and by counties for 20 irrigation states
and including a summary for the United States. This volume includes
maps showing irrigation by drainage basins in the states.

Statistics as to the drainage of agricultural land are shown for 38
states in a separate volume, which includes also a separate map showing the location of land in drainage enterprises in these states.

In addition to the regular Census reports, a number of special
studies have been published from the 1940 information. There is a
special report on cotton, showing cotton harvested by number of bales
and by counties, and showing by counties the number of farms reporting specified amounts of cotton harvested. This volume shows the
number of farms in each county that reported a bale or less, 1⅛ to 2
bales, etc., up to more than 500 bales. For each size group of farms
the report shows the acreage, the quantity produced, and the value of
all farm products sold, traded, or used by the farm household, by
major type of product. This report shows that of the 1,590,000
farms reporting any cotton harvested, one-seventh reported 1 bale or
less. These account for 5 percent of the acreage of cotton harvested

and only 1.6 percent of the total cotton produced. Three hundred and eighty-five farms reported more than 500 bales of cotton, the total being 342,000 bales, or 3 percent of all the cotton produced. These large farms reported an average yield of 1.13 bales per acre and an average of $71,000 as the gross value of product for the farm. The farms reporting less than 1 bale had an average yield of 0.16 bale per acre and their gross value of all farm products from these farms averaged only $423.

A special report on cows milked and milk produced shows by counties for 1939 and 1929 the number of farms with no cows, 1 cow, 2 cows, etc. For each of these groups of farms, the report also shows the amount of milk produced, the volume of dairy products sold, butter churned on farms, and the number of cows kept mainly for milk production. In 1939 the average number of cows and heifers milked per farm was 4.7, and 4,700,000 farms reported cows milked. More than one-fourth of these had only 1 cow and 51 percent had 1 or 2 cows, but 364 farms reported 200 or more cows, with an average of 333 cows per farm. The farms with 200 cows and over were less than one-tenth of 1 percent of all farms reporting cows milked, but they produced almost 1 percent of all of the milk and accounted for 2 percent of the whole milk sold.

A similar report on poultry gives information as to farms reporting chickens, turkeys, and eggs and, by counties, the number of chickens on hand and the dozens of eggs produced.

After the regular tabulations for 1940 were completed, a special sample of 2 percent of all farms was selected for special analysis. The report on *Farm Characteristics by Value of Product* provides information relating to the characteristics of large and small farms; the extent to which large, medium-sized, and small farms contribute to total production and account for the land in farms; and the expenditures for labor, fertilizer, etc. It describes more fully the volume and type of production of part-time farms, retirement units, and those farms which produce little more than a part of the food needed by the farm family and very little for market, in comparison with family-size farms producing for the market.

Graphic Summary of American Agriculture. The *Graphic Summary of American Agriculture* brings together in a series of maps and charts many of the significant data found in the Census of Agriculture. Following the Census of 1940, a *Graphic Summary of Crops* and a *Graphic Summary of Livestock and Livestock Products* were issued by the Department of Agriculture. The similar volumes following the Census of 1930 and 1925 covered not only crops and livestock but other subjects included in the Census as well. These publications summarize in maps like those in Figures 4 and 5 the data, by counties, showing where

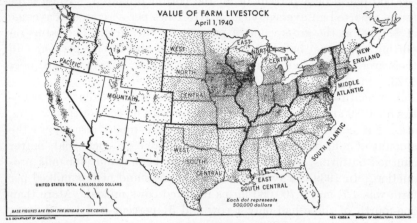

FIGURE 4

the production of an item is concentrated and where it is relatively unimportant; they also show income relationships, changes from one census to another, as well as averages and some figures per farm or per acre.

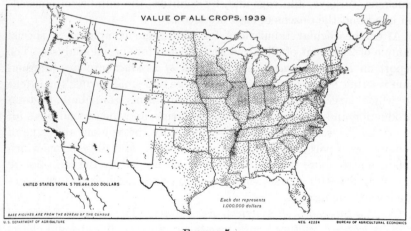

FIGURE 5

Annual Agricultural Statistics. Current statistics are published regularly in a series of reports from the Department of Agriculture.

The standard and most complete of the reports of the Department of Agriculture is the annual publication known as *Agricultural Statistics.*

Formerly published as a statistical appendix to the *Agricultural Yearbook*, this compilation of the readily available statistics relating to agriculture has grown to such size that in recent years it has been issued separately. The 1943 issue contains 614 tables. These bring together in one volume the more important statistics on grains, cotton, sugar, tobacco, oilseeds, fats and oils, vegetables, melons, fruits, tree nuts, hay, seeds and minor field crops, beef cattle, hogs, sheep, horses, mules, dairy and poultry products, farm capital and income, agricultural conservation and adjustment, and a variety of other topics, including temperature and rainfall, lumber and naval stores production, and reports on the work of the Cooperative Extension Service.

Agricultural Statistics is intended to be a permanent record which brings together the more important series of statistics prepared by the Department of Agriculture or compiled by the staff for official use. Current and historical data are presented in the tables, but the more recent issues have limited the historical information to the period since 1930. For security reasons tables showing the international trade in agricultural products and figures on United States imports and exports have not been published since 1941. Prior to that time, these, as well as comparative production statistics for the principal countries producing a given commodity, were also included.

The Crop Report. The crop report is issued by the Department of Agriculture each month in accordance with a schedule of release dates fixed at the beginning of the year. It contains the current estimate of crop acreage and prospective yields of the Crop Reporting Board, along with comments on conditions. It shows yield per acre and indicated production for the important crops, and it follows the crop production situation through from prospective plantings to actual plantings and harvest; it also shows abandonment of planted acreage and stocks on hand. Late in the year an annual summary is published which shows acreage, yield, and production of principal crops by states, with comparisons for earlier years. Other special reports deal with livestock and livestock products and with a large number of special commodities. Monthly reports, which contain the latest information on prices received and prices paid, are issued. One of the current reports that became of increased usefulness during the war was the monthly report on the number of people working on farms.

The scope of the crop reports is illustrated by the reports issued during the year on cotton.

April: Acreage, yield per acre, production of cotton lint and seed, value of production of lint, disposition and value of cottonseed, cottonseed meal used as fertilizer on cotton farms, monthly marketings by farmers, reduction from full yield per acre due to boll weevil damage and through other causes—all for the preceding year.

July: Acreage of cotton in cultivation as of the first of the month.

August: Condition as of August 1, indicated yield per acre, indicated production, commercial fertilizer used on cotton.

September: Condition as of September 1, indicated yield per acre and production, percentage of acreage abandoned since July 1, acreage left for harvest.

October: Condition as of October 1, indicated yield per acre and production.

November: Yield per acre as of November 1, probable production.

December: Yield per acre as of December 1, probable production, gross weight per running bale, acreage for harvest, acreage in cultivation July 1.

In addition to the monthly Department of Agriculture reports on cotton production, semimonthly reports on cotton ginnings are issued by the Bureau of the Census from August 1 to January 1, followed by a final report on ginnings for the crop year in April.

Reports on livestock and livestock products also provide a current picture of the developing situation. They include:

January: Cattle, sheep, and lambs on feed for market on January 1.

February: Number and value of livestock, including poultry, on farms on January 1.

March: Wool production and income, and those for mohair; the early lamb crop as of March 1.

April: Development of early lamb crop as of April 1, cattle on feed for market in the Corn Belt States as of April 1, farm production and income from meat animals during the preceding year.

May: Development of the early lamb crop as of May 1.

June: The spring pig crop and fall farrowings as indicated by farmers' breeding intentions as of June 1.

August: United States lamb crop for the current year, number and percentage of breeding ewes; cattle on feed for market in the Corn Belt States as of August 1, production of shorn wool for the current year.

October, November, December: The cattle and the lamb feeding situations as of the first of each month.

December: The fall pig crop for the current year and spring farrowings in the next year, as indicated by breeding intentions.

Situation Reports. A series of "situation" reports summarize currently the statistics and analytical studies relating to certain commodities or to certain aspects of agriculture.

These are mimeographed reports designed to give a rather complete picture of the supply, demand, price, and outlook situation for each of the more important farm products. Tables and charts contain current figures on acreage, yield, production, market movement, stocks, consumption, and prices. Comparisons with other significant periods are usually included. From time to time the results of special studies relating to the prices of the respective commodities are included. Thus persons who receive one of the two general situation reports and the situation report for the commodity of particular interest are able to keep up to date on the price situation and outlook for that commodity in relation to other commodities. There are separate "situation" reports for:

Cotton: monthly.   Poultry and eggs: monthly.
Dairy products: monthly.   Rice: annual.
Fats and oils: monthly.   Sugar: annual.
Feed: monthly.   Tobacco: four issues per year.
Fruit: four issues per year.   Vegetables: quarterly.
Livestock and wool: monthly.   Wheat: bimonthly except July and August.

Monthly reports are also published on the National Food Situation, including consumption estimates, demand and price, farm income, and marketing and transportation.

The Agricultural Situation, published monthly, is intended for more general distribution and carries regularly index numbers and other series which reflect agricultural production and economic trends affecting agriculture. Figures are given monthly for the past 12 months and annually for the past 10 years. In addition, there is a narrative summary of crop conditions, outlook, and harvest at the time of going to press, and a number of brief nontechnical articles.

The National Food Situation each month reports the index numbers of retail food prices, the distribution of food supplies, and the per capita consumption of major foods. Summaries of indications for supply, production, marketing, and consumption of major foods, along with special articles, are contained in each issue. One issue each year contains a summary for the year as a whole. Another issue appearing early in the year summarizes the outlook for consumption during that year.

The Demand and Price Situation, a monthly publication, reviews the factors affecting the demand for farm products and the general trends in the prices of farm products, wholesale prices of other products, and farm income. It also contains summaries of the price situation and the outlook for the major farm products.

The Farm Income Situation, issued monthly, contains estimates of cash farm income from marketings and government payments in the preceding month, with separate estimates of income for the principal groups of commodities. It contains estimates of income by states from sales of crops and sales of livestock and livestock products. Government payments to farmers in each state are reported twice each year, in August and February. Annual estimates of cash and gross income by states for major farm commodities, estimates of volume of agricultural production for sale and home consumption and of selected farm expenses are presented from time to time.

The Marketing and Transportation Situation, issued monthly, is divided into three parts: (1) A summary, with statistical tables, of price spreads between the farmer and the consumer, and related information on marketing charges, consumer expenditures for food products, and the share of the consumer's dollar received by the farmer; (2) summaries of the latest developments in the field of marketing and transportation which are of interest to research and extension workers, agricultural businessmen, farm leaders, and consumer groups; and (3) a special article dealing with some marketing or transportation problem of particular current significance. Each fall the outlook for marketing and transportation for the succeeding year is analyzed, and soon after the end of each calendar year the data for the past year as a whole are given, along with comparisons with preceding years.

Other U. S. Department of Agriculture Reports. Special reports cover commercial truck crops for fresh market and processing; fruit and nut crop prospects; indicated production of cranberries reported in August; seed production forecasts, and other reports on seeds; farm disposition and sales of crops; an annual report of corn acreage planted with hybrid seeds, and the monthly sales of principal field crops.

A number of weekly reports dealing with special commodities are designed primarily for the trade. These include butter production, cheese production, expected livestock slaughter, and market summaries.

The Market News Service collects and issues daily information on movements, supplies, quality, and prices of livestock, meats, wool, fruits, vegetables, dairy and poultry products, grains, cotton, tobacco, and miscellaneous products. Much of the information is gathered and released at terminal markets over the country. Temporary field stations are maintained in the producing areas of certain commodities during the heavy shipping season.

Because developments in foreign countries affect prices and markets of many products which the American farmer sells, the Department of Agriculture has maintained a small staff to collect and analyze the relevant agricultural statistics of foreign countries. This group also compiles data on imports and exports of the leading agricultural commodities. Prior to the war, these were published regularly, but during the war much of this information, including the information on foreign trade in agricultural commodities, was available currently only to government agencies.

An annual report on farm population provides estimates of the number of persons living on farms at the beginning of the year, the movement from farms to towns and cities and from towns and cities to farms, movement to and from the armed forces, and births and deaths in the farm population during the preceding year.

The Agricultural Finance Review is an annual report on current development and research in the field of farm credit, farm insurance, and farm taxation. In addition to short articles and a list of the important publications in the field of agricultural finance, it includes a statistical appendix which contains detailed data by states and geographic divisions of loans of leading lending agencies, both long-term and short-term, data on farm real estate taxes, amounts and costs of farm property insurance, indexes of net demand deposits of country banks which are member banks in the Federal Reserve System, and related information.

A somewhat different type of report is found in the series of annual reports and summaries relating to individual commodities known as the "outlook" reports. The "outlook" reports were originally developed as a result of efforts to provide late each fall the information that was needed by the Extension Service and other agencies whose members would be discussing production plans and programs with farmers during the winter and spring. They make available at that time the conclusions of experts as to probable developments in production of crops and livestock and as to probable price relationships. The tables, charts, and analytical comments bring together information that will be useful in planning for the agricultural activities of the succeeding year. Through a series of educational meetings held by state workers throughout their states, these materials are regularly put into the hands of farmers. In recent years, when agricultural production goals, both national and state, have been developed, these materials have been of assistance in shaping educational campaigns and making administrative decisions which would facilitate the achievement of these goals.

In addition to the regular and special publications issued by the Federal Government, a number of state publications deal with agricultural statistics in their own states. *The Iowa Farm Economist*, published by the Iowa State College, and *Farm Economics*, published by Cornell University at Ithaca, New York, are among the better known of these publications, but there are many others. Cooperative relationships between the U. S. Department of Agriculture and state agencies often make possible the development of state figures which parallel the national figures of the Federal Department. Other data collected primarily for state use are released in these state publications.

Unpublished Materials. The material published in special releases and in the regular publications that are currently available is that which is of most general public interest. It is impossible to publish generally all the details that must be collected in order to get at the needed figures. Consequently, a body of information is often available for use in answering special inquiries or in making special tabulations that may be desired to meet a special need. Some of the Census reports, for example, may be desired for minor civil divisions rather than for county or state units, which are the usual bases for publication. Census schedules as such are confidential, but tabulations that can be made without disclosing individual operations can ordinarily be secured through the Bureau of the Census.

Some of the current reports received by the Department of Agriculture lend themselves to special analyses to meet special needs. In other words, these reports make available a large volume of information which can be tapped for making special tabulations and analyses of special topics or for areas other than those for which data are published. The major limitation is that voluntary reports, like most compulsory reports, are considered confidential by the agencies that collect them, and, therefore, information that would disclose individual operations cannot be made available to anyone.

Using the Information for Business Purposes. Marketing analysts have used data from the farm census for a variety of purposes in market analyses, the determination of sales areas, sales quotas, farm income, consumer activities, interstate shipments, supply, and demand. They are most frequently used to calculate sales potentials for farm machinery, fertilizer, livestock, hardware, and household and electrical appliances, as well as the equipment required for specialized farm operations, such as milking machines, spraying machinery for orchards, drinking fountains for hogs and poultry, planting machinery for potatoes, and dusting machinery for cotton.

A less obvious case is that of a retail merchant selling anthracite coal, who found the available poultry data very useful in mapping his sales program. He needed to know the production of broilers within a certain area in order to determine whether his purchasing or processing of coal in the size and quality suitable for use in brooders in his territory would be warranted. From the number of chickens raised and the brooder capacity required he was able to check back to the quantity of coal required. Some time later a rationing board called for similar information in order to determine whether in two counties additional coal allowances should be made because of the extensive use of coal for brooders.

A firm manufacturing a churn suitable for farms with 1 or 2 cows and another firm manufacturing mechanical milkers suitable for the largest scale commercial enterprises found the tabulation showing number of farms with specified number of cows useful in planning for the distribution of their product. A feed salesman computed from the minor civil division and county figures the theoretical requirements of feed for the animal units in his territory. He worked out the production of the various grains in that area, calculated the differences, and set up sales quotas for his dairy and poultry feed with considerable success.

Census statistics relating to farm income are widely used. Although these figures are based on rough estimates by farmers of the value of products which they sold or traded and the value of products which were used by their households, they are useful in calculating the amount of money which will be available for sales in farm territory. By the use of crop-condition figures and price indexes, these county figures can be carried forward so that approximate current figures can be furnished without much difficulty if conditions have changed radically since the taking of the last Census.

Current reports on agricultural production and prospects are used directly or indirectly by a large number of persons who have an interest in agricultural problems or in a particular commodity. Recently persons receiving one of the minor reports were asked if they had any objection to the discontinuance of the report and of the collection of information which makes the report possible. Replies were received from farmers, wholesalers, jobbers, millers, manufacturers of end products from this commodity, warehouse operators, railroad companies, bankers, and several government offices, many of them explaining how this report was of use to them.

Farmers, farmers' cooperatives, dealers in agricultural products, sales departments of industrial concerns that sell farmers anything from soap to automobiles, publishers and radio stations who serve primarily a farm public, bankers who finance the movement of crops at harvest time, railroads that move the crops and livestock, warehousemen who store the products, and processors of agricultural products, all find considerable use for the crop reports. Many institutions that deal in farm products have their private sources of information, but they use the government reports not only as a check on their own reports, but also frequently as a base from which to start the next succeeding report.

Banking institutions find the current government estimates of crop acreages and crop prospects and of livestock numbers and production useful as a guide to the demand for funds that they may be called upon to advance for financing farmers during the producing and marketing seasons. Railroads have used the crop reports as a guide in allocating the supply of freight cars. Manufacturers, merchants, dealers, and other businessmen use crop reports in planning their production and sales so that farm machinery and supplies will be available when needed. Costly and annoying delays can be avoided through such planning, and businessmen are enabled to render more efficient service and to avoid losses.

Business interests and industries that use agricultural products as raw materials, as well as those that sell their finished product in rural communities, have an immediate interest in the crop reports. Economic forecasts and business analyses depend in appreciable measure upon crop statistics. Before the war, the sales department of at least one of the large automobile manufacturers used these statistics in locating areas of rural prosperity for planning sales campaigns. One of the large lumber companies was using crop and livestock reports as a basis for making changes in its sales program. The statistical department of one of the large soap manufacturers made extensive use of cotton and hog reports as a basis for its purchasing program.

Advertising agencies frequently use the data in planning advertising campaigns. The statistical departments of a number of mail order houses follow these reports very closely. A small circus, playing primarily in rural areas, used crop reports in planning its itinerary. Buying, production, and sales quotas and organization policies are based to a large extent upon what agricultural producers have done in the past, their present production possibilities, and the trend in types of farming in areas of interest to these industries. In the past, prospective settlers frequently made use of the governmental agricultural statistics to enable them to locate to advantage in areas best suited to the type of farming they wished to follow.

Meeting Future Needs. The agencies responsible for wartime agricultural programs found in the census reports and the current reports on agriculture a starting point which provided a large part of the information that was required. Many of their administrative needs called for more detail than had been necessary for statistical purposes, and it became expedient to broaden the reporting scheme already in operation.

Much information which had previously been relatively unimportant became important because of the regulation of certain products. The series of reports on agricultural statistics, which had been useful to a large section of the business community and agricultural interests before the war, provided a large part of the information required during the war, and the statistical programs were modified so that the need for collecting entirely new information was held to a minimum. Changes have been made, some elements of the work have been entirely abandoned, others have been streamlined, still others have been expanded, and many new items of information have been developed. With their long history and with the flexibility which has been demonstrated during the war, agricultural statistics after the war have every reason to continue to provide a public service needed by businessmen, farmers, government agencies, and others who are concerned with agriculture.

More Information. Many sources of individual reports have been mentioned, but a complete listing would go far beyond the limits set for this chapter. There are, however, a few publications that serve as a guide to the range of statistics and their use, or summarize much of the available information in readily accessible form. The more important of these are listed below:

Census of Agriculture Handbook, Uses of Agricultural Census Statistics, issued by the Bureau of the Census, describes the Census of Agriculture in 1940, the reports which have been issued, some of the ways in which these materials have already been made especially useful to businessmen, and ways in which such service can be made available to others. ($0.45 from the Superintendent of Documents.)

Census of Agriculture: Releases and reports based on the 1945 Census of Agriculture are now becoming available. For the 1940 Census, *Volume III, General Report*, is a convenient summary. ($3.00 from the Superintendent of Documents.)

Agricultural Statistics, issued annually by the Department of Agriculture, brings together the more important series of statistics prepared by the Department of Agriculture or compiled by the staff for official use. ($0.65 from the Superintendent of Documents.)

Crops and Markets, issued quarterly by the Department of Agriculture, summarizes the more recent production, market, and price statistics. ($0.30 per year from the Superintendent of Documents.)

The Agricultural Situation, published monthly by the Department of Agriculture, carries brief summaries and tables showing the price and production situation for the more important farm products and the major economic indicators relating to agriculture. ($0.50 per year from the Superintendent of Documents.)

The Crop and Livestock Reporting Service of the United States, issued by the Department of Agriculture as *Miscellaneous Publication 171*, in 1933, describes the methods used in collecting and analyzing statistical data relating to crop and livestock production and related subjects. ($0.15 from the Superintendent of Documents.)

Agricultural Economics Reports and Publications, published in March 1943, is a catalogue of the regular and special reports published by the Bureau of Agricultural Economics in the Department of Agriculture. It is available upon request to the Bureau.

Reports and Periodicals on Marketing and Distribution is a catalogue of the regular and special reports of the Office of Distribution, Department of Agriculture, including *Market News Reports* and other publications of interest to the food trade.

CHAPTER 6

WHOLESALE, RETAIL, AND SERVICE TRADES

WALTER F. CROWDER
Bureau of Foreign and Domestic Commerce
Department of Commerce

In terms of number of establishments, the wholesale, retail, and service trades represent one of the most important segments of the economy. In 1939 there were 200,573 establishments engaged in wholesaling, 1,770,355 engaged in retailing, and 646,028 establishments in the service trades. The 2,616,956 establishments in these three trades accounted for more than two-thirds of all business establishments in the Nation.

The people who gain their livelihood from the wholesale, retail, and service trades either as employees or as self-employed represent a very substantial proportion of all gainfully employed workers. The number of paid employees of wholesale establishments in 1939 averaged 1,561,948. In the same year, there were 4,600,217 full and part-time employees in retail establishments and to this total should be added 1,613,673 proprietor-owners. The total number of employees in the service trades was 1,102,047, and again to the paid employee figure should be added 652,491 self-employed proprietors. In short, there were more than 9,500,000 persons engaged in these three trades. This may be compared with the 9,747,000 persons engaged in manufacturing.

The significance of the wholesale, retail, and service trades can also be seen in the contribution these trades make to our national income. In 1943 our total national income was 147.9 billion dollars. Of this total, 6.0 billion dollars originated in the wholesale trades, 11.4 billion dollars in the retail trades, and 10.3 billion in the service occupations and the service trades. In other words, almost 20 percent of the total national income originated in these three trade groups.

Viewed in another way, business enterprises in these trades are the channels through which consumers get the greater part of the goods and services they buy. A vast network of outlets scattered throughout the country from metropolitan areas to the crossroads hamlet brings the products of far-flung industries to the very doors of consumers. The huge task of assembling the thousands of products and services demanded by consumers and of having these goods available at the right time and place and in the proper quantities for millions of individual buyers is the job of these trades.

And on the other side of the same picture, these thousands of wholesale, retail, and service establishments are the channels, the outlets, through which the products of industry and agriculture must be distributed. There are many methods or combinations of methods by which this job of distribution may be done. But by one method or another, practically all consumer goods and services reach their ultimate users through the outlets of the distributive and service trades.

Any business venture that is dependent on the distribution of goods through wholesale, retail, or service channels can have its efforts more wisely directed if those efforts are based on facts. The purpose of this chapter is to discuss briefly the governmental sources of statistics on the physical, locational, and operational characteristics of the establishments in these three trades.

WHOLESALE TRADE STATISTICS

Wholesaling occupies a strategic position in the distribution of goods. The functions which it performs are generally understood but the statistical data which reflect the magnitude, diversity, and changes in wholesaling operations are not always known to businessmen who depend on this important segment of the national economy. Every producer with a selling problem and every retailer with a buying problem should have the facts on wholesaling at hand when making business decisions.

BENCHMARK STATISTICS

The first attempt to canvass thoroughly on a nationwide basis all wholesale establishments or places of business was made in connection with the Census of Distribution for 1929. This census provided a complete enumeration of wholesale establishments, method of operation, or nature of organization so long as they were engaged in the sale of merchandise at wholesale.

In 1934 the Census Bureau conducted a second Census of Distribution as a part of the Civil Works Administration program for providing employment for unemployed white-collar workers. This Census of American Business covered, among other operations, wholesaling for the year 1933. One of the principal limitations on the use of the

Census of Distribution for 1929 lay in the inability to make comparisons with other years. The census for 1933 provided data for a depression year which could be compared with those for 1929.

A third Census of Distribution, financed, as was the second, by relief funds, was taken in 1936 and covered operations in the year 1935. This Census of Business added a third reference point for the comparison of wholesaling operations.

The Act of Congress approved June 18, 1929, provided for a Census of Distribution (now called Business) covering the year 1929 and each succeeding tenth year thereafter in connection with decennial censuses. The second decennial Census of Business was taken in the year 1940 and covered the year 1939. Thus, the two decennial censuses together with the censuses of 1933 and 1935, which were conducted as emergency work projects, provide four mileposts for measuring wholesale trade. The data from these censuses are generally comparable. Where classifications have been shifted or other changes have been made, the changes are set forth in the census volumes in which the data are published.

In addition to providing basic, comprehensive statistics for each of the four years covered, the data derived from the censuses provide a dependable base or benchmark for evaluating and projecting current statistics of a more limited nature.

Scope of the Census of Wholesale Trade. The field of wholesale trade, as defined for census purposes, is somewhat broader than the usual conception of "wholesaler." It includes all establishments or places of business primarily engaged in selling or acting as agents in selling (or buying) goods on a wholesale basis. The place of business may be a store or warehouse from which sales are made at wholesale, a sales or brokerage office, or part of an office that may be shared with others. Selling on a wholesale basis involves selling primarily to retailers, dealers, or distributors who buy goods for resale, or selling to institutional and industrial users who purchase for business use rather than for the purpose of reselling the goods in the same form. Generally speaking, those establishments engaged primarily in the sale of goods to dealers and distributors for resale or to purchasers who buy for business use are classified as wholesalers, whereas those engaged primarily in purveying goods to ultimate consumers for consumption are classified as retailers and as such are covered in the census of the retail trades.

Many businesses do not fall clearly in either the retail, the service, the wholesale, or the manufacturing categories. Since it is impracticable, as a rule, to classify any single business establishment in more than one phase of the census, the *major-portion-of-business* or the *50 percent* rule is followed for the most part. Establishments are placed in one classification or another according to their major activity. The number of establishments in which it is necessary to apply the 50 percent rule, however, is small relative to the total number of establishments. In comparing data from the various censuses, it should be noted that for borderline cases a relatively small change in sales at retail or wholesale may cause a shift in the classification of an establishment from one phase of the census to another. The same situation arises, of course, within either the retail or wholesale census, that is, a borderline establishment may be shifted from one kind of business to another, with a slight change in sales proportions.

All wholesale establishments are classified in the census by *types of operation* primarily on the basis of functions performed. Some wholesalers perform a variety of functions, such as buying, assembling, sorting and grading, warehousing, selling, delivering from stock, and extending credit, whereas others perform one or, at the most, only a few of these services. Obviously, the operating characteristics of the business vary with the functions performed. In order to present statistics so that one may work out whatever classification he deems most essential for his own purposes, all wholesale establishments are grouped into six major type classes, some of which are further subdivided as outlined below:

Service and limited-function wholesalers:
  Wholesale merchants.
  Voluntary group wholesalers.
  Converters (textile).
  Export merchants.
  Importers.
  Industrial distributors.
  Cash-and-carry wholesalers.
  Drop shippers or desk jobbers.
  Wagon distributors.
  Retailer-cooperative warehouses.
Manufacturers' sales branches (with stocks).
Manufacturers' sales offices (without stocks).
Petroleum bulk stations and terminals:
  Independent bulk stations.
  Commission stations.
  Salary stations.
  Cooperative bulk stations.
  Distributing terminals.

Agents and brokers:
  Auction companies.
  Commodity and merchandise brokers.
  Commission merchants.
  Export agents.
  Import agents.
  Manufacturers' agents:
    With stocks.
    Without stocks.
  Selling agents.
  Other agents.
Assemblers (mainly farm products):
  Assemblers of farm products.
  Commission buyers.
  Cooperative marketing associations.
  Cooperative sales agencies.
  Cream stations.
  Country grain elevators:
    Independent.
    Line.
    Cooperative.
  Packers and shippers.

In addition to type of operation, each wholesale establishment is classified by kind of business according to lines of merchandise handled or according to trade designation. The kind-of-business classification of an establishment, like the type of operation, is based chiefly on the information contained in the census reports themselves. Provision is made for self-designation of kind of business—the "designation by which the establishment is known to the trade or public." Guided largely by experience in previous censuses, all establishments were divided into 28 kind-of-business groups in 1939. These groups are further subdivided into 172 minor detailed classes. The major kind-of-business groups are shown in the following alphabetical list.

Amusement and sporting goods.
Automotive.
Beer, wines, and liquors.
Chemicals and paints.
Clothing and furnishings.
Coal and coke.
Drugs (general line).
Drugs and drug sundries (specialty lines).
Dry goods (general line).
Dry goods (specialty lines).
Electrical goods.
Farm products—raw materials.
Farm products—consumer goods.
Farm supplies.

Furniture and house furnishings.
Groceries (general line).
Groceries and foods (specialty lines).
Hardware.
Jewelry.
Lumber and construction materials.
Machinery, equipment, and supplies.
Metals and metal work (except scrap).
Paper and its products.
Petroleum and its products.
Plumbing and heating equipment and supplies.
Tobacco and products (except leaf).
Waste materials.
All other products.

Published Tabulations from the Wholesale Census. The basic statistics on wholesaling operations are derived from the separate schedules which each establishment is required to file. The data from these schedules are subject to a large number of summary tabulations and cross classifications. The most important of these are shown in the published reports of the Census Bureau, whereas special tabulations of particular value to individual concerns or trades are available for a nominal fee from the Census Bureau. A brief explanation of the nature of the data available in the published tabulations of the 1939 Census follows.

Sales, Expenses, Personnel, Payrolls, and Stocks. The basic data on number of establishments, sales, expenses, personnel, payrolls, and stocks are presented for the entire United States by 39 major and minor types of operation. Data covering the same characteristics are shown for each of the six major type-of-operation groups and by kinds of business. Similar data are tabulated for each state and for the District of Columbia, but the kind-of-business information is restricted to the 28 major groups. Data are also available for the 27 leading wholesaling cities and for the District of Columbia in as much detail as possible without disclosure of individual operations.

Monthly Employment and Sex of Employees. Data are available on the number of active proprietors and firm members of unincorporated businesses, the number of male and female employees, and the number of employees monthly, together with the average for the year. Active proprietors and firm members of unincorporated businesses are not counted as employees but are segregated in order to provide a more complete picture of the personnel of wholesale establishments. Data on these characteristics are presented for each state, and for the 14 cities having more than 500,000 inhabitants in 1940. Data for states and cities are shown by the 28 major kind-of-business groups, all types of operation combined; for the country as a whole they are given for each type of operation. Type-of-operation groups are further analyzed by kind of business. These statistics provide a measure of seasonal variation in employment of wholesale establishments for the year 1939.

Analysis of Employment and Payroll by Occupational Groups. Each wholesale establishment was asked to report the actual employment and payroll for the week ended October 21, 1939, or, if a highly seasonal business, for a week of normal employment during the active season. Respondents were requested to classify all employees during the week by occupational groups—as executives, office and clerical employees, inside selling employees, outside selling employees, warehouse employees, and all other—and to report the number and payroll for the week, full-time and part-time separately, for each class.

Data on these characteristics of the business are presented for the United States, for the nine census geographic divisions (see Chapter 12, p. 335), and for the 14 cities having a population of more than 500,000 in 1940. For geographic divisions and cities, occupational-group data are presented for each major type group by kind of business. Establishments having no paid employees and those not reporting the analysis for one week were, of course, not included. A similar tabulation is available for the country as a whole, wherein the analysis for one week is given first by 39 detailed types of operation, followed by each of the six major type groups by kinds of business.

Business Size. Wholesale merchants and, for the trades in which they appear, industrial distributors are classified by size as measured by 1939 sales. A maximum of nine sales-size groups is used in presenting the results. These groups are:

$2,000,000 and over
1,000,000 to $1,999,999
500,000 to   999,999
300,000 to   499,999
200,000 to   299,999
100,000 to   199,999
50,000 to   99,999
10,000 to   49,999
Under 10,000

A size analysis is given for each of the various kinds of business in which wholesale merchants and industrial distributors appear. For each size classification the number of establishments, sales, total operating expenses, personnel, and payroll are given. To assist in the use of the data, operating expenses are also expressed as a percentage of net sales. Size tabulations are given for each kind of business by geographic divisions. The number of size brackets used in presenting the results varies with the kind of business according to the number of establishments involved, the objective being to provide as much information as possible without disclosing information for any individual concern.

Analysis of Operating Expenses. Total operating expenses for the various kinds of business of wholesale merchants and industrial distributors are analyzed by functional divisions. Each respondent whose sales in 1939 amounted to $100,000 or more was requested to analyze his expense accounts and to report administrative, selling, delivery, warehouse, occupancy, and "other" expenses separately. Data are presented on these detailed expense items for each of the kinds of business by geographic divisions and for 14 cities. Operating expenses for some of the trades are analyzed in the summary tabulations for the businesses in the various size groups of $100,000 and more, as set forth above. In several trades, it was necessary to restrict the amount of detail by size because of the limited number of establishments involved.

Cash-Credit Analysis of Sales. Sales of service and limited-function wholesalers and of manufacturers' sales branches are analyzed on a cash-credit basis. Sales for each of the kinds of business of service and limited-function wholesalers and of manufacturers' sales branches are analyzed to show separately spot cash business, credit of 10 days or less, credit of 11 to 30 days, and credit of more than 30 days. Data on these items are shown for geographic divisions and cities of more than 500,000 inhabitants.

Accounts and Notes Receivable and Stocks on Hand. Data are presented for service and limited-function wholesalers and for manufacturers' sales branches showing the outstanding amounts of accounts and notes receivable and also stocks on hand at the beginning and end of the year. The information is given for geographic divisions and for 14 cities.

Distribution of Sales by Classes of Customers. Sales of the various classes of wholesale establishments are analyzed to show the proportions that went to retailers, to household consumers, to industrial users, to other wholesalers, to export intermediaries, and to buyers in foreign countries. Not all respondents reported their sales by classes of customers, but for those that reported, statistics are presented for the country as a whole by each of the major type groups and by kinds of business. A tabulation is given for each of the cities whose population is more than 500,000.

Sales Taxes and Sales Through Agents, Brokers, and Commission Merchants. Data on sales taxes—local, state, or Federal taxes which were collected from customers over and above the selling price of the reporting establishment and paid by the reporting concern directly to governmental taxing agencies—and sales made through agents, brokers, and commission merchants are presented in summary for the country as a whole by type-of-operation groups and by kinds of business.

Analysis of Sales by Commodities. The commodity analysis of sales is designed to show what commodities are handled in the various lines of trade and in what trades any particular commodity is found. For example, it shows what commodities and in what amounts tobacco wholesalers normally handle other than cigars, cigarettes, and other tobacco products. It also shows by what other trades, such as drugs, groceries, and confectionery, tobacco products are sold and the importance of the tobacco department in these other trades. A summary tabulation is presented by types of operation and kinds of business. Sales for the various kinds of business are analyzed by commodities in as much detail as possible. The percentage of commodity coverage is given for each trade classification (ratio of the total sales of the stores reporting commodity data to the total sales of all stores in the same kind of business). Commodities are listed in the order in which they appear in the *Standard List of Commodities* prepared by the Census Bureau.

Since not all respondents supplied a commodity itemization of their sales, two percentage calculations are made. The first is obtained by dividing the sales of the commodity by the sales of establishments selling that commodity. This percentage measures the importance of any commodity to the total sales of establishments handling it. It is unaffected by establishments not reporting sales of the particular item. The second percentage calculation measures the importance of any commodity to the total sales for the kind of business. This latter percentage can be used to determine the total sales of the commodity in each principal kind of business in which it is handled. Data on the sales by commodities are available for the major kind-of-business groups of service and limited-function wholesalers, manufacturers' sales branches (without stocks), petroleum bulk stations and terminals, and assemblers. Data are given where possible under each kind of business for geographic divisions and for New York City, Chicago, Philadelphia, Boston, and San Francisco.

Legal Form of Organization. Statistics on the number of establishments, sales, expenses, personnel, payroll, and stocks are tabulated separately for individual proprietorships, partnerships, corporations, and "other" or miscellaneous forms of organization. In summary form the data are presented for the six type-of-operation groups. Legal form data are also given for each state.

Number of Establishments Under One Ownership. The organizational structure of wholesale trade is analyzed to determine the number of establishments operated under one ownership. All ownerships are grouped in the following classes: 1 wholesale establishment only, 2 wholesale establishments, 3 to 5 wholesale establishments, 6 to 9 wholesale establishments, 10 to 14 wholesale establishments, 15 to 24 wholesale establishments, 25 to 29 wholesale establishments, and 50 or more establishments under one ownership. For each group, the number of establishments, sales, personnel, payroll, and inventories are given. Data are presented for the country as a whole by type of operation.

Age of Establishment and Year Acquired by Present Owner. Wholesale establishments are classified according to the year in which the business was established and the year under which they came under present ownership. For each age group the following information is shown: Number of establishments, sales, number of active proprietors, employees, and payrolls. The data are available in summary only for the United States.

Cities and Counties. Data are available on number of establishments, sales, personnel, and payroll for all cities having 20,000 inhabitants or more. For cities of 50,000 inhabitants or more, the basic data are available by type-of-operation groups, and each group is analyzed by kind of business.

Basic data are available showing for each county the number of wholesale establishments, sales, active proprietors, employees, and payroll. Data on these characteristics are also available for each city of 5,000 inhabitants or more within the county and for the remainder of the county.

Sources and Availability. The data on wholesale trade cited in the foregoing paragraphs are available in the published reports of the Bureau of the Census and are on sale by the Superintendent of Documents. These reports are available for inspection at the field offices of the Department of Commerce and in depository libraries in approximately 430 cities throughout the United States. The combined statistics for wholesale trade are published as *Volume II, Census of Business, 1939: Wholesale Trade.*

For those who are not interested in the statistics for all geographic divisions, separate reports are available for each state and for the District of Columbia. The state reports also contain data on the 27 leading wholesale trade centers of the country. Separate bulletins are also available on particular aspects of wholesaling as follows: *Employment by Months and Employment and Payroll for One Week; Business-Size Groups and an Analysis of Operating Expenses: Cash-Credit Analysis of Sales, and Receivables and Inventory; Commodity Sales; Petroleum Distribution—Bulk Stations and Distributing Centers.* Single copies of the following multilithed reports may be obtained without charge from the Bureau of the Census: *Summary Data on Wholesale Establishments for the United States as a Whole; Sales by Classes of Customers; Legal Form of Organization; Ownership Study; Age of Establishment and Year Acquired by Present Owner; Distribution of Manufacturers' Sales.*

CURRENT STATISTICS

Current statistics on wholesale trade are available on a monthly basis for 33 kinds of business. For each of these kinds of business, data are available on sales, inventories, and accounts receivable. These statistics have been collected on a sampling basis since 1936 and cover approximately 2,500 to 3,000 firms. Month-to-month and year-to-year changes are shown for identical concerns, that is, data for the current month are shown as a percentage of the preceding month as well as for the same month a year earlier. Statistics are also available giving the picture for geographic regions and for selected kinds of business within the geographic region. Not all kinds of business are reported for each geographic region in order to avoid disclosure of operations of individual concerns. These current statistics on *Wholesalers' Sales, Inventories, and Credits* are available on request from the Bureau of the Census, Washington, D. C.

Using these survey data as a basis, monthly estimates of aggregate sales of wholesalers raised to national totals are prepared by the Bureau of Foreign and Domestic Commerce. The figures are available by months showing dollar volume of business and are also available in index form (1935–1939 = 100) both unadjusted and adjusted for seasonal variation. This continuous series is tied in with the data from the 1935 and 1939 Censuses of Business and projections are adjusted to take into account business births and deaths in wholesale trade. The series are available for 19 kinds of wholesale business— 7 kinds selling primarily durable commodities and 12 selling primarily nondurable commodities. The estimates, both for the totals and for the several kinds of business, include the following types of wholesalers: Service and limited-function wholesalers; manufacturers' sales branches (both with and without stocks); petroleum bulk stations; agents and brokers; and assemblers. These estimates are available upon request to the Bureau of Foreign and Domestic Commerce and are published regularly in the *Survey of Current Business* prepared by that Bureau. (For current employment data in this field see Chapter 14.)

Estimates are currently prepared in the Bureau of Foreign and Domestic Commerce showing the total number of wholesale enterprises as well as births and deaths among wholesale enterprises by quarters from 1939. Estimates are also available showing the turnover of business firms in wholesaling. These data are classified by size of establishment as measured by employment.

Financial statistics relating to corporations in wholesale trade are available from annual reports, entitled *Statistics of Income*, published by the Bureau of Internal Revenue, U. S. Treasury Department. These statistics, although uneven in coverage and usually not available on a timely basis, supply an annual picture of the financial status of all incorporated businesses in wholesale trade. Tabulations are available showing number of returns, compiled receipts, compiled deductions, compiled net profit and net loss, net income or deficit, income tax, excess profits tax, total taxes, and dividends paid. Compilations are shown separately for concerns filing returns with net income and for concerns filing returns without net income.

Statistics of Income also shows data from returns with balance sheets for corporations engaged in wholesale trade. The following information is included: Number of returns; assets and liabilities at the end of the fiscal year (divided into numerous categories); compiled receipts and compiled deductions; compiled net profit or net loss; net income or deficit; taxes; and dividends paid. The above characteristics are shown both for concerns reporting net income and for those reporting no net income.

Tabulations are also available showing the distribution of balance sheet items by size of corporation as measured by total assets of the corporation by 10 asset sizes.

Wholesalers of certain products (distilled spirits, wines, fermented malt liquors, oleomargarine, narcotics, etc.) are required to purchase licenses. The number of such purchases are shown annually for the various products by collection districts and by States in the *Annual Report of the Commissioner of Internal Revenue*, U. S. Treasury Department.

Current data on the production, movement, stocks, carry-over, receipts, and disappearances at principal markets, etc., for major agricultural commodities are available from the Production and Marketing Administration, Department of Agriculture. In general, the movement of these major agricultural products is followed through the assembly, processing, and distribution stages.

COMPILATIONS FOR SPECIAL PURPOSES

Trading Area Studies. The Bureau of Foreign and Domestic Commerce has prepared wholesale trading area studies for the grocery trade and for the dry goods trade. These studies of trading areas are based on reports by individual wholesalers in wholesale centers. The reports were analyzed and the trading area boundaries for the above-named trades were drawn to conform with the business area designated by the wholesalers. The lines of demarkation are on a county basis. The maps showing the boundaries of the trading areas are available from the Bureau of Foreign and Domestic Commerce upon request.

Studies of Selected Wholesale Trades. In connection with a number of studies of the operating problems of wholesale establishments, the Bureau of Foreign and Domestic Commerce has over the past two decades collected a great deal of statistical material on operating costs in various lines of wholesaling. The statistics were developed in the process of evaluating the relative profitability of individual commodities, customers, and territories. Some of these reports are now out of print, but many of them are available from the Superintendent of Documents. *Distribution Cost Accounting for Wholesaling, 1939,* contains a list of the publications of this Bureau in this field. It also summarizes the findings and methods of earlier studies on distribution cost analyses. The more recent study, *Effective Grocery Wholesaling, 1941,* presents profit and loss data and sales analyses by commodities for approximately 100 individual wholesale grocers for a number of years prior to the war.

As a part of its investigations, the Federal Trade Commission has collected operating statistics on wholesalers as well as on the wholesale business of chains in various lines. Furthermore, the Commission has made case studies of distribution cost accounting for individual wholesale concerns which contain statistics on costs allocated to commodities, customers, and territories. These reports are available from the Commission on request.

Statistics on Listed Wholesale Corporations. All corporations whose securities are listed on the national security exchanges are required to file information with the Securities and Exchange Commission, giving their balance sheet and operating data. Registration is not required of corporations with "exempt" securities or securities admitted to unlisted trading or of companies with securities traded on "exempt" exchanges. These data on listed wholesale concerns may be obtained by writing to the Securities and Exchange Commission, Philadelphia, Pa.

RETAIL TRADE STATISTICS

Retail stores constitute the last stage in the productive and distributive process. Through them flow the great bulk of commodities on their way from mines, farms, and factories to ultimate consumers. They are the points of contact which manufacturers and wholesalers have with the buying public. The direction and flow of thousands of commodities are reflected in their sales. Every manufacturer and wholesaler must know intimately the structure and capacity of retail stores selling his goods if he is to direct his selling efforts efficiently. Retailers themselves must know what other retailers are doing if they are to measure their own effectiveness. Extensive statistics on retail operations are available for the asking.

BENCHMARK STATISTICS

As is true of wholesale trade, the most comprehensive statistics on retail trade are to be found in the various Censuses of Business. The first census of retail trade was taken as a part of the Census of Distribution for 1929, which followed a trial census of 11 cities in 1926. The second retail census was taken as a part of the Census of American Business for 1933, and the third as a part of the Census of Business for 1935. The most recent census of retail trade is part of the Census of Business for 1939.

An attempt has been made to maintain comparability in the data for the different censuses, but there have been some changes in scope and classifications. Thus, the first business census, Census of Distribution, 1929, did not include a Service Business Division. Consequently, certain automotive services, such as repair garages, painting, and tire and battery repairing, were part of the retail trade census. Later, when a separate census of service businesses was taken, these services were dropped from the retail census. Other slight modifications in scope and in classification have taken place. In the published reports of the Census of Retail Trade, 1939, is a table reconciling these minor changes in classification from year to year. This table also indicates the scope of the changes.

The Scope of the Census of Retail Trade. The field of retail trade, as defined for census purposes, includes places of business primarily engaged in selling merchandise in a "retail manner" and rendering service incidental to the sale of goods. Selling in a "retail manner," according to the Census, is selling in individual units or small quantities to personal or household consumers, from established places of business, for consumption rather than for resale. In addition to those kinds of business readily recognizable as retail stores under this general description, retail businesses such as eating and drinking places, filling stations, lumber and building-material dealers, motor-vehicle dealers, mail-order houses selling from catalogs, house-to-house sellers, roadside stands, and public markets are also included.

A retail store, however, to be counted in the Census, must operate as an established place of business open to the general public. Thus, peddlers and itinerant vendors are excluded. Places of business connected with institutions or business establishments that are open only to their members or personnel are also excluded. Restaurants and bars operated by country clubs, school cafeterias, and cafeterias operated by industrial plants for their employees are, therefore, excluded.

The major portion (more than 50 percent) of the sales or receipts must be from retail sales in order to classify an establishment, for census purposes, as a retail store. Stores doing both wholesale and retail business are classified in their entirety in either the wholesale or the retail census, according to the category in which the major portion of their sales falls. Similarly, service businesses primarily engaged in selling personal and commercial services rather than merchandise are not, in the most recent censuses of retail trade, counted as retail stores but are enumerated as service establishments by the Census of Business.

A retail store or establishment is, for census purposes, the place where the business is conducted. Each separate place of business is counted as a separate store or establishment. Thus the number of stores or establishments is greater than the number of firms, since some firms operate more than one store.

Each store is classified in a particular kind-of-business group on the basis of the activity from which it derives the principal part of its receipts. Many establishments sell such a wide range of merchandise, however, that they cannot be classified on the basis of commodity sales. Such establishments are classified on the basis of usual trade designations, such as drug, delicatessen, and variety stores.

The Census identifies 99 kind-of-business classifications. These detailed kinds of business are arranged in 11 major kind-of-business groups as follows:

Food group.
General stores (with food).
General merchandise group.
Apparel group.
Furniture-household-radio group.
Automotive group.
Filling stations.
Lumber-building-hardware group.
Eating and drinking places.
Drug stores.
Other stores, including liquor stores.

Stores are classified by type of operation into three major groups—independents, chains, and "other types."

The independent group includes single-store independents, multi-unit independents with two or three stores, local branch systems consisting of a large downtown store and smaller suburban or nearby branches operated as a unit (usually found in the furniture and department-store fields), market and roadside stands, and leased departments run by independent operators. These leased departments are usually separate departments in stores of a different kind, such as meat departments in grocery stores, millinery departments in department stores, and shoe departments in women's specialty stores.

The chain-store group includes those retail establishments owned or controlled by concerns that operate four or more units. The number of chain stores is based on a count of each retail establishment and is not a count of the number of chain store groups or firms. The group includes local chains in which all units are located in and around a single city; sectional chains in which all units are located in the same section of the country; national chains which operate in more than one section or geographic division; manufacturer-controlled chains whose principal function is to distribute the products of one or more manufacturers who own and control them; and chains of leased departments (these differ from independent leased departments only in the number of units operated under a single ownership).

The third category of type of operation—"other types"—may involve some of the characteristics of independents or chains, but it is segregated because stores in this group employ other distinct methods of retail distribution. The "other type" group consists of utility-operated stores, direct selling (house-to-house), commissaries or company stores, farmer and consumer cooperative stores, state liquor stores, mail-order houses, and a miscellaneous group including those stores not otherwise classified.

Published Tabulations from the Retail Census. The census data are the product of the classification and tabulation of the information on the schedules obtained by census enumerators from each retail establishment in the United States. A brief explanation of the nature of the data available in the published tabulations of the 1939 Census follows.

The basic data cover *number of stores, sales, number of active proprietors of unincorporated businesses, number of employees (average for year), payroll,* and *stocks on hand, end of year, at cost.* These data are classified *by kind of business, by geographic divisions, by states, by counties, and cities, by type of operations (chains, independents, etc.),* and *by legal form of organization (individual proprietorships, partnerships, cooperative associations, corporations).*

There are, of course, many possibilities for summarization and cross classification of these data. The most important of these are shown in the published Census reports; special tabulations of particular value to individual concerns or trades are available for a nominal fee from the Census Bureau. A brief description of the specialized data available in the published statistics follows.

Employment and Payroll. The information pertaining to employment and payroll have been classified and tabulated by kind of business and by geographic divisions and states to show the following data: Monthly employment (full-time and part-time) and sex of employees; number of employees and payroll—classified by occupational groups; number of proprietors, family members paid no stipulated wages, and number of employees (full-time and part-time), as well as number of paid proprietors and number of paid firm members of partnerships; and number of stores, sales, personnel and payroll classified by size groups based on average number of employees.

Although the term "employment" usually connotes only paid employees, in retail trade the extent of self-employment is so great, both numerically and relatively, that the services of proprietors and unpaid members of their families cannot be dissociated from paid employment, since the one is often in lieu of the other. Members of the families of proprietors who are regularly working in the business but who are paid no stipulated cash wage or salary are separately reported but are not included in the count of proprietors.

The method of reporting employment on the census schedules, which calls for separate figures each month of the number of full-time and part-time employees on the payroll nearest the 15th of each month during the census year, provides the basis for computing the "average number employed" throughout the year.

Legal Form of Organization. All stores in the census are classified according to the legal form of organization under which the business is operated. The four principal forms are individual proprietorships, partnerships, cooperative associations, and corporations. The statistics on legal form of organization cover the basic data on stores, sales, personnel, and payroll, analyzed by kind of business and by geographic divisions and states.

Stocks on Hand (Inventories). The information on the census schedules pertaining to the value of stocks on hand have been tabulated to show the following statistics: Value of stocks on hand at cost at the beginning and at the end of the year (covered by the census), classified by kinds of business and by geographic divisions and states; and the number of stores and sales of the stores reporting data on stocks (not all stores reported on the value of stocks on hand). Tabulations have also been made for each state, showing the values of stocks on hand at the beginning and end of year by kinds of business.

Credit Sales and Receivables. The Bureau of the Census sought to determine, by appropriate inquiries on schedules, the amount of retail business done on credit, how much of the credit extended was on open-account and how much in the form of installment credit. The schedules further called for an analysis of installment sales to show the down payment and the amount payable in installments. Another inquiry asked for the total of accounts receivable on the books of retailers at the end of the year covered by the census, and how much of the total was in the form of retail installment notes held by retailers (excluding those sold to finance companies and to banks which purchase consumer paper).

Not all retailers, however, were able to report credit sales separately from cash sales. The number reporting a distinction between open-account and installment sales was even smaller. Approximately 90 percent of all stores reported an analysis of their sales as between cash and credit in the 1939 Census, but much smaller proportions reported the further subclassifications requested.

The amount of consumer indebtedness to retailers in the form of open ledger accounts and notes held by retailers was requested for the first time in the 1939 Census. Heretofore, this information was not available, except in the form of annual estimates, based on samples, prepared by the Bureau of Foreign and Domestic Commerce.

The 1939 Census reports show for each kind of business the number of all-cash stores and their sales, and the number of cash-credit stores, with a differentiation of their sales between cash and credit. The amount of customer accounts and notes receivable at the end of the year is also available. For each kind of business, a further analysis was made of stores reporting credit sales, showing open-account and installment credit. This latter information is confined to a sample of stores with sales of more than $20,000. Still another tabulation of credit data shows, by kinds of business, an additional analysis of the sales of installment credit stores, to determine the amount of down payment and the amount of installment receivables in relation to installment sales.

Credit data comparable to those described above are available for each geographic division and state. In one set of these tabulations, data for all kinds of business are combined for each state, whereas in another set of tabulations, credit data are shown for detailed kinds of business for each state, and for each city of more than 500,000 inhabitants.

Commodity Sales. Sales of each kind of business shown in the retail census, with the exception of a few minor classifications, are analyzed by commodities and presented separately for the United States as a whole, for states, and for cities having a population of 500,000 or more. The commodity data are classified according to the 11 major kind-of-business groups.

Not all stores were able to report sales by commodities in the detail requested. Small stores frequently keep only over-all records of their sales and have no better basis for a commodity sales analysis than purchase records or invoice files. Some cash stores have separate cash registers, the receipts of which approximate rough commodity classifications of sales. Larger stores may maintain commodity sales records, but not always in the detail requested. An effort was made, however, to arrive at an accurate analysis confined to a limited number of commodities or broad commodity groups. Therefore the commodity data are based upon reports from stores which were able to analyze their sales in the detail requested on the census schedules and constitute major samples for each kind of business.

For a few kinds of business the commodity analyses are limited to a national basis, but for most classifications the data are shown for each state as well as nationally. Separate analyses also are included, wherever the sample was large enough, for each city of more than 500,000 inhabitants. For certain kinds of business, the data by states are divided into two size groups—stores with annual sales of $20,000 or more and stores with annual sales of less than $20,000.

The commodity data were classified and tabulated to show the number of stores reporting commodity data and the total sales of such stores. The size of the sample is shown by the "commodity coverage," which is the ratio of the total sales of the stores reporting commodity data to the total sales of all stores in the same kind of business.

The inquiry on commodities yielded the following data: The number of stores reporting the sale of each commodity; total sales of such stores; total sales of the commodity in such stores; percent of the commodity's sales to total sales of the *stores selling that commodity;* and percent of the commodity's sales to total sales of *all stores in that kind of business* which were analyzed.

Analysis by Sales Size. Data on all retail stores in the United States are presented by sales size (amount of annual business) classified by kinds of business. These statistics are shown for the United States in summary form and for each state. Size analyses are shown separately for independents and for chains in seven size groups. Number of stores, sales, personnel, and payroll are shown for each size group. The largest and smallest size groups are further analyzed; all stores with sales of $300,000 and over, independents and chains combined, are further classified into three size groups for each kind of business, and similar data for independent stores only, with sales under $10,000, are further classified into five size groups.

Analysis of Sales by Size of Cities. In another series of tabulations, the basic data on stores and sales are classified by city-size groups. These city-size data are subclassified by kinds of business, types of operation, and geographic divisions.

Metropolitan Districts and Small Geographic Areas. The Bureau of the Census has designated 140 metropolitan districts; these districts consist of one or more central cities and all adjacent and contiguous minor civil divisions having a population of 150 or more per square mile. The metropolitan district thus is not a political unit such as a city, but rather is an area including all the thickly settled territories in and around a city or group of cities. It tends to be a more or less integrated area with common economic and social interests. (See Chapter 12, p. 337.)

A series of 140 individual reports were published as part of the 1939 Census of Business showing a map of each district and giving the

stores, sales, personnel, and payroll within each district, and a classification of stores and sales by 11 major kinds of business groups and for
5 selected kinds of business from some of these major groups. In the
final census volumes (1939 Census), summary information is presented
for these metropolitan districts.

In addition, the data are classified and tabulated for small geographic areas as follows:

1. For each county, each city of more than 2,500 inhabitants, and for the remainder of each county:
   a. Stores and sales for each of 11 major kind of business groups and 5
      selected kinds of businesses.
   b. Stores, sales, number of proprietors and employees, and payroll for all
      kinds of business combined.
2. For each city of more than 10,000 inhabitants: Stores, sales, number of proprietors, number of employees, and payroll classified by kinds of business
   (the detail varies according to four city-size groups).

Analysis of Sources of Receipts. Although the great majority of
goods sold in retail stores is sold in the same form in which it is bought,
some of the reported sales represent receipts for repairs, storage, and
other services to customers, and a considerably larger proportion represents the sale of drinks at fountain or bars and meals. Receipts from
these four categories are classified by kinds of business for the United
States, by geographic divisions and states (all kinds of business combined), and by kinds of business for each state.

Date of Establishment of Store. The length of time stores have been
in business is shown by tabulations in which stores are classified according to the date of their establishment. For the United States, these
statistics are classified by kinds of business, subclassified by two types
of operation (independents and chains). For geographic divisions and
states they are subclassified by types of operation, all kinds of business
combined.

Negro Proprietorships. Basic data on Negro proprietorships, showing stores, sales, personnel, payroll, and stocks by kinds of business
for the United States and by all kinds of business combined for geographic divisions and states, are presented in the census tabulations.
The data are further analyzed, showing stores, sales, payroll, and stocks
for kinds of business by states.

Sources and Availability. The retail census statistics for 1939 are
published as a part of the Census of Business in *Volume I, Retail Trade,*
Sixteenth Census of the United States. This volume is released in three
parts as follows: *Part 1: United States Summary and Special Subjects;*

Part 2: Commodity Sales and Analysis by Sales Size; Part 3: Kinds of Business, by Area, States, Counties, and Cities.

For those interested only in special area reports or in special phases of retail trade, separate reports on the following subjects are available: *Individual State Reports; Types of Operation; Credit Sales and Receivables; Monthly Employment and Sex of Employees; Analysis by Sales Size; Analysis by City-Size Groups; Commodity Sales; Sales-Finance Companies and Banks' Holdings of Retail Installment Paper.*

All the above-mentioned census reports are for sale by the Superintendent of Documents, and are available at the field offices of the Department of Commerce and in depository libraries in approximately 430 cities throughout the United States.

Single copies of the following multilithed reports may be obtained without charge from the Bureau of the Census: *Legal Forms of Organization; Supermarkets and Self-Service Food Stores; Retail Trade Negro Proprietorships; Statistics for Metropolitan Districts, and for Cities of More than 25,000 Population Ranked by Retail Sales; Chain Store Organizations, 1939, 1935, 1929.*

CURRENT STATISTICS

While the census statistics described above are the only data which afford complete coverage, they are available only for the years in which the censuses are taken. In order to supply more current data to bridge the intercensal years, several governmental agencies collect figures of a somewhat more limited scope from a sample number of firms.

Sales. The Bureau of the Census compiles monthly statistics on sales of independent retail stores in 34 states, based on a sample of about 19,000 stores. These statistics have been collected since 1938. A separate release is issued for each of the states, as well as a summary release for the 34 states. The cooperating retailers report their sales for the current month, the preceding month, and the same month last year. The reported sales are then translated into month-to-month and year-to-year percentage changes.

The sales figures are classified by kinds of business and city-size groups in the individual state reports. In the summary report, the same data are presented for all 34 states combined. Copies of these monthly reports may be obtained on request from the Bureau of the Census, Washington, D. C.

The Bureau of Foreign and Domestic Commerce makes monthly estimates of the total sales of retail stores. These estimates appear in the *Survey of Current Business,* prepared in the Bureau of Foreign and Domestic Commerce. Quarterly data are available for the years 1935 through 1938; since January 1939 the estimates have been available monthly. The figures are published in the form of dollar sales and as indexes of daily average sales, both unadjusted and adjusted for seasonal changes. These estimates are prepared for 25 kinds of business.

The estimates are based on the sales of the group of "identical" stores reporting to the Bureau of the Census, on sales of a number of identical chain firms reporting to the Bureau of Foreign and Domestic Commerce, on reports of sales tax collections in 11 states, and on miscellaneous other sources.

The total sales figures referred to above are for all retail trade, including both chains and independents. In addition, the Bureau of Foreign and Domestic Commerce makes monthly estimates of chain and mail-order sales. These estimates are based on reports from more than 500 chain organizations, representing more than 60 percent of the total chain store business. Like the estimates for all retail trade, described in the preceding paragraphs, the chain-store sales data are published monthly in the *Survey of Current Business*. They are available quarterly for the years 1935 to 1938 inclusive and monthly since January 1939. The estimates are shown for 20 kinds of business and appear both in the form of dollar sales and as indexes of daily average sales, adjusted for seasonal variation.

In addition to the above aggregate sales figures, the total mail-order and retail store sales of Sears, Roebuck & Company and Montgomery Ward are reported monthly to the Bureau of Foreign and Domestic Commerce and published in the *Survey of Current Business*.

Monthly indexes of the estimated rural sales of general merchandise since 1929 are also available in the *Survey of Current Business*. These indexes are both adjusted and unadjusted for seasonal variations and are shown separately by regions for the East, South, Middle West, and Far West, as well as for the United States. These indexes are compiled from data supplied by large mail-order houses and a chain-store system which also serves the rural population.

Since the passage of the Federal Revenue Act of 1941, the Bureau of Internal Revenue has compiled statistics on the amount of retail excise taxes collected. Figures are shown separately for the amount of tax collections on "jewelry," "furs," and "toilet goods" (as defined in the Act), classified by internal revenue collection districts, states, and territories. Receipts are shown for each fiscal year ending June 30. As these excise taxes are assessed as a flat percentage of the sales price the amount of tax collected indicates the retail sales of these commodities. These data are available in the *Annual Report of the Commissioner of Internal Revenue*, for sale by the Superintendent of Documents.

Consumption Expenditures. Closely allied to retail sales figures, although there are many significant points of differences, are estimates of total consumer expenditures for all goods and services. These estimates are prepared by the Bureau of Foreign and Domestic Commerce. Originally undertaken as part of the Bureau's research on the gross national product and the national income, the estimates of consumption expenditures are of major economic significance in themselves and may be of special interest to those concerned with retail trade.

Not only does the total consumption expenditure constitute the largest single segment of the gross national product, but it also affords a measure of how successfully the economic system has achieved its end of satisfying consumer needs for commodities and service. Moreover, the detailed itemization of kinds of goods and services (which follows an approximate household budgetary classification) makes possible a much clearer understanding of the cyclical shifts in the provision of consumers goods.

Consumption expenditures by type of product, by years, for the period 1929–1942 are shown in the June 1944 issue of the *Survey of Current Business*. Current monthly estimates of consumer expenditures, divided into total goods and total services, are carried regularly in the *Survey of Current Business*.

Inventories. The Census Bureau also collects annual data on the dollar value of year-end retail inventories from the same group of stores from which it obtains sales data. Separate reports are issued for each kind-of-business classification, showing data by states, by size of store, and by size of city. In addition, there is an annual summary for the 34 states combined which gives information by kinds of business. These inventory reports may be obtained on request from the Bureau of the Census, Washington, D. C.

The Bureau of Foreign and Domestic Commerce has prepared monthly estimates of the total value of inventories in retail stores since 1933. Inventory data are presented for all types of operation in total—chains, independents, and mail-order houses combined. These estimates are shown for six major groups of nondurable goods stores and for six major groups of durable goods outlets. The data on inventories by kinds of business represent the value of stocks on hand at cost value as of the end of the reporting period. The monthly estimates appear in the *Survey of Current Business*. Together with estimates of wholesalers' and manufacturers' inventories and other data, they also appear in a monthly publication of the Bureau called *Industry Survey*. This latter publication may be obtained by writing to the Bureau of Foreign and Domestic Commerce, Washington, D. C.

Retail Births and Deaths. The Bureau of Foreign and Domestic Commerce compiles comprehensive statistics on the business population, including retail trade. The Bureau compiles current quarterly data on the number of new businesses, discontinued businesses, and business transfers; with detailed classifications of these data by kinds of business and by size of business as measured by number of employees. The basic data are derived from a wide variety of sources, including records of the Social Security Board, State taxing and licensing agencies, and trade associations. These data appear in the *Survey of Current Business*. Quarterly releases containing the information are also available on request from the Bureau of Foreign and Domestic Commerce, Washington, D. C.

Consumer Credit. Monthly estimates of total consumer credit outstanding are prepared by the Board of Governors of the Federal Reserve System. The total consumer credit is divided into installment credit, single-payment loans, charge accounts, and service credit. Installment credit is further divided into sales credit and loans.

Consumer installment sales credit outstanding, excluding automotive credit, is also classified by type of store extending the credit. Consumer installment loans outstanding are further shown by type of institution extending loan. Monthly estimates of consumer installment *credits* of commercial banks, by type of credit, and estimates of the monthly volume of consumer installment *loans* made by principal lending institution (as contrasted to amounts *outstanding*) are also presented.

The Federal Reserve System (Chapter 10, p. 292) also publishes data showing national ratios of collections to accounts receivable for department-store charge accounts, for installment accounts in department stores, and for furniture, household appliance, and jewelry stores. (These are ratios of collections during the month to accounts receivable at beginning of month.) These monthly data are shown in the *Federal Reserve Bulletin* published by the Board of Governors of the Federal Reserve System.

In addition to monthly data, the Federal Reserve publishes an annual *Retail Credit Survey*. The annual survey is based on a larger sample than that which is obtained in making the monthly estimates and the results are available in greater detail. These annual reports contain data on sales by type of transaction (cash, charge account, and installment), receivables, and collections on charge account and installment sales, variations by size of store, and changes by geographic areas for each of the 15 kinds of business analyzed. Copies of the 1942 and later surveys may be obtained on request from the Board of Governors of the Federal Reserve System, Washington, D. C.

Department-Store and Furniture-Store Statistics. The Board of Governors of the Federal Reserve System compiles a national index of monthly department-store sales, based on a sample group of reporting stores. This series began in 1919 and now includes about 1,400 stores. Each of the 12 Federal Reserve Banks also compiles monthly indexes of department store sales for its district; the data are available back to about 1919. All of these monthly indexes are presented both with and without seasonal adjustments. The Federal Reserve System also compiles weekly indexes for the United States of department-store sales, based on reports from a smaller group of stores than that included in the monthly indexes.

Data on monthly sales and stocks by major departments, in department stores, both main store and basement store, are available from the Federal Reserve. These data are presented in the form of percentage changes from the preceding month and from the corresponding month of the preceding year. Index numbers of cash, installment, and charge sales, accounts receivable, and collections during the month for installment and charge account sales of department stores are also shown monthly.

The Federal Reserve System also compiles data on the furniture-store business. Percentage changes from preceding month and percentage changes from corresponding month of preceding year are shown for the following items: Total sales, cash sales, credit sales (subdivided into installment and charge account business), accounts receivable at end of month (total and installment), collections during month (total and installment), and inventories, end of month, at retail value. These data on department and furniture stores are published monthly in the *Federal Reserve Bulletin.*

Financial Statistics. Since 1918, the Bureau of Internal Revenue of the Treasury Department has published financial statistics based on compilations of data obtained from the annual corporation income tax returns. Of course, with each change in the income tax law, the comparability of the data from year to year is affected. The extent to which the comparability of data is affected may be ascertained, however, by reference to various sections of each annual report wherein attention is directed to changes in methods of tabulation and in provisions of the Federal tax laws under which returns for a given year are filed. Of special aid is the synopsis of Federal tax laws affecting the comparability of historical data. This synopsis is shown regularly in the annual reports on *Statistics of Income*.

For the years 1918 through 1937, the data are shown in summary form only for retail and wholesale trade combined. From 1938, retail and wholesale trade are segregated and data on retail trade are further classified into 14 kind-of-business groups. For each of these kinds of business, the statistics are presented for all corporate income tax returns, and separately for returns of corporations with net income and for returns with no net income. The number of income tax returns, total compiled receipts (corresponding roughly to "gross income" on the income tax form), net income or deficit, and taxes and dividends paid are some of the data shown.

Another tabulation of the items on the income tax returns of corporations engaged in retail trade shows the amount of taxable receipts from each source, and also the detailed "deductions"; corresponding roughly to the cost of goods sold and operating expense items as classified on the income tax forms. Total deductions, net income or deficit, income tax paid, and dividends paid are also available in this tabulation.

For corporation returns with balance sheets, data are shown for the following items: Number of returns; amounts of assets and liabilities; detailed taxable receipts (income); deductions (expenses); net profit or loss; net income or deficit; and taxes and dividends paid. These data are presented separately for returns with net income and for returns with no net income. Some of the data on the returns with balance sheets are classified by size of business, as measured by value of total assets. These financial data for corporations engaged in retail trade and filing income tax returns are published annually in reports entitled *Statistics of Income*. The reports are for sale by the Superintendent of Documents.

Since the passage of the Securities and Exchange Act, financial statistics relating to corporations engaged in retail trade have also been compiled by the Securities and Exchange Commission. These compilations include data from only those companies which have securities listed and registered on national securities exchanges and which, of course, tend to be the larger corporations.

The first individual company reports were made available in 1938 and contained data for the years 1934 through 1937. Separate reports were published for chain variety stores, mail-order houses, department stores (with annual sales over $10,000,000), and chain grocery and food stores.

This series of reports contains individual profit and loss statements, balance sheets, and surplus reconciliations for each company, as well as combined profit and loss statements, balance sheets, and surplus reconciliations for all registrants (in both dollar and ratio form). Individual company reports were also issued in 1939 and 1940 and presented, in general, the same kind of data for the same kinds of businesses. In 1941 the reports were limited to manufacturing corporations engaged in the war effort. After 1941 the publication of these individual company reports was suspended for the duration of the war. These individual company reports were issued under the title *Survey of American Listed Corporations*.

The over-all statistics summarize the information from all registrants falling within the scope of the *Survey of American Listed Corporations*. These data are classified by major trade groups as follows: Chain stores; department stores; and other merchandising.

The compilations contain data on a number of aspects in the field of corporation finance, such as a detailed analysis of securities outstanding, characteristics of registered common and preferred stock issues, and a general survey of subsidiary corporations. For the merchandising group as a whole there are statistics on capitalization patterns and similar corporate financial statistics. The reports on both the *Survey of American Listed Corporations* and *Statistics of American Listed Corporations* are available in depository libraries throughout the United States.

STATISTICS FROM SPECIAL SURVEYS

Grocery-Drug Surveys. In 1927 and 1928 the Bureau of Foreign and Domestic Commerce undertook a comprehensive study of grocery retailing. This study is known as the *Louisville Grocery Survey*. Although quite old, much of the statistical information is still of significance.

The survey contains data on the elements of cost accruing to the individual commodity carried in the stock of a grocery store. Sales, turnover, gross margin, allocated expense, and net profit for 15 commodity departments in each of 26 stores analyzed in the course of the survey are shown. The survey provides detailed statistics for individual commodities in each of the 26 stores, on number of items in stock, sales value, number of sales, average value per sale, average inventory investment, annual turnover rate, gross margin, allocated operating expense, and net profit or loss.

The *St. Louis Drug Store Survey* conducted in 1931–1932 was a comprehensive survey of the retail drug business similar in scope to the *Louisville Grocery Survey*.

In the drug store survey the emphasis was placed on promotion and merchandising, whereas in the grocery survey the emphasis was almost exclusively on commodity costs and profits. Costs and profits on individual items of merchandise, however, constituted an important phase of the St. Louis survey. Detailed commodity statistics for seven drug stores are presented. The following data are included for individual commodities or groups of commodities: Number of items, average inventory value, number of sales, sales value, gross margin, turnover, average sales, allocated expense, and net profit. Most of the reports in both the grocery and drug store survey are out of print. They may be examined, however, in the field offices of the Department of Commerce and in depository libraries. Also, information may be obtained from the Government Printing Office as to the titles and prices of the booklets which are still available.

Chain-Store Survey. Beginning in 1931, the Federal Trade Commission published the results of a comprehensive survey of chain stores in all fields. The survey was made in response to a Congressional request for an inquiry into chain-store operations. The results were published in 33 separate reports. Data on prices, margins, sales, costs and profits, special discounts and allowances, and financial statistics (such as invested capital and rates of return) are some of the information included in this series of reports.

The entire series of reports is known as the *Chain-Store Inquiry*. The titles and prices of the individual reports, which are sold by the Superintendent of Documents, may be obtained on request from the Federal Trade Commission, Washington, D. C.

SERVICE TRADES STATISTICS

The service trades are an outgrowth of the trend toward expanded and more widely distributed personal incomes which has been evident over the past several decades. Many of the things which people previously did for themselves or for which they engaged a personal servant are now performed by professionals on a fee basis.

Care and dressing of the hair, for example, which was performed by the lady's maid or by the woman herself, is now done in beauty shops. The cleaning of a suit of clothes, previously done by the gentleman's valet or the housewife, is now the job of the dry cleaning plant.

Just as the individual services were diverse, so the professional counterpart found in the service trades covers a wide and heterogeneous class of businesses. Although concerns in the service trades are primarily engaged in the sale of *services* as contrasted with the sale of *goods* in the customary retailing and wholesaling businesses, they nevertheless are users of vast quantities of supplies and equipment. To the manufacturers and wholesalers of these goods they constitute a broad market.

BENCHMARK STATISTICS

In 1939 the Census Bureau canvassed the service trades as part of its regular enumeration of businesses. The canvass, covering the 48 States and the District of Columbia, was taken by enumerators who visited each business establishment during the first 8 months of 1940. The first comprehensive canvass of the service trades was in 1934 covering the year 1933, and another canvass was taken in 1936 covering 1935. These two earlier censuses were conducted as a part of the emergency work programs of those years.

Certain selected groups of the service trades were covered in prior censuses as far back as 1919. The trades on which earlier information is available are power laundries, cleaning and dyeing establishments, and hotels. Statistics for 1935 and earlier years were compiled in connection with the Census of Manufactures in so far as laundries and dry cleaning establishments were concerned. Data on hotels are available for 1929.

Because of important differences in the scope of the censuses, comparisons of the aggregates are not recommended by the Census Bureau. The Census of Service Businesses in 1939 covered lines not included in the earlier censuses, and several lines covered in the earlier years were not included in 1939. Reconciliation tabulations are available, however, that indicate the areas of comparability as between the 1935 and the 1939 Censuses.

The major types of service trades covered in 1939 are given below, together with their more important subclassifications:

1. Service establishments proper:
   a. Personal services.
   b. Business services.
   c. Services allied to transportation.
   d. Automobile repairs and services.
   e. Other repair services.
   f. Custom industries.
   g. Miscellaneous services.
2. Places of amusement.
3. Hotels.
4. Tourist courts and tourist camps.

Not all establishments generally considered as service businesses came under the census definition. Such activities as the professions (doctors, lawyers, dentists) or various scientific services, as well as establishments in the field of finance, real estate, insurance, transportation, religious and charitable institutions, hospitals and sanitariums, public utilities and government-operated enterprises are not included as part of the census of the service trades. Restaurants are included in the census of retail trades.

Service Establishments Proper. The major classification, service establishments proper, in which 106 different kinds of business are reported separately, includes the bulk of those lines of activity which are customarily thought of as service businesses. These service establishments proper were classified into the seven categories mentioned above: (1) Personal service establishments, such as barber shops, beauty parlors, power laundries, cleaning and dyeing plants, and photographic studios; (2) business service establishments, such as adjustment and credit bureaus and collection agencies, advertising agencies, billboard advertising service, dental laboratories, sign painting shops, and other establishments rendering a service to business; (3) services allied to transportation, such as stevedoring, stockyard service, and warehousing; (4) automotive repairs and services, which include automobile repair shops, automobile paint shops, automobile top and body repair shops, battery and ignition repair shops, tire repair shops, and automobile laundries; (5) other repair services (except automobile, apparel, and shoes), which include blacksmith shops, piano and organ tuning and repair service, radio repair shops, refrigerator service and repair shops, and watch, clock, and jewelry repair shops; (6) custom industries, which include cabinetmaking shops, and other custom and manufacturing establishments not covered by the Census of Manufactures, since the value of products of each is less than the required minimum of $5,000 necessary for classification as a manufacturing plant; and (7) miscellaneous services, which include circulating libraries, landscape gardening and tree surgery, livery stables, and other services which could not logically be classified in any of the other six groups.

Detailed information was obtained on several of these types of business and special tabulations were prepared for a more intensive analysis of them. The service establishments so treated are power laundries, cleaning and dyeing plants, hand laundries, and rug cleaning establishments.

A place of business to be classified as a service establishment proper must have been primarily engaged in providing service—that is, 50 percent or more of the revenue of the establishment must have been derived from the sale of service. If more than 50 percent of the total operating revenue of the establishment represented receipts from the sale of merchandise, such establishment was included in either retail trade or wholesale trade. Each unit of a chain is considered a separate establishment. Service concessions, operated independently in connection with other businesses, are classified as separate establishments. An individual's residence was considered a place of business if a sign indicated that the occupant was engaged in a service business. Businesses reporting total receipts of less than $100 for the year are not considered establishments for the purpose of the Service Census and are therefore not included.

PUBLISHED TABULATIONS. The basic data on the service trades proper which are covered in published tabulations include the following items: Number of establishments; volume and nature of receipts; number of active proprietors of unincorporated businesses; number of full-time and part-time employees; payroll; and sex of employees.

In the various tabulations these data are presented in four different ways: (1) by kind of business for the entire United States; (2) by geographic divisions and States for all businesses and for selected kinds of business separately; (3) by size of firm (using sales volume or number of employees as a base) and kind of business for the entire United States; and (4) for all businesses and certain selected kinds of business by geographic divisions and states.

EMPLOYMENT, PAYROLLS, AND RECEIPTS. Information on employment was obtained for each month during 1939 and includes data on both full-time and part-time activity. The number of male and female employees was obtained as of any payroll period ending in October. These data are shown by kind of business for the entire United States and by geographic divisions and states for all businesses and for selected kinds of business separately.

A further tabulation carries, for each type of business, the number of establishments, receipts, number of proprietors, number of employees, and total payroll, arranged by average size of establishment using number of employees as the determinant of size. These data are shown by geographic divisions and states for all types of business.

The number of proprietors, firm members, and unpaid family members is shown in tabular form by kinds of business and for all businesses by geographic divisions and states. Salaries or withdrawals are shown for proprietors, and number of family members are divided as between full-time and part-time.

The tabulation of number of proprietors is exclusive of salaried officers of corporations and other corporation executives. It is confined to the number of active proprietors (owners or partners) of unincorporated businesses whose major activity is concerned with the operation of the business. Proprietors are therefore not included in the count of employees as is true of corporation officers, nor is their compensation included in payroll.

The distribution of number of employees by sex of worker is based on one payroll period (any week in October). It is assumed that the sex ratio of employees secured on the one-period basis generally obtains throughout the year. However, as the Census Bureau points out, seasonal and other influences may affect the personnel structure of establishments to such an extent that the ratios may not be representative for the entire year.

The term "employees" represents the number of full-time and part-time employees, including salaried officers of corporations, working during any one month. The number of employees is an average for the year obtained by totaling the number reported monthly and dividing by 12. The respondents reported the full-time and part-time employees separately for the work period ending nearest the 15th day of each month. Intermittent employees who were working during the work week enumerated were thus counted as full-time for that week.

Payroll data include all compensation (salaries, wages, bonuses, and commissions) paid during the year to all employees. Compensation for proprietors or firm members of unincorporated businesses of course, is not considered as a payroll item but is shown separately. The schedule specified further that payroll data should be reported inclusive of customary deductions for Social Security tax, insurance, dues, and similar items but should not include any payment in kind such as meals and lodging.

Receipts of service establishments are analyzed by type of business for the United States and by geographic divisions and states for each type of business. Furthermore, receipts are divided into sales of service, sales of merchandise, and sales from other sources. Tabulations are presented showing the segregation of source of receipts by kind of business and by geographic divisions and states.

LEGAL FORM OF ORGANIZATION. Four forms of legal organization are distinguished in the canvass of service trades proper: (1) individual proprietorships, (2) partnerships, (3) corporations, and (4) other forms of organization. For each kind of business, the number of establishments, receipts, number of proprietors, number of employees, and payroll are shown for each legal form of organization. The basic data on number of establishments, etc., by legal forms of organization are given also by geographic divisions, states, and for large cities. For example, data are available to show for all businesses in New England (or Maine, etc.) the proportion of the totals accounted for by individual proprietorships, partnerships, corporations, and other forms of organization.

NEGRO PROPRIETORSHIPS. Basic data by kinds of business are shown for establishments having Negro proprietorships by geographic divisions, states, and selected cities.

STATES, COUNTIES, AND CITIES. Tabulations are available on a geographic basis showing the basic data (number of establishments, receipts, personnel, and payroll) for each state and the District of Columbia and by each kind of business within each state. These data are further subclassified to present for all kinds of business the basic data for each county and for each place of more than 2,500 inhabitants within each county. For cities having a population of 25,000 or more, basic data are presented for each kind of business.

Basic data for selected kinds of business are shown also for cities of 500,000 inhabitants or more as are the totals for all kinds of business. A tabulation for cities having over 500,000 persons gives employment data for all businesses and for selected kinds separately. Another tabulation for such cities shows basic data classified by volume of receipts. From this tabulation it is possible to determine, for example, the number of establishments, receipts, number of proprietors, number of employees, and total payroll for service establishments in Baltimore, Maryland, having sales of $10,000 to $15,000 annually.

Places of Amusement. The canvass of Places of Amusement covers those establishments whose primary activity consists in conducting an amusement enterprise. The Census distinguishes 23 kinds of business, the more important of which are motion picture theaters, billiard and pool parlors, bowling alleys, dance halls, professional baseball clubs, and race tracks.

Amusement enterprises such as those conducted by educational institutions, religious, charitable, or fraternal agencies, governmental or civic bodies, and nonprofit organizations are not included. Gambling places, golf and other private clubs, charter-boat fishing, and pleasure resorts primarily engaged in providing food and lodging are not covered. Legitimate theaters, athletic fields, and arenas are included only if engaged in the promotion of amusement enterprises. A combined report for an amusement enterprise and the buildings or grounds within which the enterprise is located was accepted only when they were operated as a single unit. The leasing or renting of buildings or grounds to amusement enterprises is a real estate activity and does not come within the scope of the 1939 Business Census.

Basic data (number of establishments, receipts, number of active proprietors of unincorporated businesses, average number of employees for the year, and annual payroll) are presented for the United States by kinds of business and by geographic divisions and states. For cities having a population of 100,000 or more similar data are shown for combined totals of all kinds of business.

Statistics are also presented for (1) monthly employment and sex of employees by kinds of business, by geographic divisions and states, and combined totals of all kinds of business for cities of more than 500,000 inhabitants; (2) size groups based on volume of receipts; (3) receipts based on source; (4) proprietors' withdrawals and family members employed in the business; and (5) legal forms of organization. Detailed statistics are presented for three of the more important kinds of business—motion-picture theaters, including motion-picture theaters with vaudeville; bowling alleys; and billiard and pool parlors—by geographic divisions and states. Data on seating capacity of motion-picture theaters are included.

Hotels. The canvass of hotels includes establishments designating themselves as hotels and providing hotel accommodations as their major business activity. Establishments reporting a total of less than six guest rooms, or receipts from room rentals amounting to less than $500, were excluded from the census for 1939. Hotels having six or more guest rooms, but failing to report separately the amount of income from room rentals, were not omitted unless total receipts amounted to less than $500. Apartment hotels were canvassed and classified as hotels, provided a substantial portion of their receipts was derived from the accommodation of transient guests. Apartment houses, residential hotels catering exclusively to permanent guests, boarding houses, lodginghouses, tourist homes or camps, resorts, Y.M.C.A.'s, Y.W.C.A.'s, dude ranches, club dormitories, and other similar establishments furnishing lodging and/or meals to guests are not considered hotels for census purposes.

The activities of restaurants and other eating and drinking places operated on the hotel premises by the hotel are included in the hotel reports. On the other hand, similar activities operated as concessions are included in the Census of Retail Trade. Concession rentals, however, are included as a part of the hotel receipts.

Statistics on hotels compiled from data collected in connection with the 1939 Census of Business cover the number of hotels, number of guest rooms, receipts, number of active proprietors of unincorporated businesses, average number of employees for the year, and annual payroll (both in totals and for year-round and seasonal hotels separately). These basic data are available for the United States by geographic divisions and states, and for both types of hotels combined for cities having a population of 10,000 or more.

Presentations are also included for (1) monthly employment and sex of employees for year-round and seasonal hotels, both combined and separately, by geographic divisions and states, and in totals for all hotels for cities of more than 500,000 persons; (2) size groups based on volume of receipts; (3) size groups based on number of guest rooms; (4) legal forms of organization; (5) proprietors' withdrawals and family members employed in the business; and (6) analysis of receipts based on source. In addition, the following statistics are presented by geographic divisions and states, and for cities of more than 500,000 inhabitants, for year-round hotels having 25 or more guest rooms: Guest rooms available for transient and residential guests; employment and payroll for a specific week by occupational groups; employees receiving meals and quarters; percentage of guest-room occupancy. Comparative summary statistics (1939 and 1935) for the United States, by geographic divisions and states, are shown for cities having a population of 250,000 or more.

Tourist Courts and Tourist Camps. The canvass of tourist courts and tourist camps includes those places of business engaged primarily in furnishing temporary lodging accommodations to tourists (largely motorists) in cabins or other similar structures. It does not include tourist homes (private residences furnishing accommodations to tourists), nor does it include trailer camps, dude ranches, tourist courts or camps operated by communities, or cottage colonies, catering to vacationists rather than tourists. Establishments reporting annual receipts of less than $100, or those operating less than three rental units, are also excluded. Establishments primarily engaged in retail trade (filling stations, restaurants, drinking places, etc.), although maintaining tourist cabins, are classified in the Census of Retail Trade, providing their sales of merchandise represent over 50 percent of their total annual receipts.

Detailed statistics on number of establishments, receipts, number of active proprietors of unincorporated businesses, average number of employees, annual payroll, and number of cabins and rental units are presented for the United States by geographic divisions and states.

Data are also presented by geographic divisions and states for (1) monthly employment and sex of employees; (2) size groups based on volume of receipts; (3) size groups based on number of rental units; (4) receipts based on source; (5) proprietors' withdrawals and family members employed in the business.

Sources and Availability. Statistics for the various service trades discussed above are available in the published report of the Census of Business, 1939, *Volume III, Service Establishments, and Places of Amusement, Hotels, Tourist Courts and Tourist Camps.* This volume, like the other volumes, may be obtained from the Superintendent of Documents and is available for use at the field offices of the Department of Commerce and also at depository libraries in various cities.

CURRENT STATISTICS

The available current data on service establishments, while not nearly so complete as the statistics derived from the census, nevertheless may afford some valuable aids to analysis.

Financial Statistics. The Bureau of Internal Revenue prepares certain annual tabulations showing operating and financial statistics of service businesses derived from corporation income tax returns. (See Chapter 9.) Some information relative to service trades is available for six major lines of business: Personal service, business service, automobile repair services, amusement, other services (including schools), and service not allocable. Probably the more important of the tabulations available are those presenting modified profit and loss statements and balance sheets. Data are shown separately for firms reporting net income and those reporting no net income.

These basic data are comparable with those discussed in the previous sections of this chapter on wholesale and retail trade and include statistics on gross sales, cost of goods sold, cost of operations, and other annual profit and loss items. Balance sheet items on which data are available include such categories as cash, notes and accounts receivable, inventories, accounts payable, and various other asset and liability accounts. There is also given a tabulation showing the number of corporate returns with selected receipt and expenditure items arranged by asset size for each type of business.

These data for each tax year appear in Part II of *Statistics of Income,* an annual publication of the Bureau of Internal Revenue. These reports may be obtained from the Superintendent of Documents.

Consumption Expenditures. A second source of current data on the service trades is that provided by the Bureau of Foreign and Domestic Commerce in its estimates of consumption expenditures. Annual estimates of expenditures are available for more than 100 detailed categories of retail and service businesses. Annual detailed data covering the period 1929–1942 are presented in the June 1944 issue of the *Survey of Current Business*, and quarterly estimates with less detail are available quarterly in that publication.

Although the nature of these data and the purposes to which they may be put have been explained earlier in this chapter under the section on Retail Trade, it should be pointed out that the data contain one feature which makes them peculiarly appropriate for analysis of the Service Trades. That is, the expenditures for each item are classified as between service and commodity. It is possible, therefore, to obtain an accurate picture of the current expenditures for services as well as an idea of the volume of commodities required in order to meet consumer needs.

Business Births and Deaths. In addition to data already mentioned, the Bureau of Foreign and Domestic Commerce compiles quarterly data on the number of operating business firms. Information is available on the total number of firms as well as births and deaths in such service industries as hotels, laundries, barber and beauty shops, other personal services, automobile repair, amusements, and other business services.

This information and a description of the series were first published in the March, May, and July 1944 issues of the *Survey of Current Business* and the quarterly estimates are carried currently in that publication. Statistics are presented showing the number of firms in operation as of September 30, 1929, 1933, and 1935, with data by quarters beginning with March 30, 1939. The number of service establishments classified in order of number of employees is given for 1939. These estimates are based upon the records of the Bureau of Old Age and Survivors Insurance of the Social Security Board, Unemployment Compensation, taxing and licensing records of various states, and certain statistics from the Bureau of the Census and the Bureau of Internal Revenue.

Warehouse Space. The Bureau of the Census gathers data on the space status of privately owned public merchandise warehouses which it obtains from the voluntary cooperation of over 700 warehousing firms. These statistics are given for large cities and all states and geographic divisions; they include the number of merchandise warehouse buildings operated, the amount of net usable storage space, the amount of such space occupied, and the percentage occupancy. A report is issued monthly showing both the current and previous month's data.

The Department of Agriculture has conducted a biennial census of refrigerated warehouse floor space since 1921. The reports show for the United States as a whole and for states and large cities the cubic feet of floor space available in various types of warehouses. In addition to the biennial survey, a monthly report is issued on cold storage warehouses showing the total net piling space and percentage of space occupied in public and private cold storages, apple houses, and meat packing plants. This information is available by geographic divisions and states.

USE OF THESE STATISTICS BY MANAGEMENT

The statistics compiled by governmental agencies covering the wholesale, retail, and service trades are used by manufacturers, wholesalers, retailers, and the service trades in connection with the solution of many of their production and distribution problems. They are also used extensively by advertising and marketing research concerns in servicing their clients in the above industries. These statistics are thus basic in the solution of many diverse management problems.

Market Potentials

There are numerous quantitative analyses which have as their objective the measurement of market potentials, that is, the measurement of total demand for a product. These studies may be made with different management problems in mind, but many such divergent problems have as a prevailing characteristic the fact that they can be satisfactorily met only through an estimate of what demand will be in future periods.

For example, analyses are made which attempt to determine whether or not a product should be produced and placed on the market. The product may be perfected from a designing and technical point of view; and, through other research studies, reasonable assurance may be given that it has utility and that there will be some demand if it is made available. Unless the forthcoming demand, however, is sufficiently great at the price which must be charged, the manufacture of the product may not be profitable. A study is needed to estimate the total demand at that price for such a product. Moreover, if other similar products share the market, a concern must estimate not only the total market, but also its own share of the total.

Much the same sort of problem is involved in the determination of future sales for budgetary purposes. The objective of an analysis along this line is the making of a sales forecast for a specified future period under a given marketing plan or program. Here the purpose of the study differs from that outlined in the first example, inasmuch as the product presumably has been on the market for some time.

It is not a question of whether or not to produce, but of how much the company should plan to produce over coming periods in order to meet the demand, and at the same time avoid an unnecessary surplus (under a given set of cost-price relationships).

Each concern must make such estimates. When the production period is long and roundabout, moreover, there is a greater premium for reasonably correct estimates and a greater penalty if poor ones are made. Again, as in the first case (barring a monopoly situation), two questions must be answered: First, how much in total will be purchased by consumers; and second, how much of the total business can be expected by a certain company.

Another type of problem arises in connection with territorial potentials. In addition to a forecast of total sales for production planning and budgetary purposes, it is necessary to divide the total demand among different sales territories according to their potentialities and to set sales quotas for various parts of the sales organization. Sales management is interested not only in the amount of a product which a certain sales territory should take, but also in how much it should take as compared with some other territory.

Only through studies of relative regional demands is it possible to check up on the effectiveness of selling effort, or to determine just where and in what quantity sales and advertising effort should be placed initially. Unless something is known about relative regional demands, sales efforts may be placed evenly over the total market area, with the result that, in proportion to relative demands, some parts of the market are overworked and others neglected. In general, sales effort should be distributed over the total market being cultivated by the individual concern in proportion to the sales possibilities in its various parts; and this can be done only through a knowledge of relative demands in different areas.

A knowledge of regional demands is also necessary in connection with the solution of such problems as the initial delineation of sales territories, or their subsequent adjustment in the light of changing conditions, or the most efficient location of branch warehouses and sales offices. Here again, as in the other examples given above, there are two questions in regard to regional demands: First, the total demand for a product in a given area; and second, the share of that total regional demand which an individual company can expect to obtain.

The commodity sales data in the retail census reports may be used (as described in a preceding section of this chapter) to compute the approximate total sales of a commodity made by each principal kind of business handling that commodity. The sum of the dollar sales thus derived is the approximate total sales of the given commodity made by the principal kinds of business selling the commodity.

In addition to the amounts computed by following the above method, sales of a given commodity should also be estimated for the kinds of business in which the commodity is sold in such small proportion that it is reported only in combination with one or more commodities or is not listed at all. For instance, gasoline, which is reported as a separate commodity for filling stations, is combined with oil and grease for automobile dealers and accessory stores; and with oil, tires, etc., for grocery and combination stores.

An example of the method of computing the approximate total sales of a given commodity by principal kinds of business from census data follows:

TABLE 1. SALES OF FLOOR COVERINGS BY PRINCIPAL KINDS OF BUSINESS

Kind of Business	Percent of Sales of Floor Coverings to Total Sales of Stores Reporting Sales by Commodities (1)	Total Sales of All Stores in the Stated Kind of Business (Add 000) (2)	Approximate Total Sales of Floor Coverings (Col. 1 × Col. 2) (Add 000) (3)
Total sales of these stores	....	....	$286,779 *
Furniture stores	13.0	$ 973,157	126,510
Department stores	2.6	3,974,998	103,350
Floor coverings stores	91.3	58,618	53,518
Interior decorators	10.7	27,930	2,989
Drapery, curtain, upholstery stores	2.6	15,843	412

* Caution. This total amount is limited to the principal retail outlets for floor coverings and should not be considered as the total sales of the commodity. Other kinds of businesses, such as general merchandise stores, general stores, and hardware stores, also sell quantities of floor coverings. In these other kinds of businesses, however, records of sales of floor coverings are not generally kept separately but are combined with other merchandise. Furthermore, large quantities of floor coverings are included in the catalogue sales of mail-order houses. To arrive at an approximate total figure, it would be necessary to estimate the amount of the commodity sold by each kind of business other than the principal classifications.

In addition to estimating the total demand for a commodity (as reflected in total retail sales) for the United States, the census data can also be used, in the same way, for estimating demand for a commodity for each state and county and for cities of over 500,000 inhabitants, since commodity data are available for these areas.

In many instances, however, the commodity data cannot be used, in the manner described above, to estimate the total and regional sales of a given commodity either because the commodity classifications are too broad, or the sales in other kinds of business are too important, or for other reasons. In such instances, census data can be used in other ways to estimate total sales of a commodity.

For example, by means of a special survey, it might be determined that, on the average, a given commodity accounts for a certain percentage of the total sales in a kind of business. Applying this percentage to the total sales of that kind of business gives the sales of the given commodity. Many manufacturers can use the commodity data in the wholesale census for the purpose of estimating the total sales of a given commodity. Information on the total wholesale volume of a particular commodity may afford a basis for determining total and regional demands for that commodity.

It is obvious that these techniques can be used by distributors other than manufacturers for the purpose of determining the size and location of their potential markets. Data showing actual wholesale sales by regions in a given line of trade, for example, could be used by a wholesaler in that line of trade to estimate the size of his total potential market. This approach, however, may have the weakness that sales figures may not accurately reflect the entire potential market, because some segment of it may have been neglected by wholesalers in that line of trade in a given region. To overcome this weakness, the wholesaler might estimate his total potential market by using the retail commodity data.

For example, a motor and equipment wholesaler could determine, from the retail census, the dollar business obtained by retail motor-vehicle dealers from "repairs, storage, and other services." A special survey could be made to determine what proportion of such sales are represented by parts, etc., purchased by motor-vehicle dealers from motor and equipment wholesalers and from wholesalers in other kinds of business. Similarly, the same process could be used in other retail trades that are potential markets for motor and equipment wholesalers. The total of the figures for the various lines of retail trade would indicate the total potential market for motor and equipment wholesalers.

The above examples illustrating the use of statistics in determining market potentials show, of course, how to answer the first question involved, namely: How much in total will be purchased? The second question involved still needs to be answered, namely: How much of the total business can be expected by a certain company?

In obtaining the answer to this second question a variety of techniques, ranging from rule-of-thumb judgments to elaborate statistical techniques, are used. The manufacturer or wholesaler will know from the census data the approximate total sales of his products and he will know from his own records the volume of his own sales. Thus his proportion of the total can be computed for the Nation as a whole or by regions or states. For fine subdivisions by commodities he will probably have to rely on statistics from trade associations, etc., but these statistics themselves will be computed against the background of the comprehensive census figures.

The commodity data can also be used by distributors in deciding *which* commodities to sell. A retailer, for example, can determine from the commodity sales data how many retailers in his line of trade are handling commodity lines which he does not stock. It is also possible to determine the proportion of sales which these commodities produce for those retailers who do handle them.

Wholesalers can use the commodity data in the wholesale census in a similar manner. From these data wholesalers can ascertain what lines of commodities are carried by other wholesalers in the same classification, and what portion these commodities constitute of the total sales of the houses handling them. Commodity data also show wholesalers how important each item is to the trade as a whole; they thus provide valuable information on lines of merchandise which might be added or eliminated.

Channels of Distribution

When the questions "what and how much can be sold, and where?" have been answered, the manufacturer, the wholesaler, and other distributors still need to determine the most effective channels through which they can sell their products. Statistics on wholesale, retail, and service trades provide valuable information along these lines.

Commodity data in the wholesale census can assist manufacturers in working out effective methods of distribution for their products. The wholesale census provides facts on commodity outlets showing the trade groups which handle the various items and their methods of operation. It is possible for manufacturers of electrical goods, for example, to determine what classes of wholesalers sell electrical goods, where such wholesalers are located, and how important such commodities are to their business.

Moreover, from the basic census data, the manufacturer can determine the relative sales values of different wholesale trades and various types of operation and thus can evaluate the relative importance of different kinds of outlets for his products. Such information is particularly valuable if the manufacturer is confronted with the necessity of choosing between alternative channels of distribution. A manufacturer, for example, who is deciding on whether to sell exclusively to chains or independents can determine the relative importance of these two types of operation in a particular line of trade. Similarly, data from the retail census can be used by the manufacturer and wholesaler in evaluating the relative importance, as channels of distribution, of different trades and types of operation.

Furthermore, the manufacturer and the wholesaler distributor can use the census data in evaluating the relative importance of retail stores rendering different kinds of services in various lines and areas. Thus, the proportions of credit sales and the numbers of retail stores selling for credit will indicate the relative importance of cash versus credit stores as channels of distribution. These credit data will also suggest the extent of the financial assistance necessary to carry receivables which the distributor may be called upon to extend. Likewise the information on inventories may be used to indicate to the distributor the amount of stock considered necessary by stores in different lines. Shifts in the volume of business done by firms which operate in different ways can also indicate increasing or decreasing acceptance by customers of different services and thus can guide the decision as to which types of stores, as channels of distribution, are likely to offer the most assured prospects for future growth.

The various censuses, over the period of years, moreover, indicate trends, as well as relative position at a given time. Thus management decisions can be based both on projections of past trends and on static relative position. Data on relative changes in sales in specific kinds of business, in size of stores, in location as between rural areas, small towns, and large cities, and in types of operation indicate trends which can be very valuable to distributors in formulating policies in regard to trade channels.

Another volume of the Census of Business entitled *Distribution of Manufacturers' Sales* (Volume V in the 1939 Census) is exceedingly valuable to manufacturers and others, in connection with the problem of a scientific selection of channels of distribution. This report contains statistics on the sales channels used by manufacturers in disposing of their products. It presents information, by industries, on the initial flow of goods from plants to users and consumers, showing the amounts sold through different channels of distribution.

Standards for Management

In setting up standards of performance for use in controlling operations, business management can use the statistics hitherto described in many ways. These standards can be used by the individual concern for comparing the results of its own operations with trade averages. Those differences between trade averages and the firm's operating results which may be unfavorable can be analyzed to discover their cause. Active measures can then be taken to adjust future policies and operations.

A manufacturer can determine that his own sales amount to a certain percentage of national retail sales of the types of retail stores which constitute his principal retail outlets. State by state comparison of the percentage for that state will reveal strong or weak points. Or he may determine the percentage which his sales, classified by various outlets, bear to the total sales of these outlets nationally. In other words he can measure his market penetration. Again, comparison of these relationships for smaller areas may suggest that in certain areas outlets of one kind are strong, in others weak, and so on.

The sales data can be used for setting up standards of outturn per employee and average sales per store. Data on inventories, receivables, and other credit data can likewise be used. The wholesale census statistics on operating costs can be used for standards of comparison with the individual wholesaler's own costs. Current sales indexes furnish standards by which the individual businessman can determine whether or not the sales trends in his own business are favorable as compared with the trends in his trade in his geographic area.

Other Uses

Advertising agencies, as well as others concerned with the use of advertising, have found the statistics on the wholesale, retail, and service trades to be a particularly valuable marketing tool. Data on location of stores and sales volume are used in the apportionment of the advertising budget and in the choice of advertising media so as to relate advertising effort to potential markets. Many studies made by advertising agencies on nature and location of probable customers are based on population data (Chapter 12, pp. 353 ff.) as well as on those described in this chapter. There are also many studies of the effectiveness of specific media in reaching specific markets. Finally, advertising agencies, in connection with their research and survey work, use the census statistics to set up a representative sample of stores or other units to be surveyed. Since the census shows the pattern of the "universe" to be surveyed, the size and character of the sample can be more accurately established.

The special tabulations of census-tract data which have been made by the Census Bureau (in Los Angeles County, for example) have been used to determine shifts in retail trade within a metropolitan market, as between the central business district and outlying shopping centers. Such data are particularly valuable to retailers in assessing long-term changes in consumer purchasing habits and in dealing with the resulting problems of store location.

These special tabulations of the census data, which the Census Bureau may undertake to provide to business firms on a reimbursable basis, have a very important marketing significance. This use of census data, although not widely known as yet, has promise of making a significant contribution to the analysis of the marketing problems of individual companies.

CHAPTER 7

INTERNATIONAL TRADE AND PAYMENTS

J. EDWARD ELY, *Bureau of the Census*

AND

AUGUST MAFFRY, *Bureau of Foreign and Domestic Commerce*
Department of Commerce

Statistics of foreign trade or of the movement of goods into or out of a country are one of the commonest types of statistics used in market analysis. Since all governments have always had a major interest in obtaining information on the foreign trade of their countries, both for their own use in determining and administering policy and for the use of businessmen, import and export statistics have been recorded for longer periods and in greater detail than perhaps any other type of statistics of interest to business.

The statistics of the United States foreign trade provide a very complete picture of imports and exports. These statistics are compiled in the first instance by the Department of Commerce from information on each import and export shipment received from collectors of customs at seaports, border points along the Canadian and Mexican borders, and at ports of entry and commercial airfields throughout the United States. Similar statistics on imports and exports are compiled in other countries.

Statistics of foreign trade are supplemented in the United States (and in many other countries, although not in all) by the directly related statistics of shipping and by balance-of-payments statistics. The former show in tonnage terms by what method of transportation goods are brought into or taken out of the country. The latter show all types of commercial and financial dealings between the United States and foreign countries, including not only trade in merchandise, but also purchases and sales of services, imports and exports of gold and silver, and movements of capital.

The character of these international statistics, the forms in which they are available, the agencies from which they may be obtained, and the ways in which they may be applied to business problems are discussed in detail in the sections which follow.

UNITED STATES FOREIGN TRADE STATISTICS

Scope and Coverage. United States export statistics are of great use to business in the interpretation of business activity. The statistics on exports include all commercial shipments of merchandise from continental United States or from any of the territories and possessions of the United States to a foreign country and, beginning with March 1941, include exports made under the Lend-Lease program.

Statistics on exports of gold and silver are presented separately from the statistics on merchandise exports. Shipments between continental United States and its territories and possessions and in-transit shipments of merchandise moving through the United States from one foreign country to another are similarly presented separately, rather than included in the export statistics proper.

The export figures, in addition, do not include certain relatively unimportant types of shipments out of the country, such as merchandise shipped out of the country temporarily or being returned to foreign countries after having entered the United States temporarily (exhibition goods, race horses, machinery exported for repairs, etc.); bunker coal and oil and other supplies laden on vessels engaged in foreign trade (a separate report on bunker coal and oil is provided); baggage of persons traveling abroad; and certain types of shipments having little or no commercial value or having only small value in relation to the difficulty involved in collecting statistics on them (shipments valued at less than $10 other than by common carrier, parcel post shipments valued at less than $25, etc.). A full definition of what United States export (and import) statistics include and exclude will be found in the foreword to *Foreign Commerce and Navigation of the United States*, the annual publication of the Department of Commerce containing detailed and summary statistics on United States foreign trade.

The principal part of export statistics is that covering shipment of goods which were produced within the United States. Statistics on such exports are generally labeled "Exports of Domestic Merchandise" or "Exports of United States Merchandise" (in abbreviated form "Domestic Exports"). The other type of export which is included in export statistics is exports of merchandise which originated in a foreign country and which was imported into the United States to be consumed here. For any number of reasons these goods may be reexported from the United States in the same condition in which they were imported. Tabulations of information on such reexports are generally labeled "Exports of Foreign Merchandise" or in abbreviated form "Reexports" (sometimes inaccurately referred to as "foreign exports"). Information on domestic exports is sometimes combined with information on reexports to give a total which is generally labeled "Exports (including Reexports)." The volume of reexports is very small in comparison to the volume of exports of domestic merchandise. In 1941 the value of reexports was only 2.8 percent of the total value of exports including reexports.

Statistics on both domestic exports and reexports may be further classified as exports under the Lend-Lease program (Lend-Lease exports) and non-lend-lease (commercial or "cash" exports). Information segregating Lend-Lease and other exports was in general withheld from publication during the war period, although restrictions on publication have now been removed.

United States import statistics include information on all merchandise entering the United States or its territories and possessions from a foreign country which are defined as imports by the Bureau of Customs (Treasury Department) and the Department of Commerce. Some of the types of shipments reaching the United States which are not included in the import statistics are merchandise which enters the country intransit to another foreign country, shipments to continental United States from its territories and possessions, merchandise entering a foreign trade zone, United States merchandise returned from foreign countries, gold and silver, and certain types of shipments having little or no commercial value.

Import statistics are of two general types, general imports and imports for consumption. General import statistics provide information on the total of goods arriving in the country and either (1) entering consumption channels immediately on arrival (most merchandise is entered in this fashion) or (2) being entered into a bonded customs storage warehouse. Imports for consumption, on the other hand, include information on the total of goods entering consumption channels, either (1) immediately upon arrival in the country (the most common method) or (2) on withdrawal from bonded customs storage warehouses. Through 1933 the Department of Commerce presented practically all of its import statistics in the form of general imports. Starting in 1934 most import statistics were presented in the form of imports for consumption. During the war period the Department of Commerce produced the figures on both bases for the use of government agencies, and it is likely that this practice will be continued.

Nondutiable commodities rarely, if ever, enter a bonded storage warehouse and the general-import and import-for-consumption figures for these commodities will, therefore, normally be the same. Since dutiable commodities frequently enter bonded storage warehouses at the time of arrival in the country and may stay there as long as three years, the general-import and import-for-consumption figures for these commodities for any particular period will differ to the extent that the quantity of imported merchandise entered into bonded storage warehouses is greater or less than the amount of merchandise withdrawn from bonded storage warehouses.

Intransit statistics presented by the Department of Commerce covering merchandise en route between one foreign country and another through the United States differ from the reexports described above in that there is no intention when the goods enter the country that they will remain in the United States. The intransit statistics do not include merchandise which enters and leaves a United States seaport on the same vessel and is not unladen from the vessel while it is in port.

The statistics on shipments between continental United States and its territories and possessions have, in general, the same coverage of types of shipments as that described above for United States export statistics.

United States export shipments are measured in terms of f.a.s. (free alongside ship) valuation at the point of shipment out of the United States; imports into the United States are measured in terms of the value at the principal foreign market. The value of both exports and imports includes cost of freight to seaboard.

Imports and exports are also measured in terms of the usual unit of quantity for each individual commodity—gallons, pounds, bales, number of machines, etc. As a result of the war, United States import and export shipments are also, since January 1943, being measured in terms of gross shipping weight. Because of its demonstrated usefulness, this additional unit of measurement will undoubtedly be continued.

United States import shipments are credited to the country of first origin of the commodities rather than the country of immediate shipment. Export shipments are credited to the country of ultimate destination rather than to the country in which discharged if other than country of ultimate destination.

Export shipments from the United States are credited to the United States customs district from which the carrying vessels are cleared. United States import shipments are credited to the customs district through which they enter customs. The customs districts in which imported goods enter customs may not be the same customs district as that in which the goods first arrived in the United States. Commodities may be transported in customs bond from a seaport in the United States to an interior customs district. The import is then credited to the interior customs district in which the duty is paid and the goods are "entered."

In addition to being divided into commodities of domestic or foreign origin, export shipments from the United States were classified prior to the war into approximately 1,400 commodity classifications, i.e., "cork insulation," "road rollers," "acetic acid." In order to meet war-time needs, the commodity classifications were greatly expanded to approximately 3,500, but it is likely that in the months ahead the number will be reduced considerably, principally in the military equipment categories (ammunition, firearms, etc.). The commodity schedule provides for broad classifications into 11 major commodity groups (animal products, edible; animal products, inedible; vegetable products, inedible; vegetable products and beverages; machinery and vehicles; chemicals, etc.) and into approximately 100 subgroups (rubber and manufactures, electrical machinery and apparatus, medicinal and pharmaceutical preparations, etc.). A further cross classification is provided in which the commodities are classified in 10 "economic classes" by degree of manufacture and by agricultural or nonagricultural source (crude materials of agricultural origin, crude materials of nonagricultural origin, semimanufactures of agricultural origin, semimanufactures of nonagricultural origin, etc.). The classifications of commodities into hundreds of detailed classifications, the approximately 100 subgroups, the 11 major groups, and the 10 economic classes have been made on the basis of the materials of which the articles are made, the use for which they are intended, and the extent of their refinement for manufacture. The bases on which the classifications are made vary with the commodities being classified and with the purposes for which the statistics are expected to be used.

The classifications of commodities used for United States export statistics are shown in *Schedule B, Statistical Classification of Domestic and Foreign Commodities Exported from the United States*. When the classifications are revised, usually at the beginning of each calendar year, this publication is reissued. The January 1, 1944, edition appeared for the first time in two parts: Part I, an alphabetic arrangement of the names of some 40,000 individual products for the use of shippers in locating the correct Schedule B commodity code numbers, and Part II, for persons using export statistics, showing the names of the 3,500 Schedule B commodity classifications and a list of the individual products included in each classification. This listing of the approximately 40,000 products included in the 3,500 classifications for the first time provides a clear definition of what the export commodity classifications represent.

Import statistics are classified into some 5,000 individual products as well as 11 major groups, approximately 100 subgroups, and 10 "economic classes" shown in *Schedule A, Statistical Classification of Imports into the United States*. The criteria used in setting up the classifications are similar to those outlined above for exports, except that the determining factor in most of the detailed classifications is to provide information for each commodity designated by the Tariff Act of 1930 and by the reciprocal trade agreements in force at the time the statistics are compiled. Changes in classification are incorporated in Schedule A when the publication is reissued, usually every two years.

Sources of Information. Many United States Government agencies at some time or other use United States foreign trade statistics and make them available in some form to the public. The principal agencies doing so on a regular basis are as follows:

Foreign trade statistics on each type of foreign trade shipment described above are prepared in the first instance both in detailed and summary form by the Bureau of the Census, Department of Commerce. The statistics are often rearranged, interpreted, and republished by other agencies of the Government in connection with their own particular field of work.

The Bureau of Foreign and Domestic Commerce, Department of Commerce, has as its primary responsibility the supplying of information on markets, production, and sources of supply of particular products or groups of products. In accordance with this responsibility to business, the Bureau of Foreign and Domestic Commerce recompiles and publishes much foreign trade information in a form suitable for this purpose.

The Department of Agriculture, as an agency primarily interested in statistics of agricultural production, markets, stocks, etc., recompiles foreign trade information and relates the data to other types of information. Such compilations are usually made on a crop-year basis and for that reason are particularly valuable to persons interested in agricultural products.

The Bureau of Mines, Department of Interior, has special responsibilities in regard to information on mineral production, stocks, etc. It, accordingly, relates foreign trade figures to other figures on the domestic production and utilization of mineral products and to similar statistics of other countries.

The United States Tariff Commission has as its primary responsibility the supplying of information on foreign trade, foreign production and costs, and other similar information related to tariff problems. In accordance with these functions it provides numerous special

EXHIBIT 1

16

MONTHLY SUMMARY OF FOREIGN COMMERCE

NO. 3.— EXPORTS OF DOMESTIC MERCHANDISE, BY ARTICLES — Continued

Group 7—Continued

INDUSTRIAL MACHINERY—Continued
Construction and conveying machinery—Continued

Articles	December 1941 Quantity	December 1941 Dollars	Twelve months ending December 1941 Quantity	Twelve months ending December 1941 Dollars
Self-propelled graders...no.	59	249,017	685	2,683,376
Pull or push type graders...no.	16	13,492	355	498,938
Other graders...no.	14	36,887	199	513,164
Scrapers (self loading)...no.	71	187,118	951	3,047,921
Bulldozers, angledozers, trailbuilders, brush cutters, and similar equipment...no.	132	140,156	1,343	1,601,191
Other road machinery and parts...		644,996		4,853,155
Other construction equipment and parts...no.		517,833		2,045,082
Cranes with swinging booms...no.	41	255,113	622	2,463,794
Other cranes...no.	78	296,577	501	2,298,327
Hoists...no.	885	232,554	6,962	1,546,511
Derricks, except mining...no.	5	18,007	45	96,813
Elevators, freight and passenger...no.	54	106,841	746	1,204,285
Conveyors, bucket, chain, or belt...no.	71	31,830	2,217	391,185
Other conveying equipment and parts...		630,067		4,862,772
Mining, well, and pumping machinery...		6,765,969		50,560,197
Mining and quarrying machinery:				
Coal cutters...no.	4	8,885	30	107,022
Rock drills...no.	677	119,351	7,130	1,675,294
Mine hoists and derricks...no.	47	23,897	396	255,070
Ore and rock crushing and sorting machinery and parts...		1,134,157		6,215,601
Concentrating and smelting machinery and parts...		121,282		1,174,765
Other mining and quarrying machinery and parts...		767,101		7,464,137
Well and refinery machinery:				
Petroleum and gas well-drilling apparatus and parts...		2,476,737		18,517,205
Other petroleum well and refining machinery and parts...		511,704		3,926,362
Other well-drilling apparatus and parts...		94,800		540,015
Pumping equipment:				
Centrifugal pumps...no.	1,991	389,664	15,298	2,593,368
Rotary pumps...no.	857	129,869	4,763	720,492

Articles	December 1941 Quantity	December 1941 Dollars	Twelve months ending December 1941 Quantity	Twelve months ending December 1941 Dollars
INDUSTRIAL MACHINERY—Continued				
Textile, sewing, and shoe machinery—Con.				
Textile machinery—Continued				
Other knitting machines and parts...		114,336	170,443	5,110,917
Winders and parts...		195,700	33,770	3,314,556
Carding and other preparing, spinning and twisting machinery and parts:				
Cotton...no.		233,168		2,825,317
Wool...no.		17,520		817,000
Other, including silk-throwing machinery and parts...		110,383		83,362,963
Looms and parts:				
Cotton...no.	179	67,199	5,581	582,455
Other...no.	128	58,529	818	442,717
Parts of looms...no.		83,143		727,693
Braiding and insulating machines and parts...		14,829		220,788
Beaming, warping, and slashing machinery and parts...		18,445		93,670
Dyeing and finishing machines and parts...		56,002		276,181
Other textile machinery and parts...		486,973		4,646,259
Sewing machines:				
For domestic use...no.	26,969	654,006	170,443	5,110,917
For factory or industrial use...no.	1,081	238,940	33,770	3,314,556
Sewing machine parts...		452,663		2,825,317
Shoe machinery and parts...		60,092		817,000
Other industrial machinery...		9,686,101		83,362,963
Cigarette and cigar making, and other tobacco machinery and parts...		97,815		632,702
Cream separators valued $50 or over...no.	140	16,027	2,943	230,442
Other dairy equipment and parts:				
for commercial use...		112,840		1,367,636
Bakery machinery and parts...		87,877		544,326
Flour-mill and gristmill machinery and parts...		23,688		231,299
Rice-mill machinery...		1,884		74,778
Sugar-mill machinery:				
Cane mills...no.	244	60,789	1,806	375,434
Other sugar-mill machinery and parts...no.		316,724		2,560,604
Paper and pulp mill machinery and parts...		375,571		2,113,860

EXHIBIT 2

No. 4.—DOMESTIC EXPORTS, 1941—GROUP 7—MACHINERY AND VEHICLES

COUNTRY	Motor trucks, busses, and chassis (new)—Continued						7905. Bus chassis		7906. Motor trucks, busses, and chassis (second-hand)		Passenger cars and chassis (new)			
	7903. Over 1½, not over 2½ tons		7904.3. Diesel and semi-Diesel (injection type) Over 2½ tons		7904.5. Gasoline (carburetor type) Over 2½ tons						7907. Not over $850		7908. Over $850, not over $1,200	
	Number	Dollars	Number	Dollars	Number	Dollars	Number	Dollars	Number	Dollars	Number	Dollars	Number	Dollars
TOTAL	23,699	32,188,992	1,207	4,121,164	15,754	39,673,289	145	185,524	752	458,390	62,285	38,855,637	16,387	15,625,041
Finland	48	52,937	14	26,012	86	159,788								
Gibraltar													1	902
Greece	50	49,389												
Iceland	50	44,000			4	13,935					8	5,540	216	191,554
Ireland											24	13,800		
Portugal	135	224,689	113	222,339	77	216,441	11	11,210			15	10,037	5	4,626
Spain											6	4,562	8	8,155
Sweden	44	41,838												
Switzerland	48	60,343									24	7,638		
U.S.S.R. (Russia)	2,018	4,845,987	2	15,961							3	2,024	200	193,111
United Kingdom	2,196	3,704,859	534	1,777,831	11	119,468					44	29,797	13	11,870
Canada	341	621,562	58	516,528	8,102	20,207,528	11	29,430	58	72,775	1,823	1,126,794	494	468,616
British Honduras	5	4,742			9	19,620					8	6,376	2	2,221
Costa Rica	4	5,688			3	7,684					139	98,983	62	57,985
El Salvador	3	2,594	11	16,301	3	5,709					86	70,988	71	72,346
Guatemala	26	33,190			9	12,307			1	1,000	104	75,124	91	90,072
Honduras	5	4,401	1	1,416	14	14,820			2	21,560	30	21,489	22	23,135
Nicaragua	8	10,536	1	11,012	19	42,467			13	56,724	71	50,739	35	34,213
Panama Canal Zone	48	85,874	6	113,200	487	2,063,299	1	757	7	5,369	502	348,687	187	183,358
Panama, Republic of	125	138,190			139	1,216,204					803	581,571	248	236,098
Mexico	1,669	1,861,481	8	35,428	728	921,884	73	98,770	427	159,352	5,184	3,480,873	3,290	3,179,491
Newfoundland and Labrador	65	107,202	1	1,100	89	276,804			8	2,317	421	297,431	35	34,070
Bermuda	2	3,612			35	104,207			1	250	4	604		
Jamaica	6	9,082			6	6,864					2	1,746	5	4,677
Trinidad and Tobago	1	1,343			7	53,746					16	9,995	12	11,350
Other British West Indies	8	10,245			11	47,428	1	625	16	300	28	19,136	14	13,845
Cuba	78	75,887	30	45,238	2	49,020			25	7,176	1,580	1,009,742	785	728,428
Curacao (N.W.I.)	19	17,878			10	12,090					446	312,129	105	98,364
Dominican Republic	27	23,552			7	14,976			1	400	184	123,109	31	32,749
French West Indies	2	1,149				17,604			2	1,000	4	3,080		
Haiti	18	21,471	3	9,861							86	64,724	43	41,351
Argentina	589	428,913	11	42,343	65	122,226	2	1,692	1	1,600	7,971	4,660,955	576	554,363
Bolivia	138	174,069			38	56,360			96	50,593	50	37,454	94	95,129
Brazil	468	600,010	115	246,197	243	440,778	1	1,400			7,160	4,328,711	1,023	1,003,781
Chile	526	460,718	1	4,192	47	96,525	28	21,832	5	4,533	1,776	1,208,556	540	526,372

reports on individual commodities or groups of commodities which include information on United States exports and imports.

Availability of Statistics. Prior to World War II, information on exports and imports was released to the public as soon as compiled. Immediately after the attack on Pearl Harbor publication of foreign trade statistics by the Government ceased, except for the grand total value of all exports and the grand total value of all imports. This rigid restriction on publication has now been rescinded and figures on foreign trade are being released on a current basis. It is likely that the prewar pattern of publications described below will be resumed as soon as postwar conditions permit.

Prior to the war, statistics on imports and exports were published by the Department of Commerce and other agencies in many different forms. The most common type of import and export information was information on the total quantity and total value of the individual commodities exported and imported in a particular month or a particular year. (Exhibit 1).

The next most common type of information on United States foreign trade was that showing the total imports and exports of individual commodities together with detail showing country of origin for imports or country of ultimate destination for exports (Exhibits 2 and 3). Additional information on the foreign trade of the United States, which was made available usually on an annual basis, was that showing figures on the total value of United States imports from and exports to each foreign country and further details on the commodities entering into the trade (Exhibit 4).

Material showing both commodity and country detail was available monthly in the form of hundreds of individual releases covering certain related groups of commodities. Similar figures on an annual basis appeared in the annual volume of *Foreign Commerce and Navigation of the United States*, published by the Department of Commerce.

Prior to the war, tables showing for each individual country the individual commodities imported into the United States or exported from the United States were less in demand. Such information was not ordinarily published on a monthly basis, although the information was available upon request. Information showing the total exports from the United States or imports into the United States to or from an individual country appeared in the annual publication *Foreign Commerce and Navigation of the United States* in alternate even-numbered years.

Statistics on imports and exports by customs districts through which the goods were imported or exported were in less demand prior to

EXHIBIT 3

6   No. 1.—IMPORTS FOR CONSUMPTION, 1941—SELECTED SUB-GROUP TOTALS

COUNTRY	Meat products, 0018.0-0035.5		Dairy products, 0037.0-0046.99	Fish and fish products, 0047.0-0087.9		Hides and skins, raw (except furs), 0201.0-0299.9	Leather, 0300.1-0345.9	Leather manufactures, 0350.0-0699.99	Furs, undressed, 0700.0-0728.5	Furs, dressed, and manufactures of, 0730.0-0759.9	Grains and preparations, 1020.0-109.26	Vegetables and preparations, 1191.1-125.90	Fruits and preparations, 1280.0-133.93
	Pounds	Dollars	Dollars	Pounds	Dollars	Dollars	Dollars	Dollars	Dollars	Dollars	Dollars	Dollars	Dollars
AFRICA													
Belgian Congo						75,406			13,546				
British East Africa		56,293				2,817,215	1,147	9	133,872				
Union of South Africa	100,457			2,889,336	664,776	4,020,964			11,261,332	523	210		
Other British South Africa						165,996							
Gold Coast												9	
Nigeria						2,539,529			9,803			369	
Other British West Africa		29,664				326			18,503				
Egypt	39,782					230,139	4,746	16	3,557				
Ethiopia			945			74,712			7,532				
Other French Africa						2,847							
Italian Africa													
Liberia									9,554				
Morocco	91,943					6,287	242		104			22,879	3,851
Mozambique		91,200				1,430							
Other Portuguese Africa				5,271	754	580			1,736				
Canary Islands													

COUNTRY	Nuts, 1350.0-138.14	Vegetable oils and fats, edible, 1620.0-1428.9	Cocoa, coffee, and tea, 1501.3-1521.0	Spices, 1523.1-155.59	Sugar and related products, 1570.0-1654.8	Beverages, 1711.0-177.90	Rubber and manufactures, 2011.0-2098.9	Gums, resins, balsams, n.e.s., 2102.0-2198.3	Drugs, herbs, leaves, roots, etc., 2201.0-222.40	Oil seeds, 2231.0-2240.7	Vegetable oils and fats, expressed or extracted, 2241.0-226.28	Vegetable oils and essential or distilled, 2270.1-229.58	Dyeing and tanning materials, 2302.0-2345.9
	Dollars	Dollars	Dollars	Pounds	Dollars	Dollars	Dollars	Dollars	Dollars	Dollars	Dollars	Dollars	Dollars
Calculated duty	$2,628,844	$1,711,075	$4,330	$961,666	$63,299,653	$29,952,728	$168,904	$113,703	$779,143	$12,536,365	$462,707	$440,853	$1,235,794
TOTAL	18,796,616	4,553,239	245,655,107	19,903,707	178,500,701	50,819,884	424,504,123	25,762,326	14,576,541	36,610,793	50,407,738	10,139,328	11,633,147
Europe	1,076,579	1,217,170	18,289	1,795,928	38,302,848	674,167	2,666,458	446,874		4,821	388,760	2,171,899	65,392
North America	422,252	280,093	36,948,440	5,055,240	139,834,446	10,245,542	6,770,352	1,553,970		405,190	1,339,366	1,479,416	287,791
Northern	300	12,990	52,532	3,111	1,366,699	8,615,486	417,268	13,214	560,108	250,026	55,579	17,807	17,060
Southern and West Indies	421,952	267,103	36,895,908	5,052,129	138,467,747	1,630,056	1,201,395	6,757,138	983,862	155,164	1,283,787	1,461,609	270,731

the war and were not published except in the *Monthly Summary of Foreign Commerce*, issued by the Department of Commerce, and the only information which was included was the total value of exports

EXHIBIT 4

788   No. 6.—EXPORT TRADE WITH SOUTH AMERICA—CALENDAR YEARS 1939-40

COUNTRY AND ARTICLE	1939 Quantity	1939 Value	1940 Quantity	1940 Value
BRAZIL—Continued				
CHEMICALS AND RELATED PRODUCTS—Continued		*Dollars*		*Dollars*
Other industrial chemicals........lb.	3,363,054	124,930	5,395,313	300,745
Chemical pigments................lb.		206,206		359,114
Paste and semipaste paint colors in oil, putty and paste wood filler..lb.	120,261	21,953	103,668	23,337
Nitrocellulose (pyroxylin)........lb.	91,535	191,597	67,318	145,775
Lacquers.........................gal.				
Ready-mixed paints, stains, and enamels........................gal.	103,347	200,029	94,653	180,273
Varnishes........................gal.	12,272	21,485	14,548	25,636
Phosphatic fertilizer materials..ton.	5,138	71,198	13,605	289,029
Explosives, fuses, etc.............		27,710		206,235
Soap.............................lb.	283,819	34,534	229,075	31,831
Creams, perfumes, and other cosmetics		92,146		87,405
Manicuring preparations...........		23,031		9,613
Other chemicals and related products.		55,227		344,703
MISCELLANEOUS				
Cameras..........................no.	18,616	38,712	18,275	59,393
Motion-picture films, sensitized, not exposed....................lin.ft.	4,968,751	72,608	6,757,651	95,842
Exposed motion-picture films..lin.ft.	16,643,560	316,900	16,688,413	301,908
Other sensitized films, not exposed...........................no.				
Photographic paper..............doz.	1,458,561	239,384	2,096,081	290,439
Dry plates.......................doz.	81,279	34,100	107,697	52,190
Photographic and projection goods.lb.	64,564	55,162	145,530	86,210
Other photographic and projection goods		66,969		140,955
Optical goods....................		88,712		162,684
Dental equipment and supplies.....		265,567		329,046
Other scientific and professional instruments, apparatus, and supplies		176,003		368,059
Musical instruments..............		54,684		74,127
Miscellaneous office supplies......		266,651		397,566
Toys, athletic and sporting goods..		45,673		73,400
Firearms, ammunition, and fireworks..		222,743		246,582
Books, maps, pictures, and other printed matter....................		389,234		247,670
Clocks and watches...............		50,756		121,919
Jewelry..........................		119,863		273,996
Fire-fighting equipment, except automotive fire engines..........no.	49,327	24,000	15,156	35,712
Brushes.........................doz.		28,461		24,178
Notions, cheap novelties, and specialties				
Household and personal effects.....		23,956		67,113
All other articles.................		72,700		103,450
		101,746		223,304

COUNTRY AND ARTICLE	1939 Quantity	1939 Value	1940 Quantity	1940 Value
CHILE—Continued				
VEGETABLE PRODUCTS, INEDIBLE—Continued		*Dollars*		*Dollars*
Rubber gloves and mittens...doz.pr.	1,285	4,389	2,387	10,279
Druggists' rubber sundries.........		5,590		25,529
Clothing of rubber or or of rubberized cloth.........................doz.	4,854	7,501	28,695	24,403
Rubber balloons.................gr.	12,310	-6,749	4,424	4,191
Rubber toys and balls.............		4,350		9,032
Rubber tire casings, automobile..no.	37,232	478,332	36,718	437,378
Other tubes and casings..........no.	35,197	73,041	29,801	61,845
Tire sundries and repair materials.........................lb.	17,296	5,982	16,093	6,524
Rubber and friction tape.......lb.	24,153	8,217	60,093	15,695
Rubber belts and belting.......lb.	407,371	148,698	625,278	250,391
Rubber hose and tubing.........lb.	290,894	91,187	428,685	133,488
Rubber packing.................lb.	42,657	10,597	57,787	15,239
Other rubber and manufactures..lb.		29,896		60,911
Gum rosin.......................bbl.	7,112	78,801	4,126	54,190
Wood rosin......................bbl.	5,223	53,679	6,132	59,548
Gum spirits of turpentine.......gal.	124,636	41,774	84,234	29,917
Pine oil........................gal.	42,908	*6,136	90,987	59,330
Other naval stores, gums, and resins.		3,821		28,063
Drugs, herbs, leaves, and roots, crude..........................lb.	33,015	10,698	63,557	23,033
Essential or distilled oils......lb.	3,971	7,829	13,276	48,905
Blended, compounded, or mixed perfume-flavor oils...................lb.	3,287	10,325	11,827	43,630
Vegetable dyeing and tanning extracts.......................lb.	191,613	18,410	149,777	19,982
Tobacco and manufactures.......lb.		10,383		12,969
Hops............................lb.	68,442	27,647	283,144	113,280
Other vegetable products, inedible.		14,070		41,818
TEXTILE FIBERS AND MANUFACTURES				
Raw cotton, except linters....lb.	6,264,697	646,783	5,485,920	608,249
Cotton rags, except paper stock..lb.	176,345	6,390	229,847	12,616
Cotton mill waste.............lb.	508,349	21,896	379,682	22,125
Cotton yarn for manufacturing..lb.	2,559,820	885,479	2,335,906	995,098
Cotton thread, twine, cordage, and rope.........................	99,076	33,447	231,473	219,566
Cotton cloth, duck, and tire fabric: Unbleached (gray) cloth:				
Cotton cloth (gray) cloth:.....sq.yd.				
Cotton duck...................sq.yd.	91,340	22,032	160,343	46,427
Cotton cloth (gray), medium and coarse yarn fabrics.......sq.yd.				
Finished cloth, bleached, dyed, printed, stiffened, or otherwise converted, and colored yarn fabrics:	6,209,713	331,598	5,403,486	364,942

and imports through individual customs districts each month. Annual figures providing information by customs districts were published in *Foreign Commerce and Navigation of the United States* showing for individual commodities the quantity and value exported through each customs district.

Statistics summarizing the total import and export picture in terms of broad commodity groupings or in terms of the type of commodity, such as whether or not it was a crude material, a crude foodstuff, manufactured foodstuff, a semimanufacture, or a finished manufacture, were supplied on a monthly and annual basis in the *Monthly Summary of Foreign Commerce* and *Foreign Commerce and Navigation of the United States.*

Statistics on merchandise moving intransit through the United States from one country to another were printed in *Foreign Commerce and Navigation of the United States* on an annual basis only.

Statistics on shipments between continental United States and its territories and possessions were printed in summary form without classification by commodity in each issue of the *Monthly Summary.* Detailed information on the commodities shipped on an annual basis appeared in the December issue of the *Monthly Summary.*

The *Statistical Abstract of the United States,* published annually by the Bureau of the Census, Department of Commerce, contains comparative summary statistics of United States foreign trade for extended periods beginning with the earliest official records.

In addition to the statistics described above, which were published on a regular basis, additional information on import and export intransit shipments and shipments between continental United States and its territories and possessions was available on request. Monthly information on imports and exports by Customs Districts showing commodity detail was not printed in the *Monthly Summary of Foreign Commerce* but was available on request. Similarly, figures on trade with individual countries and on shipments to and from the territories and possessions which were normally only published on an annual basis could be obtained on a monthly basis on request.

In addition to foreign trade statistics made available as such, figures on imports and exports were made available to the public in many ways by government agencies in connection with other figures on production, stocks, domestic markets, etc. Thus the Bureau of Foreign and Domestic Commerce published many releases on individual commodities in which figures on the domestic market, domestic production, etc., were compared with figures on exports and imports of the same products. Additional releases by the Bureau of Foreign and Domestic Commerce summarizing market conditions, production, etc., in individual countries contained United States export and import figures relating to the particular country. Some of these publications of the Bureau of Foreign and Domestic Commerce which are published on a regular basis are as follows:

Foreign Commerce Weekly contains frequent articles on various aspects of foreign trade.

Trend of United States Foreign Trade, a monthly publication summarizing general trends in foreign trade and trends in trade with individual countries and in individual products. Publication of this release was suspended during the war.

International Reference Service, a series of releases at irregular intervals covering, among other subjects, trade with individual countries in considerable detail. Publication of the releases in the International Reference Service series was resumed after a temporary suspension during the war period.

Summary of Foreign Trade of the United States is an annual publication of the Bureau of Foreign and Domestic Commerce summarizing United States foreign trade both in terms of trade in particular commodities and in terms of trade with individual countries and groups of countries.

The *Industrial Reference Service* is a series of publications released at irregular intervals containing information on particular commodities and industries.

Practically all releases of the Department of Agriculture containing statistical information on individual agricultural products included figures on exports and imports of these products. In addition, the Department of Agriculture follows a policy of compiling and publishing import and export statistics on a crop-year basis. The most important annual publication containing export and import figures is the annual publication, *Agricultural Statistics,* which contains a section of about one hundred pages on statistics of foreign trade on agricultural products on a crop-year basis. Additional tables in the volume contain import and export figures on particular agricultural products in addition to the information on production, prices, carry-over, etc. (Exhibit 5). The most important monthly publication of the United States Department of Agriculture containing foreign trade figures is *Foreign Crops and Markets,* published by the Office of Foreign Agricultural Relations. This publication contains statistics on monthly exports and imports of individual agricultural products compiled from Department of Commerce figures.

The Bureau of Mines of the Department of the Interior makes considerable use of United States import and export statistics in its releases on individual mineral industries. Most such releases are prepared on an annual basis and each of them covers a particular industry, such as *The Lead Industry, The Copper Industry, The Portland Cement Industry,* and *The Zinc Industry.* Such releases are later combined into chapters appearing in the *Minerals Yearbook.*

EXHIBIT 5

592   FOREIGN TRADE IN AGRICULTURAL PRODUCTS

TABLE 696.—*Imports (for consumption) of principal agricultural products into the United States, by countries of origin, 1933–34 to 1940–41*—Continued

Commodity imported and country of origin	Year beginning July—							
	1933–34	1934–35	1935–36	1936–37	1937–38	1938–39	1939–40	1940–41[1]
VEGETABLE PRODUCTS—continued	*1,000 pounds*	*1,000 pounds*	*1,000 pounds*	*1,000 pounds*	*1,000 pounds*	*1,000 pounds*	*1,000 pounds*	*1,000 pounds*
Coffee—Continued.								
British East Africa	8,488	18.370	21,743	19,760	17,311	24.609	17,289	13.768
Netherlands East Africa	11,748	28.418	13.982	45,768	35,095	9.075	6,790	17,344
Other countries	18,064	17,728	29,229	33,988	15,302	17,156	14,566	23,121
Total	1,598,107	1,552,027	1,853,138	1,760,814	1,734,137	1,965,250	2,043,773	2,534,621
Fibers:								
Cotton, raw:[19]	*Bales*	*Bales*	*Bales*	*Bales*	*Bales*	*Bales*	*Bales*	*Bales*
Egypt	101,952	78,393	67,641	80,528	45,899	49,557	69,874	66,690
British India[14]	27,167	24,973	49,010	94,997	47,250	47,285	84,105	119,242
China	21,583	3,604	25,487	49,145	20,315	30,012	0	0
Mexico	1,536	6,612	3,542	28,652	30,529	36,010	14,623	9,199
Peru	1,736	919	1,475	1,716	867	515	1,116	4,069
Brazil	0	218	7	7,547	3,229	468	3,332	2,451
Other countries	3,351	1,616	557	3,502	11,877	2,457	277	1,154
Total	157,325	116,335	147,719	266,087	159,966	166,304	173,327	202,805
Cotton, linters:[19][20]								
Union of Soviet Socialist Republics			[11]258	20,212	0	33,041	28,563	4,613
Other Europe			[11]741	1,156	21	0	0	0
Latin-American republics:								
Brazil			[11]9,455	19,772	3,991	4,833	16,719	199,118
Mexico			[11]5,584	11,585	13,784	10,297	16,562	18,226
Ecuador			[11]32	30	10	0	102	142
Argentina			[11]0	237	0	0	96	20,963
Peru			[11]0	18	0	1,214	2,708	3,215
Other Latin-American republics			[11]0	0	0	0	59	785
Total Latin-American republics			[11]15,071	31,642	17,785	16,344	36,246	242,449
Other countries			[11]0	395	0	0	0	0
Total			[11]16,070	53,405	17,806	49,385	64,809	247,062
Crin vegetal:[21]	*Tons*	*Tons*	*Tons*	*Tons*	*Tons*	*Tons*	*Tons*	*Tons*
Morocco	4,721	4,405	5,998	7,312	4,250	4,701	4,276	2,801
Other countries	5	25	179	0	5	20	18	0
Total	4,726	4,430	6,177	7,312	4,255	4,721	4,294	2,801

The United States Tariff Commission prepared many analytical studies on foreign trade containing information on United States imports and exports. A few of the more important releases of this type are:

Latin America as a Source of Strategic and Other Essential Materials, 1941.

Foreign Trade of Latin America, 1942.

The Mica Industry, 1938.

Silverware, 1940.

Italian Commercial Policy and Foreign Trade, 1922–1940.

FOREIGN COUNTRY TRADE STATISTICS

Scope and Coverage. Statistics of foreign trade for countries other than the United States are available for about 170 countries and political subdivisions as listed below. For those accustomed to think in terms of 60-odd sovereign nations the number will seem large until it is observed that it includes not only these, but also their colonies, dependencies, and mandates. Thus, for example, there are available not only data on the exports and imports of Portugal, but also of Angola (Portuguese West Africa), Macau (Portuguese colony in China), and Timor (Portuguese possession in the East Indies), and not only of the United Kingdom, but also of Aden, Kenya, Newfoundland, Sarawak, Trans-Jordan, and Zanzibar (British colonies and protectorates in various parts of the world). All of this means that statistics of foreign trade are one of the commonest types of statistical information obtainable regarding any part of the world as well as the type of data available often for the longest period of time.

It should not be supposed that the trade statistics of foreign countries are strictly comparable with each other or with those of the United States. It is true that they all consist of data on exports and imports of tangible things, but here the similarity stops. The trade statistics of some countries are widely inclusive and cover practically all goods entering or leaving a country regardless of how or by whom shipped. Others omit trade which can be recorded only with difficulty, such as parcel post shipments, or which involves complicated statistical distinctions, such as reexports of goods previously imported. Smuggled goods naturally escape recording altogether, and, where smuggling is extensive, the statistics of a country's foreign trade may be for this reason seriously deficient.

The trade statistics of some countries are available in continuous series for extended periods so that studies of long-run trends are possible. For instance, foreign trade statistics for the United States have been compiled since 1791, for the United Kingdom since 1701, for France since 1831, for Sweden since 1861, for Japan since 1868, and for Germany since 1872. Data for other countries, either because of their brief political existence or for other reasons, may cover only short periods of time. Sometimes the continuity of foreign trade statistics is interrupted by civil or international war, as the Spanish Civil War of 1936–1939 or World War II as affecting China.

In the matter of timeliness, the trade statistics for some countries are published in some form very soon after the period to which they apply. Data for others appear only after a considerable lapse of time,

Foreign Countries for Which Foreign Trade Data Are Available

British Countries and Possessions

Aden
Anglo-Egyptian Sudan
Australia
Bahamas
Bahrein Islands *
Barbados
Bermuda
British Guiana
British Honduras
British India
British Malaya
British North Borneo †
Brunei *
Burma
Canada
Ceylon
Cook Islands
Cyprus
Eire
Falkland Islands
Fiji Islands
Gambia
Gilbert and Ellice Islands
Gold Coast
Hong Kong
Jamaica
Kenya and Uganda
Leeward Islands:
  Antigua †
  Montserrat †
  St. Kitts and Nevis †
  Virgin Islands, British †
Malta

Mauritius †
Nauru
Newfoundland and Labrador
New Guinea †
New Hebrides
New Zealand
Nigeria
Niue Island
Norfolk †
Nyasaland
Palestine
Papua †
Rhodesia, Northern
Rhodesia, Southern
St. Helena and dependencies *
Samoa, Western
Sarawak †
Seychelles Islands
Sierra Leone
Solomon Islands
Somaliland, British
South-West Africa, Territory of
Tanganyika
Tonga or Friendly Islands
Trinidad and Tobago
Union of South Africa
United Kingdom
Windward Islands:
  Grenada
  St. Lucia
  St. Vincent
Zanzibar

Other European Countries and Possessions

Albania
Algeria
Angola
Austria
Belgian Congo
Belgium and Luxemburg
Bulgaria
Cameroons (French Mandate)
Cape Verde Islands
Corsica †
Curaçao (Netherlands West Indies)
Czechoslovakia

Dahomey (French)
Denmark
Estonia
Faros Islands
Finland
France
French Equatorial Africa
French Guiana
French Guinea
French India †
French Indo-China
French Morocco

Other European Countries and Possessions (Continued)

French Oceania
French Somaliland
French West Africa
Germany
Greece
Guadeloupe
Hungary
Iceland
Italian East Africa
Italy
Ivory Coast (French)
Latvia
Libya
Lithuania
Macau †
Madagascar
Martinique
Mozambique
Netherlands
Netherlands Indies
New Caledonia
Niger (French)

Norway
Poland
Portugal
Portuguese Guinea
Portuguese India †
Portuguese Timor †
Principe and St. Thomas Islands †
Reunion †
Rumania
St. Pierre and Miquelon
Spain
Spanish Morocco †
Surinam
Sweden
Switzerland
Syria and Lebanon (French mandate)
Togoland (French mandate)
Tunisia
Turkey
Union of Soviet Socialist Republics
Yugoslavia

Other African Countries

Egypt
Ethiopia †

Liberia
Anglo-Egyptian Sudan

Other Asiatic Countries

Afghanistan
Arabian Peninsula States
China
Chosen (Korea)
Iran
Iraq

Japan
Japanese Mandated Islands
Manchoukuo—includes Kwantung
Philippine Islands
Taiwan (Formosa)
Thailand (Siam)

Latin American Republics

Argentina
Bolivia
Brazil
Chile
Colombia
Costa Rica
Cuba
Dominican Republic
Ecuador
Guatemala

Haiti
Honduras
Mexico
Nicaragua
Panama
Paraguay
Peru
Salvador
Uruguay
Venezuela

* Only a negligible amount of information is available.
† Fragmentary data only are available.

the interval in all countries varying with the character and detail of the information involved. With respect to quality, it should be emphasized that the foreign trade data of all countries are only more or less accurate approximations and must not be considered as having the precision of accounting records. But in some countries better methods of collecting the original data and better methods of compiling and verifying the statistics result in more dependable figures. Adequacy of commodity classification is itself one of the most important elements in quality.

Foreign trade statistics may be compiled in greater or lesser detail, depending upon the character of the trade involved, upon the need for detail by business and other users, and upon such practical considerations as the number of persons and the amount of public money available for the work. Consider, for example, statistics of imports of soap into Latin American countries. The import statistics of Haiti, Nicaragua, and Paraguay show just "Soap," i.e., all kinds of soap lumped together. By contrast, Mexican import statistics show eleven separate classes of soap as follows:

1. Soap, toilet or bath, aromatic or perfumed.
2. Soap, toilet or bath, neither aromatic nor perfumed.
3. Soap, solely for veterinary use, neither aromatic nor perfumed.
4. Soap, solely for veterinary use, aromatic or perfumed.
5. Soap, medicated, even if perfumed.
6. Soap, washing or scouring, neither aromatic nor perfumed.
7. Soap for scouring fibers and preparing cloth, in bars weighing over 2 kilograms.
8. Sapolio, aromatic or perfumed.
9. Sapolio, neither aromatic nor perfumed.
10. Soap in flakes or powder, neither aromatic nor perfumed.
11. Soap, liquid, neither aromatic nor perfumed.

The amount of detail on imports of soap into other Latin American countries varies between the two extremes cited above.

Exports from foreign countries are generally reported on an f.a.s. basis (or f.o.b. the frontier) and imports into foreign countries—unlike imports into the United States—are based on c.i.f. (cost, insurance, freight) values. However, export values are sometimes f.o.b. the inland port of shipment, and arbitrary valuations of both exports and imports which may differ considerably from commercial values are common. The units of quantity used in foreign country trade statistics are as diverse as national systems of measurement. Weights may be net or gross, i.e., exclusive or inclusive of the weight of wrappings and containers.

These differences mean, of course, that the trade statistics of different countries are difficult to compare or add. Comparisons and summations are easiest for simple commodities such as coal, wheat, flour, and sugar and are especially difficult for complex manufactured products, such as machinery of various types. Even for these latter, however, useful data for broad groups of items may be put together by those who know the statistics.

Sources of Information. The primary sources of information on the exports and imports of foreign countries are the official publications of these countries and, for unpublished data, the official records of the government agencies responsible for the collection and tabulation of foreign trade statistics. Since these primary sources are not generally accessible to business consumers in the United States or, if accessible, are not readily usable because of language and other obstacles, several agencies of the United States Government undertake to assemble and distribute to the public in various forms the foreign trade statistics of other countries. The principal of these secondary sources is the Bureau of Foreign and Domestic Commerce of the Department of Commerce, which undertakes to provide comprehensive data on the export and import trade of foreign countries (Exhibit 6). The Office of Foreign Agricultural Relations of the Department of Agriculture is a specialized source of information on trade in agricultural commodities and the Bureau of Mines of the Department of the Interior is a specialized source of information on trade in minerals.

Availability of Statistics. The Bureau of Foreign and Domestic Commerce publishes data showing the principal exports and imports of important foreign countries and their principal markets and sources of supply in the *Foreign Commerce Yearbook*, a compendium that contains also information on area and population, shipping, agriculture and forestry, fisheries, mineral production, manufacturing production, transportation, communications, and finance. First published in 1923, the *Yearbook* was discontinued for security and other reasons with the 1939 issue, but publication was resumed in 1945 with the issuance of individual country sections. The Department of Agriculture publishes some international trade statistics (as distinguished from the trade statistics of the United States) in its annual *Agricultural Statistics*, which had its inception in 1936,[1] and in its monthly bulletin *Foreign Crops and Markets*. The Bureau of Mines publishes a certain amount of information on the trade of foreign countries in minerals in its *Minerals Yearbook*, issued in its present form since 1933.

---

[1] The statistical information in *Agricultural Statistics* was published prior to 1936 in the United States Department of Agriculture *Yearbook*.

EXHIBIT 6

General Imports and Exports of New Zealand Products[1]

Yearly average or year	Thousands of New Zealand pounds		Thousands of gold dollars		Year	Thousands of New Zealand pounds		Thousands of gold dollars	
	Imports	Exports	Imports	Exports		Imports	Exports	Imports	Exports
1901-05......	11,954	14,227	58,174	69,240	1926..........	49,812	44,339	241,996	215,400
1906-10......	15,931	18,985	77,528	92,400	1927..........	44,783	47,567	217,689	231,225
1911-15......	20,563	23,932	99,765	115,954	1928..........	44,844	54,660	218,220	266,005
1916-20......	32,356	38,180	138,593	168,102	1929..........	48,734	54,176	236,698	263,648
1921-25......	44,379	47,426	196,933	210,561	1930..........	44,340	44,209	207,607	215,145
1926-30......	46,503	48,990	224,442	238,285	1931..........	26,498	34,319	110,044	147,880
1913..........	21,654	22,578	105,377	109,887	1932..........	24,646	34,976	78,914	11?,949
1918..........	24,132	27,937	114,739	132,813	1933..........	25,581	40,409	68,054	107,600
1919..........	30,309	53,304	134,142	235,925	1934..........	31,340	46,771	75,228	112,270
1920..........	61,554	45,592	225,552	167,050	1935..........	36,317	46,052	84,332	106,937

Imports of Principal Commodities

Commodity	Quantity				Value (thousands of dollars)			
	1936	1937	1938	1939[1]	1936	1937	1938	1939[1]
Total merchandise imports.................	....	....	....	....	176,542	222,893	217,432	[2]178,288
Fish......................	....				672	827	938	768
Wheat.............1,000 bu.	420	1,641	3,555	3,194	402	1,941	3,153	1,602
Other cereals and cereal products.................					1,852	1,566	1,418	....
Oranges.........1,000 lb..	14,581	20,186	27,313	[3]24,745	500	804	1,015	[3]768
Bananas............do...	22,589	24,092	36,550	26,806	513	518	741	441
Raisins and currants....do...	12,345	13,309	10,776	12,193	1,252	1,334	1,131	1,197
Fruits, other, and nuts......					1,631	2,415	2,566	1,539
Sugar, unrefined....1,000 lb.	184,414	190,583	166,952	[4]211,748	2,390	2,604	2,076	[4]3,081
Tea....................do...	11,235	10,681	11,174	11,492	2,992	3,285	3,204	3,178

Exports of Principal Commodities

Commodity	Quantity				Value (thousands of dollars)			
	1936	1937	1938	1939	1936	1937	1938	1939
Exports of New Zealand merchandise.................	....	....	....	....	218,646	256,899	221,540	201,236
Meat, fresh, chilled or frozen:								
Beef and veal.......1,000 lb.	95,296	112,239	115,773	136,902	4,603	6,040	7,054	8,041
Mutton and lamb.....do..	390,625	387,539	407,543	449,418	40,251	43,727	43,849	40,143
Pork..................do..	67,796	67,147	58,379	52,248	6,360	6,882	6,776	5,649
Meat, other...........do....	29,519	26,966	28,042	31,038	2,690	2,712	2,475	2,902
Milk, evaporated, condensed and dried............do....	23,742	24,714	20,537	24,546	1,619	1,447	1,207	1,363
Casein................do....	9,054	8,684	4,637	4,314	777	984	385	250
Butter................do....	313,168	333,322	292,829	274,312	61,105	67,421	64,817	58,236
Cheese................do....	185,719	184,482	180,379	187,190	20,434	21,322	23,287	21,116
Fish................... do....					695	690	689	584
Apples, fresh......1,000 lb..	44,808	36,082	57,643	37,676	2,206	1,795	2,823	1,716
Peas.............1,000 bu..	279	240	277	273	485	420	494	558
Tallow...........1,000 lb.	58,453	58,106	66,333	65,267	2,506	2,572	2,059	1,648
Wood, sawn.......1,000 bd. ft..	26,978	17,642	14,529	13,135	1,057	796	697	556

Trade With Principal Countries (Thousands of Dollars)

Country of origin or destination	General imports				General exports			
	1936	1937	1938	1939	1936	1937	1938	1939
Total merchandise........	176,542	222,893	217,432	[1]178,288	220,568	258,889	223,782	[2]209,411
United States..................	22,355	27,631	26,900	20,249	11,477	18,989	5,578	10,277
Australia......................	19,709	26,179	28,090	23,206	6,295	5,894	7,321	8,144
Belgium........................	1,632	2,165	2,032	1,508	2,467	2,710	1,425	3,158
Canada.........................	13,272	18,112	19,050	15,803	4,401	6,662	4,422	3,369
Ceylon.........................	2,996	3,269	3,210	2,975	6	4	2	1
France.........................	858	923	922	839	6,567	4,028	4,337	5,701
Germany........................	2,986	3,861	4,390	3,147	1,087	3,648	3,496	1,425
India..........................	2,210	2,302	2,218	2,545	502	539	539	525
Japan..........................	5,298	6,466	4,742	3,749	6,202	12,431	2,325	1,411
Netherlands....................	839	1,066	1,059	1,110	449	510	598	911
Netherlands Indies.............	7,071	8,884	8,477	8,790	7	16	30	28
Sweden.........................	1,372	1,464	1,588	1,179	259	368	332	498

These published sources provide data on exports and imports of a limited number of principal commodities and total exports and imports distributed by countries to which the exports chiefly go and from which the imports chiefly come. Detailed information on the foreign trade of other countries such as the destinations to which individual commodities are exported and the sources from which individual commodities are imported are usually available only in primary sources and must be obtained by request to one of the government agencies maintaining a statistical service on foreign country trade statistics. Statistics for very recent periods are also available as a rule only by request to these agencies, owing to the lag between the receipt in the United States of primary sources from foreign countries and reproduction of the data in published form.

The basic arrangements of foreign country trade statistics are, of course, the same as those for United States foreign trade statistics. There are (1) commodity-by-country arrangements and (2) country-by-commodity arrangements, as illustrated below.

TABLE 1. BRAZIL: Exports of Coffee Beans, Raw, Total and to Major Markets, Annual, 1939

Class Number	Commodity and Country of Destination	Quantity in Thousand Bags *	Value in Thousand Milreis
4423	Coffee beans, raw, total exports	16,499	2,234,280
	United States	9,177	1,282,105
	Belgium (including Luxemburg)	447	64,128
	Denmark	276	35,661
	Finland	270	30,403
	France	1,638	181,871
	Germany	1,033	145,463
	Greece	75	9,446
	Italy	292	38,106
	Netherlands	606	86,361
	Sweden	818	126,685
	Argentina	381	47,203
	Turkey	106	12,825
	Union of South Africa	128	14,207
	Algeria	223	24,259
	Total, countries listed	15,470	2,098,723
	All other countries	1,029	135,557

* Of 60 kilograms each.

Business consumers of foreign country trade statistics should bear in mind that country-by-commodity arrangements, especially for current periods of less than a year, are much less frequently available than commodity-by-country arrangements. Fortunately, however, it is the latter which are most needed by business concerns with their interest in markets for, or sources of, individual commodities.

TABLE 2.   EGYPT: Principal Exports to the United Kingdom, Annual, 1939

Class Number	Commodity	Unit of Quantity	Quantity	Value in Thousand Egyptian Pounds
23A	Eggs, in shell	Thousand	67,869	164
23B	Eggs, shelled and yolk	Metric ton	625	37
48	Onions	do.	55,947	298
49A	Potatoes	do.	3,578	23
71B	Rice, bleached, even glazed	do.	9,246	100
72B	Barley	do.	251	1
78	Bran, sharps and residue of milling	do.	18,606	93
83	Cottonseed	1,000 bu.*	11,420	1,204
103A	Oil, cottonseed	Metric ton	1,445	40
120	Molasses	do.	7,275	14
169A	Cottonseed, cake	do.	174,172	611
206	Ores, metallic and rare earths	do.	62,052	56
221B1	Benzine	do.	1,667	9
326A1	Skins, tanned with vegetable substances	do.	449	66
480	Wool, raw	do.	283	18
492	Cotton, raw	1,000 bales †	649	8,189
493	Waste, of cotton yarn	Metric ton	483	15
501	Flax and hemp, raw, combed or in ton	do.	510	29
	Total value of listed exports			10,967
	All other exports			106
	Total Egyptian exports to the United Kingdom			11,073

* Converted from ardebs (ardeb = 5.62 United States bushels).
† Converted from qantars (qantar = 99.049 lb.; bale of international commerce = 478 lb.).

Because of security considerations or for other reasons, trade statistics for many countries have not been published for recent periods. Generally speaking, data are available for public use through 1939; but those for the European belligerents were withheld from publication after the outbreak of the war and those for a few countries, including Russia and Japan, were suppressed in whole or in part even before this time. Data for Far Eastern countries overrun by Japan naturally disappeared as the countries came under Japanese occupation after the beginning of the war in the Pacific. Several countries in noncombat areas, principally in Latin America, have published statistics of foreign trade throughout the war period, although frequently with certain deletions. By the middle of 1945, restrictions on the publication of trade statistics by a number of countries had been relaxed to a considerable extent and were in process of being further relaxed. With the termination of hostilities it may be expected that foreign trade data will again be available without restriction soon. Details about the availability of such data can be ascertained at any given time only by asking one of the government agencies (mentioned above) whose business it is to know what has been published and what is forthcoming and when.

The work of the League of Nations in compiling trade statistics in uniform terms is especially noteworthy. The Department of Commerce also does extensive work in this field,[2] as do also the Tariff Commission, the Department of Agriculture, and other agencies of the United States Government.

BALANCE-OF-PAYMENTS STATISTICS

Scope and Coverage. Balance-of-payments statistics, which include data not only on exports and imports of tangible things but also on all other transactions between the residents of one country and residents of other countries, are by no means as universally available as foreign trade statistics. During the interwar period there was a considerable development of balance-of-payments statistics and more or less complete data on balances of payments were published for 30-odd countries, representing all parts of the world, by the League of Nations.[3] These data consist of four general types of international transactions, as illustrated by the grouping of items in the balance of payments of the United States: [4]

1. Merchandise trade.
2. Other current transactions:
   Shipping and freight.
   Travel expenditures.
   Personal remittances.
   Institutional contributions.

[2] The Department of Commerce publication *Foreign Commerce Yearbook*, referred to elsewhere in this chapter, contains trade statistics for principal countries compiled on a uniform basis.

[3] See the annual memoranda on *Balances of Payments* issued by the League.

[4] Adapted from *The United States in the World Economy*, Table I, facing p. 216.

Interest and dividends.
Government aid and settlements.
Other government items.
Silver.
Miscellaneous adjustments and services.
3. Gold movements.
4. Capital transactions.

Because of the role of transfers of interest and dividends and of capital funds in international transactions, balance-of-payments statistics have, as their natural counterpart, data on the international investment position of a country, that is, investments by residents of the country in other countries and investments in the country by residents of other countries.   Such data for the United States appear below.[5]

TABLE 3.   INTERNATIONAL INVESTMENT POSITION OF THE UNITED STATES IN 1939, EXCLUDING WAR DEBTS

(billions of dollars)

Item	1939
United States investments abroad:	
Long-term:	
Direct	7.0
Portfolio	3.8
Total long-term	10.8
Total short-term	0.6
Total long- and short-term	11.4
Foreign investments in the United States:	
Long-term:	
Direct	2.0
Portfolio	4.3
Total long-term	6.3
Total short-term	3.3
Total long- and short-term	9.6
Net creditor-debtor position of the United States:	
On long-term account (creditor)	4.5
On short-term account (debtor)	−2.7
On long- and short-term account	1.8

Sources of Information.   The primary source of information on the balance of payments of the United States and related subjects is the

[5] Ibid., p. 23.

Bureau of Foreign and Domestic Commerce, which undertakes also to provide the business and general public with available data on the balances of payments of other countries.[6] Since 1935 the Treasury Department has collected and published statistics of certain capital movements between the United States and foreign countries as well as of the short-term international assets and liabilities of the United States. More recently the Treasury Department has undertaken comprehensive censuses of foreign holdings in the United States and United States holdings in foreign countries.

Availability of Statistics. Data on the balance of international payments of the United States were published by the Bureau of Foreign and Domestic Commerce in annual bulletins beginning with the year 1922 and continuing until 1940, when they were discontinued for security and other reasons. These annual bulletins have been supplemented from time to time by special bulletins on such subjects as United States investments in foreign countries, foreign investments in the United States, international travel and travel expenditures, and international insurance transactions. The balance-of-payments experience of the United States during the entire interwar period (1919–1939) was summarized in a comprehensive study, *The United States in the World Economy*, published by the Department of Commerce in 1943 and reprinted by H. M. Stationery Office in London in 1944. In addition to these published documents, there is in the files of the Bureau of Foreign and Domestic Commerce information of considerable variety and detail on international transactions of the United States and related subjects which can be obtained upon request.

The *Monthly Bulletin of the Treasury Department*, published since January 1939, carries current and historical data on certain capital movements between the United States and foreign countries.[7] These statistics were published in less detail during the war than previously but the lapsing of security regulations will again make it possible to publish them in full detail. The Treasury censuses of foreign holdings in the United States and United States holdings abroad, which have been in progress since 1940, are expected to yield a wealth of information on the international-investment position of the United States. Certain preliminary results have been issued in press releases, and comprehensive data will eventually be published in more perma-

---

[6] Historical data on the balances of payments of various countries, presented, so far as possible, on a uniform basis, are found in the annual memoranda on *Balances of Payments* issued by the League of Nations.

[7] Similar data were published by the Treasury in nine reports entitled *Statistics of Capital Movements Between the United States and Foreign Countries, etc.*, for January 1935 through September 1936 and for quarterly periods thereafter through the third quarter of 1938.

nent form. The *Federal Reserve Bulletin*, issued by the Board of Governors of the Federal Reserve System in Washington, is a useful secondary source of data on international capital movements and contains information also on gold production in foreign countries, gold movements into and out of foreign countries, gold reserves of central banks and governments, and other financial data for foreign countries.

SHIPPING STATISTICS

Statistics on ocean shipping and the tonnage of commodities moving in and out of the United States ports, to and from each foreign port of lading or unlading, are of vital importance in the analysis of many business problems. Statistics on United States imports and exports, described above in the section on "United States Foreign Trade Statistics," relate very largely to the water-borne commerce of the United States. While import and export statistics include shipments in or out of the country by all methods of transportation, i.e., by rail, truck, air, and parcel post, as well as by vessel, the figures for trade with countries other than Canada or Mexico are with some exceptions data on shipments by ocean-going vessel.[8]

Prior to the war such statistics suffered from one major deficiency when used as shipping statistics, namely, that the information shown for imports and exports included only the dollar value of such shipments and the *net* quantity in terms of gallons, bales, number of machines, etc., rather than the more pertinent factor, gross weight of the shipments. Beginning in 1942, as a result of war needs, information on the shipping weight of imports and exports has been compiled in addition to the value and net quantity measurements.

The statistics will provide other information needed for adequate analysis of ocean shipping such as data on movements of merchandise by vessel only, movements of merchandise on a port-to-port basis, and movements of commodities by flag of vessel, air, etc.

Statistics on ocean shipping alone were, prior to the war, principally prepared and released by the United States Maritime Commission

---

[8] Export shipments moving from the United States to Mexico or Canada by rail or truck, to be later shipped to, say, the United Kingdom, are shown in the Bureau of the Census export statistics as being exported to the United Kingdom. To this extent total exports to the United Kingdom or any other noncontiguous country include shipments which do not leave the United States by vessel. A similar situation exists in regard to import statistics which credit to an overseas country of origin imports which may have entered the United States overland from Canada or Mexico. For most commodities the volume of such export or import shipments via Canada or Mexico is very small.

and the Board of Engineers for Rivers and Harbors of the War Department. The Maritime Commission had as its primary responsibility the function of promoting the development and maintenance of an adequate and well-balanced Merchant Marine. As part of this responsibility it compiled and published information on the water-borne foreign commerce of the United States. The publication program of the Maritime Commission did not provide any substantial amount of information on ocean shipping on a monthly basis but instead provided most information on an annual basis in its *Report on Volume of Water-Borne Foreign Commerce of the United States by Ports of Origin and Destination* and its *Water-Borne and Intercoastal Commerce and Passenger Traffic of the United States*. Since the Maritime Commission was primarily interested in ocean shipping statistics for its own administrative purposes rather than in commercial imports and exports as such, the figures compiled by it differed considerably from the Department of Commerce statistics on foreign trade. The Maritime Commission figures provided information on goods entering and leaving the country in terms of the movement between individual domestic and individual foreign ports and in summary form between various sections of the United States coast (Gulf, Pacific, etc.) and various groupings of foreign ports such as west coast of South America and east coast of South America. Shipments were credited to individual ports or areas on the basis of where the goods were laden on or unladen from a vessel rather than the country of origin or the country of ultimate destination as in export and import statistics. The information provided showed the gross weight of the shipments but did not provide information on their value or net quantity.

The data on the tonnage of water-borne exports and imports compiled and published by the Maritime Commission before the war showed only very broad groupings of commodities with emphasis on bulky commodities. These groupings varied from port to port depending upon the particular commodities which represented the largest volume of tonnage in each case and the articles included in each of the categories were therefore not always homogeneous. Furthermore, the Maritime Commission commodity figures were based on reports which provided commodity information only on individual shipments with a shipping weight of ten tons or more. As a result many commodities which moved in considerable volume, but in the form of numerous shipments weighing less than ten tons, were seriously undercounted in the Maritime Commission commodity figures although the tonnage involved in such shipments was included in the total under the all-inclusive category of "general cargo" or "miscellaneous." An illustration of this was the commodity group "hides and skins" in which the United States Maritime Commission figures generally showed only half as great imports as the Department of Commerce import figures.

The Board of Engineers for Rivers and Harbors of the War Department has as one of its primary responsibilities the development and improvement of rivers and harbors. In connection with this responsibility it compiles and, prior to the war, released information on the volume of shipping inbound and outbound through individual United States ports and sections of ports to be used as a basis for determining the amount of expenditures which should be made in improving and developing rivers and harbors. These figures were published prior to the war as Part II of *The Annual Report of the Chief of Engineers of the United States War Department*. They showed the total tonnage of major commodities entering and leaving each United States port, but provided no information on where the shipments had come from or were bound to. The Board of Engineers statistics on inbound and outbound traffic included information on intransit shipping and on shipping to and from territories and possessions of the United States, as well as coastwise, intercoastal, and inland shipping.

Information on vessels entering and clearing United States ports were issued prior to the war by the Department of Commerce, the Maritime Commission, and the Board of Engineers for Rivers and Harbors in the publications described previously. Comparisons between the three sets of figures on entrances and clearances presented problems similar to those described above in regard to tabulations of cargo movements. Additional sources of discrepancy among the figures compiled by the three agencies for entrance and clearance of vessels included differences as to the size of the vessels included in the compilations, differences in the unit of measurement of the size of the vessels included (net tons, dead weight tons), definitions of vessels in ballast, method of crediting vessels to first, last, and intermediate ports of call, etc.

APPLICATION TO CONCRETE PROBLEMS OF STATISTICS OF INTERNATIONAL TRADE AND PAYMENTS

How can statistics of international trade and payments be applied to concrete business problems? To answer this question, two problems may be considered, one of market analysis and the other of investment analysis. For example, take a United States manufacturer or exporter of toilet soap who has been doing a small export business for years, shipping directly to local distributors in foreign countries. He may

EXHIBIT 7. ANALYSIS OF MARKET FOR TOILET SOAP IN COUNTRY A, 1937–1941

(All amounts in pounds)

Year	(1) Company X's Shipments to Country A	(2) Total U. S. Shipments to Country A	(3) Percent (1) of (2)	(4a) Imports from U. S.	(4b) Imports from Other Countries	(5) Total Imports into Country A	(6) Percent (4a) of (5)	(7) Domestic Production in Country A	(8) Apparent Total New Supply in Country A (5) + (7)	(9) Percent (7) of (8)
1937										
1938										
1939										
1940										
1941										

never have paid much attention to this phase of his business; but as a part of his over-all postwar program he would like to know what the foreign market for toilet soap amounts to and to what extent he may expect to expand his own export business.

Our businessman might begin with an analysis of the market in country A. First, he has the record of his own shipments to his distributor in this country over a period of years. Second, he has from government publications, or can obtain by writing, statistics of United States exports of toilet soap to country A. Third, he can get statistics of total exports of toilet soap into country A by countries of origin. Fourth, he may be able to get data on domestic production of toilet soap in country A. Now, if he sets the figures of his own shipments to country A alongside the figures of total exports from the United States to country A, he will find whether his share of this trade has been increasing, decreasing, or remaining about the same (see Exhibit 7).

This comparison shows that his share of United States exports to the market in country A actually increased during the immediate prewar period, which means that his local distributor must have been doing a pretty good job. If this trend can be explained, it may be possible to extend it and increase his share of the trade still more. Our exporter will want to inquire into this closely. Of course, if the comparison had shown the opposite trend, he would have wanted to investigate the causes very carefully and to consider, among other things, the desirability of getting different or additional distributors for his product in country A.

Now, by comparing imports into country A from the United States with imports from other sources (of which there are three—France, Germany, and the United Kingdom), the exporter can determine not only how successfully American soaps have competed with other foreign soaps in the country A market but also the size of the total country A market for imported toilet soaps. Thus, he designs the following specimen table (Exhibit 8).

Changes in the total amount of imports of toilet soap into country A during the period 1937–1941 were considerable. The trade was at a high level in 1937, fell off in 1938, picked up in 1939 and 1940, and reached its peak for the period in 1941. The exporter can readily see that these changes were related to the general business situation in country A and to the state of its trade with the United States. The market was very good in 1937 when the United States was buying relatively large quantities of raw materials from country A and in this way raising local incomes and providing dollars for purchases from the United States. The market was poor in 1938 when the oppo-

EXHIBIT 8. IMPORTS OF TOILET SOAP INTO COUNTRY A, TOTAL AND FROM MAJOR SUPPLIERS, 1937–1941

(Pounds)

Year	United States		France		Germany		United Kingdom		Total	
	Amount	Percent	Amount	Percent	Amount	Percent	Amount	Percent	Amount	Percent
1937										
1938										
1939										
1940										
1941										

site situation prevailed, then improved in 1939 and 1940 and reached a peak for the period in 1941 as the position of the country improved because of its steadily expanding exports. It is clear that the exporter will have to follow the trend of business conditions in country A and in other foreign countries if he is going to gauge the extent of these markets for his product.[9] For the present, he must make some assumption about the postwar position and may select as a figure on which to base his conclusions: (1) an average for a period of years or (2) the amount of imports in a single year, like 1937 or 1941, on the expectation that the postwar market will be at least as good as in recent good years.

He will conclude that the Germans will certainly be out of the market for a time after the war and the French probably also. Thus it may turn out that British and American exporters will divide the market for at least a few years. If this should happen and if the proportionate shares of the market should stay about the same, the exporter can easily estimate the sales in country A of all American soaps, and from this his own potential sales.

Another interesting thing which the import statistics of country A show is that foreign soaps cut into the market for United States soaps in country A in 1938 and 1939. However, comparative unit values computed from the trade figures suggest that this situation was largely the result of the import of higher priced soaps from other countries while lower priced United States soaps continued to compete, rather unsuccessfully, with domestic soaps which were also in the lower price ranges. The exporter should perhaps push his own fancy soaps in the country A market, but first he should have a look at domestic soap production in country A.

The figures on domestic soap production in country A fill out the picture very nicely. It is clear that domestic production has been increasing rapidly and has taken an increasing proportion of the total market. As a matter of fact, if the trend shown by these figures continues, the market for imported soaps in country A is going to remain pretty small, even if total consumption continues to increase. It may be worth while for the exporter to look into the possibility of taking advantage of this trend by getting a tie-up with a local soap manufacturer and putting in some capital under a management contract

<hr>

[9] The hypothetical analysis in this chapter is highly over-simplified to illustrate the application of foreign trade statistics. A variety of other information is required for a complete market analysis, such as information on import duties and import restrictions, exchange controls, documentary requirements, sanitary regulations, quality and price standards, selling outlets, and credit conditions and practices.

with a view to manufacturing and marketing his soaps in country A under his own brand names. But should he make an investment in country A? Should he make an investment in soap manufacturing specifically?

In order to answer the second of these two questions the exporter will need, among other things, additional statistics of foreign trade. He already has a measure of the extent of the market for both the normal and the present sources of raw materials for soap making for country A. The stub of the table on page 221 of *Agricultural Statistics* for 1942, which is reproduced below (Exhibit 9), provides a convenient check list, and the Department of Commerce can supply statistics of imports into country A of all these items showing countries of origin over a period of years. Finally, he should look at the export statistics of country A to find out whether the recent rapid growth in domestic soap production there has been accompanied by the development of export outlets, especially in neighboring countries. If so, the possibility of developing export outlets for a production venture in country A would be a factor in his calculations.

EXHIBIT 9. Fats, Oils, and Rosin Used in the Manufacture of Soap

Hard oils (tallow class):
  Slow lathering:
    Tallow, inedible.
    Whale and fish oils.
    Grease.
    Palm oil.
    Tallow, edible.
    Oleostearine.
    Lard.
  Quick lathering:
    Coconut oil.
    Palm-kernel oil.
    Babassu oil.
Soft oils:
  Cottonseed-oil foots and other foots.
  Olive oil, foots and inedible.
  Soybean oil.

Soft oils (*Cont.*):
  Cottonseed oil.
  Corn oil.
  Castor oil.
  Linseed oil.
  Peanut oil.
  Sesame oil.
  Oleo oil.
  Rape oil.
  Olive oil, edible.
  Neat's-foot oil.
  Perilla oil.
  Tung oil.
  Sunflower oil.
  Other oils.
Rosin.

To answer the question "Should an investment be made in country A?" it will be necessary to go beyond trade statistics to data on various types of payments between the United States and country A and to the record of American and other foreign investments in that country. Our soap manufacturer would want answers to the following questions at least: What is the general character of the commercial and financial relations between country A and the United States on the one hand

and all the rest of the world on the other? What is the present amount of foreign investment in country A? To what extent are investments being made currently in country A by foreigners, or to what extent are foreigners withdrawing their investments in country A? What fixed claims are there on the dollars which are available to country A as a result of its sales of goods or sales of services to the United States and other countries? What has been the general earnings record of United States and other foreign capital in country A? What has been the record with respect to the freedom of transfer of earnings on foreign investments in country A? What has been the course of rates of exchange for the dollar in country A?

It is improbable that complete answers to all of these specific questions can be obtained from any source. However, the information on balances of payments and on international investments from government sources, which are available on request, should go far to establish the essential facts. Suppose the manufacturer finds upon inquiry that there is no evidence of a chronic shortage of dollars in country A, although it did get into difficulties with respect to dollar payments, in common with many other countries, during the 1930's. As a matter of fact, country A defaulted interest and sinking fund payments on its dollar bonds during the depression, but a settlement has recently been reached with the bondholders providing for the resumption of service on terms considerably easier than the original ones. This settlement has had the effect of reducing to a reasonably small percentage fixed claims on the dollars obtained by country A through its dealings with the United States and other countries. He finds further that there were restrictions placed by country A on the transfer of earnings on foreign investments into dollars and other foreign currencies but that these restrictions were temporary and were relaxed as soon as the depression conditions which were fundamentally responsible for them had improved. There has been no arbitrary or long-continued restriction of the transfer of earnings or other funds out of the country. On the whole, earnings on United States and other foreign capital in country A have been high, which is typical of investments in underdeveloped countries. It appears that there is a current movement of foreign capital, including United States capital, into country A, and this fact indicates a general confidence not only in investment opportunities in country A, but also in the possibility of withdrawing earnings and capital from country A as desired. The rate of exchange in country A for the dollar, that is, the rate at which local earnings are converted into dollars, has over a long period of years varied within wide limits. It takes twice as many units of country A's currency to get a dollar as it did in 1929, but this change in the value of country A's currency was the result of the scarcity of foreign means of payment during the depression and of a forced depreciation of the currency in terms of dollars. The rate has been stable for a number of years and country A has accumulated a substantial amount of gold and foreign exchange which can be used to stabilize its currency after the war. Government and other authorities on these matters warn that there can be no certainty that the currency of country A will not again be depreciated at some time in the future or that there will not again at some time be restrictions on the transfer of earnings and other funds out of country A. Whether these unfavorable circumstances reappear will depend, they say, very largely upon the success of the United States and of other industrial countries in maintaining high levels of production and employment and of maintaining in this way a market for the exports of country A at good prices.

On the basis of all this evidence, the manufacturer would apparently be warranted in concluding that an investment in country A would represent a reasonable risk.[10]

[10] There are obviously many other considerations outside the realm of international trade and payments which would affect the decision to make an investment in a foreign country, of which the chief, perhaps, would be taxation.

CHAPTER 8

TRANSPORTATION AND OTHER PUBLIC UTILITIES

FRANK L. BARTON AND PATRICIA VAN DERAA
Bureau of the Budget

One of the largest groups of Federal statistics available is in the field of transportation and other public utilities.

Public utilities, which may be briefly defined as those economic activities given regulation because they are "peculiarly affected with a public interest," are subject to Federal regulation under the inter-state commerce clause of the Constitution. As a by-product of such Federal regulation, many of the most important series of Federal Government data are compiled and made available to the public.

This chapter indicates the most important data currently available in that field. Little or no mention will be made of information gathered by the various war agencies because of its temporary or incomplete nature and because it is not generally available to the public.

Retaining the traditional distinction, transportation statistics will be discussed as a group with attention being given to the individual kinds of transport, including rail, water, motor, and air. Pipelines, freight forwarders, express companies, electric railways, private car companies, and the Pullman Company will also be included. The electric power utilities and the communications industries will, of course, comprise the other group.

TRANSPORTATION STATISTICS

Railroads. Railroads were made subject to the first of the Federal regulatory agencies, the Interstate Commerce Commission, by the Act to Regulate Commerce of 1887. During the fifty-odd years of railroad regulation, numerous comprehensive statistical series have been developed; some of these are published for varying periods of years as far back as 1890 in the principal statistical publication of the Interstate Commerce Commission, issued annually under the title *Statistics of Railways in the United States.*[1] The rail statistics mentioned here are contained in that publication.

[1] Sold by the Superintendent of Documents ($1.50).

222

The Commission has divided operating railroads (those whose officers direct the actual transportation service) into three classes, according to annual revenues: Class I, having revenue above $1,000,000; Class II, above $100,000 but not more than $1,000,000; and Class III, below $100,000. Class I railway statistics are very important relatively since on Class I railways originate about 95 per cent of total rail freight tonnage and about 99 percent of the passenger traffic. Aggregate data are available for all Class I roads and many of the items for individual lines.

ROADWAY AND TRACK. The number of railroads, miles of road owned, miles of single or first main track, and miles operated are given by classes. All track (including main line and other than main line track) is shown for Class I railroads by miles of track operated, by kind of track, method of control, and by district.[2] The number of crossings (railroads crossing highways) in each state with each kind of protection is given for Class I railways and for switching and terminal companies.

The ICC statistics show miles of road constructed and abandoned annually, by class of railroad, for all line-haul rail carriers.

EQUIPMENT. With the railroads' need for additional facilities during the war, many persons have become increasingly conscious of railroad equipment and its uses. Data on equipment for all steam railways covers locomotives, cars, and floating equipment (like that in use in New York harbor). It is shown by kind, by class of railway, and by district. The significant aspect of these data is that they give the age of equipment—much of it was built in the first decades of this century—and the decline in the number of units in the possession of the railroads. In addition to information on freight, passenger, and switching locomotives, detailed statistics are gathered on both freight and passenger cars. Railways, as the ICC discloses, own highway vehicles in addition to railway equipment.

TRAFFIC. Among the most-used data on the railroads are those on freight traffic carried. For each Class I line-haul railway information is gathered annually on tons of freight carried, ton-miles, and average length of haul. Revenues, both average per ton and per ton-mile, are tabulated for the Class I carriers. These figures are especially useful to those interested in evaluating rail securities and in analyzing trends in rail traffic.

---

[2] The ICC has designated three "districts," defined roughly as Western, the area west of the Mississippi River; Southern, east of the Mississippi and south of the Ohio River; Eastern, the remaining area north of Southern District. "Regions" are subdivisions of districts.

In addition, information is shown for revenue freight originated,[3] terminated, and total carried, by carloads, tons, and average load. These figures are shown for five major commodity groups by districts. Revenue freight is also given by tons originated and by tons carried, with revenue for each of 157 groups of commodities. A comparatively recent addition to ICC statistics is a table on tons of revenue freight originated and terminated, in carloads, by the five major commodity groups and by states for Class I line-haul railroads.

Despite the vast amount of traffic movement information, there is a serious weakness in the statistics available: the flow of traffic is not adequately shown, that is, traffic originating in one location cannot now be traced to its destination.

A widely used series of statistics on weekly freight carloading is compiled by the Association of American Railroads. Covering the week from Saturday to Saturday, this report gives cars of revenue freight loaded, including less-than-carload traffic. The information is published widely and used to indicate general business conditions. To obtain this weekly release (release CS-54), write the Association of American Railroads, Transportation Building, Washington, D. C.

OPERATION. The most useful of the ICC rail carrier operating statistics for Class I railroads fall into six groups.

1. Train-miles, by kind of service and by district.
2. Locomotive-miles, by kind of service and by district.
3. Car-miles, by kind of service and by district.
4. Train-mile and car-mile averages, by district.
5. Averages per mile of road and per mile all track.
6. Operating averages for freight service, showing net ton-miles per train-mile and related data.

EMPLOYMENT. Railroad employment is closely related to other railway statistics. The ICC shows employees as of the middle of the month, by class of railway, and by seven occupational groups for all steam railways.

The annual average number of employees is given, with total compensation, average compensation per employee, and average compensation per hour for all Class I line-haul railways. In addition, for this same class of carriers, data are published by 128 occupations, on number of employees, total time paid for, total compensation, and average compensation per hour, or day.

[3] Defined as shipments not identified as having had previous line-haul transportation by other rail carriers.

ACCIDENTS. Both employees and nonemployees are subject to railroad accidents. Along with increased travel incident to the war, the total number of accidents has increased. These casualties are reported by all steam railroads to ICC by kind of accident, giving number of persons killed and number injured. The number of employee casualties while on duty, both killed and injured, by kind of accident, is reported separately.

FUEL. The railroads are the greatest single group of users of fuel. The amount of fuel received and unit cost per ton or gallon is given for Class I line-haul rail carriers for bituminous coal, fuel oil, Diesel oil, and gasoline. Consumption of fuel, including electricity, is shown by locomotive and by rail motorcars. These data are further refined to show use by kind of fuel, motive power, service (of which freight and passenger are the most important), and district.

FINANCE. The ICC requires that carriers subject to its jurisdiction keep accounting records in accordance with uniform accounting procedures prescribed by the Commission. Consequently, financial data of all the railroads within a class are comparable.

Operating revenues are tabulated by individual accounts (freight, passenger, mail, express, and so on) for each of the three districts. Average revenue per ton of freight originated and per ton-mile and average haul, in miles, are included. Two interesting subgroups of revenue are: (1) average revenue per ton and (2) average haul per ton originated for all classes of steam railways taken as a system.

Operating expenses are published, as assigned or apportioned to each class of service, types of which are given in the preceding paragraph. In addition to being shown by district, the data are shown by groups of accounts, such as the groups pertaining to maintenance of way and structures and maintenance of equipment. Operating expenses are given in considerable detail by individual account within each group. For instance, the group on maintenance of way and structures is broken into 104 detailed accounts. Percent of total expenses for each account is shown, even though it is only one one-thousandth of one percent. Railroad operating ratios (ratio of operating expenses to operating revenues) and maintenance ratios are also given. Railway tax accruals are published by states for Class I line-haul railways and for lessors. United States Government taxes charged to railway tax accruals, by kind of tax, are shown in a separate table.

Without going further into detail, it is sufficient to say that detailed railroad financial data include (1) income and profit and loss; (2) dividends and interest; (3) balance sheet; (4) capitalization; and (5) receiverships and trusteeships.

COST STUDIES. The ICC has carried on some outstanding work in the field of cost finding. The costs ascertained are the costs to the railroads of rendering rail service in the various rate territories of the United States. Although the subject is a technical one, the ICC report on rail costs—*Rail Freight Service Costs in the Various Rate Territories of the United States*, published as Senate Document 63, 78th Congress—is easily understood.

GENERAL SUMMARIES OF ICC STATISTICS. Summary tables are published annually showing selected statistics on the development of steam railways. The tables contain data from 1890 until the present time on number of railroads, miles of road, amount of equipment, investment, capitalization, revenues, and the various measures of passenger and freight traffic. These tables are exceedingly valuable and show the relative size and importance of the transportation plant during the past fifty-odd years.

MONTHLY RAIL TRANSPORTATION SERIES. The statistics discussed above are mostly on an annual basis, but the following series are available monthly for Class I roads only: (1) revenues and expenses; (2) selected income and balance sheet items; (3) tons and carloads originated, terminated, and carried with freight revenue, by commodities, states, and regions; (4) train-miles, car-miles, locomotive-miles, gross and net ton-miles, and train-hours in road freight service and road passenger service; (5) revenue tons and ton-miles, revenue passengers and passenger-miles with freight and passenger revenue; (6) locomotives and cars assigned, by class of service; (7) quantities of fuel and power purchased and consumed and cost by class of service; (8) summary of accidents, by class of accident; and (9) summary of number of employees, by classes of employment, service time, and amount of compensation.

Current data on transportation statistics contained in the ICC release, *Monthly Comment on Transport Statistics*, are supplemented with comments couched in brief, understandable language. This useful report is available upon request to the Interstate Commerce Commission, Bureau of Transport Economics and Statistics, Washington 25, D. C. Likewise, additional data on the statistics mentioned concerning railroads may be obtained at this address.

Water Carriers. Three Federal agencies are chiefly responsible for statistics in the field of water transportation: the Interstate Commerce Commission, the Board of Engineers for Rivers and Harbors of the War Department, and the United States Maritime Commission. These data cover physical plant and operating statistics; foreign trade statistics are discussed in Chapter 7.

The Interstate Commerce Commission, by the Transportation Act of 1940, was empowered to regulate common and contract water carriers engaged in interstate commerce, excepting bulk carriers of three products or less.[4] The ICC classification of water carriers is based on revenue; carriers having annual revenue of more than $500,000 are Class A; those having more than $100,000 but not more than $500,000, Class B; those of less than $100,000, Class C. The publication of the ICC on water carrier data is entitled *Selected Financial and Operating Statistics from Annual Reports of Carriers by Water*.

As Class C water carriers are relatively unimportant, statistics mentioned here pertain only to Classes A and B. The more numerous and important series are collected annually. Data on floating equipment in possession of the carriers are published by number of units of equipment, dead weight carrying capacity, class of service, and area served. The areas are five in number: Atlantic and Gulf Coasts, Great Lakes, Mississippi River, Pacific Coast, and Intercoastal. Tons of freight carried and the revenue derived therefrom by carriers in the five areas are reported under the same commodity classification used for railroads.

Selected annual financial and operating information for Classes A and B water carriers is published by areas serviced and by individual carriers. Two quarterly series gathered by the ICC from water carriers may be mentioned: (1) freight revenue and passenger revenue in each area served and (2) tons of revenue freight moved and number of passengers carried.

Under authority given by various acts of Congress, the Corps of Engineers, War Department, gathers data on type of vessels, passengers, freight, and tonnage from vessels plying navigable waters. Statistics on water carriers under this authority are collected by the district offices of the Corps of Engineers and published annually in *Report of the Chief of Engineers, U. S. Army, Part 2, Commercial Statistics, Water-Borne Commerce of the United States* (compiled in the Office of the Board of Engineers for Rivers and Harbors). "Part 2," the short title for this volume, is usually 1,500 pages in length. This material is extremely detailed and gives for each individual navigable channel a description of the waterway, annual exports and imports by commodity classes, coastwise receipts and shipments, internal shipments (traffic between a port and a tributary waterway), intraport receipts and shipments, and local (port) traffic.

Other reports describing ports, port facilities, traffic, and floating

[4] For an exact definition of water carriers exempted from ICC regulation, see the Interstate Commerce Act, Part III, Section 303.

equipment are prepared by the War Department, but distribution of most of these was restricted for the duration of the war.

The third agency mentioned as gathering statistics on water carriers is the United States Maritime Commission. Although at present the gathering of these statistics on common carriers by water is in the hands of the War Shipping Administration presumably later on the information will again be collected and disseminated by the Maritime Commission.

Two annual reports on cargo movements of the Maritime Commission should be mentioned. *Water-Borne Foreign and Domestic Commerce of the United States*, available for each calendar year from 1921 to 1940, is a simple report showing for United States ports grouped by districts (Atlantic, Gulf, Pacific, Great Lakes), total commerce, foreign commerce, intercoastal commerce, and commerce with noncontiguous territories such as Alaska, in long tons. Data on individual commodities are not given.

More detailed data on commodities are given in the *Report on Volume of Water-Borne Commerce of the United States by Ports of Origin and Destination*, available for fiscal years from 1922 to 1937. The commodity tables in this report contain annual summaries of cargo, in long tons, loaded and discharged at each domestic port together with similar summaries of the activities of foreign ports in commerce with the United States in the same period. Summaries of United States port activities are given, with segregation of the principal import and export commodities moved through each port, and the distribution of these commodities among foreign ports of origin and destination. Similar treatment is given foreign ports in commerce with the United States.

On passenger traffic the most useful Maritime Commission report is *Water-Borne Passenger Traffic of the United States*, available for calendar years from 1923 to 1937. Shown in this report is the number of arrivals and departures by ports, with origin, destination, and type of cruise.

For those desiring information on our fleet of merchant vessels, the following Maritime Commission publication, available annually from 1929 to 1936, is recommended: *American Flag Services in Foreign Trade and with United States Possessions*. It lists the steamer lines and companies, with number and gross tonnage of vessels, and indicates the types of service rendered by each line, along with ports of call, both United States and foreign.

During the war large numbers of vessels have been constructed, many of which no doubt will be added to American commercial fleets later. After the war, this publication, probably in some revised form, should continue to be a useful one.

Motor Carriers. With the passage of the Motor Carrier Act of 1935 by Congress, numerous common and contract motor carriers engaged in interstate commerce were brought under regulation of the Interstate Commerce Commission. The number of regulated motor carriers is greater than the number of rail carriers and other transportation agencies subject to ICC regulation.

For reporting and accounting purposes motor carriers are divided into three classes by the ICC, according to annual gross operating revenue: Class I, revenue above $100,000; Class II, revenue from $25,-000 to $100,000; and Class III, revenue below $25,000. Motor carriers of property and motor carriers of passengers, as well as those combining both functions, are included.

In this discussion attention will be confined to the data on Class I motor carriers, with property carriers and passenger carriers given separate treatment. The data are published by the ICC in *Statistics of Class I Motor Carriers*, beginning in 1938.

The important annual statistics for carriers of property [5] include the number of units and cost of revenue equipment owned classified by type of equipment, by kind of property carrier service, and by geographic areas.[6] Information published on revenue freight owned includes data on the number of units by type of equipment, capacity, and kind of property carrier service, for each area. Needless to say, the total equipment in use by motor carriers has shrunk during the war years, owing mainly to military needs for such equipment and to lack of tires.

The perennial question of whether the trucking industry is subsidized because of its use of public highways illuminates the need for figures on taxes paid by the industry. Operating taxes and licenses paid by

---

[5] These have been subdivided to show returns separately for carriers engaged preponderantly in intercity service and those mainly in local service. Those in intercity service have been further divided into common carriers of general freight, common carriers of commodities other than general freight, and contract carriers, operating owned equipment exclusively or principally. Carriers of property preponderantly engaged in intercity service operating with owned equipment and with purchased transportation in an amount in excess of 3.75 percent of their total operation and maintenance expense are shown separately.

[6] For motor carriers the ICC has designated these geographic areas: Eastern district, embodying New England region, Middle Atlantic region, and Central region; Southern region; and Western district, including Northwestern region, Midwestern region, Southwestern region, Rocky Mountain region, and Pacific region.

property carriers are published by kind of tax (gasoline tax, corporation tax, and others), and kind of property carrier service, for geographical areas. Closely related are operating revenues by source of revenue. Income and balance sheet statements are published by kind of service and area.

The petroleum industry has benefited by the development of trucking. The extent of the use of petroleum products by property carriers is shown in the ICC data on fuel and oil consumption, given by kind of property carrier service and by area.

Intercity freight service is a large segment of the business of property carriers. The extent of this business may be learned from the data on tons carried, vehicle miles, and revenue received, by kind of property carrier service and area.

Employment data show average number of employees and total compensation, by kind of employment, by geographic areas, and by kinds of property carrier service.

In addition to the annual statistics just described, the following quarterly statistics may be noted as important for Class I motor carriers of property:

1. Revenue and expenses, by areas.
2. Truck and tractor miles operated and tons of revenue freight transported, by common and contract carriers and by areas.
3. Operating ratios by areas.

For Class I motor carriers of passengers, information is made available by the ICC on approximately the same items as mentioned for property carriers with the necessary differences: traffic and capacity are shown in terms of passengers and by kind of passenger service (intercity and local).

Quarterly statistics for these passenger carriers, by kind of passenger service by areas, cover revenue, expense, and net income; bus-miles operated; and number of revenue passengers carried. Monthly series of statistics are compiled on passenger revenue, vehicle-miles operated, and revenue passengers carried.

OTHER STATISTICS RELATED TO MOTOR TRANSPORTATION. The Public Roads Administration has available considerable data on highways, including data on mileage, surface type, expenditures, the motor vehicles which use highways, gasoline consumed by those motor vehicles, and related information. The information can be segregated roughly into the following major groups: motor-fuel consumption and taxation; motor-vehicle registration and taxation; motor-carrier taxation; the financing of state highways, including the analysis of state highway debt; the mileage of existing highway systems; and the construction of highways by widths and surface types.

Public Roads Administration publishes data on these subjects in the form of tables on large unbound sheets. Annual figures for each state are available on a variety of subjects in each major group. Requests may be made to Public Roads Administration, Washington 25, D. C.

Air Carriers. The rapid development of air transportation has been of increasing importance to the businessman. The significant position attached to air power in the war and the resultant training of personnel, and aircraft production point to a surge in the availability of air transportation after the war.

Prior to 1938 Federal regulation in this field was divided among the Interstate Commerce Commission, the Post Office Department, and the Bureau of Air Commerce in the Department of Commerce. However, the Civil Aeronautics Act of 1938 provided for the Civil Aeronautics Authority and centralized Federal control and the collection of statistical data in that agency. By Reorganization Plans III and IV, effective June 30, 1940, the Civil Aeronautics Board and the Civil Aeronautics Administration constituted the Civil Aeronautics Authority, which was placed in the Department of Commerce. The Civil Aeronautics Board, however, performs its rule-making, adjudicative, and investigative functions independently of the Department.

Air transportation statistics published by the Civil Aeronautics Administration are found in the *Civil Aeronautics Journal*, published monthly by the Information and Statistics Service of the Civil Aeronautics Administration, Washington 25, D. C.

The monthly data show revenue miles flown, revenue passengers carried, revenue passenger miles flown, express carried by pounds, express pound miles flown, passenger seat-miles flown, and revenue passenger load factor percentages. These data are shown separately for the sixteen domestic operating airlines and by routes of each airline.

The *Journal* also carries the "Semi-Annual Air Carrier Operations Statistics" of domestic lines by routes. These data are similar to those given on a monthly basis, but in addition the months operated by each line and route are shown. The revenue passenger load factor percentages are not shown by routes but are consolidated by carrier line. Passenger seat-miles flown are not included.

The "Annual Air Carrier Operations Statistics" are also published in the *Journal*. The itemization of the data is the same as in the semi-annual statistics with the addition of mail pound-miles flown.

"Progress of Civil Aeronautics in the United States" may be found in the January 15, 1944, issue of the *Journal*. For the two years prior to this date, these tables were published separately in multilith form. It is contemplated that in the future these statistics will be published by the Civil Aeronautics Administration in a loose-leaf statistical handbook. Annual totals since 1936 on operations, equipment, personnel, gasoline and oil consumed, and accident data are given.

Other data in the same publication show private flying operations, certificates granted, airports and landing fields, and production of civil aircraft for domestic consumption excluding aircraft produced for the United States military services or those exported for civil or military use. Annual totals are given on aids to air navigation—airways, mileages, communications, and airway lighting, including weather reporting aids.

A list of scheduled air carrier aircraft in service and in reserve is published semiannually. The tables show, by airline, the identification and approved type certificate numbers of the aircraft; the make, model, year of manufacture, and seating capacity of the aircraft; and the make, model, and horsepower of the engines. The last such list available is that of 1941. Similar tabulations have not been published since the outbreak of the war because of security reasons, although current records are maintained.

The *Aircraft Yearbook of the Aeronautical Chamber of Commerce*, Washington, D. C., publishes air transport routes semiannually, showing routes operated by each airline, airline distance of each route, services offered (mail, passenger, and express), the number of trips daily, and the total of unduplicated route mileage of domestic air carrier operations.

The Civil Aeronautics Board also computes and makes public certain data which should be of interest to the businessman in the field of air transportation. Certain operating data are found in the Civil Aeronautics Board's *Recurrent Reports*. These are made monthly and show aggregates and data for individual airlines for the current month and for the corresponding month the year previous with percentage of increase. These reports show revenue mileage for mail, passengers and property; mail and property only; passenger and property only; express and freight; and charter flights. The reports also show total nonrevenue mileage and the percentage of nonrevenue miles to miles flown.

Traffic statistics are subdivided into revenue passenger miles, available seat miles, revenue passenger load factor, average revenue passenger load (persons), average available seats, number of revenue passengers carried, average length of journey over the carrier system, mail pounds, mail pound miles, average mail load, express and excess baggage by pounds, pound miles, average load, and average revenue load in pounds.

There are also data on weighted average route mileage in operation, average number of one-way trips operated daily over the system, average daily utilization of owned aircraft in hours, and average daily total miles per aircraft.

From 1939 through 1941 the Civil Aeronautics Board published semiannually two reports, *Station to Station Airline Traffic Survey* and *Origination and Destination Airline Traffic Survey*. The data in these studies cover the month for which the particular study was made. These studies were discontinued during the war but will possibly be resumed after the war.

The *Station to Station Airline Traffic Survey* contains several maps showing route numbers and stations operating for domestic airlines, average passenger traffic per day between stations, and average mail and express carried between stations. The first series of data shows how the station ranks by average daily passenger load and by mail and express rankings, average daily load by revenue passengers, mail pounds, and express pounds. A condensed alphabetical station summary gives rankings by average daily load and gives the number of scheduled flights and average load per flight. Data on the seasonal variation of revenue passenger miles are shown by airline and selected routes by month. Average deviation and range are also given. Average traffic per flight by carrier is shown by route number and by direction. These data include average traffic per flight on route between stations, average traffic per flight entering and leaving route stations, and average traffic per flight by flight number within each carrier's route.

Statistics of Other Common Carriers and Transport Agencies. The group is made up of pipelines, freight forwarders, the Railway Express Company, electric railways, private car companies, and the Pullman Company. The statistics for each are described separately in the materials which follow.

PIPELINES. This specialized means of transportation is less conspicuous than either rail or motor transportation but is important, nevertheless. Pipelines subject to Federal regulation transport crude oil, gasoline and other refined petroleum products, and natural gas.

The Hepburn Act of 1906, under which the Interstate Commerce Commission was given authority to regulate interstate pipeline operations for petroleum, exempted pipelines used for transportation of gas, either natural or artificial. In 1938 the Natural Gas Act placed control over pipelines handling gas under the Federal Power Commission.

For petroleum pipelines subject to its jurisdiction, the ICC has assembled adequate data published as *Statistics of Pipe-Line Companies*. The more important annual series disclose, by company, miles of line operated, divided into gathering lines and trunk lines. The latter item is further divided into those used for crude oil and those for transporting refined products.

The amount of either crude or refined oil transported is shown in units of barrels; the data show amounts originated, received from connections, barrels terminated, and deliveries to connections. The annual number of barrel-miles of crude and refined oils is given for trunk pipelines. Average and total number of employees with corresponding figures for compensation are given and also data on the financial condition of each company.

FREIGHT FORWARDERS. Forwarders are not common carriers in the sense that railroads and motor carriers are common carriers, although forwarders were made subject to regulation by the Interstate Commerce Commission in 1942. An example will show how the forwarder performs its functions and obtains its revenue. Less-than-carload shipments of freight are obtained from various shippers in a locality, consolidated into a carload, and shipped in the name of the forwarder at the carload rate. At destination the car is unloaded and the several shipments turned over to the proper consignees.

The forwarder obtains its revenue from the spread between the relatively high less-than-carload rate paid it by the shipper and the lower carload rate paid by the forwarding company to the railroad. The shipper generally pays no more than the railroad would charge for less-than-carload service and receives an expedited service that usually insures delivery well ahead of the regular rail schedule.

On both an annual and a quarterly basis the ICC publishes, for forwarder operations, transportation revenue; amount of transportation purchased by type of transport (forwarders utilize the services of various kinds of transportation agencies); tons of freight handled; and number of shipments received from shippers. Selected financial and operating statistics are available annually.

EXPRESS COMPANIES. In reality there is only one railway express company in the United States: Railway Express Agency, Inc., the capital stock of which is owned by 70 Class I railroads. There is in effect between Railway Express and each of about 400 carriers agreements in standard form which designate the Agency as the exclusive agent for carrying on express service over its lines. After expenses are deducted from revenue, the remainder is apportioned among the carriers party to the standard agreement according to the volume of express handled on each line as measured by gross express revenues. Annual figures on inventory value of equipment owned and mileage covered by operations in each state are available through the ICC.

Data similar to those obtained by the ICC on railroad employment are shown for the express agency. Financial data, too, are also maintained in some detail.

ELECTRIC RAILWAYS. As motor transportation has increased in importance this form of transportation has dwindled in recent years. Electric railways, however, still occupy a place in the transport picture.

The ICC publishes annually *Selected Financial and Operating Statistics from Annual Reports of Electric Railways.* These statistics, for individual carriers, follow the ICC pattern for steam railroads but in lesser detail.

PRIVATE CAR COMPANIES. In accordance with the Interstate Commerce Act, persons furnishing railway cars or protective service against heat or cold to or on behalf of any carrier by railroad or express company subject to Part I (devoted to railroad regulation) of the Interstate Commerce Act are requested to file reports with the ICC. Reports began with 1942. The data are published by ICC in *Selected Statistics from Annual Reports of Private Car Owners.*

Private car companies, also called private car lines, or private car owners are divided by the ICC into three classes for making annual reports: those owning 1,000 cars or more; those owning 100 but less than 1,000; those owning less than 100 cars, from which no annual report is required.

Refrigerator cars and tank cars are the types of equipment most commonly furnished by private car lines. These private cars are usually identified by the letter "X" in the number appearing on the car.

Annual statistics published for private car owners, identified by type of car, include investment in transportation property, equipment owned, and mileage made. Selected financial and operating statistics are also available. The quarterly statistical series include cars owned, by type of car; revenue receivable, by basis of payment and type of car; and serviceable and unserviceable cars, by types.

PULLMAN COMPANY. Several tables are devoted to the Pullman Company in *Statistics of Railways in the United States.* The general balance sheet and income account are given. Average miles of railroad over which operations were conducted, number of revenue passengers, and units of various kinds of Pullman equipment, considered together, give insight into the importance of Pullman operations.

COMMUNICATION STATISTICS

Two important publications on communication statistics are published annually by the Federal Communications Commission. The first, *Statistics of the Communications Industry in the United States*, contains summary data and data for individual communications common carriers. For the standard broadcast stations and networks, statistics are not shown in detail because these companies are not common carriers and their reports are not of public record. More elaborate figures are shown, however, for the broadcast stations and networks in the second annual document, namely, *Financial and Employee Data Respecting Networks and Standard Broadcast Stations*.

Telephone. Telephone carriers reporting to the Federal Communications Commission receive over 95 percent of the gross operating revenues received for telephone service in the United States. These carriers are divided into four classes according to average annual operating revenue: Class A, exceeding $100,000; Class B, exceeding $50,000 but not more than $100,000; Class C, exceeding $25,000 but not more than $50,000; and Class D, $25,000 or less.[7] The most important data are obtained from Classes A and B carriers.

Geographical grouping is maintained for the purpose of statistical analysis of the telephone industry. The United States is divided into three districts—Eastern, Southern, and Western. These in turn have been subdivided into nine regions.

On a state basis there are annual data based on reports of Class A and Class B carriers disclosing miles of wire in cable and aerial wire, number of central offices, average number of local and toll calls a month, number of business and residential telephones, and operating taxes. With the exception of the last item, on which data are available since 1934, the information is available since 1938.

Data covering the following items show the development of Class A carriers through the years since 1926: number of carriers, investment in telephone plant, various reserves, capitalization, total surplus, interest on funded debt, dividends declared, local and toll service revenue, operating expenses, operating ratio, operating taxes, and net operating income. Additional items show miles of wire and pole lines, number of telephones, average number of calls per month, number of employees at end of year, total employee compensation, and average compensation per employee for each year.

---

[7] Carriers having average annual operating revenues exceeding $50,000 are required to file annual reports. Those having annual operating revenues exceeding $250,000 are required to file monthly reports of revenue and expenses.

Annual data beginning in 1938 are available on radiotelephone service reported by telephone carriers, showing the number of chargeable calls and gross revenue from calls between fixed stations in overseas service, including transatlantic and transpacific calls. Similar information is given for calls in mobile service, consisting mostly of ship telephone service through land stations located in the United States. The number of vessels with radiotelephone service is indicated.

One of the oldest of the statistical series on telephone carriers contains annual figures on number of employees of Class A telephone carriers, according to occupation and weekly rate of compensation as of the end of each year.

In conjunction with the foregoing annual statistical series for telephone carriers the FCC publishes monthly a report entitled *Summary of Monthly Reports of Large Telephone Carriers in the United States.* The gross operating revenues of telephone carriers included in this report cover approximately 95 percent or more of the revenues of all telephone carriers in the United States. In addition to the Class A carriers, a group of large carriers reporting voluntarily are included, bringing the number of carriers covered in the monthly report to about 100. The series begins in 1933 and discloses operating revenues, operating expenses, net operating income, revenue from message tolls, and average message tolls per day.

Statistics of the Communications Industry in the United States contains annual data for individual Class A and Class B telephone carriers, approximately 90 in number, with summaries covering all carriers, the Bell system, and the major geographical subdivisions of the industry. The reports are based on items from balance sheets, income statements, plant operating statistics, and employment data. By the use of the excellent general index in the document, information by subject and for each company is easily located.

Telegraph, Cable, and Radiotelegraph. Statistical information relating to this telegraph service is obtained by the FCC from annual reports filed by land-wire telegraph carriers, often called telegraph carriers; carriers engaged in the ocean cable business; and radiotelegraph carriers. These statistics are included in *Statistics of the Communications Industry in the United States.* Monthly reports are required of those carriers having annual operating revenues in excess of $50,000, from which monthly statistical data are compiled and published by the FCC.

A list of the carriers reporting to the FCC is published, showing the type of carrier service rendered and the type of report filed with the regulatory agency.

For large wire-telegraph and radiotelegraph carriers annual aggregate figures are shown, beginning in 1926, for the number of carriers, selected financial statistics, miles of wire in cable and aerial wire, number of revenue messages transmitted, number of employees at end of June, total employee compensation, and average compensation per employee for the year.

The FCC annual data regarding revenue messages transmitted by large wire-telegraph and radiotelegraph carriers are ample. The messages are classified according to class, number of messages in each class, number of words in each class, and amount of revenue. The information is presented separately for landline telegraph carriers and ocean cable carriers. The series begins with 1937.

Annual employment information for these large carriers begins with 1916 and gives the number of employees, classified according to occupation and aggregate monthly rate of compensation for each occupational group.

The monthly statistics published on telegraph and radiotelegraph are patterned very closely after those published monthly for telephone carriers, which are discussed in the preceding section.

Also similar to annual data for telephone carriers are those for individual telegraph, cable, and radiotelegraph carriers, covering balance sheet items, income statement, and general operating statistics. The series begins in 1934. Individual companies are listed in the general index of *Statistics of the Communications Industry*.

Broadcast Stations and Networks. Standard broadcast stations reporting to the FCC are grouped geographically for statistical purposes into three districts—Northern, Southern, and Western. These districts have been further subdivided into seven regions.

Statistics published on the broadcasting industry, as mentioned previously, are found in *Statistics of the Communications Industry*, with more detailed data available in the report entitled *Financial and Employee Data Respecting Networks and Standard Broadcast Stations.*

Financial data published are extensive, with most of the series beginning with the year 1937. Currently shown are data on revenues, expenses, and income of radio networks, including 9 key stations of major networks, 23 other stations managed and operated by the networks, and 819 other standard broadcast stations showing revenue from the sale of broadcast time to major networks, regional networks, and other networks and stations.[8]

[8] Number of stations in the groups mentioned in this discussion vary slightly from year to year.

Other figures on the sale of time show non-network time sales to national, regional, and local advertisers and sponsors. Also available are data on revenue from the sale of talent under contract to the respondent and commissions and fees received for placing talent. Miscellaneous data published cover sundry broadcast expenses, payments by networks to foreign stations, commissions paid to regularly established agencies, representatives, and brokers, total broadcast expenses of networks and stations, and broadcast income before Federal tax deductions.

For 851 standard broadcast stations considerable annual data are published, including broadcast revenues, expenses, and income, by broadcast region, state, class, and time on the air according to stations affiliated with major networks and those not so affiliated. Additional statistics on the same basis as shown for networks are available for this same group of stations by annual revenue groups, according to total time sales. The revenue groups are classified in multiples of $25,000, beginning with $25,000 and ending with $250,000. Separate groups are shown for stations with revenue of $250,000 to $500,000; over $500,000 to $1,000,000; and $1,000,000 or more. Revenues of stations with time sales of less than $25,000 are considered to be received from local advertisers. The number of stations is shown for each classification.

Data are available annually for the 851 stations on revenue, expenses, and income, classified by the number of stations operated by the same respondent, by size of community, class of station, number of stations in each size of community, and by metropolitan districts. Data similar to those for the 851 standard broadcast stations are published for stations having annual revenue of $25,000 or less.

Unique among statistical series are those published by the FCC on the group of standard broadcast stations reporting loss from broadcast operations. These number approximately 195 stations. The items shown are similar in general to those shown for the 851 stations, allowing a careful analysis of the unprofitable operations.

Three important groups of annual statistics are available on tangible property of the broadcasting industry. The first relates to tangible property of all standard stations and networks, showing cost of the property to the licensee, depreciation to date, and depreciated cost. These figures apply to 851 broadcast stations, 4 major networks, and 3 regional networks.

The second group pertains to tangible broadcast property of the 851 standard stations according to type of network served. Included is a classification of property intended for broadcast service, showing original cost, depreciation, and depreciated cost. The stations are classified as to class and time on the air.

In the third group, cost to licensee, depreciation to date, and depreciated cost are shown by broadcast region and state. The states are grouped into seven broadcast regions, and the regions are grouped into the three districts established for statistical purposes by the FCC.

Mention of employment and employee compensation data completes the discussion of FCC statistics for the broadcasting industry. Monthly data are published on number of employees and total employee compensation of the 851 stations by class of station and time on the air. Similar figures are given for 4 major and 6 regional networks, in addition to those given on the same basis for the 851 stations by broadcast regions.

Several series are available on employment and compensation based on one week in October. Typical is the series showing number of full-time employees and average compensation paid by standard broadcast stations, by occupational class, for each of the years 1939 to 1942 and the percent change in weekly compensation for each year.

A final word on communications statistics: To obtain the professional attention of those handling the data, address your inquiry to the Federal Communications Commission, Accounting, Statistical and Tariff Department, Washington 25, D. C.

ELECTRIC STATISTICS

The principal source of statistics on electric utility operations is the Federal Power Commission. The Securities and Exchange Commission also publishes reports of studies made by its Public Utilities Division primarily for the use of the Commission. Federal Power Commission statistics are published as separate reports or as part of a rate service and a statistical information service.[9]

Federal Power Commission. The statistical information service includes monthly reports on electric energy production by electric utilities and industrial establishments. Production data by states are shown separately for energy generated by water power and energy generated by fuels. Total energy production of industrial establishments is estimated from monthly reports of about 800 generating plants representing 85 percent of the 1943 industrial production of energy. Monthly reports of electric energy production are received from practically all electric utilities. Prior to 1945 this series was limited to

[9] For publications or information address Federal Power Commission, Washington 25, D. C.

production of electric energy for public use. The inclusion of information on the industrial generation of power improves these data for use as a general business indicator. The annual reports of electric energy production, also a part of the statistical information service, present annual summaries of energy production for public use and end-of-year figures on installed generator capacity and number of plants by class of ownership and by type of prime mover, as well as retrospective monthly information on energy production.

The Commission's report *Electric Power Requirements of Industrial Establishments, 1939–1942 (Actual), 1943 and 1944 (Estimated)* presents annual data on the industrial use and generation of electricity in the United States, starting with the period for which the FPC began the collection of these statistics. The information in this report shows the number of kilowatt-hours purchased and maximum kilowatt demand of purchases, the number of kilowatt-hours generated and the maximum generated demand, the number of kilowatt-hours sold or delivered to others, the number of kilowatt-hours used in industrial operations, and the rated capacity of industrial generating plants summarized (1) by states, (2) by major industry groups by states, and (3) by minor industry classifications. Approximately 21,000 manufacturing, extracting, and government establishments report this information. These plants represent in excess of 90 percent of the total electricity consumed by manufacturing and extracting industries in the United States.

Detailed information on the consumption of fuel in the production of electric energy for public use by public utilities is obtained from the same utility reports in which information on the production of energy is supplied. The monthly report shows for each state consumption of coal, oil, and gas in the production of energy by public utilities and coal and oil stocks on hand at the end of the reporting period. The annual report presents, in addition to retrospective monthly data, kilowatt-hour production by each kind of fuel. (See Chapter 4 for a full discussion of fuel consumption statistics.)

In 1940 the FPC began the publication of a series on electric power requirements and supply in the United States.[10] For purposes of this study, the principal electric utility operating systems in the United States (and a few large industrial generating plants) were divided into 48 power supply areas which were later also combined into eight power supply regions. At the present time summary information by the 48 power supply areas and the eight power supply regions is furnished

---

[10] In 1935 the FPC conducted a National Power Survey and published a report presenting an analysis of the Nation's power resources and power requirements.

monthly, and detailed monthly information by companies is available annually. Information contained in these reports is based upon data furnished by the utilities on actual and estimated electric energy requirements, peak demands, reserve requirements, and capacity.

A comparison of capacity and demand indicates the over-all condition of the industry to meet requirements for electric power. However, under conditions unlike those assumed, capacity may be different from the reported figure. Although power supply areas have been selected because they represent the physical boundaries within which utility operation may be integrated, there are within these areas limitations on existing interconnection facilities. Estimates of future requirements are the utilities' own.

Of assistance particularly in connection with the Commission's study of electric power requirements and supply is the *Directory of Electric Generating Plants,* which was published in 1941 based on data compiled as of June 30, 1940. All electric utility plants of 1,000 kilowatt capacity or more are listed, by states, under each utility by which they are operated. A map showing the location of the generating stations and the principal interconnections accompanies this directory. Distribution of the directory is at present restricted. There have been, however, since the date of publication substantial changes in the generating capacity of electric utility systems, and it is expected that the Commission will bring this publication up to date shortly.

Also a part of the statistical information service is the Commission's monthly report on revenues and income of privately owned Class A and Class B electric utilities. Utilities in Classes A and B are those which have an annual electric revenue of $250,000 or more. On the basis of both assets and revenues, these companies comprise in excess of 95 percent of the privately owned electric light and power industry. Together with the Commission's annual report *Statistics of Electric Utilities in the United States,* there is available extensive information to determine the earnings and financial position of the electric utility industry. The annual report contains for each operating company financial information consisting of a balance sheet, income and earned surplus, capital stock and bonds, electric operating revenues by classes or service, electric operating expenses, and utility plant. This information is available on an annual basis beginning with the year 1937 and is presented according to the Commission's Uniform System of Accounts.

Published as a separate report and as a part of the Commission's *Statistics of Electric Utilities in the United States, 1943* are composite statements of the balance sheet, income and earned surplus accounts, electric operating revenues, and electric operating expenses of Class A and Class B privately owned electric utilities for the years 1937 through 1943. These composite statements are the total of the individual annual operating utility reports to the Commission and are not consolidated to eliminate duplications. No attempt has been made to render these reports directly comparable on a year-to-year basis.

In addition to the financial information just described, the report *Statistics of Electric Utilities in the United States* presents physical data for individual operating companies. Generating capacity is classified by type of prime mover and by number of plants within certain specified limits. Generation, by type of prime mover, energy purchases, and interchange-in are also shown. Disposition of this energy is shown in energy sales, interchange-out, company use, and losses. Both structure and circuit miles are shown for transmission lines, classified by voltage and supporting structures. Transformer capacity and special equipment capacity are given separately for substations classified as transmission and distribution. Information on distribution systems shows miles of overhead and underground lines, number and capacity of transformers, and number of meters. For street lighting and signal systems there are shown number and capacity of transformers and number of lamps.

For the year 1942 the Commission also published in a report similar to that prepared annually for private utilities financial and operating information for municipal utilities selected on the basis of complete filings.

The uses which may be made of data contained in the Commission's *Statistics of Electric Utilities in the United States* are too numerous to recount completely here. However, the Commission itself has used this information in studies it has prepared for publication. One of these is *Electric Utility Cost Units and Ratios*. In this report, the Commission developed a comprehensive analysis of electric utility costs. Ratios of plant investment reflect type of prime mover and size of plant. Operating expense units are related to station size and to plant factor. Operating ratios are divided on the basis of principal source of power, i.e., fuel generation, hydro generation, or purchased power. Financial ratios are based upon the entire operations of the utility companies, but in the development of these ratios those companies having a high proportion of assets represented by other than utility plant investment are excluded. The results of this study afford a useful measure of an individual utility's own performance, but not without investigation as to the underlying causes for variation from the average.

Another study published by the Commission illustrates the use which may be made of information presented in *Statistics of Electric Utilities in the United States.* This is the Commission's report on *Electric Sales Statistics, 1938* for privately and publicly owned utilities. Data summarized in this report are helpful in indicating the extent to which electricity is used and the distribution of service among the various classes of customers. Care should be taken, however, in interpreting the relationship revealed in such a study. For instance, in analyzing the average revenue per kilowatt hour, reference should be made to rate schedules before conclusions are established as to the trend in rate levels.

The Commission publishes a *National Electric Rate Book* and individual rate books for each state summarizing the rates charged by publicly owned and privately owned electric utilities in communities of 1,000 inhabitants or more. Rates for rural service are excluded.

Typical bills computed from schedules contained in the rate book are of assistance in analyzing rate levels. The Commission began the publication of such studies with a preliminary report presenting "typical" bills for residential service in effect January 1, 1935, in cities of 50,000 inhabitants or more, followed by a series of state reports presenting typical bills for residential service, commercial lighting service, commercial power service, and industrial service. Annual publication of the state series was discontinued with the reports for January 1942.

Industrial and commercial service bills especially are "typical" only under specified conditions of use. A mere comparison of bills, however, is subject to severe qualifications. Consideration should be given in making such comparisons to differences in customer density, source of power, and adequacy of service. The study of *Electric Utility Cost Units and Ratios* previously described is helpful in explaining differences in rates.

Based upon the detailed tabulations of typical bills in effect in 1935, the Commission itself prepared a study on *Comparative Rates of Publicly and Privately Owned Electric Utilities* (1936) which contains, in addition to summaries of bills for electric service, information on those factors accounting for differences in rates such as taxes paid by privately owned utilities, taxes and cash contributions of publicly owned utilities, and "free services" rendered by publicly owned utilities. This study was last brought up to date with publication of the report *Rates, Taxes, and Consumers Savings, Publicly and Privately Owned Electric Utilities (1935–1937)*, and expanded to include information on rate reductions.

The statistical information service currently published by the Federal Power Commission includes three studies which were made in anticipation of their continuance on an annual basis. Publication was interrupted by the war. One of these studies is on *Electric Construction Budgets—1943 and Electric Construction Expenditures—1942*. Expenditures, actual for 1942 and estimated for 1943, are shown by states and classes of ownership for generator plant, divided by type of prime mover; transmission plant; distribution plant; and general plant.

Another of the special reports included in the statistical information service is *Movement of Electric Energy Across State Lines and International Boundaries, 1941*. This publication contains a tabulation, by states, showing kilowatt-hours received and delivered during 1941 across state lines and international boundaries.

The third of the suspended annual reports included in the statistical information service is *Installed Water Power Capacity in the United States and Outlying Territories.* This report presents summaries as of January 1, 1941, of installed water power capacity of plants of 100 horsepower or more (1) for each state, divided between utility and industrial and (2) for each state, classified by size of plant within certain specified limits. Water wheel capacity is included whether or not electric generating equipment is installed.

Nonrecurring reports published by the FPC include *Electric Power Statistics 1920–1940*, also a part of the statistical information service. This report brings together all the historical data collected by the Government on production of electric energy, capacity of generating plants, and consumption of fuel in the production of electric energy. For the twenty-one years 1920–1940, data are presented in a form directly comparable with the current annual reports and in substantially the same detail. Graphic illustrations effectively portray the major development and growth of the industry.

With a few exceptions, the preceding discussion has been concerned with the periodic statistical reporting system of the FPC. In order to complete discussion of its statistical activities, however, reference is made to special surveys of the Commission. Some of these, now out of print, are *The Use of Electric Power in Transportation (1936); The Cost of Distribution of Electricity (1936); Power Requirements in Electrochemical, Electrometallurgical, and Allied Industries (1938); Electric Rate Uniformity (1936); and Rural Electric Service (1936).*[11]

Securities and Exchange Commission. Under the authority of the Public Utility Holding Company Act of 1935, the Securities and Ex-

---

[11] The principal private source of electric-utility operating statistics is the Edison Electric Institute. Information collected by the Institute is regularly available to both members and nonmembers, in an annual statistical report, monthly report of sales data, and weekly report of electric energy output.

change Commission regulates the financial practices of holding-company systems controlling gas and electric utilities. In connection with its activities in this field, the Commission has made available studies [12] which are of widespread interest but which were prepared primarily for the use of the Commission staff.

One of these studies, chiefly of an informational character and published annually as of August 31, gives a list of registered public-utility holding companies and their subsidiaries, showing corporate relationship. The information on which this report is based is obtained from registration statements and annual supplemental registration statements submitted by the holding companies.

The SEC publishes annually a report, *Security Issues of Electric and Gas Utilities*, showing for each company whose securities were offered publicly or sold privately during the years covered by the report (1) the price at which each security was offered to the public or sold privately, (2) the price paid by the underwriters if underwritten, (3) the net proceeds to the issuing company, and (4) the market price range. Data contained in this report are obtained from records of the Commission, with the exception of information on the market price range.

For the year 1938 the Commission began publication of an annual report, *Financial Statistics for Electric and Gas Subsidiaries of Registered Public-Utility Holding Companies*. This report shows for each company the principal income account and balance sheet items, together with the Commission's calculations of about a dozen financial ratios which are generally comparable between companies and which are useful to the investor. In August 1940 the Commission made available a similar report covering the years 1930–1940, particularly because the information was related to the problem of depreciation. Publication of the comparative reports was discontinued with the issuance of the report covering the years 1930–1942. These reports included only operating electric and gas utilities that are subsidiaries of registered public-utility holding companies whose assets are 5 million or more and whose securities are in the hands of the public.

[12] For publications or information address Securities and Exchange Commission. Philadelphia 3, Pennsylvania.

CHAPTER 9

ACCOUNTING STATISTICS [1]

WILLIAM W. COOPER

Bureau of the Budget

Selecting the statistical data to be presented in this chapter has involved several difficulties because of the heterogeneity introduced by the variety of purposes for which accounting data are collected and because of the confidential character of much of the information. In order to reduce this heterogeneity as much as possible we shall have to delimit the term to transactions reflected at some point in the books of account.

Accounting statistics then fall into two general categories: financial data and cost data. By financial data is meant the usual total company (as distinct from plant or product statements) profit-and-loss statements, balance sheets and buttressing schedules, such as analyses of surplus, and cost of sales. In short, the very familiar type of data which is found in stockholders' reports or income-tax returns. It is to these types of statistics that we shall primarily address ourselves. Eliminating cost statistics, i.e., such things as commodity costs and product profit-and-loss data, will enable us to reduce the field to manageable proportions. Moreover, little will be lost by this reduction. There are few recurrent cost series in the Federal Government. Most of the cost information is collected only once or at infrequent intervals for particular purposes, such as letting a contract or setting a

[1] The author wishes to express his gratitude to Messrs. Ralph Krapp, Irwin Friend, and Walter Louchheim, of the Securities and Exchange Commission; Henry M. Long, of the Federal Communications Commission; E. G. Craig, of the Federal Power Commission; E. M. Whitcomb, Howard Barker, and William Corey, of the U. S. Tariff Commission; William H. England and J. W. Adams, of the Federal Trade Commission; Rexford Parmelee and Saul B. Sells, of the Office of Price Administration; Edward White and William Turner, of the Bureau of Internal Revenue; Frederick C. Dirks and Miss Susan Burr, of the Board of Governors of the Federal Reserve System; and Samuel Nakasian, of the Bureau of the Budget. These persons devoted valuable time to reading the text and offered many helpful comments and criticisms. The author alone is, of course, responsible for errors or deficiencies.

price ceiling or tariff. Such information is of little general interest or use. The arbitrary character of most cost computations makes the cost figure as such of less importance than the changes in cost. Such costs, and such changes, are exceedingly difficult of interpretation under even the best circumstances but we shall attempt to cover the relatively few cases where these statistics are reasonably comparable, broad, and continuous enough to be of interest.

How to treat the great amount of information which is designated as confidential has been, if possible, even more of a problem. There seems little point in describing data which are not, and probably never will be, made public. The various procurement agencies, for example, collect vast quantities of both cost and financial information in connection with the negotiation, renegotiation, and termination of war contracts. No discussion of this information has been included, since in all probability none of it will be made public. A discussion of some of the data collected by the Office of Price Administration has been included even where the data are not now publicly available, since publication of statistical totals may be undertaken at some future date.

Series such as those formerly maintained by the Securities and Exchange Commission and Federal Trade Commission have been included, although publication and perhaps collection of data have been discontinued. Nonpublication may result from lack of personnel, wartime security regulations, interruption in the agency's work, or other factors. Which programs will be resumed or continued and which will be made public, and hence worth treating, must consequently rest on judgment and guesses as to the future nature of Federal activity in the field of accounting statistics.

Uses of the Data. A great many uses are made of accounting statistics by the Federal Government. They may be collected by particular agencies to set or review maximum or minimum prices; collect taxes; negotiate, renegotiate, and terminate contracts; regulate stock flotations and market activities; set and review public utility rates; and adjust claims or pay subsidies. Other agencies may also find these same statistics useful for their purposes. Supplemented by other statistics they may, for example, serve to indicate broad levels of economic activity for over-all policy formation and review covering such activities as devising new tax or borrowing programs, adjusting banking policy, reviewing the workability of laws, regulations, and administrative procedures.

Similarly, private persons may find these statistics of considerable value. Business firms may find them useful in controlling and directing sales activity. The sales of a given firm, to cite one illustration, may be compared with the sales of an industry over the past and causes for variation analyzed. Through these techniques, errors of the past and possible means of improvement may be discovered. For example, the sales for a given firm may be increasing, but comparison with sales for the industry may disclose that its relative share of total sales is declining. This in itself may be an indication of trouble ahead. Perhaps relationships between sales in one industry and those in other industries may be discovered. If sales at one level of industrial activity have a marked effect on sales at some other level, careful study and statistical analysis may help avoid errors based on inadequate information. Correlations may even exist with the level of general business activity.

Many other applications may be found. Sales quotas may be set by geographical regions through the use of data on sales and inventories of potential customers. Selling and promotional activity may be guided by studies of the sales, profits, and financing operations of potential buyers. Inventory controls may be adjusted on the basis of predictions as to future activity resulting from such studies, and long-range financial or construction programs may be carried out, discontinued, or modified in the light of developing trends.

Financial statistics alone will not, however, prove adequate in many of these analyses. Major reliance will probably rest on other series discussed in this book. Not that financial statistics are unimportant. A manufacturer of textile machinery in analyzing his potential markets may, for example, prepare a spot map of textile mills to obtain a geographical picture of the distribution of potential customers. Definite clusters will be found at particular points on the map. But the mere existence of textile mills is not sufficient without some measure of their activity. Data on dollar sales by industry, region, and company will prove valuable as a further index of potential sales. Profitable firms, and, more particularly, firms with increasing profits, are likely to prove better customers than unprofitable ones. Information on financing programs and capital expansions may also prove useful. A supplier of raw materials may also find leads through studies of inventory data (such as inventory turnover) of potential customers.

There are other uses which may be made of accounting data without the same need for supplementary statistics—except, perhaps, for weighting purposes. For gauging the efficiency of his operations, the businessman may want to compute various expense, sales, and profit ratios for comparisons with competitors or with industry averages. In the few cases where reliable cost information is available, he may find the data useful in setting standard costs as targets for his own operations. Where individual company information can be obtained, the businessman may rank the data and hence be able to judge himself by the use of various indexes.

Financial statistics are of outstanding importance to investors. Although the investor may find aggregates useful in indicating general areas of investment or reinvestment, his decision to invest or reinvest must ultimately be made with respect to an individual company. For this purpose he must have individual company data. He can, of course, obtain company reports in some cases, or he can refer to one of the various private investment services, but most Federal statistics will be of limited usefulness to him because usually they do not reveal individual company data.

With these potential users in mind, we may describe the most important sources of Federal financial statistics available for public use.

BUREAU OF INTERNAL REVENUE

Although processing and publishing financial statistics has only recently been recognized as a continuing responsibility of the Federal Government, certain major statistics derived from Federal administrative programs have been available for a long time. Among them are the statistics derived from Federal income tax returns published annually as *Statistics of Income*.[2] These important statistics were first published in 1916 on specific direction from Congress, and every subsequent Revenue Act has carried forward a provision requiring the preparation of these statistics. From the point of view of the Government, these data are valuable in arriving at estimates of national income and income distribution, individual and corporate savings, etc.; they form the basis of important decisions affecting tax and banking policy, budgetary policy, and numerous other decisions of broad economic policy; and finally, since the coverage is practically universal for corporations and extremely broad for individuals, these statistics provide important benchmarks for checking and adjusting other statistical series.

Statistics of Income are published annually in two volumes: Part I is compiled from individual income tax returns (including partnerships and sole proprietorships), fiduciary income tax returns, estate tax returns, and gift tax returns; Part II contains statistics compiled from corporation income and declared value excess profits tax returns, corporation excess profits tax returns, and personal holding company returns. It is with Part II that we shall be primarily concerned.

[2] Sold by the Superintendent of Documents.

For corporations the coverage is practically complete. Naturally there is some fluctuation from year to year and a change over the whole period. For the long and turbulent span covered by these statistics, however, the fluctuation is surprisingly small. For the last published report, 1940, more than 500,000 corporation reports have been filed and processed. Even during the war period the figures have remained fairly constant.

Corporate data cover the bulk of the business community in terms of dollar volume. By far the greater number of businesses, however, are conducted as sole proprietorships or partnerships. Data on these two categories may be found in Part I but are more scanty than data for corporations. Partnership profit and partnership loss, business profit and business loss are shown by net income classes; and various frequency distributions in terms of sources of income and distributions by states are also shown. Most of the data for partnerships are, however, shown by profits distributed to the individual partner. Data on business profits must be interpreted with care, since reports on individual income tax returns may cover profits on more than one business enterprise. Coverage is not universal, as in the case of corporations. Difficulties arise both in terms of legal exemptions and because of the tremendous problems of enforcement in small business enterprise. The Bureau endeavors from time to time to include more extensive data, but the lack of such information as balance sheet data on partnerships and proprietorships arises from limitations of administration or law and is not likely to be overcome for the mere sake of better or more complete statistics. Within these limits, though, it would be of considerable value if the Bureau could publish more complete statistics on the various items of income, cost, and expenses now included in the tax returns.[3]

The data on corporations in Part II are much more extensive, including balance sheet data and distribution by states as well as fre-

[3] Supplemental studies have been issued from time to time. The Works Progress Administration in cooperation with the Division of Research and Statistics issued in 1938 a volume entitled *Statistics of Income Supplement, Compiled from Federal Income Tax Returns of Individuals for the Income Year 1934*. In 1940, three volumes, *Statistics of Income Supplement Compiled from Income Tax Returns for 1936, Individual Incomes*, were issued, divided into 4 sections: Section I, "Distribution and Sources"; Section II, "Income of Husbands and Wives Filing Separate Returns"; Section III, "Patterns of Income"; and Section IV, "Capital Gains and Losses." These tables contain many valuable analyses but, unfortunately, they do not contain corporation data. A similar study from the 1936 tax returns was made on a selected sample of small corporations. Although still available in the source book prepared by the project, corporation data have never been published.

quency distributions by income and asset classes. Specifically, tables of major interest on corporate financial data contained in *Statistics of Income* include the following: (1) data by states for the current year showing number of returns, net income and tax and dividend data; (2) profit-and-loss data by major and minor industrial groups; (3) business income and deductions, capital gains and losses, income and excess profits taxes, and dividends (by types) by major industrial groups; (4) balance sheet and profit-and-loss data by major industrial groups; [4] (5) frequency distributions by total asset classes (for corporations filing balance sheets) showing both balance sheet and income-and-expense data cross classified for selected balance sheet and profit-and-loss items by major industrial groups; (6) balance sheet, and profit-and-loss and tax data for corporations filing excess profits tax returns, classified by different methods of computing the tax; and (7) historical data, including a summary table from 1909 to date, net income classes from 1937 to date, and profit-and-loss and balance sheet from 1926 to date classified by major industrial groups.

The data contained in *Statistics of Income* are summaries of more detailed tables compiled by the Bureau of Internal Revenue and maintained in a *Source Book*. For corporations these data are available from 1926 to date; for individual returns the data are recorded from 1927 to date. There is only one copy of the *Source Book* available and it is not open to public inspection without the approval of the Secretary of the Treasury. A *Synopsis of the Data and Classifications* describing the data contained in the *Source Book* is, however, prepared and may be obtained from the Statistical Section, Income Tax Unit, Bureau of Internal Revenue, Washington, D. C. In general, the data contained in the *Source Book* are the same as those contained in *Statistics of Income* except that they are presented in more detail.

Although income tax statistics are of great value for many purposes, there are shortcomings from the point of view of the business user. Not the least important is the fact that the data are not current. Generally, about two years elapses between the time the income tax reports are filed and the data are published. This lag in publication may limit the use of these data for purposes of current analysis, but the data are still invaluable for benchmark purposes and general

---

[4] These data are, of course, only for corporations filing balance sheets. Two errors should be guarded against here: first, balance sheets are not obtained in all cases, although the Bureau has become more insistent on the filing of balance sheets in recent years. Furthermore, the corporation's own balance sheet is acceptable in lieu of filing Schedule L on Form 1120, provided the balance sheet is prepared on the same basis as the tax return.

economic analyses. Coupled with more current data, they provide a broad basis for checking and adjustment and for the establishment of trends.

Other limitations should, perhaps, be noted. In order to assure publication of the statistics, even within this rather lengthy interval, the data are drawn from the unaudited, rather than the audited, returns. For errors peculiar to a particular firm, the lack of auditing and adjustment may not prove serious since, to some extent, it is possible to depend on cancelling out of errors in large aggregates of data. If a constant error is present the problem is somewhat different. If, say, business concerns in general increase their depreciation charges in anticipation of the tax authorities paring them down, this fact should be given careful consideration. Even here, however, the problem is not serious if only comparisons are to be made, and if the error is *constant* from year to year. Moreover, tax laws, regulations, and administrative practices change from time to time. The user should familiarize himself with these factors. The picture is frequently complicated by changes in accounting and business practices.

These comments apply with particular emphasis to the various expense categories and balance sheet items. The Bureau is obviously not as much interested in the *classification* of a particular item of expense as it is in determining whether it is an appropriate deduction in arriving at taxable net income. This is even more true in connection with balance sheet items. Since the income tax form does not provide for total current assets or total current liabilities, the sums of current assets and current liabilities reported (and hence total fixed assets and liabilities) may be incorrect and the important working capital total impaired, although total assets and liabilities may be correct. Again, tabulating instructions may change. Starting in 1940, for example, all reserves shown in the liabilities section of the balance sheets, except reserves for bad debts, depreciation, and depletion, were included in surplus reserves, and hence in net worth. For this reason differences between net worth in 1940 and prior years should be interpreted with caution.

The major and minor industrial groupings are based on the *Standard Industrial Classification*, a system of classification developed in the Federal Government and used in a great many statistical series.[5] The user of Federal statistics should familarize himself with both the system of classification used and the method of application. Rather than use the major product produced or sold by a company in a given

---

[5] Sold by the Superintendent of Documents.

year and freezing the classification of the firm in an assigned industry, as is done in some of the other accounting series described in this chapter, the Bureau classified each company on the basis of the commodity accounting for the greatest percentage of dollar sales in each year. This method of classification may create difficulty when comparisons are desired between years for given industries because the relative importance of commodities change. The finer the classification used, the greater the danger that fluctuations may result from classifications rather than actual financial changes in the affected firms.

SECURITIES AND EXCHANGE COMMISSION

The Securities and Exchange Commission under the full disclosure provisions of the various securities acts is another important source of financial statistics. These statistics, while valuable to business users in general, are of particular interest to investors. They are one of the few places in the Federal Government where detailed data on individual companies are available to the public.

SEC statistics are available in a variety of forms: (1) The files of the Commission, which are open to public inspection, constitute a valuable storehouse of data on all corporations which have securities registered on national exchanges or which offer public issues of securities; (2) major statistical series, such as the *Survey of American Listed Corporations;* (3) other regularly prepared reports such as the quarterly release on corporate working capital, corporate and individual savings, and cash balances; and (4) miscellaneous studies, statistical series, and publications which are released from time to time.

Under the various securities acts which the Commission administers, practically all corporations which make substantial public offerings of securities must file registration statements and annual reports with the SEC. During the year, if any substantial change occurs in finances or corporate structure, if new issues are offered, old ones retired or refinanced, the affected corporation must file an interim report qualifying its last previous statement. In addition, all prospectuses, as well as requests for "proxies" and supporting data, must be filed. These statements are examined by Commission experts to determine whether full and fair disclosure has been made in accordance with SEC rules and regulations,[6] necessary adjustments are made, and the state-

[6] Copies of the Commission rules, regulations, and reporting forms and instructions may be obtained at any SEC office or by writing to the Securities and Exchange Commission, Philadelphia, Pa. Bound volumes of Commission decisions, rules, and reports may be obtained from the Superintendent of Documents.

ments are filed in a bound docket available for public inspection.[7] The Commission maintains public reference rooms in its Philadelphia, New York, and Chicago offices, where interested members of the public may examine these reports.[8] Photocopies of these materials may also be obtained at the cost of photostating.[9] In addition, members of the Commission staff will render interpretative and advisory assistance to the public with respect to these statements in the light of the law and SEC rules, regulations, and instructions.

In order to carry out more effectively its responsibilities for full disclosure, a Commission-sponsored WPA project was begun in 1937 known as the *Survey of American Listed Corporations*. The purpose was to make available, in convenient form, part of the data on file with the Commission. These data were tabulated by individual companies classified into selected industry groups on the basis of the *Standard Industrial Classification*. In 1939 the project was changed to emphasize selected defense industries and renamed *Survey of American Listed Corporations and Study of Selected Defense Industries*. It was discontinued in February 1943, although certain studies of selected items and industries have been carried forward since that date.

The emphasis of the *Survey* is on complete data for individual companies registered with the SEC, and it covers all listed companies except those subject to the jurisdiction of the Interstate Commerce Commission (railroads), Federal Communications Commission (communication companies), insurance companies, banks and trust companies, bank holding companies, bondholders' protective committees, voting trusts, and foreign issuers other than Canadian and Cuban. It contains data on 2,125 consolidated companies (which include 11,748 named subsidiaries, making a total of 13,873 companies) [10] from 1934 to 1941, inclusive. These compilations cover 141 industry groups available in 166 published reports, and cover all the data submitted by the filing corporation in its registration statement and annual reports. The data cover both financial and nonfinancial information. The financial information consists mainly of balance sheets, profit-

---

[7] All data are available to the public unless a request for confidential treatment is requested by the filing corporation and granted by the Commission. The Commission rarely grants such requests. During the war the SEC had to withhold certain information in accordance with security regulations.

[8] Listed corporations (i.e., corporations with stocks listed on registered exchanges) file copies of the statements with the exchanges on which the securities are listed. These are generally available for public inspection.

[9] Requests should be addressed to the Administrative Division, Duplicating Unit, Securities and Exchange Commission, Philadelphia, Pa.

[10] Individual company data are generally available only on a consolidated basis.

and-loss statements, selected expense items, and surplus reconciliations. Summary tables show total assets, volume of business, etc., by industry. These tables are followed by comparative historical tables (for the period covered by the report) showing these same items for each company in the industry group. Certain nonfinancial items are also given for each company. These include such items as the date when the company's fiscal year ends, place of annual meeting, number of active and inactive subsidiaries, as well as data on funded debt and equity issues; for each registrant, parent and subsidiary company relations are given as well as the percent and level of control. In addition to data for individual companies, industry balance sheets and profit-and-loss statements as well as selected expense items and surplus reconciliations are given. These are followed by tables of selected percentage ratios and information on security issues outstanding;. also remuneration data (showing by individual registrant the total remuneration to each of the three highest paid officers, directors, or employees, and the total remuneration of all officers and directors).

In addition to the *Survey*, summary volumes were issued from time to time as the *Statistics of American Listed Corporations*. Two volumes or parts of this series were released before the project was discontinued. These volumes do not attempt to give data for individual companies, but instead present summary tables, frequency distributions, charts, and interpretative analyses.

Part 1 of the *Statistics* covers the year 1937 alone for 1,961 corporations. It includes detailed analyses of securities outstanding; classifications of the corporations as to industry, size of sales, geographic location, periods of incorporation (age), and stated subsidiaries; frequency distributions of certifying accountants; capitalization patterns; detailed financial statements (balance sheets, profit-and-loss statements, and surplus reconciliations) classified by industry, size, capital structure, return on invested capital, and profit experience groups. In addition, financial and operating ratios are presented, cross classified by industry, size, capital structure, profitability, and income leverage.

Part 2 of the *Statistics of American Listed Corporations* covers 1,495 corporations in summary tables for the years 1935 to 1939 and includes practically all companies for which financial data were presented in Part 1 and which had securities registered during the period 1935–1939, including even successor corporations, in cases of reorganization or merger, when the data are regarded as reasonably comparable throughout the period. The analysis covers only financial data but in more detail than in Part 1. As in Part 1 and the *Survey*, the data were tabulated only after processing by Commission experts. In addition, wherever feasible and desirable, adjustments were made to preserve intraindustry and interindustry or year-to-year comparability. Consolidated statements were used wherever filed by registrants, and subsidiary companies were eliminated, so far as possible, to avoid double counting. Each chart and table is accompanied by explanatory material.

Specifically, the data included in Part 2 consist of (1) detailed financial statements classified by major and minor industry groups, by type of capital structure (in 1937) and by asset size (in 1937); (2) principal financial statement items classified by rate of return on invested capital and asset size groups; (3) a summary analysis of earned and capital surplus; and (4) frequency distributions of selected financial ratios classified by industry, amount of total assets at end of 1937, amount of net sales in each year from 1935 to 1939, type of capital structure at end of 1937, and rate of return on invested capital in each year from 1935 to 1939. In addition, certain charts and summary analyses and interpretations are presented.

In addition to the *Survey* and *Statistics of American Listed Corporations*, two volumes on registrants and named subsidiaries were issued, one for 1938 and one for 1942. These show the registrants and their parents or subsidiaries by levels of corporate structure, percentage of control, and interlocking ownership. It is planned to revise and release these studies every few years. The results of study of the return on invested capital for the years 1936 through 1941, for 878 individual manufacturing companies (including 6,500 subsidiaries) were released in 1943. This was followed by a four-volume study of 1,106 manufacturing companies classified into 75 industry groups, covering the period 1936–1942. This study is usually referred to as *Data on Profits and Operations*, although the full title is *Survey of American Listed Corporations, Data on Profits and Operations, 1936–42*. Only selected data on profits and operations are presented; these include net sales; operating profit; provision for war and related contingencies provided out of income; net profit before income taxes; net profit after income taxes; selling, general, and administrative expenses; maintenance and repairs; depreciation, depletion, amortization, etc.; intangible assets; net worth; net profit before income taxes as a percent of net worth; and net profit after income taxes as a percent of net worth. The data are presented both by combined industry totals and for individual companies for each of the years covered in the study. A similar study covering the years 1942 and 1943 has been completed and published. The 1942 data are revised to take account of renegotiation adjustments which were not known at the time of the original study.

The statistics in these studies have several marked advantages from the point of view of both the business user and the investor. They are the only major Federal statistical series on financial data (exclusive of industries subject to regulatory commissions such as public utilities and railroads) which give figures both for aggregates and for individual companies. Many of these data, even in aggregate form, are not elsewhere available. In addition, careful review and examination is given to each statement filed by the registrant in discharge of the Commission's responsibility for "full and fair disclosure." This assures a maximum of accuracy and comparability. Finally the Commission, in its various rules and regulations, has tried to allow full scope to established commercial practice. This is more likely to result in a truer picture of operations than when reports are filed under preconceived legal standards such as obtained in the computation of "taxable net income" under the Internal Revenue Code.

There are, however, several disadvantages. Most of the volumes are now out of print, although copies are available both in Commission offices and in depository libraries. In addition, photocopies may be obtained from the SEC in Philadelphia at a cost of ten cents per page, or seven cents per page for all copies over 100 in a single order.

Discontinuance of the project, with the exception of *Data on Profits and Operations*, is itself a serious disadvantage since these data are now of interest largely as background or historical material. Unincorporated business is not included and, from the very nature of the corporations subject to SEC jurisdiction, small business is inadequately represented. Nonetheless, the study constitutes an important source for users of accounting data. Despite the limited number of companies, more than 50 percent of total corporate assets in the United States are represented in the group. Wherever individual company data or painstaking accounting treatment are desired, this material will prove of great value. The fact that individual company data are presented in elaborate detail makes it relatively easy for the user to supplement these data by surveys either of his own or from other sources in order to secure whatever sample he may require.

The SEC also prepares a quarterly compilation on corporate working capital as well as certain statistics on public utilities resulting from the administration of the holding-company act. The quarterly release on working capital is an outgrowth of the Commission's studies of the volume and composition of individual and corporate savings, begun in 1942. The report on working capital covers the detail of the working capital items (including some 16 current asset and liability items) for more than 1,000 registered corporations. This series was only recently begun by the Commission, and the first release was made on June 9, 1944. This covered the years 1939–1943, and the figures were "blown up" by keying them into *Statistics of Income* and other statistical series. Statistical tables are presented for all United States corporations, for registered corporations, for manufacturing corporations (in total and for manufacturing corporations in war and nonwar industries), for manufacturing corporations with assets under $5,000,000, for manufacturing companies with assets from $5,000,000 to $100,000,000, and for manufacturing corporations with assets of $100,000,000 and over, as well as for railroads, public utility systems, and trade corporations. This series will be carried forward quarterly, and copies of the regular release as well as more detailed data for various industrial and size groups may be obtained on request from the SEC.

Although lacking in individual company information, these reports are of interest in view of the importance of current data on corporate working capital, particularly in the reconversion period which lies ahead. For purposes of current analysis this series has marked advantages because of the speed with which the data are collected, processed, and released. Publication is usually within two months after the close of the quarter.

The SEC has made extended studies of particular fields of industry such as the Insurance Industry,[11] Protective and Reorganization Committees, and Investment Trusts and Companies.[12]

FEDERAL TRADE COMMISSION

The Federal Trade Commission has long been active in the field of financial and cost statistics. The Commission has devoted itself to specific studies designed for particular purposes. However, in 1940 a regular program of collecting, processing, and publishing corporate financial reports was undertaken under the title of *Federal Trade Commission Industrial Corporation Reports*, commonly referred to as *Industry Reports*.

[11] Temporary National Economic Committee, Monographs No. 2 *Families and Their Life Insurance*, No. 28 *Study of Legal Reserve Life Insurance Companies*, No. 28-A *(Statement on Life Insurance)*. Other studies were also conducted by the Commission for the TNEC. Cf., e.g., Monograph No. 29 *The Distribution of Ownership in the 200 Largest Nonfinancial Corporations*, and Monograph No. 30 *Survey of Shareholdings in 1,710 Corporations with Securities Listed on a National Securities Exchange.* (Sold by the Superintendent of Documents.)

[12] A list of these studies may be obtained from the Annual Reports of the Securities and Exchange Commission (also cf. *The Work of the Securities and Exchange Commission, May 1944*, prepared by the SEC) or by writing to the Commission in Philadelphia.

As noted in the previous section, the coverage of the SEC series was limited to corporations subject to Commission jurisdiction. The Federal Trade Commission reports were designed to supplement the SEC statistics by broadening the coverage and by asking for certain data which were not obtained by the SEC.[13] As the title indicates, these statistics were confined to manufacturing companies. Unincorporated enterprises were not included in the series, and data were published in aggregate form only. Both listed and unlisted corporations were covered in these reports.

The Federal Trade Commission first requested some 900 of the principal corporations operating in 76 manufacturing industries to file financial reports of their 1938 and 1939 operations. In 1941 a series of separate reports for each industry was published in pamphlet form.[14] These covered, for 1938 and 1939, selected financial ratios; principal assets and percent of increase or decrease; principal liabilities, capital, and surplus, and percent of increase or decrease; combined detailed balance sheets and percent of increase or decrease; and, for the year 1939 only, combined detailed statements of income and expense, earned surplus, and investment (by types of equity interests). Since reliable data on cost of goods sold were not obtainable in all cases, a supplementary schedule was usually prepared covering the corporations from which reliable data were obtained. Explanatory text is included in each report.

For the year 1940 the coverage was extended to some 4,500 corporations. A similar series of reports was prepared, but distribution was not made outside the government. Further work was then suspended.

The fact that the project was of such short duration is probably its major shortcoming from the point of view of the business user. As a result of the development of other war activities, the project was discontinued and the Commission did not execute its plans for obtaining more adequate coverage and for preparing more detailed tabulations (by size groups, geographical areas, etc.). Despite these drawbacks, however, this series constitutes the only source of this type of information for many industries.[15] The Commission exercised a great deal

[13] The main additional items requested by the FTC are subdivisions of sales between domestic and foreign; an analysis of cost of goods sold; and certain analyses of selling, general, and administrative expense and plant account.

[14] Copies may be obtained from the Federal Trade Commission, Washington, D. C.

[15] The pamphlets are arranged in convenient form for each industry. A list of these pamphlets and the industries covered (as well as other Federal Trade Commission publications) may be obtained from the *List of Available Publications of the Federal Trade Commission*, copies of which may be obtained on request to the Federal Trade Commission, Washington, D. C.

of care in the preparation of these reports, and they contain certain types of information (such as analysis of cost of goods sold, and details of cash, etc.), which are not elsewhere available.

In addition to the *Industrial Corporation Reports*, the Trade Commission has made numerous investigations of selected industries. Some of these investigations are incidental to regular Commission functions; others are undertaken in order to service other agencies which call upon the Commission to furnish expert assistance. Frequently these surveys are exhaustive in character, involving elaborate field studies and extensive analyses and interpretations of both cost and financial data. The FTC gives somewhat heavier emphasis to financial data than the Tariff Commission, which we shall discuss in a later section.

While few of these studies have as yet been made public it may be well to list the more important studies that the Commission has made during the past five years. Most of the studies cover the years 1936–1942.

Subject of Study	*Number of Companies Covered*
1. Household furniture industry (including trends in unit costs and prices for typical items).	67 *
2. Biscuit and cracker industry (including comparative costs. The study covers wholesale baking companies, wholesale and house-to-house companies, house-to-house and retail chain grocery companies).	60
3. Bread baking industry (including plant costs. Study covers wholesale bakeries, house-to-house bakeries, and chain grocery bakeries).	375
4. Phosphate rock mining industry (including cost and price data).	12
5. Fertilizer industry (including cost and price data).	20
6. Paperboard Inquiry:	
a. Manufacturers of paperboard (exclusive of those manufacturing containers and other paper products).	28 *
b. Manufacturers of paperboard containers and other paper products (both studies include extensive plant and product cost data).	18 *

* Through 1941 only.

OFFICE OF PRICE ADMINISTRATION

As the agency responsible for the Government's price control program, the OPA has had a broad program for the collection of cost and financial statistics. Much of this information, however, is collected for the administrative purposes of drafting, revising, and reviewing of a price regulation and the processing of an application for price adjustment. The information is thus extremely limited in scope and will never be made public. Such data are consequently of little interest to the potential business consumer of government statistics.

There are two general categories of statistics collected by OPA, however, which possess considerable interest—the general financial statistics program, known as OPA Forms A and B administered by the Financial Reporting Branch of the Accounting Department and certain periodic reporting programs (covering mainly plant or product costs) maintained in a few of the price branches.

With the passage of the Emergency Price Control Act of 1942, it was decided to set up a broad program for the collection of financial statistics in the Accounting Department. This program ultimately replaced the financial statistics program of the Federal Trade Commission and Securities and Exchange Commission. To meet the wartime needs of price control special forms, to be known as OPA Forms A and B, were designed and the coverage was extended to all corporations in the fields of manufacturing, mining, and construction, with total assets of $250,000 or above. Form A, consisting of detailed financial statements and buttressing schedules (including analyses of business structure, cost of sales, surplus, property and reserve accounts, and compensation of officers and employees), was collected annually; and Form B, consisting of a profit-and-loss statement, balance sheet, and statement of cost of sales, was collected quarterly. In order to reduce, as much as possible, difficulties arising from the production of more than one product by a single company, emphasis was placed on obtaining these data from the operating subsidiaries rather than from parent corporations, particularly where the latter acted primarily in the capacity of holding companies.

These returns were collected on a voluntary basis, from about 18,000 companies, covering their operations for the fiscal years 1941 and 1942. In 1943, however, it was decided to revise the program. Coverage, because of the asset limitation, had proved inadequate in many industries, and difficulties in obtaining and processing the information were slowing down the operations of the price branches which needed more complete and rapid information in order to keep abreast of a rapidly changing picture. Simplified forms which could be filled out by both small and large firms (unincorporated as well as incorporated) were devised, and it was decided to construct representative samples for each industry. In addition, more adequate coverage was extended to the wholesale and retail trades,[16] and it was decided to invoke the man-

---

[16] A sample of 2,000 independent retail stores was included. For this group, however, a special form was designed consisting of a simple profit-and-loss statement and balance sheet. At present only annual data, covering the years 1941, 1942, and 1943, are being collected from this group.

datory powers of the statute where necessary to maintain the adequacy of the samples. When the samples are finally constructed it is expected that between 30,000 and 50,000 respondents will be included.

After the returns are received, they are reviewed and adjusted by OPA accountants, and certain of the data are tabulated by industry groups. From Form A, the annual return, both profit-and-loss and balance sheet as well as cost of sales items are tabulated. Since balance sheet data are not collected quarterly, only the profit-and-loss and cost of sales data are tabulated quarterly.

The information from Forms A and B is available in individual company form to OPA and in aggregate form to other Federal agencies. Unfortunately, tabulations are not now available to the public, although it is possible that such release may be made in the future.[17] The data would not only furnish a valuable record of American industry during the war, but would also be useful in filling the gap between discontinued series (such as SEC and FTC) and whatever program is instituted after the war. Several reports were, however, made (primarily from these data) by the OPA Division of Research, known as the *War Profits* series, and are available in depository libraries throughout the country. The following is a list, complete to 1944.

1. *Profits of 1735 Large Industrial Corporations, 1939–1941.*
2. *Profits of 200 Important War Contractors, 1939–1941.*
3. Part I: *Comparative Profits of 200 War Contractors and 1559 Other Large Industrial Corporations, 1939–1941.*
   Part II: *Profits of Consolidated Corporations and "War" Subsidiaries, 1939–1941.*
4. *Corporate Profits in the First Six Months of 1942, Including a Comparison of War Contractors and Others.*
5. *Profits—First Quarter, 1942 and 1943, of 750 Large Industrial Corporations.*
6. *Profits, 1939–1942, of Wholesale Food Grocers.*
7. *Profits, 1936–1942, of Women's Hosiery Manufacturers.*
8. *Profits, 1936–1942, of Fruit and Vegetable Canners.*
9. *Profits, 1936–1939, of Meat Packers.*

OPA surveys for purposes of establishing, revising, or reviewing maximum price regulations usually include cost data for the product in question and over-all profit-and-loss data for the companies covered in the survey. These usually cover the base period (1936–1939) and current figures to date. Most of these surveys are single time in character, but some of them are brought up to date from time to time. While we cannot hope to cover all these types of data (and there would

---

[17] OPA has no general policy on the release of such statistics. It does not engage in the collection and publication of statistics as an end in itself but in order to meet its own administrative needs. Some data may be obtained on request.

be little point in doing so) there are a few series on cost and financial statistics maintained in certain of the price branches that may be of interest. Such series are maintained on coal (bituminous and anthracite), rubber, pulp, and newsprint. Inquiries concerning these data should be addressed to the particular price branch of the Office of Price Administration, Washington, D. C.

Since 1943 the OPA Solid Fuels Price Branch has maintained a series of monthly sales, cost, and realization statistics, by mine, for coal mines (bituminous and anthracite) [18] producing in excess of 50 tons daily. These data cover more than 2,000 mines and are made available in aggregate form to members of the industry.

Beginning in 1941, the Paper and Paper Products Price Branch of OPA has obtained monthly cost and sales data, by grades of pulp, from all manufacturers in the industry. This is supplemented by a quarterly statement of profit and loss (on a total company basis from Forms A and B) as well as certain other information such as inventories, pulpwood receipts, and sales through agents. In 1942, a similar program was instituted by the Price Branch for producers of newsprint. From this universe of 13 manufacturers are obtained quarterly statements of the cost of manufacture for each newsprint mill and a quarterly statement of profit and loss, both by mill and by company. These data, like those for coal mines, are available in aggregate form to members of the industry.

[18] This covers about 2,000 bituminous mines (about 90 percent of the total volume of commercial coal and 50 percent of captive) and about 68 anthracite mines (which includes more than 90 percent of total volume). The data on bituminous coal are arranged by district and by type of mine, underground (hand loaded and machine loaded are shown separately) and strip, showing labor and other mine costs, realization and inventory, for coal sold on the open market and otherwise. For anthracite mines, annual data are available for 1942, quarterly data for 1941, 1942, 1943, and the first half of 1944; monthly data will be available for the last half of 1944. This information is tabulated by field (northern, eastern, middle west, middle, and southern) and the culm banks showing production cost, sales realization, inventory, net operating income, other income and other charges, and net income before and after taxes. Average realization by size of coal and in total is also shown. The Bituminous Coal Division of the Department of the Interior obtained similar data on bituminous coal mines (including annual returns from some 10,000 smaller mines) from 1936 to 1943, and statistics for these years are available in various public hearings and news releases. Data on sales and realization in aggregate form were also released in the annual chapters of the *Minerals Yearbook*, published by the U. S. Bureau of Mines (sold by the Superintendent of Documents). Additional statistics drawn from these sources showing analyses by producing districts, price areas, and type of mines may be obtained from the Bureau of Mines, Department of the Interior, Washington, D. C.

The Rubber Price Branch has, since early in 1942, obtained departmental profit-and-loss statements on a quarterly basis from some 50 rubber manufacturers.[19]

From time to time other periodic reporting systems are set up as materials grow tight, volume declines, costs increase, or subsidy programs are undertaken. As the situation eases, or new programs are assumed, these reporting systems are abolished or changed beyond recognition.

UNITED STATES TARIFF COMMISSION

For some 20 years the Tariff Commission has been engaged in making industry studies which have required the collection, compilation, and analysis of a great variety of accounting statistics. Frequently these data include both cost and financial information; but primary emphasis is placed on cost data. No series as such on cost or financial statistics are maintained by the Tariff Commission, but many of these studies contain information extending over a considerable period.

Prior to 1934 the work of the Commission was mainly concerned with studies of comparative costs between domestic and foreign producers. The Commission's work for that period is summarized in its study *Range and Variety of Costs*,[20] which also serves as a general index to the material covered in the various surveys undertaken during that period. Since that time, however, the Tariff Commission has devoted itself largely to studies of domestic industries, frequently at the request of some other Federal agency. While a great deal of this information reposes in the Commission's files, summaries have frequently been prepared and are available in mimeographed and published form.

It would be impossible, within the space available here, even to catalogue the numerous studies prepared under Commission auspices. Since cost information becomes rapidly obsolete because of changing patterns of production and costing techniques there is little reason for showing the entire range of studies. The following list of studies con-

[19] These cover tires and tubes (original equipment and replacement equipment by sales to the U. S. Government, private brand owners, and others), mechanical rubber goods, vulcanized rubber footwear, heels and soles, drug sundries, and coated and combined fabrics. The sample has fluctuated from time to time and is now in process of revision.

[20] Sold by the Superintendent of Documents. Although temporarily out of print, copies are available in depository libraries. An index of similar studies covering more recent periods is available in *Investigations Ordered under Provisions of Section 336, Tariff Act of 1930* (United States Tariff Commission, Office of the Secretary, Washington, D. C.).

ducted during the past five years will, however, give a general indication of the type of data available in Commission files:

Subject of Study	Number of Companies Covered	Years * Covered
1. Cigars	43	1941–1942
2. Concentrated citrus juice	15	1943–1944
3. Hermetically sealed canned crabmeat	12	1939–1940
4. Fresh crabmeat	22	1939–1940
5. Dried whole eggs	25	1943
6. Canned meat products	15	1943–1944
7. Fluid milk distribution	48	1943
8. Beet sugar	10	1940–1942
9. Sugar cane farm costs, Puerto Rico	102	1941–1942
10. Sugar cane refining, United States	9	1940–1942
11. Raw sugar cane, Puerto Rico	20	1941–1942
12. Refined sugar, Puerto Rico	5	1941–1942
13. Packaged tea	6	1940–1942
14. Wool, sheep, and lambs (ranches)	326	1940–1943
15. Glass containers (Mason jars)	15	1942
16. Crude petroleum, United States	2,884	1939–1941
17. Crude petroleum, selected California pools	170	1939–1942
18. Crude petroleum, selected United States pools, except California	440	1939–1942
19. Douglas fir doors	7	1938–1941
20. Douglas fir logs	8	1940–1941
21. Douglas fir sawmills	55	1940
22. Douglas fir sawmills	32	1941
23. Western pine lumber	87	1941
24. Ponderosa pine millwork	22	1938–1941
25. Pine box shook	56	1941
26. Red cedar shingles, domestic	56	1940–1941
27. Red cedar shingles, Canadian	18	1940–1941
28. Sulfite and sulfate pulp	22	1939–1940
29. Cotton cloth in the gray coarse and gray fine goods	41	1941
30. Gray carded cotton cloth (coarse goods)	36	1942
31. Bed linen (finished)	5	1942
32. All wool worsteds (including costs for clean, sort, top, and yarn)	16	1943–1944
33. Wool knit coating and other knit fabrics	9	1943
34. Fabrics with wool and rayon warp and filling	8	1943–1944
35. Fabrics with various combinations of wool and other fibers	6	1943–1944
36. Carded cotton yarn made from regular cotton and carded cotton yarn made from cotton waste	19	1941
37. Civilian woolen fabrics (including costs for yarn)	25	1942
38. Combed cotton yarn	12	1941
39. Military woolen and worsted fabrics	15	1941–1942
40. Spun rayon yarns and rayon blended yarns	10	1941–1942

* Including only partly completed years. These cover studies completed through September 1, 1944. An elaborate survey of the cotton textile industry is now in process under OPA auspices which will collect financial data from 1936 to date and current cost information for all major textile constructions. These surveys are for the purpose of adjusting prices in accordance with the so-called Bankhead Amendment.

Unfortunately because of the limitations of security regulations and personnel, very few of these studies have been printed for public distribution. In no event are data available in other than aggregate form. The Tariff Commission will undoubtedly remain an important source of cost data in the postwar world, and more of this information may then be available for public release. Inquiries should be directed to the United States Tariff Commission, Washington, D. C.

FEDERAL RESERVE SYSTEM AND COMMERCE DEPARTMENT

The Federal Reserve System in the *Federal Reserve Bulletin* [21] and the Commerce Department in the *Survey of Current Business* [22] present a great variety of statistics, including statistics derived from accounting data, which are of interest to businessmen. Analyses of the sources and uses of corporate funds have been prepared for some time by the Federal Reserve Board and constitute a field of interest for users of accounting statistics. This material is not published regularly, but photostatic copies may be obtained on application to the Board of Governors of the Federal Reserve System, Washington, D. C. These include detailed figures for 890 selected large manufacturing companies (with assets in excess of $5,000,000) in 16 industrial groups for the years 1936–1942.[23] This material is kept up to date with analyses for 500 large companies covering over half of all manufacturing activity. These data are further supplemented by a similar analysis of Class I railroads and lessors, Class A and Class B telephone companies, and Class A and Class B electric power companies. In conjunction with the Robert Morris Associates, another series of analyses are now in preparation for some 2,000 medium- and small-sized manufacturing and trade companies for the years 1939 through 1943.

[21] Issued monthly by the Board of Governors of the Federal Reserve System, Washington, D. C.

[22] Sold by the Superintendent of Documents. Biennial supplements are also issued which show historical series in convenient form, present a record of adjustments, and indicate where earlier revised data may be obtained.

[23] Illustrative data from these tabulations were published in *Dun's Review* for August 1944. Similar data were prepared for 100 large companies from 1926 to 1940 and released to the National Bureau of Economic Research. These data were published in *The Financing of Large Corporations, 1920–1939*, by Albert R. Koch (New York: National Bureau of Economic Research, 1943).

CONCLUSION

While we have not covered the entire range of financial statistics available in the Federal Government, we have included the most important series. Even in normal times it would be a difficult task to discover and describe such statistics. Not only are the various kinds scattered throughout several agencies, on the basis of administrative needs, but the picture is one of continuous change and adaptation. For this reason a completely satisfactory statistical system can hardly be said to exist. The confidential character imposed on these data militates further against the establishment of such a system, as well as limits the usefulness of the data to potential users of the results. To this picture has been added the rapidly changing characteristics of a government at war, further limiting the possibility of establishing such a system and further subordinating the data to administrative needs and confidential treatment.

There are, however, brighter sides to the picture The war made clear the need of the government for speedy and reasonably complete financial information on wide sections of the American economy. It has become increasingly apparent that this need is likely to continue into the foreseeable future. Since most of the readjustment will have to be undertaken by private firms acting in their individual capacities, there is every reason to make such statistics available to the general public in order to enable business firms and investors to make their decisions as intelligently as possible on the basis of relevant information.

Although the data now available will undoubtedly be of great value to private users, there are obvious improvements which can be made in these statistics. One promising area lies in further coordination and integration of existing statistical systems. Progress can be made in securing uniformity of accounting treatment and industry classification. Every effort should be made to secure speedy collection and release of information, even to the extent of sacrificing detail and accuracy. Considerable care and judgment will have to be exercised, however, in determining to what extent detail and accuracy can be sacrificed without making the results misleading. A single reported figure on corporate profits would, for example, be both meaningless and dangerous. In view of the variety of definitions employed by various firms, accounting surveys must nearly always obtain enough data to assure comparable treatment between firms in the computation of desired items.

If, as we have predicated, private users are to be the mainstay of postwar readjustment, it would seem worth while to afford them broader and more complete indications of the limitations of these statistics in order to enable them to avoid possible errors of interpretation. A step in this direction would result from careful explanations of the methods employed in collecting and tabulating data in order to provide potential users with adequate safeguards against errors in interpretation.

CHAPTER 10

MONEY, CREDIT, AND BANKING [1]

EDWARD T. CROWDER
Bureau of the Budget

The economic system under which we live has been described by the phrases "money economy" and "credit economy." The first emphasizes that economic life today centers around the making and spending of money. The second suggests several ideas: that present-day money-making activity relies heavily on the borrowing and lending of funds; that a large proportion of business transactions involve deferred rather than immediate payment; and that the great bulk of our payments themselves are made not in the form of coins or paper money but through a bookkeeping system of bank accounts and checkbooks.

Our money and credit economy relies on a rather elaborate mechanism for providing a medium of exchange and for facilitating the flow of funds among lenders and borrowers. This mechanism includes a group of financial agencies and enterprises by which cash is manufactured and circulated, deposits are held, checks are cleared and collected, and funds are made available to businessmen, farmers, the government, and other borrowers. Among these financial institutions are private or cooperative enterprises such as commercial banks, savings banks, and building and loan associations, together with a number of governmental or quasi-governmental agencies.

The present chapter is concerned with various types of statistics arising from the operation of this financial system. These statistics bear a close relation to those discussed in the previous chapter on corporate financial accounting. While that chapter may be said to deal with the measurement of ordinary business by dollars-and-cents standards, the present chapter is concerned with money and credit and with those special financial institutions which provide and deal in money and credit rather than in commodities.

---

[1] The writer is greatly indebted to a number of staff members of various Federal agencies who have patiently supplied information and have made critical comments on the manuscript. He is, in the usual manner, alone responsible for the shortcomings which remain.

The field of money and credit is wide, and no attempt can be made here to cover exhaustively the statistics which bear on it. Some of these are discussed in other chapters of this book. In this chapter particular emphasis will be placed upon the commercial banking system, which is rightly regarded as the pivot of our financial mechanism, providing our major form of currency, the checking account, and furnishing a source of long-term and short-term credit to which the business community in general, including other financial enterprises, turns for loans. Attention will also be given to various other agencies of long- and short-term credit, including the government credit agencies, which particularly in recent years have supplemented on a large scale the activities of private agencies. Other topics include statistics of currency, the money market, and the securities market. Limitations of space will permit little more than passing mention of the broad field of public finance.

USES OF STATISTICS OF MONEY, CREDIT, AND BANKING: A GENERAL COMMENT

The statistics about to be described are of varied kinds. They include data on the number, size, and location of banks; bank assets, liabilities, and earnings; loans and investments of banks and other lending institutions; interest rates; the volume of deposits and the rate at which they are spent; the volume of coin and paper money outstanding; and other subjects.

Certain of these data lend themselves to direct uses. Thus persons interested in a particular bank may compare its financial statements with combined statements for a large group of banks. A knowledge of the number of banks, their characteristics, and location may be useful to those who look to banks as their customers, as is a similar knowledge of any other business. Statistics on interest rates are obviously useful to borrowers and lenders.

But beyond such direct uses, statistics of money, credit, and banking have a peculiar significance to the businessman, the economist, and the government in that they are especially useful for general economic analysis. Money and credit are in a sense the lifeblood of our economic relationships, and the operations of financial institutions are valuable indexes of economic developments. The availability and distribution of credit, the price at which such credit may be had, the effective supply of purchasing power within the community, and the rate at which it is spent—these and related matters are of widespread interest to all who would understand and attempt to forecast economic conditions.

SOURCES OF DATA: AGENCIES AND PUBLICATIONS

It will be helpful before we enter into a discussion of specific types of data to refer to certain agencies which are leading sources of Federal statistics in this field; to indicate their general responsibilities which give rise to these statistics; and to identify certain major publications in which the statistics appear. Other publications will be mentioned later in connection with particular types of data.

Treasury Department. The responsibilities of the Treasury Department that bear on the operation of the financial system include the manufacture and issuance of coin and paper money; the management of our monetary reserves of the precious metals; the surveillance of international capital movements; the control of certain foreign exchange transactions; the management of the Exchange Stabilization Fund; the supervision of a large segment of our commercial banking system (and of certain other financial institutions); and in a broader sense the management of the Federal finances, including the collection of taxes, the disbursement of funds, and the management of the public debt.

Statistics on Federal Government finance are presented annually in the *Annual Report of the Secretary of the Treasury on the State of the Finances.* Current data, including figures on receipts and expenditures, assets and liabilities, the public debt, and government corporations and credit agencies, together with miscellaneous monetary statistics, appear in the monthly *Bulletin of the Treasury Department.* Daily figures on assets, liabilities, receipts, and expenditures appear in the *Daily Statement of the United States Treasury,* supplemented by a detailed analysis of cumulative receipts and expenditures for the current month and fiscal year and for corresponding periods in the previous year. Special tabulations appear periodically in the *Daily Statement,* including statements dealing with the public debt and with government corporations and credit agencies. The monthly *Circulation Statement of United States Money* gives data on money in circulation. The *Annual Report of the Director of the Mint* gives statistics on mint operations, metallic money, and the precious metals.

The office of the Comptroller of the Currency was established in the Treasury Department in 1863 at the time of the inauguration of the National Banking System. The Comptroller supervises the national banks, as well as certain other financial institutions in the District of Columbia. The *Annual Report of the Comptroller of the Currency* contains statistics covering the banking system generally and particularly the banks and other financial institutions supervised by the Comptroller. The statistical content of the published annual report has been drastically cut as a wartime measure. Three times a year or more the Comptroller issues the *Abstract of Reports of Condition of National Banks* containing statistics based on balance sheet reports of national banks.[2]

Federal Reserve System. A leading Federal source of banking and financial statistics is the Board of Governors of the Federal Reserve System. Essentially the "system," established in 1914, comprises twelve regional "bankers' banks" known as Federal Reserve Banks; a central authority in Washington known as the Board of Governors, flanked by certain other central bodies; and the "member banks," including all the national banks in continental United States and those banks under state supervision which have chosen and have been permitted to join. The varied functions of the Federal Reserve System include services to the member banks, centralized control over credit conditions, and bank supervision.

The *Annual Report of the Board of Governors of the Federal Reserve System* has been a source of statistical data on the Federal Reserve Banks and the member banks, and of selected other banking, financial, and business statistics, although the report for 1944 has appeared without the usual statistical section. The monthly *Federal Reserve Bulletin* gives currently the more important banking and financial statistics, generally with comparative data for back periods. Included are current figures for plotting in *Chart Book I, Federal Reserve Charts on Bank Credit, Money Rates, and Business* and occasional special articles containing statistics. The *Member Bank Call Report* presents three or more times a year statistics derived from balance sheet data reported by member banks. Various statistical releases are distributed currently. Also, monthly reviews containing some financial data are distributed by the various Federal Reserve Banks.

The Board of Governors published in 1943 a volume entitled *Banking and Monetary Statistics*. This was designed "for the purpose of making available in one place and on a uniform basis statistics of banking, monetary, and other financial developments." While major emphasis is placed on the Federal Reserve Banks and the member banks, the coverage is wide. Most of the series extend from 1941 back to 1914,

[2] Of these Treasury Department publications, the annual reports of the Secretary, of the Director of the Mint, and of the Comptroller of the Currency are sold by the Superintendent of Documents. The others are distributed by the Department without charge. Other Treasury publications are described in *Publications of the Treasury Department as of May 15, 1944*, prepared by the Department in mimeographed form.

though some data are carried back to earlier dates. The Board of Governors plans to issue supplements from time to time bringing the material up to date. The volume will be found a useful companion to current issues of the *Federal Reserve Bulletin*. Particularly valuable are the extended textual discussions dealing with the significance of the figures, sources of data, the adjustment of data, and related matters. Constant use has been made of this volume in the preparation of the present chapter.[3]

Federal Deposit Insurance Corporation. A third leading source of information on our banking system is the Federal Deposit Insurance Corporation, established after the banking crisis of 1933 to administer a national program of bank deposit insurance. The insurance program includes the national banks, the state member banks, and the bulk of the nonmember banks. The Corporation has supervisory powers over the insured banks and particularly over the nonmember insured banks. The *Annual Report of the Federal Deposit Insurance Corporation* presents statistics on the banking system as a whole, on the insured banks, and on the insurance and supervisory program, with financial data on the Corporation itself. Occasionally special reports containing statistics appear in the annual report. The extended "Explanatory Notes" for the statistical tables are particularly useful. Balance sheet statistics for insured banks appear in the semiannual *Assets and Liabilities of Operating Insured Banks*. Recently the Corporation was made responsible for the supervision of the Federal credit unions (formerly under the Farm Credit Administration); and the Corporation now issues an annual publication: *Federal Credit Unions: Annual Report of Operations.*[4]

Securities and Exchange Commission. The Securities and Exchange Commission, established in 1934, has various supervisory responsibilities in the field of investment finance. Chapter 9 describes the corporate financial data made available by the Commission. Statistics relevant to the present section include those dealing with the issuance of securities, with security trading, and with securities dealers and brokers. The *Annual Report of the Securities and Exchange Commission* has been an important source of data, but its statistical content was cut greatly during the war. The monthly *Statistical Bulletin*, a recent publication dating from July 1942, presents data currently, as do certain statistical releases. *Selected Statistics on Securities and on*

---

[3] The above-mentioned publications of the Board of Governors are distributed by the Board. *Banking and Monetary Statistics*, the *Chart Book*, and the *Bulletin* are for sale; the others are distributed free of charge.

[4] These publications of the FDIC are available free of charge from the Corporation.

Exchange Markets, published by the Commission in 1939, contains useful back data.[5]

Other Agencies. Although the present chapter is primarily concerned with statistics provided by the above agencies, certain other agencies deserve passing mention. The extensive statistics on agricultural finance provided by the Department of Agriculture are discussed in the chapter on agricultural statistics (Chapter 5). Data on nonfarm mortgage finance published by the Federal Home Loan Bank Administration and the Federal Housing Administration are treated in the chapter on construction and housing statistics (Chapter 13).

The Department of Commerce is the source of a variety of statistics bearing on our financial system, including financial statistics of state and local governments, farm and nonfarm mortgage data, statistics on the balance of international payments, on employment and payrolls of banks and other financial institutions, on credit sales and receivables, on consumer loans, and on gold movements. Only in part do these statistics fall within the scope of the present chapter, and certain consumer credit data formerly obtained by the Commerce Department are, as indicated below, now obtained by the Federal Reserve System. Many of the statistical series of Federal agencies discussed in this chapter are available in the Department's *Survey of Current Business;* the *Statistical Abstract of the United States* contains a useful annual compilation of banking and other financial statistics.

CURRENCY IN CIRCULATION

A convenient point at which to begin the discussion of specific series is money itself, in the familiar sense of coins and paper bills. Figures on currency in circulation (including both coins and paper money) reflect the changing demands of the public and of business for hand-to-hand money, as affected by the volume of retail trade and other factors. Changes in currency in circulation may have important effects on bank reserves.

The basic source of information on money in circulation is the *Circulation Statement of United States Money*, a single sheet published monthly by the Treasury Department, giving figures as of the last day of the month. For each type of currency (Federal Reserve notes,

[5] The annual reports for 1942 and 1943 were mimeographed and given limited distribution by the Commission, although earlier reports were printed and were sold by the Superintendent of Documents. The *Bulletin* and the releases are distributed free of charge by the Commission. A pamphlet, *The Work of the Securities and Exchange Commission* (May 1944), distributed by the Commission, gives further information on its publications and releases.

national bank notes, minor silver coins, etc.) the *Circulation Statement* gives the following information: the total stock; the amount of this which is held by the United States Treasury for various purposes; the amount held by Federal Reserve Banks; and the amount "in circulation," by which is meant simply the amount outside the Treasury and the Federal Reserve Banks. Some of this, of course, is in the hands of commercial banks, or has been lost, or for some other reason is not in circulation in the popular sense. The statement gives the amounts of gold and silver held by the Treasury as well as the amounts of paper money "backed" by these metals. Totals for all types of currency are given for selected dates, with per capita figures for currency in circulation. Further detail on the distribution by denominations of the several types of paper money outstanding and in circulation is provided by a second monthly sheet published by the Treasury Department entitled *Monthly Statement: Paper Currency of Each Denomination Outstanding*.

In addition to presenting Treasury circulation figures monthly in the *Federal Reserve Bulletin*, the Board of Governors has made certain refinements. A daily "money in circulation" figure is estimated by using the Treasury statements and certain other sources. Wednesday figures form part of the weekly statement on "Member Bank Reserves, Reserve Bank Credit, and Related Items" discussed below. The Board also derives a monthly figure for "currency outside banks" by subtracting from the Treasury "circulation" figure an amount representing vault cash held by commercial and mutual savings banks. The resulting figure, which more nearly approximates true circulation, appears in the *Federal Reserve Bulletin* in the regular table entitled "Deposits and Currency—Adjusted Deposits of All Banks and Currency Outside Banks." The *Bulletin* also presents weekly and monthly circulation figures adjusted for seasonal variation, bringing out more clearly the longer term variations.

Other sources of circulation data may be mentioned. The *Annual Report of the Secretary of the Treasury* gives historical data on the stock of money and money in circulation. The *Survey of Current Business* gives an unadjusted monthly circulation figure and a weekly average of daily circulation estimates. *Banking and Monetary Statistics* gives a great many back data including June 30 figures from 1860.

Since the great bulk of our payments are made by check, the significance of hand-to-hand money should not be overestimated. Statistics of money in circulation should be considered in their relation to the banking system, and they will be referred to again in the discussion of certain banking statistics.

NUMBER AND CLASSIFICATION OF BANKS

The user of banking statistics will do well to familiarize himself with the general outlines of our banking system, since these statistics reflect various functional or other classifications into which banks fall.

Banks are distinguished by function as "commercial" and "mutual savings" banks. The former are those which hold demand deposits and make short-term self-liquidating loans. This class includes ordinary "banks," trust companies, "industrial banks," and "stock" savings banks (which usually hold demand deposits). Mutual savings banks are organizations without capital stock which, in general, hold only time deposits. On June 30, 1944, there were in the United States approximately 14,600 banks, of which all but about 550 were commercial banks, accounting for approximately 90 percent of the total deposits.

Of the commercial banks, slightly over 5,000 were national banks chartered by the Federal Government and supervised by the Comptroller of the Currency. These held over half of all commercial bank deposits. The remainder were largely "state banks" chartered and supervised by the state governments. (There were also a very few unchartered "private" banks.) All the national banks (exclusive of a few in the United States possessions) and over 1,700 of the state banks (including three mutual savings banks) were "member banks" of the Federal Reserve System. Member banks accounted for over 85 percent of all commercial bank deposits. All member banks together with the majority (about 6,500) of the nonmember banks were participants in the deposit insurance program under the Federal Deposit Insurance Corporation. The insured commercial banks accounted for over 98 percent of commercial bank deposits. Of the mutual savings banks, 192, holding 66 percent of the mutual savings bank deposits, were insured.

Banks may be classified in other significant ways. Most are single independent units, but some of them operate one or more branches. Some separately incorporated banks are joined together by common ownership or control into "groups" or "chains." There are furthermore the familiar classifications by size and location, the latter having a special significance for member banks, since legal reserve requirements are different in different classes of cities.

The publications of the Federal bank supervisory agencies contain a great deal of information on the number and classification of banks presented in conjunction with financial data similarly classified to show, for example, the number and total loans of insured commercial banks for individual states. Information on changes in the banking structure may be derived from administrative statistics on bank authorizations, conversions, suspensions, etc. The *Federal Reserve Bulletin* gives quarterly information on changes in the number of banks, branches, and additional banking offices during the year by type of change (new organizations, suspensions, etc.). Once a year the *Bulletin* presents detailed data on banks and branches and on group banking by states as of the end of the year. Both the FDIC and the Board of Governors give, in their annual reports, detailed annual data on changes in the banking structure, as well as data on number and classification of banks and branches. *Banking and Monetary Statistics* gives extensive data on the banking structure, going back in part to 1835.

BANK ASSETS AND LIABILITIES

A considerable share of available banking statistics is derived from balance sheet reports known as "call reports" submitted to supervisory authorities as of designated dates. Data derived from these reports lend themselves in various ways to economic analysis. They throw light, for example, on the flow of bank credit into various loan and investment channels; the amount, distribution, and nature of bank deposits; and the relationships among asset, liability, and capital accounts.

Call reports are in practice required of all insured banks regularly as of the end of June and December. Member banks must make one or more additional reports per year. National banks report to the Comptroller. Generally speaking state member banks report to the Federal Reserve System and nonmember insured banks to the FDIC, although nonnational banks in the District of Columbia report to the Comptroller. Virtually identical report forms have been adopted by the three agencies.

Aggregate figures based on the call reports are published by each of the three agencies following call dates. The Comptroller publishes the *Abstract of Reports of Condition of National Banks* and the *Abstract of Reports of Condition of National and Nonnational Banks in the District of Columbia*. The figures for national member banks are combined with those for state member banks and published in the *Member Bank Call Report* by the Board of Governors. For the June and December call dates the FDIC combines member bank figures with those for insured nonmember banks for its publication *Assets and Liabilities of Operating Insured Banks*. Call report data appear also in the annual reports of the three supervisory agencies and in the *Federal Reserve Bulletin*.

Call report data on individual banks are not published by the Federal agencies. A supplement to the Comptrollers' annual report, entitled *Individual Statements of Condition of National Banks*, giving limited financial data on individual national banks, was last issued for December 31, 1941. Annual reports of the Board of Governors for 1937 and prior years gave limited data for individual state member banks; and such data for several subsequent years were made available in mimeographed form. Each member bank is required to publish locally an abridged version of its call report, and most nonmember banks are subject to a similar publication requirement by the state.

An abundance of statistical data based on the Federal call reports is available. The most comprehensive tabulations are those of the FDIC covering insured commercial banks. The issue of *Assets and Liabilities* for June 30, 1944, gives over 90 balance sheet and "memorandum" items for operating insured commercial banks classified by state and cross classified by type (national, state member, nonmember). Another table gives aggregate data (some 20 items) for insured mutual savings banks. Other tabulations with varying coverage and criteria of classification may be found in the several publications of the supervisory agencies.

Still more comprehensive call report figures are compiled by the three supervisory agencies, covering banks not regulated by the Federal Government. Of these "all bank" tabulations, the most elaborate have been those of the Comptroller, who has been required by law since 1873 to compile data on state banks. The annual reports of the Comptroller present data on "all active banks in the United States and possessions" based on the national bank call reports and call report data for state banks collected from the state banking supervisors. The 1943 report presents detailed year-end data for "all banks," national banks, and banks other than national, the last group classified as state commercial banks, mutual savings banks, and private banks. Aggregate data for all banks covered are presented by individual states. Semiannual releases give summary all-bank data for June 30 as well as for December 31. The fuller annual reports prior to the wartime curtailment gave asset and liability data by state and by type of bank for the year-end and the midyear. The FDIC also gives in its annual report asset and liability data for all banks classified by functional type and insurance status. All-bank data also appear in the *Federal Reserve Bulletin*.

For many users the *Federal Reserve Bulletin* will prove an adequate source of call report data. Regular monthly tables give selected information for various classes of banks, with comparative back data, and special tables appear from time to time. Extensive tabulations based on call reports appear in *Banking and Monetary Statistics*, including data on national banks from 1863, on member banks since 1914, on insured banks since 1934, and on all banks since 1914.

The information derived from the call reports is not sufficiently current to serve the purposes of week-to-week analysis. In recognition of this fact the Federal Reserve System has obtained since 1917 weekly statements of condition from a group of cooperating member banks in selected cities. Figures from 1919 through 1941 on a substantially comparable basis are available in *Banking and Monetary Statistics*. The banks today number almost 400 and together account for over half of the total loans and investments of all commercial banks. Changes in their assets and liabilities may be assumed to reflect with considerable accuracy banking developments in larger cities, though not those in smaller places. The weekly reports are obtained as of the close of business each Wednesday. A mimeographed statement, *Condition of Weekly Reporting Member Banks in Central Reserve Cities*, is released on Thursday and appears in the financial press on Friday. A second statement, *Condition of Weekly Reporting Member Banks in Leading Cities*, released the following Tuesday, appears in the press on Wednesday. The latter release shows about 30 asset and liability items for the banks grouped by Federal Reserve Districts. Weekly reporting bank data are carried regularly in the *Bulletin*, and selected items appear in the *Survey of Current Business* and in the weekly supplement to the *Survey*.

As noted above, the call reports are valuable as an index of the uses being made of bank credit. Bank statistics have been markedly improved in recent years in this respect. The *Assets and Liabilities* report of the FDIC for June 30, 1944, shows for operating insured commercial banks the following classification of "loans, discounts, and overdrafts (including rediscounts)":

Commercial and industrial loans (including open market paper).
Loans secured by agricultural commodities, covered by purchase agreements of the Commodity Credit Corporation.
Other agricultural loans (excluding loans on farm land).
Consumer loans to individuals:
    Retail automobile installment paper.
    Other retail, repair, and modernization installment loans.
    Personal installment cash loans.
    Single payment loans to individuals.

Loans to brokers and dealers in securities.
Other loans for the purpose of purchasing or carrying securities.
Real estate loans:
  On farm land.
  On residential properties.
  On other properties.
Loans to banks.
All other loans (including overdrafts).

Securities are analyzed under thirteen subheadings. The weekly
member bank tabulations are less detailed on the whole, but they currently, in connection with loans for purchasing or carrying securities,
distinguish between government and other securities—a significant distinction in the present period of heavy Treasury financing.

Annual statistics on the condition of banks as revealed by reports
of bank examiners have been prepared by the FDIC. Beginning with
the annual report for 1938, tabulations covering examinations made by
all three of the Federal supervisory agencies have been available.
These show examiners' deductions from assets and from capital, and
related information. Both absolute and relative figures are given.
Banks are classified according to "net sound capital" ratios, amounts
of deposits, and other criteria. These tabulations, unlike those based
on the call reports, involve the summation of data collected by examiners as of different dates throughout the year. Balance sheet data are
treated in terms of a very few categories. The annual report for 1940
carries tables dealing specifically with banks examined by the FDIC
itself from 1933 through 1940.

It should be said by way of caution that bank asset and liability data
are available in a confusing variety of forms, and the precise contents of
any table should be noted carefully—for example, whether it covers *all*
banks, or all *member* banks, or all *insured commercial* banks. Roughly
comparable figures may differ because of the inclusion or exclusion of
banks in the United States possessions. Changes in classification of
items must be reckoned with in analyses of data covering a period of
time. Careful attention should be paid to footnotes and available
textual explanations.

BANK EARNINGS, EXPENSES, AND DIVIDENDS

Statistics covering bank earnings, expenses, and dividends are available for all insured banks. No individual bank figures are published
by Federal agencies. These statistics throw light on the ability of
the banking system to continue to do business on a sound basis and

to attract new capital.[6] Individual bankers will find the published aggregate data helpful in interpreting their own financial results.

National banks (and District of Columbia banks) report to the Comptroller semiannually on earnings, expenses, and dividends. State member banks report in the same manner to the Federal Reserve System. Other insured banks report annually to the FDIC. Earnings, expense, and dividend data for national and District banks appear in the Comptroller's annual report, and midyear earnings data for these groups of banks are issued in press releases. Member bank data appear semiannually in the *Federal Reserve Bulletin*, with a special annual presentation of operating ratios. Insured bank data appear in the annual report of the FDIC. Historical tabulations may be found in *Banking and Monetary Statistics*, including national bank data back to 1869 and a particularly detailed analysis of member bank data.

The FDIC gives annual data on the largest group of banks. The annual report for 1943 gives an analysis of earnings, expenses, and dividends of insured banks consisting of 36 items. The data are given separately for different classes of banks.

FEDERAL RESERVE BANK STATISTICS

The twelve Federal Reserve Banks, located at key financial centers in the twelve Federal Reserve Districts, play a vital role in American finance. These banks, though owned by the member banks in their respective districts, are quasi-public institutions carrying out national credit policies determined by the Federal Reserve authorities in Washington. Statistics on the operations of the Reserve Banks give information both on the policies of the System and on the financial situation in terms of which these policies are framed.

Each week the Board of Governors issues a release, *Condition of the Federal Reserve Banks*, showing individual and combined statements of condition for the twelve banks as of the close of business on Wednesday. These appear in the financial press on Friday, and both weekly and end-of-month figures appear in the *Federal Reserve Bulletin*. Year-end statements are carried in the Federal Reserve annual report. The condition of the Reserve Banks can be traced on a year-end basis back to 1914 in *Banking and Monetary Statistics*. Selected series appear in the *Survey of Current Business*.

The Reserve Bank statements indicate from week to week, among other things, the amount of gold certificates or other funds held by

[6] See *Banking and Monetary Statistics*, p. 257.

these banks as a reserve against their note and deposit liabilities; the amount of loans outstanding; holdings of government securities of various types; outstanding liabilities in the form of Federal Reserve notes; amounts due to member banks and to other depositors; and the ratio of reserves to note and deposit liabilities. Changes in the item "discounts and advances" reflect largely greater or lesser borrowing by the member banks in order to maintain legal reserves. Increased borrowing of this type tends to indicate a tighter credit situation. Changes in securities reflect sales or purchases initiated by commercial banks, as well as "open market" purchases or sales through which the Federal Reserve Banks may deliberately pump funds into, or drain funds out of, the market. Changes in the reserve ratio are to be interpreted in the light of the legal requirement of reserves to be kept against notes outstanding and deposits. Changes in Federal Reserve notes outstanding are intimately related to changes in money in circulation, since these notes constitute the bulk of all money in circulation.

Other tabulations concerning the operations of the Reserve Banks may be found in the Federal Reserve publications. These include tables dealing with loans and securities held, classified by maturity dates; with Federal Reserve notes and the security held against them; with the annual volume of certain operations of the banks; and with earnings and expenses.

The Board of Governors prepares weekly a statistical summary, derived largely from the Wednesday statements of the Federal Reserve Banks and the *Circulation Statement*, designed to facilitate the analysis of changes in the banking situation. The statement consists of two groups of items. The first group are described as items "supplying" member bank reserve funds and include Reserve Bank credit outstanding (as evidenced by various types of Reserve Bank assets), the Treasury gold stock, and the stock of coin and paper money for which the Treasury is primarily responsible. The second group are described as factors "using" member bank reserves and include, in addition to member bank reserve balances with the Reserve Banks, money in circulation, cash held by the Treasury, and several other items. The total of the "supply" items is equal to the total of the "use" items. An additional figure is appended representing the excess of member bank reserve balances over the legally required amount. These items are closely interrelated, and, as in a balance sheet, changes in one or more items are balanced by changes in one or more others. An analysis of the upward or downward movements of the items listed in the statement throws light on the nature of the changes that have been taking place in the banking situation.[7]

These weekly summaries appear regularly in the *Federal Reserve Bulletin* in a table entitled "Member Bank Reserves, Reserve Bank Credit, and Related Items." A somewhat abridged version is released each week with the Federal Reserve Bank statements on Friday, and in these releases changes in the various use and source items are given in terms of absolute increases and decreases for the past week and the past year. The summary is also prepared as of the end of each month and in terms of monthly and yearly averages. The *Federal Reserve Bulletin* carries end-of-month and monthly average figures. The annual reports of the Board of Governors give end-of-month figures for the latest year and year-end figures for previous years. *Banking and Monetary Statistics* gives weekly data from 1922, annual averages of daily figures and end-of-month and call date figures from 1914, and monthly averages of daily figures from 1917.

DEPOSITS

Special interest attaches to statistics on bank deposits. They represent liquid purchasing power at the disposal of the community. Geographical distributions of deposits may throw light on the distribution of purchasing power. Statistical series showing the use of deposits have been developed, and special studies have been made of deposit ownership.

Much information on the nature and distribution of deposits is available from the call reports in the form of regular tabulations of assets and liabilities as well as special tables. Certain other sources of deposit data deserve mention. The *Federal Reserve Bulletin* carries a monthly tabulation showing the deposits and reserves of member banks, based on semimonthly reports required of these banks for the administration of legal reserve requirements. The *Survey of Current Business* reports monthly the deposits of New York State savings banks. As indicated below, Postal Savings deposit data are carried monthly by both of these publications as well as by the Postal Savings System annual report. The FDIC has from time to time made "special calls" for information on deposits of insured banks. The annual report for 1941 gives statistics for the special call as of September 24, 1941. Tables are included giving information on the distribution of deposit accounts and of deposits by size of account and by other criteria.

[7] See the discussion in *Banking and Monetary Statistics*, pp. 360 ff., or in the *Federal Reserve Bulletin*, July 1935, pp. 419 ff.

To provide a measure of the total volume of means of payment outstanding the *Federal Reserve Bulletin* regularly carries a table, "Deposits and Currency—Adjusted Deposits of All Banks and Currency Outside Banks," showing monthly figures for deposits of several categories; for "currency outside banks" (meaning currency in circulation minus vault cash for commercial and mutual savings banks); and for two aggregates of deposits and currency. The first of these, "total deposits adjusted and currency outside banks," excludes deposits owned by banks and cash items in process of collection. The second, "total demand deposits adjusted and currency outside banks," excludes these same factors and also U. S. Government deposits. These series are carried for selected call dates back to 1892 in *Banking and Monetary Statistics*.

Although various published tabulations of the call report data give a great deal of information on the nature of deposits, relatively little is known of the make-up of the largest single category, namely, deposits of "individuals, partnerships, and corporations." The marked increase in this figure during the war has caused interest in the question of who owns the deposits and which groups of owners have enjoyed the greatest increases. Answers to these questions have important implications in the determination of both wartime and postwar fiscal and credit policies. Several studies of the ownership of demand deposits have been made recently by the Federal Reserve System, and it is planned to continue these surveys periodically. A recent survey by the Securities and Exchange Commission dealt with the distribution of demand deposits of "individuals" among various types of holders.[8]

Somewhat related to deposit statistics, as well as to certain other categories of statistics discussed in this and other chapters, are the quarterly estimates made by the Securities and Exchange Commission of the volume and composition of saving by individuals and unincorporated businesses. Figures are given for "gross" and "liquid" saving. Gross saving is distributed among seven major categories, among which are "currency and bank deposits," "savings and loan associations," and "securities." These estimates first appeared in 1942, but the data have been carried back to 1940. Figures appear quarterly in the SEC *Statistical Bulletin* and in releases.

[8] For reports on the Federal Reserve studies see *Federal Reserve Bulletin*, August 1943, pp. 713 ff.; October 1943, pp. 917 ff. and 930 ff.; May 1944, pp. 432 ff.; November 1944, pp. 1069 ff.; and April 1945, pp. 331 ff. For the SEC study see Irwin Friend, "Individuals' Demand Deposits, June 1942–43," *Survey of Current Business*, June 1944, pp. 14 ff.

DEBITS AND DEPOSIT TURNOVER

Related to deposit statistics are statistics on "bank debits," which means the total of debits to deposit accounts by check or otherwise. When debits for a given period of time are divided by average bank deposits (against which the debits are made) during the same period, we have a measure of "deposit turnover." Bank "clearings" (or the value of checks passing through clearing houses) are similar to debits but fail to include checks or other debits which do not pass through a clearing house.

Statistics on debits are a good index of total payments in our economy. The information which debits figures give on the activity of deposits is relevant to the determination of banking and credit policies. Because debits cover speculative and other transactions not arising from current production and trade, and for other reasons, one should be very cautious in attempting to draw inferences from them as to general business conditions. "Deposit turnover" figures (which have been suggested as an index of business confidence) should also be used with great caution.[9]

The Board of Governors issues monthly a mimeographed release, *Bank Debits—Debits to Deposit Accounts Except Interbank Accounts*, giving monthly data for reporting banks in 334 leading centers, by Federal Reserve Districts and by individual centers. This series was changed from a weekly to its present monthly basis in 1942; the number of centers was increased and banks were added in centers previously reporting. A table in the *Federal Reserve Bulletin* gives four monthly debits series based on these figures: for all reporting centers; for New York City; for 140 other centers; and for the remaining centers. Two annual rates of deposit turnover are computed: for New York City and for the 333 other centers. An annual mimeographed release, *Bank Debits to Deposit Accounts Except Interbank Accounts*, gives monthly debits for districts and for the individual centers.

A second type of debits figures is also provided by the Board of Governors. These are debits to *demand* deposits (except interbank and U. S. Government deposits) for the weekly reporting member banks. The regular weekly release *Condition of Weekly Reporting Member Banks in Leading Cities* gives data by districts and separately for New York City and for Chicago. These figures are included with the

---

[9] See *Banking and Monetary Statistics*, pp. 230 ff.; and Elmer C. Bratt, *Business Cycles and Forecasting*, Richard W. Irwin, Inc., Chicago, 1941, Revised Edition, pp. 623 ff., 701 ff., 709. See also "Significance of Bank Debits as an Index of Changes in Business Activity," *Federal Reserve Bulletin*, March 1941, p. 211.

weekly reporting member bank data published in the *Bulletin*. A separate table gives two monthly series (for New York City and for 100 other cities) with annual rates of deposit turnover computed for each.

Historical tables in *Banking and Monetary Statistics* give debits of the first type (debits to total deposits) by individual reporting centers yearly from 1919; and of the second type (to demand deposits, for weekly reporting member banks) by districts and separately for New York and for Chicago weekly from 1935. Estimated debit and turnover data for all commercial banks annually since 1919 are also given. The *Survey of Current Business* and the weekly supplement to the *Survey* carry selected Federal Reserve debits series.

SHORT-TERM INTEREST RATES AND THE MONEY MARKET

Our knowledge of interest rates charged by banks is limited. A group of member banks in 19 leading financial centers reports quarterly on new short-term commercial and industrial loans made at different rates of interest during a 15-day period. Average rates are compiled by the Board of Governors and published in the *Bulletin* as well as in the *Survey of Current Business*. Several averages are computed: for the 19 cities as a group, for New York City, for seven other northern and eastern cities, and for 11 southern and western cities. Averages are weighted in terms of the volume of loans at different rates and the relative importance of the different cities. Although the current reporting program has been in effect only since 1939, reports on interest rates have been made by banks since 1919, and figures fairly comparable to the present series have been computed back to 1928. Back figures are presented in *Banking and Monetary Statistics*.

These averages reflect rates charged by large metropolitan banks and are not representative of rates at other banks. The low rates at large metropolitan banks appear to reflect, in part, a tendency for larger banks to charge somewhat lower rates, but they probably reflect mainly the larger size of loans made and the types of business of the borrowers to whom these banks typically lend.[10] A rough measure of average rates of interest earned by banks may be derived from reported figures on loans and on income from loans. Ratios are computed and published by the three supervisory agencies. Such ratios may be found, for example, in the FDIC annual report for 1943, the *Federal Reserve Bulletin* for May 1944, and the annual report of the Comptroller for 1941.

[10] See *Banking and Monetary Statistics*, p. 426.

Certain other types of short-term rates are also available from Federal sources. The rates charged by the Federal Reserve Banks in their extensions of credit to commercial banks (and in certain cases directly to the business community) are published every month in the *Federal Reserve Bulletin*. Historical data appear in *Banking and Monetary Statistics*. The same is true of the rates at which the Federal Reserve Banks agree to buy short-term Treasury securities and bankers' acceptances. Changes in Reserve Bank discount and buying rates are among the devices available to the Reserve System for effectuating its credit policies.

The Federal Reserve Bank of New York collects data on certain "open market" money rates in New York City. One of these rates, the rate on "prime commercial paper" of 4- to 6-months maturity, represents the (very low) interest rate at which large borrowers of unusual credit standing can obtain funds by marketing their promissory notes, usually through special middlemen known as commercial paper dealers. The rate on 90-day "prime bankers acceptances" reflects the cost of financing foreign trade and other transactions through bills of exchange of high quality drawn against banks. Rates are also published indicating the cost to New York Stock Exchange members of funds borrowed on security collateral. These rates are carried by weeks, with monthly and yearly averages, in the *Federal Reserve Bulletin*, and monthly averages appear in the *Survey of Current Business*. The Board also issues a monthly mimeographed release, *Open-Market Money Rates in New York City*, presenting weekly and monthly data prior to the publication of the *Bulletin*. With the aid of certain other sources the Board of Governors has prepared tables of short-term open market rates monthly from 1890 and weekly from 1919. These appear in *Banking and Monetary Statistics*. Yields of short-term Treasury securities are discussed in a later section.

Information on the volume of short-term lending may be found in statistics discussed elsewhere in this chapter, including those on commercial banks and the Federal Reserve Banks and on government securities. Two additional monthly series on borrowing in the short-term money market may be mentioned here. The first of these shows the volume of commercial paper outstanding, based on reports by the leading commercial-paper dealers. The other shows, on the basis of reports by makers of bankers' acceptances, the volume of bankers' acceptances outstanding, classified to show how they are held and the basis on which they have been drawn. These figures are reported in the *Federal Reserve Bulletin*. Commercial paper figures are carried back to 1918 and bankers' acceptance figures to 1924 in *Banking and*

Monetary Statistics. Both series are compiled by the Federal Reserve Bank of New York. The bankers' acceptance data prior to August 1936 were compiled by the American Acceptance Council.

THE SECURITIES MARKETS

A considerable body of statistical data on the securities markets, much of it originating from private sources, is available. Our knowledge of these markets has been substantially increased in recent years, especially through the statistical activities of the Securities and Exchange Commission.[11]

Statistics on the issuance of new securities provide information on the procurement of long-term capital by corporations and by governmental and certain other agencies. The Securities and Exchange Commission compiles, chiefly from its own files and from the financial press, monthly figures on the estimated proceeds of new securities offered for cash in the United States. The Commission states that these figures cover substantially all new issues offered for cash in amounts over $100,000 and with maturities of more than one year. These figures are published monthly in the *Statistical Bulletin* of the Commission. Estimated gross proceeds are shown by type of issuer (four types of corporate issuers and five types of noncorporate issuers), by type of security (common stock, preferred stock, corporate bonds and notes, and noncorporate bonds and notes) and by six types of offering (indicating whether the issue is public or private, registered under the Securities Act of 1933 or unregistered, and if unregistered, the reason for nonregistration). A further analysis is given of the estimated net proceeds of all *corporate* offerings, and of the offerings of each of four major types of corporate issuers, showing how the funds are to be used (plant and equipment, working capital, retirement of funded debt, retirement of other debt, retirement of preferred stock, and "other" purposes). The annual report of the SEC for 1943 presents roughly the same information by years from fiscal year 1935 and by months for fiscal year 1943, supplemented by a table dealing with private placements of securities. Selected series on securities issuances from the SEC appear monthly in the *Survey of Current Business.* The *Federal Reserve Bulletin* carries SEC data on proposed uses of proceeds, and *Banking and Monetary Statistics* carries proposed use figures monthly back to 1934. The last two publications also carry Department of Commerce figures on

---

[11] See the section on "Securities Markets and Corporations," by R. W. Goldsmith, in *Statistical Activities of the American Nations* (Inter-American Statistical Institute, Washington, D. C., 1941), pp. 558 ff.

foreign issues. Statistics on "new issues" through June 1938 may be found in *Selected Statistics on Securities and on Exchange Markets*.

Issues registered with the SEC under the Securities Act of 1933 comprise only a minor fraction of total issues, excluding, as they do, Federal, state, and local issues, issues of common carriers, intrastate issues, and certain other categories. Moreover, registration indicates intention to issue rather than actual issuance, and some securities are registered for purposes other than immediate sale. Very full information, however, is available on these registered issues. Quarterly registration figures appear in the *Statistical Bulletin*, with analyses by nature and purpose of registration, types of securities, major industrial groups, methods of distribution, groups to be solicited, and uses of proceeds. Registration data were analyzed in much greater detail in annual reports of the SEC prior to 1942, certain data being classified by some 50 industrial groups. The presentation is greatly curtailed in the reports for 1942 and 1943. Background data on registered issues may be found in *Selected Statistics*.

The SEC has given us more comprehensive figures than were previously available on the total volume of trading on securities exchanges, as well as detailed information on specific types of trading.[12] The *Statistical Bulletin* gives monthly data on volume and value of trading on each of 24 securities exchanges, separately for stocks, for bonds, and for rights and warrants (the volume of bonds being measured by the face value). Collection of volume and value figures began in 1934. Summary data are published in annual reports. Other series on particular categories of trading appear in the *Statistical Bulletin* or separate releases. Selected SEC series on trading on exchanges appear in the *Survey of Current Business*, and background "trading" data may be found in *Banking and Monetary Statistics* and *Selected Statistics*. Statistics dealing with the registration, under the Securities Exchange Act of 1934, of issues for trading on exchanges may be found in the SEC annual reports. Certain statistics on international securities transactions are referred to below.

Federal agencies have made certain contributions to the information available on prices and yields of long-term securities. The SEC monthly *Statistical Bulletin* contains indexes of weekly closing prices of common stocks on the New York Stock Exchange for each of 27 industries, together with a composite index for the group of industries. The Treasury Department computes an average yield of "high grade corporate bonds," currently based on five issues. Daily figures and

[12] Idem, p. 560.

monthly averages of daily figures are published currently in the Treasury *Bulletin;* weekly averages appear in the *Federal Reserve Bulletin.* Related to bond yields as an indication of the cost of obtaining long-term capital are certain figures on the cost of flotation of securities under the Securities Act. The classification, discussed above, of proceeds by proposed uses shows the cost of flotation in the form of commission and discounts and other expenses of flotation. The Commission also has made special tabulations dealing with the cost of flotation, as in the 1943 annual report and in separate releases. Federal series on prices and yields of government securities are discussed below in connection with the Federal public debt.

Quarterly tables are published in the SEC *Statistical Bulletin* showing the underwriting and syndicate-managing activities of investment banking houses. These show individually for some 75 houses and for the residual group, the number of issues underwritten and the extent of their participation in such issues. These data are classified for each firm by type of security (bonds, preferred stock, and common stock). For some 25 houses that lead in the management of underwriting syndicates (and for the residual group) further information is given as to the number and value of issues managed and the extent of their participation in them. The figures apply to registered issues offered during the quarter. Earlier data on underwriting are available in *Selected Statistics.*

The Securities Exchange Act of 1934 requires the registration with the Commission of security dealers and brokers with certain exceptions. Statistics on registered dealers and brokers have been published somewhat irregularly. The annual reports of the Commission for 1943 and 1942 contain limited tabulations showing by state (New York City separately) and by form of organization, the number of registrants, the number of branch offices, and certain data on personnel. The report for 1941 gives a more detailed classification, including an analysis by four types of business engaged in (dealer, broker, combination, "other"), cross classified according to type or types of credit extended to customers (carrying margin accounts, selling on partial payment contracts, and six other categories, including houses extending no credit). Data on number of registrants are carried back in this report to 1935 by years. An elaborate analysis of registrations as of June 30, 1938, appears in *Selected Statistics.*

Further information on the activities of stock brokers is provided by reports to the Board of Governors beginning in 1935 by all member firms of the New York Stock Exchange carrying margin accounts for their customers. These reports show various "debit balances" and "credit balances." Most significant of the items are "customers debit balances," which represents credit extended to customers principally for carrying securities purchased on margin, and "money borrowed." The latter figure comprises one of several sources of information on "brokers loans," or loans made to brokers. Selected items from the reports, which are now made semiannually, appear in the *Federal Reserve Bulletin* and the *Survey of Current Business*, with estimates for key items for months falling between the semiannual reports. *Banking and Monetary Statistics* carries debit and credit figures from 1931.

CONSUMER SHORT-TERM CREDIT

Consumer credit may take the form of purchases "on credit" or of cash loans. Statistics dealing with the extension of credit to consumers by merchants are discussed in Chapter 6. The present discussion is concerned with statistics on the activities of financial institutions in extending short-term consumer credit directly in the form of cash loans or indirectly by purchasing from others the obligations arising from credit sales.

The Board of Governors presents in the *Federal Reserve Bulletin* monthly estimates of consumer credit outstanding by major types. Included are estimates of installment loans and of single payment loans. Installment loans are further classified as loans by commercial banks, by small loan companies, by industrial banking companies, by credit unions, and by miscellaneous lenders, with a separate series for repair and modernization loans. For the four major types of lending agencies, figures are given on volume of loans made during the month. The *Bulletin* also carries monthly data on consumer installment *credits* of commercial banks, including purchased installment paper as well as direct loans. These installment credits are classified into five types. Both amounts outstanding at the end of the month and volume extended during the month are shown. Several monthly releases are also issued by the Board of Governors. *Consumer Credit* gives estimated amounts outstanding at the end of the month by major components. Another, *Consumer Installment Loans*, gives loan volume, amounts outstanding, and repayments, for the four types of lending agencies. The release *Consumer Installment Credit in Commercial Banks* gives loan volume and amounts outstanding by type of loan and by Federal Reserve District. Some of the consumer credit series are carried currently in the *Survey of Current Business*. Much of the

Federal Reserve work in this field is a continuation of series prepared through August 1942 by the Department of Commerce.[13]

The above-mentioned series are derived from reporting samples of respondents. Call report data on consumer loans to individuals for all reporting banks are also available. A bird's-eye view of the operations of lending agencies in the field of consumer installment credit was obtained in 1941 through a compulsory registration of persons extending such credit. Summary statistics on the installment credit extended by various types of lending agencies as of September 30, 1941, are presented in the *Federal Reserve Bulletin* for May 1942, p. 435.

Especially full data are available for one type of agency lending directly to the consumer, namely, the credit union. Credit unions are cooperative associations which make personal loans to their members and in which members invest their savings. Of the approximately 9,100 credit unions active at the end of 1943, about 3,900 were "Federal" credit unions chartered by the Federal Government under legislation of 1934 and supervised by the Federal Deposit Insurance Corporation. Aggregate financial and other statistics on the Federal credit unions are published annually by the FDIC in its *Federal Credit Unions: Annual Report of Operations*. The first such report of the FDIC, covering the year 1941, appeared in 1942. Earlier data may be found in the annual reports of the Farm Credit Administration, which supervised these associations until 1942. Statistics of all credit unions have been compiled for each year beginning with 1931 by the Bureau of Labor Statistics of the Department of Labor on the basis of statistics of state and of Federal credit unions. These appear in articles published in the *Monthly Labor Review* as well as in separate publications.

A monthly statistical release entitled *Sales Finance Companies* is published by the Board of Governors. Responsibility for the series was transferred to the Board early in 1945 from the Census Bureau. Sales finance companies participate indirectly in the extension of consumer short-term credit by purchasing from dealers installment paper based on retail sales, especially the sales of automobiles. They may also finance sales at wholesale in a similar manner and may make direct business and personal loans. The series currently covers approximately 200 reporting companies accounting for the bulk of the sales

---

[13] See the *Survey of Current Business*, November 1942, pp. 15 ff., for monthly data on loans outstanding from 1929 through August 1942, with a discussion of methods of estimating and sources of data. The series on consumer installment credit of commercial banks is discussed in the *Federal Reserve Bulletin*, October 1942, pp. 992 ff., and some back data are given. Revisions of consumer credit statistics are discussed in the *Bulletin*, December 1944, pp. 1177 ff.; and January 1945, pp. 27 ff.

finance business. The indexes published in the releases are useful for indicating trends in the various types of sales financing. The absolute figures must be used with care because of incomplete coverage and because the sample is not identical from month to month. The series in its present form dates from January 1942. Prior to that it covered only automobile sales finance.[14]

GOVERNMENT CORPORATIONS AND CREDIT AGENCIES

The Federal Government supplements the work of private financial enterprises through the activities of certain government corporations and other agencies whose functions include the making of loans, the provision of capital through stock purchase, and the provision of insurance. As this is written, the publication program for current statistics on these agencies is undergoing revision.

Statements of the assets and liabilities of the so-called government corporations and credit agencies have appeared in the past in the *Daily Statement of the United States Treasury* for the last day of each month showing the condition of the agencies as of the close of the preceding month. (It should be noted that the corporations and agencies covered are not necessarily engaged primarily in credit or other financial activities.) Beginning with the statement as of September 30, 1944, which appeared in the *Daily Statement* for November 15, 1944, these data are to appear quarterly. The tabulation for September 30 gives approximately 50 balance sheet statements for individual or grouped corporations, agencies, or programs. The statements are presented in terms of a common classification of assets, liabilities, and capital, which includes a detailed subdivision of loans and investments.

Less detailed balance sheet data for the corporations and other agencies have appeared monthly in the past in the *Bulletin of the Treasury Department*, together with additional data showing for certain of them the sources and uses of funds. The *Bulletin* will henceforth carry balance sheet data and data on sources and uses of funds quarterly. Consideration is being given by the Treasury to the publication of quarterly income and expense statements, required of the agencies under the new program.

Statistics on government corporations and credit agencies based on Treasury Department data have appeared in the *Federal Reserve Bul-*

---

[14] A section on "Sales-Finance Companies and Bank Holdings of Retail Installment Paper" appears in the *Sixteenth Census of the United States: 1940, Census of Business, Vol. I, Retail Trade: 1939, Part I,* pp. 787–814. It was also published as a separate pamphlet.

letin, the *Survey of Current Business*, the *Annual Report of the Secretary of the Treasury*, and *Banking and Monetary Statistics*. Information may also be found in reports and releases of the individual agencies themselves. The *Survey of Current Business* carries current series on loans by the RFC and by agencies supervised by the Farm Credit Administration, based on compilations by these two agencies.

Extensive background statistical data on 30 agencies or groups of agencies were compiled by the Treasury Department in response to Senate Resolution No. 150, of June 27, 1939, which required the Department to submit financial statements for these agencies covering the period from the time of their organization through June 30, 1939. The resulting report, entitled *Financial Statements of Certain Government Agencies* (S. Doc. 172, 76th Cong., 3d sess., 1940, in two parts), is voluminous and contains balance sheet and income and expense data for each agency or group, accompanied by textual discussion.

The Postal Savings System is not included in the tabulations for government corporations and credit agencies. Detailed information, including the number of depositors and amount of deposits for each participating post office as of the fiscal year-end, is presented in the annual report to Congress entitled *Operations of the Postal Savings System*. Less detailed monthly data on the Postal Savings System are carried currently in the *Federal Reserve Bulletin* and the *Survey of Current Business*. Back data from 1911 may be found in the Postal Savings annual reports and in *Banking and Monetary Statistics*.

THE FEDERAL PUBLIC DEBT

Special attention is due the Federal public debt as an influence of outstanding importance in the market for funds. A great mass of information on the public debt, including data on debt outstanding, offerings, issuances, retirements, interest, maturities, and prices and yields, may be found in the regular publications of the Treasury Department, and selected data appear in the *Federal Reserve Bulletin*, the *Survey of Current Business*, and *Banking and Monetary Statistics*. Only a few features of these data will be discussed here.

The basic source of current information on debt outstanding is the Treasury *Daily Statement*, which prints in the issue for the first of each month a "Statement of the Public Debt" as of the close of the preceding month. For each outstanding issue this statement gives descriptive material, the amount issued, the amount retired, and the amount outstanding. Supplementary data on contingent liabilities are given. Moreover, the *Daily Statement* carries a statement of receipts and expenditures on account of the public debt, with detailed statements for the public debt accounts cumulatively for the current month and for the current fiscal year.

Daily price and yield data (with monthly averages) for individual outstanding issues appear in the monthly Treasury publication *Prices and Yields of Public Marketable Securities Issued by the United States Government and by Federal Agencies*. Selected price and yield data by individual issues appear in the Treasury *Bulletin*.

Several current series are available showing prices or yields of different types of government securities. The Treasury *Bulletin* carries average yields for taxable long-term Treasury bonds and for partly tax-exempt long-term Treasury bonds. In addition to these two series the Board of Governors publishes also, in the *Federal Reserve Bulletin*, the average yields of 3-month Treasury bills, 9- to 12-month certificates of indebtedness, 3- to 5-year taxable Treasury notes, and taxable Treasury bonds due or callable in 7 to 9 years, and an average price of long-term Treasury bonds. These series are all available on a weekly basis and the two Treasury Department averages are available on a daily basis. The *Survey of Current Business* carries monthly figures for most of these series.

Both the Treasury Department and the Board of Governors present periodic tabulations dealing with the distribution among major groups of investors of interest-bearing securities issued or guaranteed by the Federal Government. The most elaborate data on private holdings are those derived from a survey conducted monthly since 1941 by the Treasury Department covering the holdings of reporting groups of commercial banks, stock savings banks, mutual savings banks, life insurance companies, and other insurance companies. The Treasury *Bulletin* shows from month to month the holdings of the several groups of banks and insurance companies; of United States Government agencies and trust funds and of the Federal Reserve Banks; and of all other investors (including nonreporting banks and insurance companies). The holdings of public marketable securities are shown by individual issues. Additional detail on the holdings of different classes of commercial banks is given twice a year. The reporting banks and insurance companies hold substantially all of the government securities held by banks and insurance companies in the United States. Quarterly data from the survey from 1941 appear in the Treasury Department annual report for 1943. Further periodic estimates of *total* holdings by different groups of investors are presented by the Board of Governors in the *Federal Reserve Bulletin* and by the Treasury Department in the Treasury *Bulletin*. Background data may be found in

Banking and Monetary Statistics and the Treasury Department annual report for 1943.

INTERNATIONAL FINANCIAL STATISTICS

An annual publication of the Department of Commerce entitled *The Balance of International Payments of the United States* (discussed in Chapter 7) analyzes the international financial, as well as commercial, transactions of persons in the United States. It brings together a variety of data relative to international finance, including long- and short-term capital movements and movements of the precious metals. This annual publication is suspended because of the war, the last issue having appeared for the year 1940.

In preparing these analyses the Department of Commerce relies in part on certain statistics based on compulsory reports required by the Treasury Department. Since the end of 1934 the Treasury Department has required reports of banks and bankers and security dealers and brokers, from which have been compiled statistics of international capital movements and the foreign exchange market. These reports were at first required weekly, but since the middle of 1942 they have been required only monthly. The statistics from 1935 through the third quarter of 1938 were published in a quarterly Treasury Department bulletin entitled *Statistics of Capital Movements Between the United States and Foreign Countries and of Purchases and Sales of Foreign Exchange in the United States.* Beginning in 1939 publication has been on a monthly basis in the Treasury *Bulletin.*

The data through the year 1941 were published in considerable detail in tables dealing with short-term liabilities to, and claims against, foreigners as reported by banks; security transactions; foreign debit and credit balances as reported by security brokers and dealers; foreign exchange transactions; and related matters. Data were analyzed by foreign countries or areas. Publication of detailed tabulations was, however, suspended for the duration of the war, and the *Bulletin* currently carries only a monthly summary of the "net capital movement to the United States," which analyzes this net movement into movement in short-term banking funds, in brokerage balances, in transactions in domestic securities, and in transactions in foreign securities. Data are given by years from 1935 and for recent months, with a cumulative figure from 1935. No country or area analysis is given. The *Federal Reserve Bulletin* carries a cumulative analysis of net capital movement, supplemented by current figures on banking and brokerage balances outstanding. *Banking and Monetary Statistics* carries useful back data by countries and areas. Weekly figures for outstanding short-term liabilities and assets are carried back in this volume, on the basis of earlier reports from New York City banks, to May 31, 1929, for liabilities and to March 31, 1931, for assets.

Statistics on imports and exports of gold and silver were formerly published currently by the Department of Commerce (in the *Monthly Summary of Foreign Commerce of the United States*) but this practice was discontinued for reasons of security in 1941. Statistics by countries are available through the calendar year 1941. Statistics on total imports and exports and on trade with certain countries are allowed to be released with a 12-month (or in certain cases a 6-month) lag, and the Department plans a program of monthly releases in accordance with this timing schedule. Some data since 1941 have already been published on a delayed basis in Census Bureau releases bearing the title *Report No. FT 850: United States Exports and Imports of Gold and Silver*.

Foreign exchange rates are released monthly by the Board of Governors and published in the *Federal Reserve Bulletin*. The published figures are monthly averages of daily noon buying rates for cable transfers in New York City certified by the Federal Reserve Bank of New York for the use of the customs administration. Because of present curtailment of the foreign exchange market, rates are no longer certified for a number of countries. Monthly averages are published currently for only eleven countries, but back data in terms of yearly averages of certified rates are still published regularly in the *Bulletin* for thirty-five countries. Selected rates appear in the *Survey of Current Business*. *Banking and Monetary Statistics* gives, from various sources, monthly and yearly averages for approximately forty countries for varying periods. The *Foreign Commerce Weekly* of the Department of Commerce gives exchange rates (selling rates for sight drafts on New York) for sixteen Latin American countries, giving monthly averages and latest available quotations. A balance sheet for the Exchange Stabilization Fund appears quarterly in the Treasury *Bulletin*.

In addition to the statistics already mentioned the *Federal Reserve Bulletin* brings together a variety of foreign financial data including data on the condition of central banks and commercial banks, money rates, security prices, gold production, and gold reserves of central banks and governments. In conjunction with its tabulations in the field of international and foreign financial statistics *Banking and Monetary Statistics* carries useful discussions of the data.

CONCLUSION

Among the various types of economic data, the statistics of money, credit, and banking are unusually full. Moreover, substantial improvements have been made in them in recent years. The availability of data in this field reflects in part the recognized public interest in the operation of financial institutions—a public interest which early in our history led to the collection of reports from banks incident to public control.

Responsibility for further improvement in this area of statistics does not lie wholly with the Federal Government but is shared by the states and by nongovernmental bodies. Federal agencies should, of course, continue to give attention to remaining gaps in our data which can appropriately be filled in by improvements in the Federal reporting system. In the attempt to refine and extend our knowledge of financial processes, they should give due consideration to the technique of procuring current reports from selected samples of respondents. Federal influence should be used as in the past to promote uniformity in state statistics.

The present division among three agencies of responsibility for the collection and publication of Federal banking statistics calls for careful coordination of the several programs to avoid unnecessary duplication and to insure that the published data are readily comparable and of maximum usefulness. A substantial amount of coordination already exists and further progress by the agencies should be looked for. If responsibility is to continue to be divided in this field, serious consideration should be given to the possibility of a joint publication program as a means of obtaining a better balanced and better integrated body of Federal banking statistics.

CHAPTER 11

PRICES

LESTER S. KELLOGG [1]
Bureau of Labor Statistics
Department of Labor

Prices are the gauges of business in a free enterprise economy. They regulate the flow of both producer and consumer commodities and they determine profits. Low prices may force a producer to the wall; high prices may squeeze the working man even when dollar earnings are nominally high. It is not at all surprising, therefore, that ethical judgments have frequently been made on what constitutes "just prices" and that prices are the best known and most widely used statistics in the written record of man's social development.

PRICES IN HISTORY

For early times scattered prices are available for the major foodstuffs, or for those crops and staples which were the mainstays of ancient economies. Even in the *Bible*, prices are frequently mentioned. In the era of the Roman Empire and in the Dark and Middle Ages which succeeded it, "just prices" were the foundation of business ethics, and their disregard the basis for the earliest regulatory laws of usury. Since the beginning of the industrial revolution in the Western World there has been increasing and, at times, concentrated attention to prices in all aspects, ranging from voluminous collections of records to complicated analyses relating to currency, "general" price levels, international trade, the role of price in profits, and its potentialities as a tool of economic control. The state itself has recognized the enormous impact of price in our economy. Tariffs, working through prices, have long imposed artificial barriers to free trade; utility and transportation rates have long been controlled, and largely in terms of a "fair" rate of return; responsibility has been assumed for preventing

[1] The author wishes to acknowledge with gratitude the assistance of Louis Weiner and Galen B. Price, Jr.

precipitous declines in farm prices; and government agencies are established in all warring nations to stem inflation.

For the past 100 years in all the civilized world there have been records of prices which, though not statistically complete, are sufficiently comprehensive to be useful, both for businessmen and economists. There is not room to list these records or describe many of them. That there was interest in such records, however, and that they were currently of importance to traders with commodities to sell, is evidenced by many kinds of historical data, business records, and the press. Of some interest in this respect is the small book, *Benner's Prophecies of Future Ups and Downs in Prices*, first published in 1871.[2] Samuel Benner, an Ohio farmer, compiled material and wrote with the object of giving "brief, full, and clear exposition of the ups and downs in prices for certain products and commodities in the markets of our country, to all who are struggling in the same for a competence."

The emergence of organized commodity markets, of both local and national importance, has done much to stimulate the development of price records. In the United States a tremendous impetus to the development of such data has resulted from the expanded functions of government departments, both state and national, and with the establishment of various agencies to administer specific legislation. The price data which have been developed have been collected in different ways and have been treated so as to serve the varied purposes for which they were intended.

Nature of Prices and Index Numbers. Early price information was reported in frontier fashion. Prices simply meant the amount of the customary monetary unit necessary to obtain the usual amount of the commodity in question—the number of cents necessary to obtain a dozen eggs; or at wholesale, the amount in dollars and cents necessary to obtain a case. There was little detailed physical specification of the item being purchased, so that the price of a dozen eggs simply meant the number of cents, pence, lire, or centimes required to purchase a dozen eggs (white or brown, large or small, and strictly fresh or not) at a specified time and place. There was no problem of specification except full measure, no problem of trade-mark or trade-name, and none of the problems of detailed description which are now employed in comprehensive grade labeling.

Detailed knowledge of the nature of a price becomes important when business operations require greater precision. In this respect, prices are not different from other business statistics. As business becomes more complex and as administrative direction becomes more

[2] Robert Clarke & Company, Cincinnati, Ohio, 1871.

refined, there is greater need for complete knowledge of the nature of the facts that are being used to guide it. Current interest in prices may require even greater specialization—it may require prices for a number of sizes, varieties, stages of production and distribution, and by trade-mark or highly advertised name. To illustrate, a person may want to know the price of roasted Brazilian coffee, in hundred-pound bags, on the 15th of last month in the New York market. Or again, he may want the price to a retailer of Maxwell House coffee, ground for a percolator, in one-pound jars, 24 jars to the carton, at wholesalers' warehouses in Chicago. Depending upon the purposes for which information is to be used, caution must always be exercised to be sure that the prices being examined have the characteristics—both the precise commodity and of the correct method of combination—necessary for the kind of conclusions to be drawn.

Available records for early years usually give prices in terms of the purchases and sales of a given individual or of a sale in a given market. Historically there was little or no consideration given to representing all sales or of an *average sale*. The increased number of sales and the variation in prices for essentially the same commodity in the same market during a short period of time has made the concept of average prices important. Average prices may represent, statistically, the arithmetic average, the median, or the modal price of the sales of all varieties of a commodity during a given period. Average prices, on the other hand, may refer only to sales of a particular variety of the commodity, or to prices at a given time in the market, or to a certain stage in the production or distribution of the commodity.

Prices of a commodity at its several distribution levels refers to prices of the producer or manufacturer, of the wholesaler or other intermediate distributor, or of the retailer. Further expansion of prices at any of these levels is possible. For instance, at the retailer level prices might be those of independent or of chain food retailers.

Prices might also represent one of several different levels of reality, such as market quotations, catalogue or list prices, contract prices, cash prices, discounted cash prices, or realized prices. Each of these prices has its special significance with reference to groups of commodities. Prices may also reflect the time characteristics of the commodity or of the market; for instance, a single price may result from an auction or it may simply reflect the number of times during a business period that prices are collected.

For many purposes, even more general information concerning prices is desired. Interest may be focused not on the price of a single, narrowly defined commodity or on the average price of such a commodity, say in a number of markets, but rather on the general trend of prices over time. We may be interested in the *movement* of meat prices; we may want to compare *changes* in the prices of raw cotton and wool with those of the fabrics made from them; prices of consumer goods with prices of producer goods; or we may need an over-all measure of wholesale price changes for all commodities combined. Obviously, some sort of averaging procedure is required in such cases in order to combine the prices of a wide variety of commodities. *Index numbers* are merely the results of such an averaging procedure.[3]

Index numbers, and average prices or price composites as well, are always constructed to serve a specific purpose. This purpose determines the commodities included, their specifications, the location of the reporting markets, the stage of production or distribution, the conditions of sale, the frequency of price collection, and the weights or measures of importance, used in combining the various commodities. It cannot be emphasized too strongly that each of these characteristics of an average price or price index must be scrutinized carefully before the prices or index numbers are used. To use an index number of wholesale food prices to represent retail food prices, or of all building materials to represent lumber, without knowing the necessary qualifications or the problems involved may be as serious as treating a person with appendicitis for stomach ache. The specific purpose to be served must determine whether actual average prices for individual commodities or index numbers of prices for groups of commodities are used.

WORLD WAR I—STIMULANT TO PRICE COLLECTION AND ANALYSIS

The great need for statistical data during the First World War provided a previously unequaled stimulation to the collection, analysis, interpretation, and use of statistical information. Prices held a high priority among the data which were essential to the control of the war economy.

Recognizing that "facts are our masters now," the price collection and analysis work of the War Industries Board was developed on an

---

[3] Index numbers were invented by G. R. Carli, an Italian whose work on the subject appeared in 1764. Major development of index numbers of prices has taken place, however, mainly since the turn of the 20th century. Though private agencies developed and regularly maintained several price index numbers, the greatest contributions have been made in America since World War I by several departments of the United States Government. Price data and price indexes of various kinds are now regularly published and are continuously available.

unprecedented scale [4] and, though greatly reduced at the end of the war, set standards which served as stimulants to broader and better price work by Government agencies in the postwar era. Recession from the peak of data collection activity that had been reached during the war followed the Armistice, but the framework for a comprehensive pattern of information had been developed. This general framework was expanded and filled in during the period from 1920 to 1940. At the beginning of the Second World War, as a result, there was more information on prices available for consideration by the Congress and its committees, for administrative agencies, and for the war agencies than had ever before been available for guidance in any economic emergency.

Price collection between the two wars developed as a result of the needs of business and agriculture, the expansion of the Government's program, and the numerous and important Congressional investigations of our economy, together with those conducted by various regulatory commissions. The two regular Government departments in which price work has had greatest development are the Department of Agriculture and the Department of Labor. Outstanding among the commissions whose special investigations have added much to our price information are the Federal Trade Commission and the Temporary National Economic Committee. Many other departments and commissions, however, have developed important data. The following is a brief review of the price work of the Government agencies whose functions require them to conduct and maintain price information.

PRICES IN AGRICULTURAL MARKETS

Prices Received by Farmers. The most widely used series of prices currently collected by the Department of Agriculture is "Prices Received by Farmers." These prices are, as their name indicates, the prices that farmers receive for their products at the farm. They represent the estimate of the average price of all grades and classes of commodities being sold in local farm markets about the 15th of each month. The grades and classes may vary from one season to another, and even from one month to another, but since these prices represent the amounts

---

[4] In his summary of the 56 price bulletins issued in 1919, Wesley C. Mitchell, Chief of the Price Section of the War Industries Board, said: "There has been no other revolution in prices at once so sudden, so violent, and so widespread as the revolution that accompanied the War of 1914–1918." For this price record of World War I, see *Price Bulletins 1–57*, of the War Industries Board, distributed by the Superintendent of Documents.

which the farmers get for their products in the local markets, they represent the first price at which a product changes hands. Subsequently, there may be other prices for the product as it is traded in markets farther along in the distribution process, that is, in markets nearer the ultimate consumer.

The prices are reported as an average for each crop for the United States, as well as an average for each state where the crop is of importance. These prices are released monthly,[5] in dollars and cents, for the customary physical unit of sale. Average actual prices are also published for the 5-year period August 1909 to July 1914, in order to provide an easily accessible basis for comparison over a long period of time.

Prices Paid by Farmers. In order to gauge more completely the living conditions of the agricultural population, the Department of Agriculture collects prices for the commodities which go into the living of farmers—prices which farmers pay. Each month voluntary responses by storekeepers all over the country provide the basis for the calculation of the indexes of average prices paid [6] for foods, clothing, operating expenses, furniture and furnishings, building materials for house, building materials for other than the house, farm machinery, equipment and supplies, seed, and fertilizer, which are commonly included in the purchases of farmers. These prices represent the most commonly purchased items in the stores in which farmers buy. Occasionally the actual average prices for many of the commodities are published in addition to the index numbers derived from them.

Each month these prices are combined with farmers' interest and tax payments into the index number of "Prices, Interest, and Taxes Paid by Farmers," which is one of the factors used in establishing parity prices. This index number is considerably different from the consumers' price index of city wage earners and salary workers as computed by the Bureau of Labor Statistics, in that among other things it does not include rents, utilities, and many of the services which are consumed by city workers. To measure the full impact of economic changes upon farmers, farm taxes and interest payments have been added to this index to provide an over-all index of expenditures of farmers. These indexes, with a base of August 1910–July 1914 = 100 unless otherwise indicated, and are regularly published in releases of the Department of Agriculture.

[5] *Agricultural Prices*, monthly release of the Bureau of Agricultural Economics, U. S. Department of Agriculture, Washington, D. C.

[6] These are also regularly published in *Agricultural Prices*.

Wholesale and Market Prices. To expand price information as a guide
to agricultural policy, the Department of Agriculture also collects and
publishes regularly wholesale or market prices for the important farm
products.[7] Wholesale prices differ from prices paid by farmers in that
they reflect the amounts at which products change hands in the commercial markets and organized produce exchanges. The market price
is sometimes considered the first commercial transaction. In order
to obtain these prices, regular field workers of the Department, located
at the country's major markets, regularly report the prices at which
commodities, by variety and grade, are sold in each market period—
usually daily. These prices are regularly reported in the press for the
commodities which are currently in the market. On the basis of combinations of these figures, it is possible to compute United States averages
for short periods of time.

PRICES IN COMMERCIAL MARKETS

Wholesale Prices. The importance of wholesale prices in the United
States has long been recognized. The first major examination of wholesale prices, aside from sporadic private studies, was that conducted
for the Senate Committee on Finance in 1891 and 1892. The results
of the study were made public as a result of the order of March 3, 1893,
in Senate Report 1394 and has been widely known since as the Report
of the Aldrich Committee. Investigations of this committee resulted
in a compilation of average prices and price relatives for more than
200 articles important in trade between 1860 and 1891.

The Bureau of Labor considered that wholesale price information
was of major importance in the analysis of the welfare of the working
people and as a consequence in 1902 began the collection and publication of its series of wholesale prices. The index of wholesale prices
was continuously maintained thereafter by the Bureau, and in 1914
series of price relatives and index numbers by finely divided groups of
commodities were published back to 1891, the period of the Aldrich
Report. Since that time the index of wholesale prices has continuously
been published on a monthly basis and through cooperative efforts
private and Government agencies have produced a wholesale price
index running back to the Colonial Period of the United States, as
shown in Figure 1. At the present time, the Bureau of Labor Statistics
publishes the wholesale price index based upon some 890 commodities
and nearly 2,000 quotations, with the year 1926 = 100.

[7] Summarized annually in *Agricultural Statistics*, Department of Agriculture;
available in local releases currently; see Chapter 5.

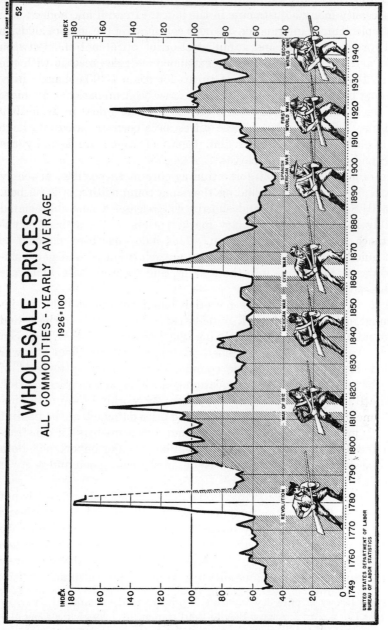

WHOLESALE PRICES
ALL COMMODITIES - YEARLY AVERAGE
1926=100

UNITED STATES DEPARTMENT OF LABOR
BUREAU OF LABOR STATISTICS

FIGURE 1

During the 1930's and the war period following 1939, there have been
of necessity many adjustments in the index. In addition, a great deal
of supplementary information has been collected for purposes of analysis
and for the guidance and administration of price control. Between
1938 and 1941 the BLS greatly expanded its price records with the
result that continuous series of prices for some 10,000 commodities,
running back in many cases to 1865, have been prepared as averages
and in terms of relatives based on the average prices in 1935–1939
and also 1926. Graphs of these prices have been prepared and have
been photographed on microfilm, copies of which are held by the
BLS and the National Archives.

In order to keep this information as current as possible, a weekly
wholesale price index, including the same commodities, is published.
The BLS has prepared, and shortly will release, a new abbreviated
weekly index based on primary market prices of 125 articles of importance in civilian consumption. This index has been planned to
add quickly old commodities as they are reintroduced and new commodities as they come into the market, and to drop those which are
no longer of importance.

A daily index of basic raw materials based on August 1939 was instituted in January 1940 as a guide to control of markets in the period
of rapid price movement following the beginning of the European
War. This index was maintained continuously throughout the war
period, although many of the commodities since the latter part of
1941 have been under strict allocation control, as well as price control.

The Bureau is currently and continuously working toward the improvement and extension of its wholesale price data and, at the present
time, is making plans for price series and index numbers for construction and auxiliary machinery which will be of major importance, both
in domestic and in international trade, in the conversion and postwar
periods.[8]

The Term "Wholesale Prices." The term "wholesale prices" is not
a clear description of the type of prices actually included in wholesale
price indexes. The BLS Wholesale Price Index measures prices in
primary markets, i.e., at the first commercial transaction for each
commodity in the form in which it is priced. The prices, therefore, may
be those reported for commodities in primary agricultural markets;

---

[8] For a history of price developments in primary markets during the war, see
Wartime Prices, Part I, August 1939 to Pearl Harbor, by John M. Blair and Mel-
ville J. Ulmer, of the Bureau of Labor Statistics, U. S. Department of Labor,
Bulletin 749, Washington, D. C., 1944. Part II of the history, which deals with the
period Pearl Harbor to June 1944, will soon be published.

they may be prices quoted by manufacturers or importers, or they may be prices paid by wholesalers, as well as prices paid to wholesalers. They are not prices charged by wholesalers as that term is generally used in marketing. They do not in the main, therefore, represent prices paid by retailers; they represent prices paid by large buyers—distributors or large industrial users. Depending on the nature of the commodity and the source of the price information, a price reported by the BLS may represent an actual sale, as prices on organized exchanges for raw commodities, or the quoted price at which a manufacturer stands ready to sell his product at a given time. Most finished products, for example, are quoted on this basis. Prices are reported after the deduction of all applicable trade and cash discounts, and are treated as cash prices.

Care must be exercised in comparing these wholesale prices with unit value figures obtained by dividing the total value of product by the number of units sold. The prices are quotations for carefully defined grades and types of commodities, as determined by detailed specifications, whereas the unit value figure represents an average of a number of types and grades. For example, the BLS reports a price on "Pillow cases, 64 × 64 count, plain, bleached, 45″ × 36″, per dozen, no quantity specified, f.o.b. mill, manufacturer to jobber and wholesaler; seller's list price subject to current cash and trade discounts; weekly, Tuesday." The price collected is further identified by brand name, if a branded article, and by manufacturer's model or type number. The unit value figure which can be secured from data in the Census of Manufactures, for example, would relate to all pillow cases, including all sizes, types, brands, and qualities. Obviously, this unit value would vary with changes in the type, brand, or quality of pillow cases sold. The BLS figure, on the other hand, would vary only as a reflection in price of changes in the demand or supply of the pillow cases priced. Each of these types of "price" has its unique applications and should not be used for applications for which it is not fitted. For example, the unit value figure which can be obtained from the Census of Manufactures figures on total sales is useful as a measure of changes in the dollar value realized by manufacturers per unit of the commodity sold, without any distinction between changes due to price factors and those due to variations in quality and specifications; the quoted price is useful as a measure of changes in primary market prices due to the market demand and supply situation for a particular commodity.

Wholesale Prices Published. Wholesale prices have in the past been published on a monthly basis in index number form as an all-commodity index, and 9 major groups and 51 subgroups. These major groups are: Farm products; foods; hides and leather; textiles; fuel and lighting materials; metals and metal products; building materials; chemicals and alllied products; and housefurnishing goods. These data are released in mimeographed form each month. Average prices and index numbers are reported in a printed publication, available each half-year, upon request to the BLS.

During the war emergency the BLS constructed a number of special index numbers and price series for the use of the war agencies. In 1940 index numbers of prices of strategic and critical materials were constructed for the use of the Army and Navy Munitions Board and the Office of Production Management. With the growing shortages of many raw materials early in the war, scrap prices were collected and an index number of scrap prices was constructed. With the aid of representatives of the machine tool industry, an index number of machine tool prices was introduced in March 1941.

Building Materials Prices. The commodity group "Building Materials" provides one of the best illustrations of the ways in which group price data can be used. The BLS assembles more than 1,000 building material price series, of which 147 are used in the computation of the wholesale price index. Comparable prices at retail for 44 different building materials are also collected from dealers in 50 cities located in the 48 states and the District of Columbia.[9] These retail prices from over 700 dealers represent local prices to general contractors, f.o.b. job site, less trade and cash discounts.

Retail Prices. Wage earners and workingmen can usually buy under the modern marketing system only at retail. The great significance of the wellbeing of working people demanded that the movements in retail prices, as well as those in wholesale prices, be examined. The *Eighteenth Annual Report of the Commissioner of Labor* for the year 1903 described in great detail the studies which had been made in the last decade of the nineteenth century on the cost of living, and also gave in detail a summary of prices of goods at retail for the years 1890–1902 in the United States.

In order to obtain these retail food prices, agents of the Bureau of Labor collected some 5,300 schedules or statements of prices for the years 1890–1903 from more than 800 retail merchants located in 33 states. Prices were secured for 30 different foods of various grades

[9] These series represent a continuation of the data collected for the Temporary National Economic Committee and published in Monograph 33, *Geographic Differentials in Prices of Building Materials.*

and descriptions for each month of the 14 years 1890–1903. These prices are shown for each year, for each food, for each community, and by groups of states, for these periods. For the United States as a whole, and for each group of foods, price relatives are shown with an average price of 1890–1899 = 100.

Retail food prices have been collected regularly by the BLS since the period of this report and are now collected monthly in 56 cities, located in 37 states and the District of Columbia. They are collected for each of 78 foods and are reported as the *Retail Costs of Foods*, each month, showing by city and by food average prices and relative changes.

Consumers' Price Index.[10] In the period 1903–1918 the wholesale price index and the retail cost of foods were the two major criteria for measuring the economic welfare of workingmen. During World War I, the wholesale price index was the major criterion for the adjustment of wages. In 1918, however, dependence upon food prices at either wholesale or retail alone was recognized as not a sufficient guide to wage adjustment. At that time an investigation of the cost of living of workers in war centers (mainly shipbuilding areas) was undertaken by the BLS. Based upon the information from this study, a complete consumers' price index was prepared, with six major components representing food, clothing, housing, house furnishings, fuel and light, and miscellaneous. The index, based upon information collected at that time, was carried back to 1913 and has been maintained continuously to date. (See Fig. 2.) During this period the consumers' price index has been the official index of the cost of living of wage earners and lower-salaried workers in the United States and has been used as a guide to wage adjustment and in union wage contracts.

Early in the 1930's, recognition of the defects of the consumers' price index that had been developed during World War I became increasingly apparent. To overcome the weaknesses of the index and to provide information on the income and expenditures of the people of the United States, large surveys were undertaken through the cooperation of several Government agencies. These surveys provided the basis for a complete revision of the consumers' price index which was published in 1937. At first, based on data collected quarterly, it was published four times each year, but with the advent of the war it has been calculated on a monthly basis.

[10] Prior to September 1945 this index was known as the Cost of Living Index for Moderate Income Families in Large Cities.

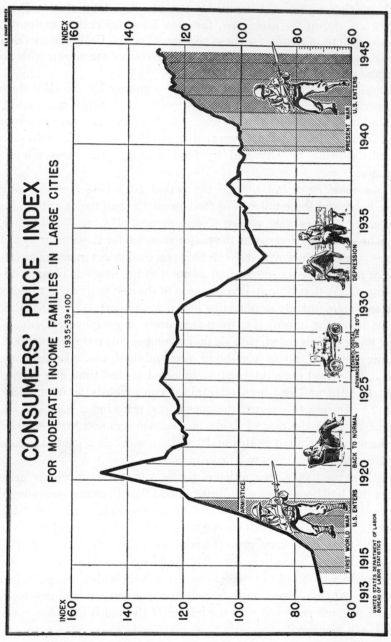

CONSUMERS' PRICE INDEX
FOR MODERATE INCOME FAMILIES IN LARGE CITIES
1935-39 = 100

UNITED STATES DEPARTMENT OF LABOR
BUREAU OF LABOR STATISTICS

FIGURE 2

As it is currently and regularly reported, the consumers' price index represents average changes in prices for living essentials in large cities.[11] Food prices are collected each month in 56 cities (the index of food costs). Prices of other goods and services are collected in 34 large cities, for four quarterly dates (March, June, September, and December) and in 21 of these cities for a restricted group of items in the intervening months. In order to calculate a monthly index, data on rents are collected from some 70 to 80 thousand tenants in 72 cities, 50,000 of which, in 34 cities, are used in the index. The 56 cities in which food prices are collected represent 81 percent of the population of cities of more than 100,000; the 34 large cities represent 72 percent of the population of the same size cities. Separate indexes are also calculated for 39 additional cities of varying sizes. These latter, however, are not included in the official national consumers' price index. Used locally, these separate city indexes provide a basis for comparing the movements of the cost of living from time to time in the cities for which indexes are calculated.

Prices upon which the consumers' price indexes are based are collected by representatives of the BLS who call upon merchants, department store representatives, buyers, and merchandisers (tenants, in the case of rents), and obtain the prices which are actually charged for articles of given specifications. Specifications of articles included in the list are developed from surveys of what working families actually buy, as determined in surveys of family expenditures. In this way the articles priced are considered to be similar to those which are currently purchased by wage earners in the United States. The stores from which prices are obtained are those commonly patronized by wage earners and their families. Consumers' price indexes for the United States are published each month about the middle of the month following the date to which they apply. They are released in mimeo-

[11] The BLS index indicates average changes in retail prices of selected goods, rents and services, bought by families of wage earners and lower-salaried workers in large cities. The items covered represented 70 percent of the expenditures of families who had incomes ranging from $1,250 to $2,000 in 1934–1936.

The index does not show the full wartime effect on the cost of living of such factors as lowered quality, disappearance of low-priced goods, and forced changes in housing and eating away from home. The President's Committee on the Cost of Living has said that 3 to 4 index points should be added to take account of these changes since they cannot be measured for index number purposes.

It does not measure changes in *total* "living costs," that is, *in the total amount families spend for living.* Income taxes and bond subscriptions are not included.

graphed form and are summarized by commodity group and city in an annual printed summary.[12]

Intercity Differences in Living Costs. The consumers' price index was developed to measure changes from time to time in prices of goods and services purchased by wage earners; it was not developed to provide comparisons between places, although it has frequently been used incorrectly for this purpose. Since the consumers' price index endeavors to measure changes in the cost of articles typically purchased by wage earners in each city covered and since typical purchases vary from city to city, it is obvious that there is no necessary correlation between cities in the index. For instance, the consumers' price index measures changes in the rents for homes in which wage earners live in Buffalo, N. Y., and Atlanta, Ga. Housing in these cities is not comparable and no effort has been made to compare them in the official index. The official consumers' price index, therefore, should not be used to make intercity comparisons of levels of cost of living. As a further example, the consumers' price index for June 15, 1944, on a 1935–1939 basis was 121.8 for Boston and 129.3 for New Orleans. These figures indicate that the cost of living in Boston had risen 21.8 percent from the 1935–1939 average while in New Orleans it had risen 29.3 percent in the same period. It does not indicate that New Orleans is a more expensive place for wage earners to live than Boston. It is entirely possible that Boston may be more expensive than New Orleans. In any case, there is no indication in these figures as to relative costs. The only indication given by the figures is the change within each city from the base period.

An index for measuring intercity differences in the cost of living is one of the large gaps in government price data. The BLS plans to provide this information in the near future but no such indexes are published at present. The only information available is based on a study by the Works Progress Administration in March 1935, which priced a "maintenance" budget in 59 cities. The BLS, in cooperation with the Works Progress Administration and later alone, prepared, until June 1943, estimates of the cost-of-maintenance budgets in 33 of the 34 cities in the official consumers' price index (excluding Savannah, Ga.) by applying the Bureau's indexes of living costs, which show changes in the costs from time to time, to the cost as estimated in 1939

---

[12] For a description of the computation of the consumers' price index and of the changes in the index due to rationing and wartime restrictions see *Changes in the Cost of Living in Large Cities in the United States, 1913–41,* by Faith M. Williams and Stella Stewart, Bulletin 699, Bureau of Labor Statistics, 1941; and *Cost of Living Indexes in Wartime,* by Faith M. Williams, Frances R. Rice, and Emil D. Schell, in *Journal of the American Statistical Association,* December 1942, Vol. 37, pp. 415–424.

by the Works Progress Administration. These indexes have not been calculated since June 1943 because the methods are inadequate during the war period when significant changes have taken place in living standards.

Special Price Studies. In addition to the regular price reports issued by the Department of Agriculture and the Department of Labor as described above, special studies of prices and their relationships to various aspects of the economy are being conducted almost continuously, both by administrative departments of Government and by special commissions or committees of the Congress. There are certain regular price series which are collected by administrative departments by virtue of the areas of the economy over which they have been given special kinds of responsibility. For instance, the Department of Commerce has regularly produced an index of prices (unit values) of imports and exports, based upon declared values at port of entry of imports and port of exit of exports. The Department of the Interior has maintained, through the Bureau of Mines, average mine values or sales realization prices of minerals, including coal.

For rates of major utilities, the Federal Power Commission publishes typical monthly bills for electricity by city, by type of consumer, for January 1 of each year.

Prices of special kinds of equipment purchased by railroads have been regularly maintained by the Interstate Commerce Commission. These prices represent the average unit cost to the railroad by type of equipment. Average cost figures are also secured for coal and other supplies. On the basis of such prices for machinery, the Commission has provided an index of machinery prices.

The Federal Trade Commission has for a long period of time conducted special studies in the distributive characteristics of prices. It has, for instance, conducted studies in the differences in milk prices as between different locations. Outstanding among its special investigations has been the investigation of prices charged by independent grocers and chain grocers.

During the period of wartime, the Office of Price Administration has become the source of a great deal of price information which is the basis for its operations in establishing price controls and enforcing its decisions.[13] These data for particular industries and groups of commodi-

---

[13] The BLS has been the official price collection agency for many of the price studies required by OPA. Basic to many of these studies are data of a wide variety which have never been published and which are rich resources for analysis of price relationships. Among these data are several studies which have gone behind prices to margins. Of greatest volume are the margin data for retail and wholesale food distributors.

ties will become invaluable as time goes on as a record of control decisions during a period of complete economic mobilization. They will undoubtedly be incorporated with the price records of regular government agencies when the war ends and the great masses of war-collected information can be brought together.

With the increased amounts of Government purchasing, beginning in the depression years and continuing throughout the war, there has been a continuously more insistent demand that records be maintained · and reports provided on prices paid by the Government. If prices of the major portion of the product of the country are to be recorded, it is necessary that prices paid by governmental agencies be reported, since Government purchases have amounted to as much as 60 percent of the country's production during the war period. Moreover, in periods of price and production control, in which the Government has found it necessary to operate more extensively since the beginning of the depression, it is important that detailed knowledge of current market prices, as well as of prices paid by the Government, be maintained in order that government operations can be timed so as to strengthen rather than to weaken markets. By proper timing not only of Government purchases but also of sales of Government surplus and products made on relief projects, it was frequently possible to show the effects of the proper timing of purchase and sale upon the markets. As the distribution of Government war surpluses becomes a more pressing problem, this same characteristic will again reveal itself. In order not to weaken markets, but to support them and thereby to maintain the highest possible employment levels, it will be necessary for Government agencies to watch the current trends of prices and to know how the prices they are paying and charging relate to these trends.

Early in the war, in order to gain greater control over the prices they were paying for munitions and as a guide to improved procurement, both the War and Navy Departments established internal price reporting systems. These systems have been maintained and improved, and from them both the War and Navy Departments are currently producing for administrative uses indexes of prices paid by the Army and Navy, as well as average prices by commodities. These price data have been collected for a wide range of munitions and non-munitions items purchased by the military services, covering the whole range of their purchases from the largest airplanes to the smallest (but very voluminous) quartermaster items. Great stress is put upon the use of average prices and the trends of price movements as determined from these munitions prices by the War Department in its Army Service Forces manual, *Prices in War Contracts*. In addition to their use in relative pricing for procurement and in the provision of trends of prices, these munitions prices have provided the bases for budget estimates, which were completely lacking at the beginning of the war. As a result of this work, a detailed summary of contract prices, together with contract conditions, will provide the basis for immediate use should further need of procurement of military items on a wide scale develop. There was no such record or guide for procurement left from World War I.

Gaps in Price Information. There are great gaps in our present price information. On the information side, gaps exist in (1) retail prices, (2) prices of goods exported, (3) prices of goods imported, and (4) prices of comparable goods in foreign countries. On the analysis side, there are gaps in the relationships between prices and costs, and prices and volume of distribution. Gaps on the information side can be closed by plans now in the making and by the work which will have to be done in arranging for postwar international settlements. Gaps in analysis can only be closed over a much longer period of time and through the cooperative efforts of business and research agencies. Foresight in perceiving and comprehending the problems involved in these gaps will aid most in closing them.

USES OF PRICE DATA

There are many uses which can be made of Government price data by business, trade associations, labor unions, and individuals. These uses expand as ingenuity develops them and as acquaintance with the available information increases. Indeed, the usefulness of these data increases rapidly as problems of individuals, labor, and business are brought to the attention of the specialists who are responsible for the collection and treatment of data. A number of these uses will be illustrated.

Economic Indicators. The most general use of the most general kind of price data is as an indicator or barometer of general business conditions. The Index of Wholesale Prices (prices in primary markets) has, over a long period of time, given an accurate description of the trend of business. The Department of Agriculture's Indexes of Prices Received by Farmers has likewise given a good picture of the trend of agricultural prosperity and depression. For the short run and during periods of rapid change, it is preferable to watch indexes with fewer commodities which are more sensitive to changing conditions. An index of this type is the Daily Index of 28 Basic Commodities. During the war period the majority of wage earners in the United States have become acquainted with the Consumers' Price Index for this purpose. Graphs of the Index of the Cost of Living from 1913 to 1920 and from 1939 to 1945 have been widely published and posted as indicators of the extent of price stability in the United States during World War II (see Fig. 3).

The greatest value of a general price index to the average business-man lies in its use as a general guide for administration. Many large business organizations maintain elaborate staffs to provide current information on economic factors affecting the particular business for the guidance of management. The average small businessman cannot hope to maintain a staff for this special purpose, but with the expenditure of a very small amount of time, perhaps less than one hour a month, he can maintain a record of a selected number of indexes which are applicable to his business. Such general indicators, it should be emphasized, are mainly useful in giving a well-rounded picture of general business activity and serve as a supplement to detailed specialized information about his own business.

The operator of a small grocery store may even find great value in keeping up to date on general price movements. A grocer might follow the following price series: Wholesale Price Index (BLS), Food Group Index, Prices Paid by Farmers (BAE), Food Group of Consumers' Price Index (BLS) nationally and for the nearest city for which it is published. A method of making this information most helpful is to make simple charts for a period of 10 years previously, posting the data by months. The indexes mentioned above are clearly related and might be plotted on the same chart or each might be given its own chart. Current data and data for back periods can be secured by writing directly to the agencies listed, telling them what is wanted and for what purpose. Once the charts are drawn up for the back period data, the current data can be plotted as it becomes available each month.

With these data before him, the grocer has an excellent measure of general price movements in the commodities in which he is most vitally interested. The wholesale price index, as the most general of the indexes listed, would give him an idea of the direction of price movements in primary markets of all commodities. In other words, it is a picture of movements in the general price level. The food index group would measure primary market prices for the commodities which he sells, whereas the index of prices paid by farmers, or the food group of this index, and the food group of the consumers' price index would give him an idea of national movements in retail prices of the type of commodities that he handles. The Index of Prices Received by Farmers would serve as a measure of changes in the prosperity on a national

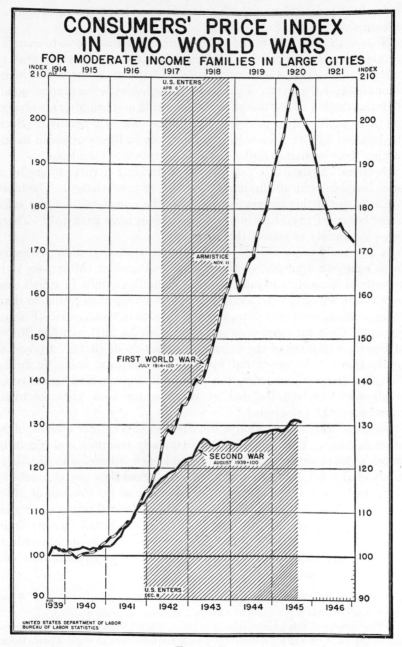

CONSUMERS' PRICE INDEX
IN TWO WORLD WARS
FOR MODERATE INCOME FAMILIES IN LARGE CITIES

U.S. ENTERS
APR 6

ARMISTICE
NOV. II

FIRST WORLD WAR
JULY 1914=100

SECOND WAR
AUGUST 1939=100

U.S. ENTERS
DEC. 8

UNITED STATES DEPARTMENT OF LABOR
BUREAU OF LABOR STATISTICS

FIGURE 3

basis of the people (farmers) who may form an important group of his customers.

None of these indexes would provide direct information as to changes in this grocer's costs or selling prices since they are obviously general indexes. The grocer's own records would have to do that. Frequent comparison of the trends of prices he is paying with the graphs would indicate whether or not the prices he is paying and charging are changing more rapidly than prices in the United States generally.[14] Such information will be of increasing importance to businessmen in maintaining their businesses under postwar competitive conditions.

Deflators. Deflation is the process of dividing a value figure by a price index in order to eliminate the effect of price change. The most common use of this process is to answer the question, "Are my sales larger because I've sold more or because prices have gone up?" There is a wide variety of uses of this technique.

It is usually impossible to obtain all the statistical data necessary for a complete appraisal of the economic situation. Moreover, it is sometimes impossible to add the various kinds of units in which economic data are collected. Price indexes, which are more available than other kinds of economic data, may be helpful in these cases. For instance, if the total value of production in a year in the United States is known, a measure of the physical production or change in physical production can be calculated by dividing the total value figure by the price index.[15] Likewise, the change in the physical quantity of retail sales can be calculated by dividing the total value of retail sales by a retail price index.

Guides in Purchasing. One of the simplest uses of price data involves average prices. Purchasing agents frequently maintain and regularly watch series of average market prices and price indexes, both at wholesale and at retail, for comparison with the prices they pay as guides to their own purchasing efficiency. A late issue of the *Journal of Marketing* describes the use of the index of wholesale food prices as a rough guide to the movement of prices paid by restaurants.[16] Large chain grocers compute average prices and indexes of commodities which they sell, for comparison with retail price indexes of similar items sold in the general market.

[14] Differences between the retail and wholesale indexes do not represent differences in price levels and cannot be used as a measure of profit margins.

[15] The reverse of this process, the division of a total value figure by a physical volume figure, results in a measure of price change known as an implicit price index.

[16] "Appraisal of the BLS Index of Wholesale Food Prices in Wartime," by Malcolm D. Taylor, *Journal of Marketing*, July 1944, pp. 32–42.

Wage Adjustments. Index numbers have their widest general use as the basis for wage adjustments. Wage adjustment clauses based upon the consumers' price index are frequently included in wage contracts. For instance, in one contract the following clause was introduced:

> Wages in effect July 7, 1938, will remain consistent for the period July 8, 1939–December 31, 1939. The corporation will recognize an advance in the cost of living, as evidenced by labor statistics, for the ____ area, published by the Department of Labor for low-salaried workers on the following basis: If during this July–December period the cost of living has advanced beyond the cost of living on July 1, 1937, the corporation will make an adjustment for the period January 1, 1939–June 30, 1939, as follows: When the percentage advance is sufficient, calculated on the basis of forty cents per hour, to turn out one cent, all wages will be advanced one cent per hour.

And again:

> Wage rates shall be adjusted automatically to the cost of living in the following manner: The basis shall be the quarterly cost of living index in ____, issued by the Bureau of Labor Statistics. Effective at pay period following publication of the index, wage rates shall be increased or decreased by the same percentage as the index has changed from quarter to quarter.

Escalator Clauses. Frequently in long-term contracts for the production of machinery or construction, price indexes are used for adjusting both material and labor costs. Such adjustments, usually called escalator clauses, have been used by some corporations for a long time and were used commonly in the early part of the war; they have been frowned upon during the period of price control because they are alleged to have inflationary effects. If properly used, however, escalator clauses may be of great advantage to both parties of a contract. In periods when the trend of prices is very uncertain, when it cannot be foreseen whether prices are likely to advance or decline, it may be advantageous to permit a contractor to commit himself at current prices for only the amount of materials which is necessary for current production and to permit him to make an adjustment upward or downward for subsequent commitments, depending upon the movement of prices. If it is assumed that it is good business to keep prices as low as possible, and if it is further assumed that the ordinary contractor is not a price speculator and does not plan on making his profits on changes in prices, an escalator clause may be used to great advantage. Escalator clauses provide the means by which, therefore, a contractor may shift the risk of price changes from his own shoulders to the shoulders of the buyer. Many private agencies, during the later

period of the war, have contracted for the construction of plants in
the postwar period. In view of the uncertainties of postwar trends of
prices, they have relied upon price escalator clauses to take care of
this phase of their problem.

A clause in use currently in a long-term contract of one of the
country's largest manufacturers follows:

> Any price or prices for ____ established pursuant to the provisions of
> · · · this Contract shall be subject to variation as follows. In the event
> that the average of the All-Commodity Wholesale Price Index Number of
> the Bureau of Labor Statistics of the United States Department of Labor
> during any period of four (4) successive weeks shall vary by ten percent
> (10%) or more from said All-Commodity Wholesale Price Index Number
> for the week in which any such price or prices, respectively, shall have been
> established under the provisions of said Section · · ·, then such price or
> prices, with respect to ____ supplied during each period of four successive
> weeks thereafter shall be increased or decreased as the case may be by a
> percentage which shall be the average of the percentage of any such varia-
> tion of said All-Commodity Wholesale Price Index Number during each
> period of four (4) successive weeks, and said price or prices respectively
> shall continue to be so adjusted whenever and so long as the variation in
> said All-Commodity Wholesale Price Index Number first above mentioned
> shall be ten percent (10%) or more.

Similar to the use of price index numbers in escalator clauses, but
without necessary formal arrangement, many large manufacturers
watch the movement of index numbers as a guide in price adjustments
for their subcontractors. Large manufacturers cannot afford to see
their subcontractors fail. It is necessary for them, therefore, to be
watchful of price changes in order that failure of subcontractors may
not result from loss due to price changes.

STUDIES OF CONSUMER INCOMES AND EXPENDITURES

The amount of the nation's income which has been distributed to
consumers and the way in which those consumers have used that income in the United States provides a pattern of a democratic economy
in a period of freedom, and also may provide the guides to fiscal and
price policy. An inquiry into consumer incomes and expenditures, as
mentioned above, was made by the Bureau of Labor Statistics in 1918
as a guide to the construction of its consumers' price index.

The most comprehensive and complete study ever conducted in any
country on the patterns of expenditures and incomes was that by the
Bureau of Home Economics and the Bureau of Labor Statistics, with
the cooperation of WPA, the National Resources Committee, and the

Central Statistical Board, in 1934–1936.[17] The study of incomes covered the 12-month period from July 1935 through June 1936. As described in the National Resources Committee Report:

> It shows estimates of the incomes received by all of the Nation's income-spending units—by the 29 million families of 2 or more persons, by the 10 million "single" individuals living alone or as lodgers, and by the 2 million persons living in institutions and in quasi-institutional groups. For family incomes, this broad national picture is traced in more detail to show the flow of the income stream to farms, villages, and cities, to different geographic regions, to different occupational groups, to families of different size, and—in the South and in Northern cities—to the white and Negro population.

Schedules on income were secured from 300,000 American families, showing the income received by each family from all sources. Schedules were obtained from 60,000 families showing detailed expenditures during an entire year for the development of the family expenditure patterns. Extreme care in both these studies was exercised in the construction of the samples in order to guarantee complete representativeness of the great variety of factors which affect both income and expenditures.

In addition to the general volumes on incomes and expenditures that were published by the National Resources Committee, individual volumes for each of the urban communities were produced by the Bureau of Labor Statistics and additional volumes, representing the findings for the rural and farm areas, were produced by the Bureau of Agricultural Economics as a result of these studies. These reports have provided one of the richest sources of information for American marketing and distribution that has ever been produced.

Changes in patterns of both income and expenditures have been associated with the war. In the last quarter of 1941 and the first quarter of 1942, the Bureau of Human Nutrition and Home Economics of the Department of Agriculture and the Bureau of Labor Statistics conducted another survey based on a very much smaller number of families.[18] The reports on this study provided the only statistical indi-

[17] For description of these studies see the three volumes: *Consumer Incomes in the United States, Their Distribution in 1935–36*, National Resources Committee, Washington, 1938; *Consumer Expenditures in the United States, Estimated for 1935–36*, National Resources Committee, Washington, 1939; and *Family Expenditures in the United States, Statistical Tables and Appendixes*, National Resources Planning Board, Washington, 1941.

[18] For description of results see: *Spending and Saving of the Nation's Families in Wartime*, Bulletin 723, U. S. Dept. Labor, Washington, D. C., 1942; *Income and Spending and Saving of City Families in Wartime*, Bulletin 724, U. S. Dept. Labor, Washington, D. C., 1942; and *Rural Family Spending and Saving in Wartime*, Miscellaneous Publication 520, U. S. Dept. Agr., Washington, D. C., June 1943.

cator to the impacts of the war on this phase of the economy. With the increased production following full conversion to war products and the continued restrictions on civilian goods, there were noticeable changes in the income and consumption patterns as the war situation deepened. The need for additional surveys of consumer expenditure and patterns was apparent to organized labor, as well as to the business and the Government agencies responsible for production of war materials, for fiscal policy, and for price control. Studies planned late in the year 1943 were never completed. As this volume goes to press, a check on prices paid by consumers, based upon a nationwide sample, together with an over-all check on expenditures, is being conducted by the Bureau of Labor Statistics.

CONCLUSION

The whole field of price data and collection maintenance and of the measurement of income and expenditures is one involving a great complexity of subject and method. With the recognition that prices are the backbone of a competitive system, it is essential for every businessman that he make the most advantageous use of all available price information. To get greatest benefit from price data collected by governmental agencies, he would always do well to put his questions as simply and directly as possible to one of the major price collecting agencies of the government. These agencies are invariably aware of the general program of price work and the history of price information that exists in Government files. Questions put to these agencies with sufficient explanation to indicate the problem of the businessman receive helpful answers.

In practically all collection of price data by governmental agencies, reports received from respondents are confidential. Data for individual respondents, therefore, are not available, but summaries, averages, index numbers, and price relatives on many other bases are available and can frequently be provided to give answers to bothersome questions in need of solution.

CHAPTER 12

POPULATION

PHILIP M. HAUSER

Bureau of the Census
Department of Commerce

In the last analysis production and distribution have as their purpose the satisfaction of human wants. Recognition of this fact is commonplace in the business and industrial world and is sometimes expressed in the phrase "people are markets." From the standpoint of statistics this is a shorthand way of saying that facts about people are facts about markets, at least consumer markets. Widespread as the acceptance of this statement may be, there is very little understanding of the facts about people that are most relevant to management and marketing purposes, or of the significance, import, or usefulness of such facts as are available.

In the very nature of things, the Federal Government has almost a monopoly on the collection, compilation, and publication of the general facts about the American people. This is not to say that other sources of population data have no significance, but it is difficult to imagine how any single business enterprise or even a combination of enterprises could hope to marshal even the minimum facts about all the people, by localities, in as vast a nation as the United States. Although several agencies of the Federal Government, through their administrative or statistical operations, collect some facts about some part of the population of the United States, only one department has a systematic program for collecting, compiling, and publishing facts about all the people in the country and that is the Department of Commerce through the Bureau of the Census. Because of the predominant role of the Bureau of the Census in the field of population statistics, the materials in this chapter are in the main restricted to a consideration of the basic population data made available by that Bureau and of their import for industrial and business use.

STATISTICS ON THE NUMBER OF INHABITANTS

Total Population. Perhaps the most important fact about people as markets is their number. This does not mean that it is not important to know many things about their composition and characteristics, but their total number in any given area is a basic datum for any analysis involving production goals or marketing potentialities. The intense interest in the shifts of population occasioned by World War II is certainly one measure of the importance attributed by industrial and business enterprises to the basic facts about the number of inhabitants in a given locality.

The facts about the total number of people in the nation and in its various subdivisions have periodically been made available since the founding of this republic. The Constitution of the United States provides that an enumeration of the population "be made within three years after the first meeting of the Congress of the United States and within every subsequent term of ten years" (Art. I, Sec. 2). Provision is made for such a census of the population in order to apportion representatives in Congress among the states in accordance with their populations. The Census of Population and in fact the Census Bureau have their origin in this constitutional requirement, which makes the census a vital instrument in the maintenance of our democracy. In the course of the years since the first Census of Population, taken in 1790, however, population and other census statistics have had increasing usefulness not only to the Government but also to business and industry—a usefulness which far transcends the original constitutional purpose of the population canvass.

The facts about the total population of the nation; each of its political subdivisions, including states, counties, cities, towns and villages, and minor civil divisions; and certain other convenient economic, social, or statistical units, such as regions, geographic divisions, metropolitan districts, urban and rural areas, census tracts, city blocks, and enumeration districts, were collected in the most recent census—the Sixteenth Decennial Census of Population taken as of April 1, 1940—and, in the main, have their counterpart in each of the preceding censuses of the United states.[1] Most of the basic facts on the number of inhabitants in the nation as a whole and its various subdivisions as of April 1,

---

[1] For convenience, references to sources of materials will uniformly be to the latest data available. The latest published census volumes and releases frequently contain historical data for comparisons. Convenient guides to the census statistics of the past are available in the following: *Topical Index of Population Census Reports: 1900–1930* and *Index of Data Tabulated from the 1930 Census of Population, Including Unemployment*. A convenient guide to published and unpublished data for small areas of the 1940 Census is available in the *Key to the Published and Tabulated Data for Small Areas*. These three publications have been issued by the Bureau of the Census. More exact references to historical data can be obtained by writing to the Director of the Census, Washington 25, D. C.

1940, are recorded in the *Sixteenth Census of the United States, 1940, Population, Volume I—Number of Inhabitants*, which is also available as a series of separate bulletins, one for each state and the District of Columbia and a summary for the United States. The summary bulletin, in addition to statistics for the United States, contains convenient summary figures for the states, regions, and divisions, for cities, for counties, and for metropolitan districts. In addition to statistics on the number of inhabitants for each of the political subdivisions of the states and for the metropolitan districts, Volume I of the Population Census shows the urban and rural population as well as the land area and population density of each county, and gives the location of each minor civil division and city or town by county. Moreover, the volume contains maps showing the boundaries of the minor civil divisions of the states and of metropolitan districts, and is generous in its presentation of historical data and of absolute and percentage changes in population from census to census.

Volume I of the Population Census is supplemented by three important bulletins possessing considerable value for business purposes. The first is *Population—Special Report on Institutional Population*, which contains data on the number of persons 14 years old and over who, at the time of the census, were inmates of private or public institutions, such as prisons and reformatories, local jails or workhouses, mental institutions, and homes for the aged. For many types of market analysis, particularly for smaller communities, it is desirable to subtract from the total population of the area the institutional population, a figure which can be obtained from this bulletin. (The characteristics of the institutional population can also be obtained from this bulletin.)

The second bulletin, entitled *Population—Unincorporated Communities*, contains information on the total population of unincorporated places, information difficult to compile because of the absence of fixed legal boundaries. This special bulletin shows the population of each unincorporated community in the United States having 500 or more inhabitants for which separate figures could be compiled, and indicates both the minor civil division and county in which the unincorporated place is located. The population of institutions containing 100 or more persons is excluded from the population shown for the unincorporated places.

The third publication, which for business purposes may be regarded as a supplement to Volume I of the Population Census, is entitled *Areas of the United States: 1940*. This volume contains information on the total land and water areas of the states, counties, cities, and minor civil divisions and presents the results of the first complete remeasurement of the United States made since the Census of 1880. For the determination of administrative, management, or sales districts, land area will frequently be found to be an important and useful factor.

Trends. The facts available at any one census about the number of inhabitants constitute only part of the story useful to business contained in the total population figures. Another and equally important

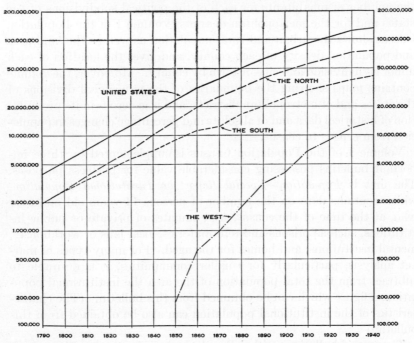

FIGURE 1.   Growth of the Population of the United States and Regions: 1790 to 1940.

part is that made available through historical comparisons of the data, that is, the facts on changes in total population or trends in growth. One hundred and fifty years of census taking have recorded the growth of the population of this nation from 3,929,000 persons in 1790 to 131,669,000 in 1940. Such a great change in the total number of inhabitants has profoundly affected the course of our industrial, business, and economic development as have also the important population changes from decade to decade. (See Fig. 1.)

The connection between over-all national population growth and the conduct of a specific business enterprise may at first thought seem quite remote. A moment's reflection, however, brings sharply to mind the import of such basic national trends. Although since 1900 the population of the nation has increased by over 55 million persons, or by 73 percent, the rate of national population growth during this period has greatly declined. During the intercensal decade between 1930 and 1940, the population of the United States increased by less than 9 million persons. This represents an increase of 7.2 percent, a rate of increase less than one-half that shown in any previous decade since the first census in 1790, and an absolute population increase smaller than any since the decade 1860 to 1870.

The import to business of the considerable decline in the rate of the population growth of the nation in recent decades is perhaps made clear by contrasting the absolute increase in the population between 1920 and 1930 with that between 1930 and 1940. In the former decade the total population of the United States increased by over 17 million persons, in the latter by a little less than 9 million persons. The difference represents a population greater than that of the entire state of Illinois in 1940. That is, if the population between 1930 and 1940 had increased by the same amount, not to mention the same rate, as between 1920 and 1930, the nation would have had an additional population equivalent to that of the entire state of Illinois. Translation of the human wants represented by a population of this size into terms of production and distribution would dramatically illustrate the production and marketing opportunities lost to the American industrial and business community as a result of the decline in the population growth of the nation.

This over-all picture, which has its counterpart in the various separate political units and markets of the nation, affects not only business and industry in general, but specific businesses and industries. The brief outline of national trends sketched above can be reproduced from the census volumes for the various regions, geographic divisions, states, counties, or cities of the nation.

Estimates of the Future. Total population figures for the present and for the past have an important value in themselves, but they have an even greater value if some effort is made to interpret their implications for the future. Although predictions in human affairs are always hazardous, the analysis of trends in the total population growth of the nation, a region, a state, a county, a metropolitan district, or a local community within a city is an important aspect of any attempt to evaluate the future market. Such projections have been made for the nation as a whole—the most widely accepted are those, projected to A.D. 2000, prepared for the National Resources Planning Board by Warren S. Thompson and P. K. Whelpton, of the Scripps Foundation

for Research in Population Problems.[2]   These estimates project not
only the total population, but the age, sex, and color composition of the
population to the year 2000. They dramatically portray the anticipated continued decline in the population growth of the United States.
They are important, if properly interpreted, as a general long-run
guide to business and industry in pointing to the disappearance of the
old days of rapid population growth.

While projections this far into the future are not too reliable for small
areas within the nation, some projection preferably based on additional
knowledge with respect to local political, social, and economic factors
might well become at least one page in the book of facts of enterprises
interested in a local market and can be made from the data readily
available from the Bureau of the Census.[3]

Current Estimates.   The Decennial Census of Population, although
eagerly awaited each decade to provide benchmark statistics on the
number and distribution of the inhabitants of the nation, soon outlives
its usefulness as far as total population figures for localities are concerned, particularly under rapidly changing conditions.   To meet the
need for current or annual statistics on the size and distribution of the
population, the Bureau of the Census has from time to time prepared
intercensal and postcensal estimates of the population of the nation
as a whole and, as far as possible, of its component parts.

The intercensal estimates relate to periods between two censuses
already taken, and a number of them have been made from time to
time.   A series of such estimates are published in the appendix of the
volume *Vital Statistics Rates in the United States, 1900–1940* (Table I,
pp. 884 ff.).   The postcensal estimates, more difficult to make, relate
to periods after one census but before the next. Such national
population estimates have been prepared semi-annually since the
1940 Census.

Although it is relatively easy to make postcensal estimates of the
total population of the nation even during the war, it is not so easy to
estimate the population of the states, cities, and counties of the country.   Even in normal times adequate data are not available on internal
movements of people, and such data are an important element of
local population estimates.   Various methods have been devised, however, which produce reasonably satisfactory results in normal times,

[2] Warren S. Thompson and P. K. Whelpton, *Estimates of Future Population of the
United States, 1940–2000*, U. S. Government Printing Office, Washington 25, D. C.

[3] For an example of one type of projection for local markets, see Philip M. Hauser,
"Wartime Population Changes and Postwar Prospects," *The Journal of Marketing*
January 1944, pp. 238–248.

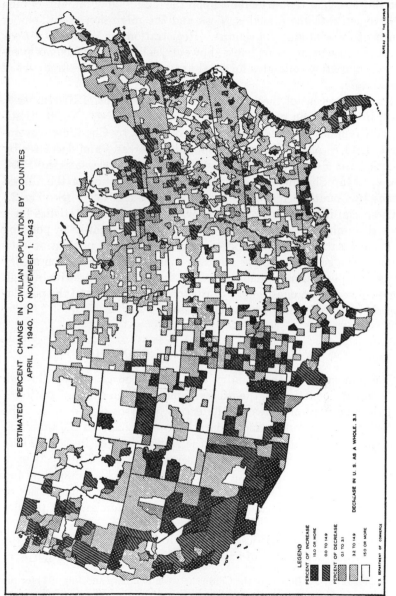

FIGURE 2

but they prove completely inadequate during periods of rapid population shifts such as that attendant upon the induction of millions of men and women into the armed services and the migration of millions of persons to war production centers.   Registration for *War Ration Book One* and subsequent ration books, however, solved the problem of post-censal population estimates for local areas for at least the first part of this decade.

The most recent of these estimates are available as of November 1, 1943, in the Bureau of the Census release Series P-44, No. 3, "Estimated Civilian Population of the United States, by Counties: November 1, 1943." A map picturing population increases and decreases by counties was also prepared (Bureau of the Census release Series P-44, No. 4, "Map Showing Changes in Civilian Population of the United States, by Counties: April 1, 1940, to November 1, 1943"). (See Fig. 2.)

Of special interest, not only in providing population statistics for a limited number of metropolitan areas but also primarily in pointing to a more satisfactory method of obtaining current population estimates is the series of sample censuses of congested production areas.[4] These sample censuses made possible the preparation, with a high degree of accuracy, of estimates of the total population and the population characteristics of the areas canvassed.

FACTORS IN POPULATION GROWTH

The population of the country as a whole can grow only through net immigration—that is, the excess of immigration over emigration—and through natural increase—the excess of births over deaths.   The statistics on immigration and emigration are available in the Immigration and Naturalization Service of the Department of Justice.   These statistics may have direct value for certain specialized interests such as producers and distributors of foreign language books, newspapers and movies, and the production and distribution of other commodities or services intended primarily for various types of foreign-born populations.

Vital Statistics.   Statistics on births and deaths, available in the Bureau of the Census, are of value for business and industrial purposes

---

[4] Conducted by the Bureau of the Census between February and July 1944 for the Committee for Congested Production Areas of the Executive Office of the President in the following areas: Charleston, S. C., Detroit, Mich., Hampton Roads, Va., Los Angeles, Calif., Mobile, Ala., Muskegon, Mich., Portland, Oreg.-Vancouver, Wash., Puget Sound, Wash., San Diego, Calif., San Francisco, Calif.   Releases containing the results of these censuses are available upon request.

not only because they are the important component in the total population growth of the nation, but also because of their inherent value for various specialized production and distribution problems. Statistics relating to births and deaths for the nation and its various political subdivisions are given annually in the volumes *Vital Statistics of the United States* and in the *Vital Statistics—Special Reports* series. The latest published data are for 1942. The annual volumes contain statistics on births and deaths by both place of occurrence and place of residence. Data on both births and deaths are also currently available in the *Monthly Vital Statistics Bulletin,* which contains a preliminary report on current birth and death statistics for each state and for Baltimore, Chicago, Boston, New Orleans, New York, and the District of Columbia. Comparisons for the preceding month and the corresponding month of the preceding year are also given.

In addition to a large number of special reports containing detailed analyses of various aspects of natality and mortality, two other publications merit special attention. The first is the volume *Vital Statistics Rates in the United States, 1900–1940,* which contains tables covering general mortality rates, infant mortality rates, maternal mortality rates, stillbirth rates, and natality rates, showing time trends by geographic areas and race and other characteristics of the population. This volume also contains a comprehensive discussion of basic qualifying factors in vital statistics and of the interpretation and definition of various types of fertility and mortality rates and indexes. The second report, *Vital Statistics of the United States, Supplement 1939–1940, Part III,* makes use of the population data from the 1940 Census to present birth and death rates for counties and cities. Ordinarily, vital rates for small areas are not computed because of the lack of adequate current population statistics.

Birth and death statistics, particularly the former, have a direct bearing on many types of industrial and business activity. Manufacturers and distributors of commodities designed to meet the needs of pregnant women, of infants, and of the growing child are becoming increasingly aware of the importance of observing not only current data, but also trends in the birth rate. This includes not only enterprises in such fields as clothing, food, perambulators, toys, health, and housing, but also publishing, school supplies, recreation, and education. The death statistics have a somewhat more restricted business value, but are not overlooked by the more alert members of the producer, distributor, and professional enterprises which cater to the needs of the bereaved and the deceased.

The wide cyclical fluctuations in both fertility and mortality and the predictability of peaks and valleys in the numbers of children at various ages which can be obtained from following and analyzing fertility and mortality statistics make it possible to adapt specialized producing and distributing facilities to the ebbs and tides of human reproduction. In fact, at least one large concern engaged in both productive and distributive activities is said to have been well rewarded for anticipating the boom in babies preceding and immediately following our entrance into the war.

Internal Migration. The most important single factor in the changing population of local areas within the nation is frequently internal migration—the movements of people from farm to city, from state to state, from small cities to large cities, and so on. There are no statistical series available which directly measure on a current basis the movements of people within the nation. The 1940 Population Census, as one of its more important innovations, however, did make available facts on the movements of people between 1935 and 1940. These data, although now far from current, do throw considerable light on the volume and character of internal population movements and describe trends which will continue to have significance for some time to come. The statistics are set forth in a special report entitled *Internal Migration, 1935 to 1940*.

As a measure of long-term internal population shifts, the statistics as presented in a special report for 1940 entitled *State of Birth of the Native Population* will be found useful. These statistics make possible an analysis by states, regions, and divisions of the extent to which the population born in a given state were resident in that state or other states; thus, they measure the net gain or loss caused by interstate movement from time of birth to the time of the 1940 census. For example, the maps in this report show at a glance that the population born in the "Dustbowl States" were to a large extent resident in other states in 1940, and that a relatively large proportion of the population resident in the "Pacific Coast States" in 1940 were born in other states. Among the states the net movement of population from time of birth to the time of the census ranged from a net gain of 3,146,000 persons by California to a net loss of 856,000 by Pennsylvania. Statistics on state of birth are also presented for urban and rural areas and separately for cities of 100,000 or more. Comparable data are presented back to 1850 in some of the tables.

Further facts on internal migration are made available from time to time in the form of estimates on "net" migration, as in the releases of Series P-5a, Nos. 10–18, for each of the geographic divisions. These estimates show the net movements of people between 1930 and 1940 in and out of the several geographic divisions of the United States.[5]

Estimates on the net movements of people from and to the farms of the nation are made on an annual basis by the Bureau of Agricultural Economics of the Department of Agriculture. The latest of these estimates available are those as of January 1, 1945, entitled *Farm Population Estimates*.

These estimates of migration, although they are indirectly derived from total population figures, are useful in indicating at least the net volume and direction of population movements.

AREAS FOR WHICH POPULATION STATISTICS ARE AVAILABLE

Although for many purposes national statistics and national trends are of considerable importance for the businessman, statistics for various subdivisions of the nation may have even greater importance, particularly for enterprises serving local markets or concerned with the adaptation of production, distribution, or service practices to conform with the needs of local markets. Most statistics in the Census have been made available historically for the various political subdivisions of the country, that is, for the states, counties, incorporated places, and minor civil divisions. The latter, of which there are approximately 52,000, are the elemental subdivisions of counties or cities, such as townships, precincts, wards, parishes, and beats.

For many production and marketing purposes population statistics for political subdivisions have considerable utility, but more often political boundaries do not coincide with markets or meet the need for broad generalization with respect to the major subdivisions of the nation. The types of areas other than political units for which population statistics are made available are briefly described in the section which follows.

Regions and Geographic Divisions. To provide a better basis for presenting over-all statistics for areas smaller than the country as a whole and yet not as numerous as its 49 major political subdivisions, the Bureau of the Census has in most instances summarized the data for the states by three and four broad "regions" and nine "geographic divisions," each of which comprises combinations of states. The three regions are the North, the South, and the West, but for some purposes the North is further divided into the Northeastern and the North Central States. The North is defined to include four of the geographic

[5] See also, Henry S. Shryock, Jr., "Internal Migration and the War," *Journal of the American Statistical Association*, Vol. 38, No. 221, March 1943, pp. 16–30

divisions, namely, the New England States, the Middle Atlantic States, the East North Central States, and the West North Central States. When the North is divided into two regions, the first two of the geographic divisions make up the Northeastern States and the latter two the North Central States. The South includes three of the geographic divisions, namely, the South Atlantic States, the East South Central States, and the West South Central States. The West includes two of the geographic divisions, namely, the Mountain States and the Pacific States. (See Fig. 3.)

FIGURE 3. Map Showing Census Geographic Divisions of the United States.

The regions and geographic divisions, although they are not political subdivisions of the nation, have considerable utility for statistical purposes not only because they make data more manageable than is possible separately for each of the 48 states and the District of Columbia, but also because the various combinations of states tend to be fairly homogeneous with respect to population type and economic and cultural organization. For a broad over-all picture of the major elements in the national market, the statistics for the regions and geographic divisions are useful analytical tools.

Urban and Rural Areas. One of the most significant and revealing ways of classifying the American people for purposes of general economic and social analysis, including market analysis, is the classification of the population into urban and rural groups. This division of the population has become increasingly useful in the course of the years as the nation has shifted from a primarily agricultural and rural economy to a predominantly industrial and urban one. Although the Census, in the course of its history, has used several definitions of urban and rural areas, the comparative historical figures available in the 1940 Census volumes are based on the definitions used in the 1930 and 1940 Censuses.

The urban area is in general made up of cities and other incorporated places having 2,500 persons or more. (For exceptions to this rule see *Sixteenth Census of the United States, 1940, Population, Volume I— Number of Inhabitants*, p. 10.) The rural area of the United States is defined as that part of the nation not included in urban area and is further subdivided into rural-nonfarm and rural-farm population. The rural-farm population is that living on farms (outside of urban areas) without regard to occupation. The rural-nonfarm population includes persons not resident in cities having 2,500 or more inhabitants and who do not live on farms.

Practically all of the population statistics presented in the census volumes are shown for urban and rural parts of the United States, the regions or geographic divisions, and the states. In Volume II of the *Sixteenth Census Reports on Population* urban and rural statistics are also shown by counties.

Metropolitan Districts. Among the more valuable recent innovations in census practice has been the recognition of the importance for statistical purposes of defining and making data available for metropolitan districts. This follows from the fact that urban communities, more perhaps than any other type of area, are focal units in the consideration of local markets. Certainly the large aggregations of populations in our cities constitute the largest and most accessible markets for most of the goods and services produced by our economy.

The political boundaries of our cities are the products of historical circumstances and, in the main, therefore, do not conform with the economic and social entities of which they are usually the central part. The census "metropolitan district" is a result of attempts to define this economic and social entity. It is recognized that the census definition which is necessarily objectively and arbitrarily achieved can at best be only an approximation of the real unit desired; but it is a valuable approximation which has been found increasingly useful for many purposes, including general business and marketing analysis.

In the 1940 Census of Population a metropolitan district was defined for each city of 50,000 or more inhabitants, although two or more such cities sometimes fell in one district. In census usage, the metropolitan district, in general, consists of a central city or cities and all adjacent and contiguous minor civil divisions or incorporated places having a population density of 150 or more per square mile. (For exceptions to this rule see *Sixteenth Census of the United States, 1940, Population, Volume I—Number of Inhabitants*, p. 4.)

Volume I of the Population Census, 1940, gives the population, land area, and population density for each metropolitan district. This volume shows total population figures not only for the central city or cities, but also for each of the minor civil divisions of which the metropolitan district is made up; it contains comparative figures for 1930 (except for seven districts for which complete figures are not available) and a map of each district showing the central city or cities and minor civil divisions. More detailed statistics for metropolitan districts are shown in Volume II of the Population reports and in a number of the special reports based on the 1940 Population Census.

Census Tracts. For many purposes of local market analysis the metropolitan district and the city, or its political subdivisions, are frequently too large to be of maximum service. Local political units, that is, wards, precincts, etc., within a city or metropolitan district often change boundaries so frequently that historical comparisons cannot be made and neighborhood trends, therefore, cannot be ascertained. To meet the need for comparative data for small areas within the city or metropolitan district the Bureau of the Census has encouraged the establishment of "census tracts" in the larger cities.

"Census tracts" are small areas, designed in cooperation with local committees so as to include, as far as possible, equal numbers of inhabitants or equal areas. In laying out the tracts, an attempt is also made to delineate areas with fairly homogeneous populations.

In the 1940 Census both population and housing statistics are shown for 10,461 census tracts in or adjacent to 60 cities. The cities for which census tract information is available include all cities of 250,000 or more inhabitants and some smaller ones. A series of 58 bulletins entitled *Statistics for Census Tracts—Population and Housing* covers the 60 tracted cities and contains most of the population statistics described as available for small areas (see below). These bulletins also contain maps showing the boundaries of the census tracts which can be used to considerable advantage in market analysis.

City Blocks. To meet the needs of housing and construction interests, the Bureau of the Census for the first time made certain limited information available in the 1940 Census by city blocks for each of the 191 cities having 50,000 or more inhabitants in 1930.

The statistics presented by blocks relate primarily to housing and at least three items are considered worthy of special mention here.

The first of these is the information on number of "occupied dwelling units" which, as more fully explained below, is equivalent to the number of "families." The second is the number of dwelling units occupied by nonwhite inhabitants. The third is the average monthly rent or rental value of dwelling units. (See Chapter 13.) The item of rent is one of the most valuable indexes of purchasing power available for market analysis—certainly for local market analysis.

The statistics for city blocks are available in a series of bulletins, one for each of the "block cities," which also contain maps permitting the identification and location of each block within the city. (See also page 348.) For census tract cities, statistics are presented for combinations of blocks making up the census tracts as well as for the individual blocks.

Enumeration Districts. The enumeration district is the smallest census administrative area used in the decennial canvass of the population. To conduct the vast administrative operation necessary to enumerate the population of the United States, the nation was divided into approximately 150,000 enumeration districts. The location of each of these districts was described and shown on maps to indicate to each enumerator the area within which the canvass was to be made. In rural areas the minor civil division and the enumeration district often coincided, but many minor civil divisions were made up of two or more enumeration districts.

Population data were not published for the enumeration district, as such, but limited statistics of the characteristics of the population as described in the following pages, as well as total population figures, may be obtained by enumeration districts from the Bureau of the Census for the cost of transcribing the data. Maps showing the boundaries of the districts (unless copyrighted) may also be purchased at nominal cost. These data are often useful for local market analysis, particularly for cities that do not have census tracts and for outlying portions of metropolitan districts. Although historical comparisons of population cannot be made by enumeration districts, because their boundaries change from census to census, the data available for any one census are often used by many types of business enterprises.

CHARACTERISTICS OF THE POPULATION FOR SMALL AREAS

For many production and marketing purposes, information about the composition and characteristics of the population of an area is an important tool for the determination of policy and the conduct of business operations. Certainly for some types of commodities designed for class markets, it is as important to know the kind of people in a market as it is to know their total number. Moreover, since for many business purposes information is desired for local markets, it is especially important to know what types of data are available for local areas. It is for this reason, and because census tabulations for practical reasons vary considerably in amount of detail for "small" and "large" areas, that separate sections are given below on the statistics relating to characteristics of the population for these respective types of areas.

The "small area" tabulations of the population census are of two basic types: (1) those made for enumeration districts and (2) those made for all urban places including subdivisions such as wards of cities of 50,000 or more, or census tracts in tracted cities, and counties, including separately the rural-nonfarm and rural-farm parts of counties. These tabulations are, of course, consolidated to provide metropolitan district, state, and national totals.

All of the published population statistics [6] available for "small areas" from the 1940 Census may be found in Volume II of the *Sixteenth Census Reports on Population—Characteristics of the Population* (in 7 parts) and in the bulletins for census tract cities described above. The statistics in Volume II are also available as a series of separate bulletins, one for each state, the District of Columbia, and the United States.

The statistics on the characteristics of the population available for minor civil divisions and incorporated places of 1,000 to 2,500 inhabitants are published in the full detail in which they were tabulated in Volume II of the Population reports. These data give for the approximately 52,000 minor civil divisions the age (in 10-year intervals) and sex composition of the population, sex and race, nativity of white persons, and farm and nonfarm residence. Similar information is on hand in unpublished form by enumeration districts and can be made available, together with maps showing the boundaries of the enumeration districts, at the nominal cost of transcribing or reproducing the materials.

The information tabulated for the small areas other than minor civil divisions and enumeration districts includes (by sex, race, and nativity) the characteristics age; citizenship; school attendance; years of school completed for persons 25 years old and over; country of birth of foreign-born white; employment status of persons 14 years old and

---

[6] For family statistics for small areas, see pp. 348 ff. For housing statistics, especially rent and value statistics for small areas, see Chapter 13. Data on the characteristics of inmates of institutions are given in the 1940 Population bulletin *Special Report on Institutional Population*.

over; and for employed workers data on class of worker, major occupation group, and industry. Data are also given for potential voters.

Because of the tremendous mass of material, it is not possible, even in the publications devoted to small areas, to present for each area all of the information which is tabulated. In general, the plan has been followed of showing more detailed information for large areas in the census volumes than for "small areas." For a quick picture of the type of information that is available for the various types of "small areas," reference should be made to page XII of Part 1 of Volume II of the reports on Population. For a quick determination of the unpublished statistics, available usually at the nominal cost of transcription, one need only compare the information published for the given area of interest with that available in Volume II for the state as a whole. If the statistics are available for the state, they have been tabulated for all of its counties by rural-farm and rural-nonfarm areas, urban places of 2,500 inhabitants or more, metropolitan districts, and with the exception of certain materials showing minor races, by race, for census tracts. These data can be obtained by addressing an appropriate communication to the Director of the Census. The nature of some of the more important data tabulated for the "small areas" of the nation and some indication of their usefulness to business is given in the paragraphs which follow.

Sex. Many of the goods and services of modern life—for example, clothing, publications, hair dressing, and toilet articles—are produced and distributed primarily for the use of one or the other of the sexes.

The mobility of the population and the nature of modern migration, together with war, which still takes a heavier toll of men than of women, have caused marked changes in the sex composition with the passage of time and considerable variations in the proportion of the sexes from area to area within the nation. The variation of the sex ratio (number of males per 100 females) within the nation is indicated by the range of 125.4 for the state of Nevada in 1940 to 91.9 for the District of Columbia.

For most business purposes, data on the number of persons of each sex in a given market is quite sufficient and may readily be obtained from Volume II of the 1940 reports for Population.

Age. Age is another population characteristic which is closely associated with the nature of consumer demand. All other things being equal, production and distribution goals would certainly be different for a population with an average (median) age of 16 years, the actual average (median) age in 1800 for the United States, and that with a median age of 29 years, the actual average age of the American people in 1940. Age statistics will become increasingly important to watch in the years that lie ahead because of the rapidity with which the proportion of older persons in the American population is increasing.

Statistics relating to the age of the population are available in considerable detail (by 5- and 10-year age groupings) for the small areas of the country and permit detailed analysis with respect to the various age classes that are of greatest significance for marketing purposes.

Color or Race. Because of differences in economic level and in consumer habits, statistics on color or race are frequently important market indicators, especially for local markets. The number and proportion of nonwhite persons by specific nonwhite race are available in considerable detail for the small areas of the nation in Volume II of the Population reports and in a special report entitled *Characteristics of the Nonwhite Population by Race.*

Nativity. Information is also available on the nativity of the white population and on the place of birth of the foreign-born white population for the small areas of the nation. Of the white population 90.3 percent were native and 9.7 foreign born in 1940. Between 1930 and 1940, the number of foreign-born white persons decreased from 13,983,-000 to 11,419,000 or by more than 18 percent.

For specialized interests, such as those represented by the foreign language press, statistics relating to the foreign-born population still possess considerable value. It may be expected, however, in light of the fact that the median age of the foreign-born white population was 51 years in 1940, that unless our immigration policy is considerably modified, the foreign-born population will rapidly disappear from the American scene.

Education and School Attendance. Among the items which made their first appearance in the 1940 Census of Population is one which possesses considerable importance for marketing purposes, namely, highest grade of school completed. The 1940 Census schedule contained a question, asked of each person, on the last full grade completed in the regular school system, public, private or parochial school, college, or university. For small areas the statistics based on this question are restricted to persons 25 years old and over, that is, adults practically all of whom have completed their formal education.

The statistics are presented both in tables showing the median year of school completed and in terms of frequency distribution showing the number of persons who have completed the various years of school in grade school, high school, or college. The data on education should possess considerable value for producers and distributors of many commodities such as books and magazines, the consumer demand for which is directly related to educational attainment. The data are useful also as a general index of the economic, cultural, and social status of the population of an area, and as such an index it may possess greatest value for general marketing purposes.

Data are also presented for persons 5 to 24 years old showing school attendance by age of child. These data may prove useful for special marketing groups interested in the school child at various age levels as a potential consumer.

Labor Force. Among the characteristics of the population useful for market evaluation are the labor force data, including employment status, class of worker, and the occupational and industrial affiliation of workers. Although the volume of employment and the status of persons in the labor force are subject to considerable change with swings in the business cycle, the statistics available for any one point of time, as those for the 1940 Census, nevertheless possess value in indicating the economic character of the community.

Information is available in the census for small areas showing the employment status of all persons 14 years old and over based on work activity during the week preceding the census—that of March 24 to 30, 1940. The census tabulations permit the classification of the population into two broad groups, namely, persons in the labor force and persons not in the labor force. Within each of these broad categories further subclassification of work status is presented.

In addition to statistics giving the basic employment status classifications described above, information is available for employed workers on class of worker, major occupational group, and industry group. The class of worker statistics show whether the employed persons in the labor force were wage or salary workers, employers, own account workers, or unpaid family workers. The occupational statistics for small areas show the broad occupational class of employed workers in 12 occupational groupings, such as professional, farmers and farm managers, and domestic service workers. The industrial affiliation of workers is shown in 44 broad classes of industry, including such designations as coal mining, logging, and chemicals and allied products.

The array of statistics for each of the small areas of the nation describing the work status and occupational and industrial affiliation of the population has important direct and indirect uses for management and marketing purposes. From the management standpoint, statistics on the available and potential labor supply is at least one factor in determining policy and practice with respect to such matters as plant location, expansion, and personnel recruiting. The industrial statistics reported in the 1940 Population Census may also be useful as indirect indexes for industrial marketing purposes. Perhaps the most important use of these statistics lies, however, in their description of the work status and occupation of the population because these characteristics frequently point to important differences in cultural level, consumer habits, and purchasing power.

POPULATION STATISTICS FOR LARGER AREAS

Most of the information available for "small areas" is shown only in limited cross classification, that is, rarely are statistics shown in combination with characteristics other than sex, color, and nativity of the population. It is highly desirable for many purposes to have the census information available in more detailed cross classification. For example, for a number of purposes statistics on occupation are much more meaningful if presented by age than for the total population without regard to age composition. It is not possible, however, within the limits of Census Bureau appropriations and other practical considerations to tabulate population statistics in detailed cross classification for small areas. The more detailed tabulations, therefore, are reserved for the larger areas of the nation, that is, the country as a whole, the states by urban and rural areas (or combinations of states as regions or geographic divisions), and large cities and metropolitan districts. The detailed cross tabulations of the Population Census are available in Volume III, entitled *The Labor Force—Occupation, Industry, Employment, and Income* (5 parts), and Volume IV, *Characteristics by Age— Marital Status, Relationship, Education, and Citizenship* (4 parts); and in a series of special reports and bulletins. Volumes III and IV are also published as separate bulletins, one for each state, the District of Columbia, and the United States.

Labor Force. Volume III of the Population Census reports presents detailed information on the labor force, including cross classifications of a number of personal characteristics with occupation, industry, employment, and income.

In this volume, the data for the states and cities of 100,000 inhabitants or more are presented in a series of seven groups of tables (some tables are restricted to the state or to cities having 250,000 inhabitants or more). The tables contain detailed cross classified statistics relating to the following major subjects: employment status and class of worker, occupation, wage or salary income, industry, hours worked, employment during 1939, and duration of unemployment.

These detailed cross classifications add greatly to our knowledge of the economic characteristics of the population and are valuable marketing tools not only in presenting data for the specific large areas to which they relate, but also in providing background for better interpretation of the more simple statistical tabulations made available for smaller areas.

Income. Worthy of special mention and available only for large areas are the wage or salary income data presented for the first time in the 1940 Population Census. The 1940 population schedule contained inquiries directed at all persons 14 years old and over (except inmates of specified institutions) with respect to the amount of money wage or salary income received in 1939. Those who received more than $5,000 in wage or salary income were asked to report only that they received over that amount. No attempt was made to obtain entrepreneurial income or any income other than receipts from wages or salaries. In order to identify those persons whose incomes were for all practical purposes restricted to money wages or salary, persons 14 years of age and over were also asked to report whether they had received $50 or more from sources other than wages or salaries in 1939.

Although statistics relating to the income of the population are of great value as a direct index of purchasing power, it is important to realize the limitations for marketing purposes of the census statistics on income. Since no attempt was made to obtain amount of income from sources other than wages or salary the income data presented may be quite misleading for any given area if what is desired is an index of total or relative purchasing power. Despite this limitation, however, the income statistics are worthy of close attention for the large areas for which the data are made available, that is, the states, urban and rural areas, and cities having 100,000 or more inhabitants.

The usefulness of the census income statistics may be greatly increased if advantage is taken of the relationship of money wages or salary to other characteristics of the population as contained in the census volumes. For example, money wage or salary income is presented for workers classified by volume of employment in 1939, sex, and occupation. Since occupational statistics are available for "small areas" as well as "large areas," the income data by occupation published for "large areas" provide some basis for evaluating the purchasing power of various occupational groups shown in the "small area" statistics. Of even greater value than the relationship between wage or salary income and occupation is that of family wage or salary income and rent. This relationship and its potential use are further discussed in Chapter 13.

Population Characteristics. The more detailed tabulations relating to the personal characteristics of the population are presented in Volume IV of the Population reports, *Characteristics by Age*. This volume contains considerable detail on the age composition of the population cross classified by marital status, relationship, education, citizenship, and some limited information on the labor force.

In both Volumes III and IV, in addition to the detailed cross tabulations described, comparative data are liberally presented from earlier census reports.

Special Reports. A series of special reports presents data on special subjects based largely on sample tabulations. These will be found useful not only for the specific large areas to which they relate, but also, as in the case of the other large area tabulations, as a basis for interpreting the less detailed tabulations available for smaller areas. Most of the special reports are based largely on tabulations of cross sections of the population scientifically seclected to represent the total population. The statistics were tabulated in considerable cross classification but only for relatively few areas, usually the regions or geographic divisions, sometimes the states and larger cities, and in no case for cities with less than 100,000 inhabitants.

These special reports may be broadly classified into two categories, (1) those relating to general population characteristics and (2) those relating to labor force characteristics.

The first of these groups of special reports includes eight bulletins. A series of three of these relates to the *Nativity and Parentage of the White Population*, and are subtitled *General Characteristics, Country of Origin of Foreign Stock*, and *Mother Tongue*. The remainder comprise *Characteristics of the Nonwhite Population by Race; Differential Fertility: 1940 and 1910; Education, Occupation, and Household Relationship of Males 18 to 44 Years Old;* and finally two bulletins to which reference has already been made—*Internal Migration 1935 to 1940* and *State of Birth of the Native Population*.

The second group of special reports, those relating to the labor force, is made up of seven bulletins. Three of these deal primarily with detailed tabulations of the personal characteristics of the population 14 years old and over both in and out of the labor force as follows: *Employment and Personal Characteristics, Employment and Family Characteristics of Women*, and *Characteristics of Persons Not in the Labor Force, 14 Years Old and Over*. The last gives for persons 14 years old and over not in the labor force at the time of the census not only their age, sex, color, and household relationship, but also, for those with previous work experience, months worked in 1939 and usual major occupational group. The remaining four bulletins in this group contain detailed tabulations on specialized subjects as follows: *Wage or*

Salary Income in 1939, Occupational Characteristics, Usual Occupation and *Industrial Characteristics*.

For various specialized types of management and marketing problems, time may be well spent in the study of these special reports.

Current Statistics. As is to be expected, there are not many data made available currently on the detailed characteristics of the population. Such current data as can be compiled on the composition of the population are restricted to age, sex, and color estimates for the country as a whole and to employment status and general characteristics of persons in the nation's labor force.

The first of these estimates is based on projections of the population from the last census through the use of life tables prepared by the Census Bureau. The most recent report of this character is *Estimated Population in Continental United States, by Age, Color, and Sex: 1940 to 1942*, released on March 29, 1944. Worthy of mention is the release *Estimated Civilian Population by Age and Sex for Selected Areas, November 1, 1943* (Series P-44, No. 15), which presents estimates of the civilian population by age and sex for 39 selected metropolitan areas. These estimates resulted from a special project in which an analysis was made of applications for *War Ration Book Four*.

The current statistics relating to the labor force are based on a monthly canvass of approximately 30,000 households representative of the population of the country as a whole. On the basis of this sample survey there is issued the *Monthly Report on the Labor Force*, which gives by sex the following information relating to the labor force: employment status, including the employed classified by nonagricultural and agricultural employment, the unemployed and persons not in the labor force. From time to time special reports are issued giving more detailed characteristics such as age and color and certain other special subjects such as hours worked during the census week, type of nonworker, characteristics of the unemployed, month-to-month changes in labor force activity, and other characteristics of persons in and out of the labor force. (See also Chapter 14.)

This monthly sample operation is still in process of development and it is hoped that it will be possible to present for the nation as a whole estimates of more detailed general characteristics of the population from time to time. A recent example of one such estimate is the release on *Marital Status of the Civilian Population: February 1944* (Series P-S, No. 1).

Sample censuses such as those conducted for the congested production areas described above may in the course of time make possible the preparation of current estimates of population characteristics as well as total population of at least the larger areas of the nation. At the present time the various problems involved in the preparation of such estimates are under intensive study in the Bureau of the Census.

STATISTICS ON FAMILIES

Number of Families. Although human wants are resident in individual persons, the family, from a marketing standpoint, is often the more important consumer unit. A large proportion of goods and particularly of durable consumer goods, such as refrigerators, furniture, and automobiles, are in a real sense used by families rather than by individuals. For this reason statistics on the number of families in the nation and in its various subdivisions and on family size and composition are important data for industry and business.

Statistics relating to families and households are available both in the Census of Housing (see Chapter 13) and in the Census of Population taken in 1940. Figures on the number of families for states, cities, counties, minor civil divisions of the United States, and the various special statistical areas including regions, geographic divisions, metropolitan districts, and urban and rural areas are available in Volume I, Census of Housing, 1940, *Data for Small Areas.* Family data for census tracts are available in the individual bulletins *Statistics for Census Tracts* for the 60 tracted cities. Furthermore, for the first time in the history of the census, certain statistics including data on the number of families have been tabulated and published by city blocks. These data are available in individual bulletins for cities having 50,000 or more inhabitants in 1930 and are known as *Supplements to the First Series Housing Bulletins; Block Statistics for Cities.* As in the case of general population statistics, unpublished data on the number of families can be made available by enumeration districts at the nominal cost of transcribing the information.

The family data in the housing reports are not identified as statistics on "families" but appear in the various tables as figures on "occupied dwelling units." The term "occupied dwelling unit" as used in the 1940 Housing Census is defined as the living quarters occupied by one "household." The "household" comprises the "private household," which includes related family members who constitute the "family," together with lodgers, servants, or hired hands, if any, who regularly live in the home; and the "quasi-household," which is made up of a group of unrelated persons such as those living in a boarding or lodging house, an institution, or a school. Since "occupied dwelling units" do not include "quasi-households" the number of "occupied dwelling units" reported in the Housing Census is approximately the same as the number of "private households" in the 1940 Census (or as "families" in the 1930 Census), and, with few exceptions, for very small areas, may safely be used as statistics on the number of families.

Family statistics, like statistics relating to the total number of inhabitants, become increasingly significant when historical comparisons are made. For example, the number of families in the United States increased from 16,188,000 in 1900 to over 35 million in 1940; that is, the number more than doubled. If a comparison is made of the rate of growth of families with the rate of growth of population in the country, further interesting facts emerge. Since the turn of the century, while the number of families increased by 117 percent, the total population increased by only 73 percent. During each decade in this 40-year period, the number of families increased considerably more rapidly than the total population.

At first glance, the more rapid increase in the number of families than in the total population may appear to be contradictory. This seeming paradox is resolved when we analyze the changes that occurred in the size of the average family during the period under consideration. The average size of the American family in 1940 was about 3.8 persons as compared with 4.1 persons in 1930 and 4.7 persons in 1900. It is the decrease in the average size of the American family that accounts both for the greater percentage increase in the number of families than in population and for the slower decline in the growth of families than in population. These facts possess considerable significance for business, industrial, and marketing purposes, as noted below.

Historical comparisons for the nation as a whole and for its various subdivisions can be made back to 1850, for each decennial census since that date has included information on the number of families and the number of dwellings.

Characteristics of Families. From both the production and marketing standpoint it is important to have not only information about the number of families but also about their characteristics. Limited data on the characteristics of families are available in Volumes I and II of the 1940 Census of Housing. In Volume I and in the *Supplements to the First Series Housing Bulletins* containing block data for cities, the color or race of families can be obtained from the statistics on occupied dwelling units showing "dwelling units occupied by nonwhite." This information is available for most of the political subdivisions and census areas.

In Volume II of the Housing Reports additional information may be obtained on the size of households by color of head for the regions, geographic divisions, states, metropolitan districts, and cities of 50,000 inhabitants or more. This additional information also may be obtained for urban places of less than 50,000 with a significant number of non-whites, for counties, and the rural-farm portions of counties for the southern states. Data relating to value of home and rental are also available in these housing volumes. (See also Chapter 13, pp. 366 ff.) Similar statistics are also available by census tracts in the bulletins entitled *Statistics for Census Tracts*.

More detailed cross tabulations of the characteristics of families are available for relatively large areas in a series of eight bulletins based on tabulations of a sample of the population. Information on tenure, size of family, number of children, labor force status of children, number of lodgers and subfamilies, number of persons in the labor force, family employment status, and family wage or salary income are shown for states, cities of 100,000 or more, and metropolitan districts of 200,-000 or more in the bulletin *Population and Housing: Families, General Characteristics, 1940*. This bulletin also includes information about the heads of families who are shown by race, nativity, parentage, citizenship, sex, marital status, age, highest grade of school completed, migration status and 1935 residence, employment status, and major occupation group.

Information on types of families, classified by various characteristics of families and their heads, is available for the United States, regions, urban and rural, and for cities of a million or more in a bulletin *Population, Families—Types of Families*. The term "type of family" is applied to the classification of families by sex, marital status, age of head, and number of children under 18 years in the family. Statistics are presented on the various types of families cross classified by family size, number of children under 10 years old, tenure and monthly rental value of home. Heads of families are shown by type of family cross classified by the head's race, nativity, and highest grade of school completed. Wives of family heads are shown by age, labor force status, and number of children under 10 years old. Statistics are also shown for families by type of family cross classified by family wage or salary income and receipt of other income, and by employment status and major occupation group of head. Additional detail on family composition is available in the bulletin *Population, Families—Size of Family and Age of Head* and *Population, Families—Employment Status*.

For good indications of the purchasing power of families a series of three bulletins is available. The bulletin on *Family Wage or Salary Income in 1939* presents data for the United States, the regions, and cities of a million or more; the bulletin *Tenure and Rent* for regions, cities of a million or more, and metropolitan districts of 500,000 or more; and the bulletin *Income and Rent* for regions and metropolitan districts of a million or more. *Income and Rent*, which gives the relationship between rent and wage or salary income, is particularly important for interpreting the rent statistics available for small areas.

Finally, for those interested primarily in farm families, a bulletin on *Characteristics of Rural-Farm Families* presents data on families by tenure, occupation of the head, and value or rent of house cross classified by selected housing characteristics, family characteristics, and characteristics of the head for the United States, regions, and geographic divisions.

Current Statistics. Current statistics on the number of families in the United States have been much in demand for business as well as other uses. Although postcensal estimates of the total number of families in the United States have not as yet been made which possess the same precision as those on total population, the Bureau of the Census, to meet demand for the data, has prepared a release on the *Estimated Number of Families in the United States: 1940 to 1960* (Series P-1943, No. 2). These estimates, which will undoubtedly be revised as better data become available, are worthy of the attention of all enterprises interested in the family as a consumer unit. The release contains a discussion of the methods used in making the estimates; presents estimates under peacetime and wartime conditions; and presents high, medium, and low estimates which permit the user to exercise his own judgment in the light of his own problems. It is possible that in the near future more detailed current family statistics, including estimates of new family formation, will be made available as a result of the sampling studies being conducted in the Bureau of the Census.

Statistics on Marriage and Divorce. Of considerable interest to many types of enterprises, particularly to those interested in durable consumer goods for which families are the primary consumer units, are statistics relating to marriage. Each marriage, at least potentially, represents a new household with a new set of wants. The new households affect not only industries and distributors in fields such as housing, furniture, household equipment, electrical appliances, and utilities, but also, because of changes in consumer habits and purchases which accompany family living, the general market.

It is rather surprising in light of the fact that marriage statistics have considerable general social significance as well as important marketing uses that the United States has not had, and does not now have, adequate and complete current national statistics in this field. Moreover, it is perhaps just as surprising that the United States does not have current national statistics on divorce.

Although marriage statistics can in a spotty manner be reconstructed back to the year 1867, the historical series is full of inadequacies. In more recent times the Bureau of the Census has published marriage and divorce statistics beginning in 1922 and continuing until 1932, when the series was discontinued as an economy measure. In 1939 the collection and publication of statistics on marriage and divorce was resumed by the Census Bureau for the decennial census period, that is, for the years 1939 and 1940. This program, for lack of funds, was discontinued at the close of the decennial census.

Beginning in 1944 the Bureau of the Census is again resuming the preparation of data on marriages based on summary reports received directly from most of the counties, cities, or towns in all of the states and the District of Columbia. This series of statistics was initiated in 1937 and maintained by the Home Owners' Loan Corporation until the series was transferred to the Census Bureau in January 1944. The first of the releases based on this series was issued on July 4, 1944, under the title *Marriages in the United States: 1914 to 1943* (Series PM-1, No. 1). The second of the releases based on this operation was issued on August 14, 1944, and entitled *Marriage Licenses Issued for Cities of 100,000 or More: January to June, 1944 and 1943* (Series PM-2, No. 1). It is contemplated henceforth to issue monthly data on marriages even though their quality on the present restricted basis of collection leaves much to be desired.

Statistics for Territories and Possessions. The decennial census of population includes a census of the outlying territories and possessions of the United States. The territories and possessions are becoming increasingly important for marketing and other purposes. In general, more detailed statistics are available for the larger territories and possessions than for the smaller ones. Bulletins containing statistics on the number of inhabitants entitled *Population—First Series* are available for Alaska, American Samoa, Guam, Hawaii, Panama Canal Zone, and Virgin Islands. In addition, bulletins containing statistics relating to the characteristics of the population entitled *Population— Second Series* are available for Alaska, Hawaii, and the Virgin Islands (population and housing). For Puerto Rico, a series of three bulletins is available (Population Bulletin Nos. 1–3) in bilingual form, Spanish and English.

USES OF POPULATION STATISTICS FOR MANAGEMENT AND MARKETING PURPOSES

The benchmark and current statistics made available by the Bureau of the Census on various aspects of the population of the United States have important uses and implications for management and marketing purposes. To some of these, brief reference is made here, not to exhaust the subject but rather to provide a general framework which may be helpful in suggesting adaptations of the data for various business and industrial purposes. Although the value of current population statistics is highlighted during periods of rapid change such as those occasioned by severe depression, drought, or war, close observation of trends in population growth even in more normal times will undoubtedly be found a profitable pursuit for successful sales management.

Markets have literally moved away from many localities of the nation since the 1940 Census and into other areas at rates which have strained their public and business resources. There has been considerable variation in the extent to which business has moved with the moving market.

Such adaptations as are made in marketing practices to conform with rapidly shifting population should, however, be made with some knowledge of basic long-time trends against the background of which changes may be adjudged as merely temporary or relatively permanent.

For example, although many metropolitan centers grew very rapidly during the war, some undoubtedly will experience postwar losses of population, whereas others have much better prospects of retaining their wartime population growth. Such changes as may be made in dealing with the shifting market in delineation of sales territories, allocation of sales quotas, disposition of sales force, and allocation of advertising lineage can be made more efficiently and with proper safeguards if the postwar population prospects of specific communities can be anticipated.

Although many factors enter into the future of any community, reasonably good insurance against the future may be obtained at the small cost of analyzing and projecting population and other trends in a given area. For example, on a regional basis, it is clear that the shifts in population occasioned by the war represent in the main a continuation of previously observed trends. The relatively rapid wartime growth of the South and the West, and particularly of the metropolitan areas located within these regions, is in keeping with the trend in evidence during preceding decades. This is not surprising upon analysis because the South and the West are less industrialized and urbanized than the North and, relative to the North, are still in a developmental state. The fact that rapid wartime expansion in business and industry in the West and in the South is in keeping with previously observed trends can be interpreted as indicating that the wartime population growth of the South and the West is likely to endure. On the other hand, although it may be true that markets in the South and West are expanding more rapidly than in the North, this should not obscure the fact that the North still contains the bulk of the population and the purchasing power of the nation. Although the northern market may not increase as rapidly, it will, nevertheless, contain a greater marketing potential than the South and the West for many years to come.[7]

The great increase in the labor force of the nation undoubtedly has had important effects on business and industry. This follows not only from the increased purchasing power attendant upon the increased number of workers but also upon the important changes in consumer habits. The latter is particularly true in the case of women whose consumption and purchasing habits undoubtedly undergo great change as their status changes from that of housewife to that of worker. Moreover, the business or industrial executive may be interested in labor force statistics not only from the standpoint of the labor force as consumers, but also from the standpoint of labor as an element in production or in providing services. From the management standpoint, the volume of employment and unemployment, the availability of various types of skill, the potential labor supply, and the personal characteristics of workers are among the types of data which have great usefulness in the determination of recruiting, training, wage, and other policies.

Trends in the development of individual metropolitan districts may also have important short-run implications for business practices. American cities have for some decades, in general, been emptying at their centers and growing rapidly at their peripheries. The decentralization of population within a metropolitan district has called for and, for many types of enterprises resulted in, the decentralization of sales outlets. The census tract and block statistics described above have potentially great value for following population shifts within the urban community or the metropolitan district and should prove a powerful tool for enterprises interested in local distribution problems.

The large difference in the rates at which the population and families have been growing in the country as a whole and in its component

[7] Philip M. Hauser, "Wartime Population Changes and Postwar Prospects," *The Journal of Marketing,* January 1944, pp. 238–248.

parts also merits the attention of businessmen. To the extent that
there will be declines in production or distribution of commodities
paralleling the decline in the rate of population growth, differential
declines may be expected among commodities intended primarily for
individual consumption and those produced primarily for consumption
by family units. It should be emphasized, of course, that a declining
rate of population or family growth does not necessarily imply a decline
in the volume of production because higher purchasing power and increased level of living can more than offset decreases in rates of growth.
The differences in the rates of population and family increase are
sufficient, however, to justify separate analysis of these data by production and marketing interests.

Determination of Sales Areas and Quotas. Population data may be
used successfully by market analysts in the delineation of sales areas,
the evaluation of the marketing potential for general and class markets,
the determination of sales quotas, the disposition of sales force, and
the allocation of advertising. In the highly competitive days which
lie ahead, it may safely be asserted that the producer or distributor
who is able to reach his market with the smallest expenditure of time
and energy will have a marked advantage over less efficient competitors.

Census data on land area and population are primary factors which,
for many types of commodities, will be found quite useful in the delineation of sales territories. In fact, a number of enterprises have
successfully used census data in this manner. Depending on the character of the commodity to be distributed, it is possible in addition to
these primary data to plot on a map the characteristics of the population which have the greatest relevance for the specific distribution
problem involved.

Perhaps the best single item worthy of consideration for this purpose,
in addition to total population, is the combined index of contract or
estimated rent. (See Chapter 13, p. 368.) This index of the purchasing
power of a community, particularly when interpreted in the light of
the relationship of rent to wage or salary income (see Census bulletin
Families: Income and Rent), is, despite its numerous limitations, a most
valuable economic index.

Within a census tract city, for example, it would be quite illuminating
to plot on a census tract map the total population and contract or
estimated median rental of each tract as reported in the census volumes,
alongside the actual sales of, or organization of sales forces for, a given
commodity. Such a map would reveal at once facts of vital interest
to the market analyst, such as high purchasing power communities
with relatively small sales, and low purchasing power communities

with unduly large disposition of sales forces. With the aid of such a map it would be possible intelligently to adjust sales territories and quotas and to spot areas which for one reason or another require special attention. Other data can, of course, be added to such a map as, for example, the educational level of the population, color or race, age, and occupational or industrial composition. The use of population census data on maps in conjunction with other census data, as, for example, that in the Census of Business or the Census of Housing (see p. 364), and with sales data has in the experience of many enterprises been found an exceedingly valuable analytical device.

Market Surveys. Many of the modern advances in the technique of distribution have flowed directly from information obtained from market surveys. It is, therefore, of considerable importance efficiently to plan market surveys. It is almost unnecessary to point out that census data will be found to have great value in the design of such surveys, especially in the preparation of a sample design.

Market surveys employ various types of sample design to obtain desired information in a quick, efficient, and economical manner. A commonly used type of sample design is that usually referred to as the "quota" or "in-ratio" method of sampling. Although this method of sampling is subject to many pitfalls and requires caution in use,[8] a prerequisite for its use is a knowledge of the characteristics of the population to be sampled. Such characteristics, if at all available, are generally to be found in the census volumes.

If more rigorous sampling designs are employed as in area sampling, again the census data will be found to provide valuable information useful for efficient sample design.[9] Since in area sampling it is necessary to use relatively small population clusters, widely dispersed, the census data of greatest usefulness for sampling purposes will be the statistics for the very smallest areas—those for counties, minor civil divisions, city blocks, and enumeration districts. These statistics, as has been outlined above, may be readily obtained from the Bureau of the Census and make possible at least the first steps in the selection of sample areas.[10]

[8] See Philip M. Hauser and Morris H. Hansen, "On Sampling in Market Surveys," *Journal of Marketing*, July 1944.

[9] Morris H. Hansen and W. Edwards Deming, "On Some Census Aids to Sampling," *Journal of the American Statistical Association*, September 1943, Vol. 38, pp. 353–357.

[10] It will be found in designing area samples that for most purposes even the city block or the enumeration district are units too large for efficient results, but these units may be used as a basis for efficient subsampling to complete the sample design.

It is appropriate to call attention to the fact that in addition to the published and unpublished census statistics useful for sample design purposes in market surveys, the Bureau of the Census has conducted important researches in the field of area sampling which merit the attention of persons interested in this field.[11]

Matching Studies. A recent development in the use of census statistics opens up new mines of information to market analysts which may well merit further exploration. This development is the "matching study" in which the Bureau of the Census compiles summary statistics based on information obtained in census schedules for lists of consumers furnished by the business enterprise. Several such studies have recently been conducted at the expense of interested business concerns (on a cost basis), which have been found to possess considerable marketing usefulness.

In one study, for example, a publisher was interested in obtaining a comparison of the characteristics of subscribers to a given publication with those of the general population. The publishing company furnished to the Bureau of the Census a list of its subscribers, which were matched to census schedules. The information on the schedules for the subscribers was first transcribed and then transferred to punch cards along with information about the subscribers furnished by the business enterprise. Tabulations were then prepared by the Census Bureau which showed in summary form the characteristics of the subscribers as reported to the Bureau of the Census in correlation with the characteristics of the subscribers as known to the publisher. This type of tabulation, of course, does not violate the confidential nature of the data collected by the Census Bureau because information is not made available in a form which would permit the identification of individual persons or families. The characteristics of the subscribers as obtained from such a summary tabulation were then compared with the characteristics of nonsubscribers in identical areas. The resulting analysis proved quite enlightening and was used with telling effect in the sales promotion work of the publication.

Such matching studies have their maximum value if they are made while the census data are still "fresh," immediately after the conduct of the census. However, a number of enterprises are still greatly interested in the conduct of such special studies, even though the 1940 population census is badly out of date, and requests continue to be received in the Bureau of the Census calling for cost estimates on

[11] Morris H. Hansen and William N. Hurwitz, "On the Theory of Sampling from Finite Populations," *The Annals of Mathematical Statistics*, Vol. XIV, No. 4, December 1943, pp. 333–362.

such projects. As business and industry become increasingly aware of the potentialities of this type of market analysis, a considerable increase in requests for matching studies may be expected.

SUMMARY

The population census has its primary legal basis in its use for the apportionment of representatives among the states. As has been indicated, however, the scope and character of the contemporary population census permit uses which far transcend its original constitutional function. The decennial census of population and related reports and the various current types of information compiled and published by the Bureau of the Census represent a considerable investment of public time and money. This investment in the long run can be justified only in the uses which not only government agencies but also various types of private and public interests, including industrial and business interests, make of the data.

The major barrier to the more widespread utilization of population statistics is ignorance of what they are and how to procure them. This is a barrier which is in part attributable to poor marketing practices on the part of the government producers of statistics, and government agencies are increasingly attempting to apply the proper remedial measures. Despite the difficulties which may be involved in keeping informed as to the population statistics which are available, it may be stated with confidence that the businessman will make a profitable investment in allocating time and energy sufficient to know them and to use them.

CHAPTER 13

HOUSING AND CONSTRUCTION

HOWARD G. BRUNSMAN

Bureau of the Census
Department of Commerce

Most of the bread that is sold on any day is consumed on the day of sale or the following day. There is no significant inventory of bread in the hands of consumers. The sale of bread for any day is an excellent measure of the consumption of bread. This factor simplifies the problem of compiling statistics on consumption of bread. The same factor of low consumer inventory also applies to many of the perishable consumer goods. Unfortunately, it does not apply to housing. Most of the housing that is being used for shelter today was produced three years, five years, or ten years ago. Much of it was built twenty, thirty, and even fifty years ago. There is no close relationship between housing being produced in any period and the housing being consumed through use during the period. Thus, if we want to know the type and characteristics of the housing being consumed, it is not sufficient to know the characteristics of the housing produced during a given period. In addition, we must know the characteristics of the housing that was in existence and available for use at the beginning of any given period.

Another peculiar characteristic of housing is its relative immobility. The housing and real estate market of any area would fluctuate far less if more of us lived in trailers. If a housing surplus developed the trailers could be moved to an area of greater demand. We do not live in trailers, however, and our houses are not mobile. The housing shortage in Philadelphia cannot be relieved by transferring to Philadelphia the housing surplus in Scranton. These two peculiar characteristics of housing—its durability and its immobility—result in tremendous fluctuations in the home building industry.

This result is readily demonstrated by the problem of war housing in the United States. War workers moved to a group of war production centers from rural areas and from other urban places. There was no substantial increase in the number of homes required by these workers but they wanted the homes near their new places of employment.

359

The number of new homes built each year usually represents not more than 2 or 3 percent of the existing supply of homes in an area. An increase of 10 percent in demand for housing in a war center represents only a moderate increase, but it would result in a demand equivalent to normal building in a three to five year period. To supply these additional homes in a period of less than a year would require a tremendous increase in construction activity. The increase in demand in war centers was accompanied by a decrease in demand in other areas. A decrease in demand of 3 or 4 percent may result in complete elimination of demand for new homes in the area, and the home building industry in such an area would show a tremendous decline.

The characteristics of housing and of the home building industry outlined above result in greater interest in data relating to the inventory of existing housing, in the more exact measurement of activity of the home building industry and, in data for local areas such as counties, metropolitan districts, cities, and even city blocks.

BENCHMARK DATA

Inventory of Housing. In view of the importance of the data relating to the inventory of housing it is fortunate that the 1940 Census of Housing was included with the inquiries of the Sixteenth Decennial Census. All of the 37,325,470 dwelling units in the continental United States were covered by this enumeration. The basic results of the census are presented in Volumes I to IV of the *Sixteenth Census of the United States Reports on Housing.* In general, the quantity of data presented for an area varies with the size of the area, ranging from a single line of data for a ward in a city of 10,000 inhabitants to the many pages of data for a city of 100,000 inhabitants or more.

Volume I of the Housing reports presents data for the smaller areas. It contains information for each city or other incorporated place with 1,000 inhabitants or more, for each ward in cities with 10,000 inhabitants or more, and for the townships or other minor civil divisions of each county. Data also are shown separately for the rural-farm dwelling units in each minor civil division.

In Table 1 there is presented a summary of housing data for the United States as a whole. Basic data of the type shown in this table are available in Volume I of the Housing reports for each of the smaller areas of the United States. The number of occupied dwelling units is an indication of the number of families in the various small areas, and is of particular importance since the family represents the basic unit of consumption for many items (see Chapter 12). Home owners represent the principal market for lawn mowers and many types of goods that are associated with the more stable type of family. Tenants may represent the better market for other types of commodities.

TABLE 1. CHARACTERISTICS OF HOUSING FOR THE UNITED STATES, 1940, AS PRESENTED IN VOLUME I OF THE HOUSING REPORTS OF THE SIXTEENTH DECENNIAL CENSUS

Item	United States	Urban	Rural-nonfarm	Rural-farm
All dwelling units	37,325,470	21,616,352	8,066,837	7,642,281
Occupancy				
Occupied	34,854,532	20,596,500	7,151,473	7,106,559
Vacant, for sale or rent	1,864,383	918,297	510,676	435,410
Percent of all dwelling units	5.0	4.2	6.3	5.7
Vacant, not for sale or rent	606,555	101,555	404,688	100,312
State of Repair and Plumbing Equipment				
Number reporting	35,026,442	20,063,571	7,659,437	7,303,434
Needing major repair or no private bath	17,233,101	5,735,611	4,892,086	6,605,404
Percent of reporting units	49.2	28.6	63.9	90.4
Needing major repair	6,413,727	2,298,890	1,636,491	2,478,346
Percent of reporting units	18.3	11.5	21.4	33.9
With no private bath	15,852,098	4,673,900	4,649,282	6,528,916
Percent of reporting units	45.3	23.3	60.7	89.4
Contract or Estimated Monthly Rent of Nonfarm Dwelling Units				
Reporting nonfarm dwelling units	29,129,996	21,239,794	7,890,202	....
Average monthly rent	$27.45	$30.83	$18.35	....
Occupied dwelling units	34,854,532	20,596,500	7,151,473	7,106,559
Tenure				
Owner-occupied units	15,195,763	7,714,960	3,698,076	3,782,727
Percent of all occupied units	43.6	37.5	51.7	53.2
Tenant-occupied units	19,658,769	12,881,540	3,453,397	3,323,832
Persons per Room				
Number reporting	34,447,032	20,364,883	7,064,895	7,017,254
1.51 or more persons per room	3,085,922	1,170,633	786,855	1,128,434
Percent of reporting units	9.0	5.7	11.1	16.1
Mortgage Status				
Reporting owner-occupied nonfarm dwelling units	10,611,259	7,275,576	3,335,683	....
With mortgage	4,804,778	3,682,839	1,121,939	....
Percent of reporting units	45.3	50.6	33.6	....

Volume I of the Housing reports contains three measures of the quality of housing or of its occupants. These measures are the number of dwelling units needing major repairs or lacking a private bath, the number of dwelling units with more than one and one-half persons per room, and the average contract or estimated rent of the nonfarm dwelling units in the area. These three factors may be used to measure the effective market for many household appliances, for household equipment, and also for various types of consumer goods that are used by the family as a whole. The best market for consumer durable goods is usually the areas with the lowest relative number of dwelling units containing more than one and one-half persons per room, the lowest relative number of dwelling units needing major repairs or lacking a private bath, and the highest average monthly rent of nonfarm units.

Certain of the Federal housing agencies have defined as "substandard" any dwelling unit that lacks a private bath or that needs major repairs. The definition is certainly not an exact one. Many dwelling units that are defective in either of these elements are still adequate for most living purposes, whereas a considerable number of dwelling units that are not "substandard" according to this definition are totally unsuited for occupancy. Nevertheless, various studies have demonstrated that the number of such "substandard" units in an area is closely associated with the number of unsatisfactory dwelling units in the area. According to the statistics presented in these reports one-half of the dwelling units in the United States need major repairs or lack a private bath, nine-tenths of the rural-farm units, more than five-eighths of the rural-nonfarm dwelling units, and more than one-fourth of the urban units. The number of dwelling units with more than one and one-half persons per room represents 9.0 percent of all occupied dwelling units in the United States, 5.7 percent of units in urban areas, 11.1 percent in rural-nonfarm areas, and 16.1 percent in the rural-farm areas of the United States.

The average monthly rent of urban and rural-nonfarm dwelling units in the United States was $27.45. This figure includes estimated rental value of owner-occupied and vacant dwelling units as well as the contract rent of tenant-occupied dwelling units. The average monthly rent for all urban dwelling units was $30.83 as compared with an average of $18.35 for all rural-nonfarm units. Many marketing people consider this average rental figure the best single measure of the quality of the consumer market of a small area. Of course it must be used with caution. Because of the greater protection from the weather and more complex heating equipment required in northern climates, the rentals are considerably higher in the North than in the South. Statistics relating to a few additional characteristics are available in Volume I of the Housing reports for the rural-farm portion of each minor civil division, county and state. These additional characteristics include lighting equipment, running water, and toilet facilities.

The basic housing data for 1940 have been tabulated and published by city blocks for the cities that had 50,000 inhabitants or more in 1930. There are approximately one-half million blocks in the 191 cities for which these block tabulations have been prepared. The tabulations include all the nonfarm items outlined above and in addition a distribution of dwelling units by year built. These data are published in a series of *Supplements to the First Series Housing Bulletins,* a separate supplement for each of the cities and for each of the five boroughs of New York City. To assist in analyzing and interpreting these detailed data by city blocks the Census Bureau has prepared a series of analytical maps [1] presenting in graphic form the more important of these housing characteristics. (For example, see Fig. 1.) Included in the series are maps for average rent, state of repair and plumbing equipment, year built, nonwhite households, persons per room, owner occupancy, and mortgage status.

Volume II of the 1940 Housing reports contains the most important data from the 1940 Housing Census. The statistics are presented in considerably more detail than in Volume I but are given for fewer areas. Table 2 indicates the more important additional characteristics for which data may be obtained from Volume II of the Housing reports. These data are presented for each urban place with 2,500 inhabitants or more and for each county, metropolitan district, and state. They are also available for the rural-nonfarm and rural-farm areas of each county and state and for the urban total of each state.

It is unnecessary to elaborate on the use of these data in analyzing the inventory of housing in an area. Although radical changes have taken place since April 1, 1940, in many areas of the United States the homes that were in existence at that time still represent a predominant portion of all dwelling units. Wartime conditions have caused radical changes in a few areas, but the wartime shortages of material and equipment have prevented changes in most other areas.

[1] The maps for each city of 100,000 inhabitants or more are presented in a separate bulletin of Analytical Housing Maps. Copies of the maps for the larger cities may be obtained on request from the Bureau of the Census. Maps for the smaller cities have not been published but photographic prints of them may be obtained at cost from the Bureau of the Census.

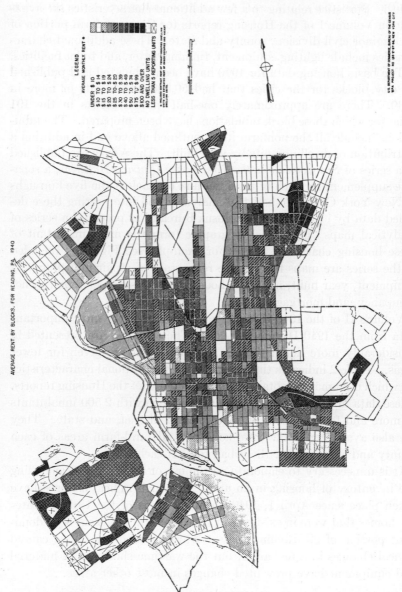

FIGURE 1.   Sample Map Showing Average Rent by Blocks.

TABLE 2. ADDITIONAL CHARACTERISTICS OF HOUSING FOR THE UNITED STATES, 1940, AS PRESENTED IN VOLUME II OF THE HOUSING REPORTS OF THE SIXTEENTH DECENNIAL CENSUS

Item	United States	Urban	Rural-Nonfarm	Rural-Farm
All dwelling units	37,325,470	21,616,352	8,066,837	7,642,281
In 1-family structures	24,908,955	10,658,732	6,852,115	7,398,108
Percent of all dwelling units	66.7	49.3	84.9	96.8
In 5-family or more structures	3,928,298	3,845,425	76,558	6,315
Percent of all dwelling units	10.5	17.8	0.9	0.1
Built 1930 to 1940	5,528,096	2,193,222	2,044,993	1,289,881
Percent of reporting units	15.9	11.1	27.0	17.6
Built 1899 or before	8,058,942	4,550,178	1,484,256	2,024,508
Percent of reporting units	23.2	23.0	19.6	27.6
Median age (years)	25.4	26.1	20.2	28.1
With running water in dwelling unit	25,796,314	19,999,176	4,457,113	1,340,025
Percent of reporting units	69.9	93.5	55.9	17.8
With private flush toilet in structure	21,966,878	17,674,398	3,429,973	842,507
Percent of reporting units	59.7	83.0	43.2	11.2
With private bathtub or shower	20,606,386	16,505,350	3,220,249	880,787
Percent of reporting units	56.2	77.5	40.8	11.8
With electric lighting	28,915,486	20,379,352	6,185,089	2,351,045
Percent of reporting units	78.7	95.8	77.8	31.3
With 1 or 2 rooms	4,522,767	2,471,295	1,134,973	916,499
Percent of reporting units	12.3	11.6	14.3	12.2
With 8 or more rooms	3,593,455	1,738,544	752,637	1,102,274
Percent of reporting units	9.8	8.1	9.5	14.6
Median number of rooms	4.73	4.78	4.61	4.70
Occupied dwelling units	34,854,532	20,596,500	7,151,473	7,106,559
Total population	131,669,275	74,423,702	27,029,385	30,216,188
Population per occupied dwelling unit	3.78	3.61	3.78	4.25
With 1 or 2 persons in household	11,307,742	7,112,558	2,446,028	1,749,156
Percent of occupied dwelling units	32.4	34.5	34.2	24.6
With 8 or more persons in household	1,713,160	734,918	327,552	650,690
Percent of occupied dwelling units	4.9	3.6	4.6	9.2
Median size of household	3.28	3.16	3.21	3.81
With mechanical refrigeration	15,093,346	11,339,901	2,718,532	1,034,913
Percent of reporting units	44.1	56.0	38.7	14.9
With radio	28,048,219	18,386,121	5,502,730	4,159,368
Percent of reporting units	82.8	91.9	79.0	60.2
With gas or electric cooking	18,613,580	15,857,109	2,304,759	451,712
Percent of reporting units	54.2	78.2	32.7	6.5
With central heating	14,346,835	11,749,595	1,893,194	704,046
Percent of reporting units	42.0	58.2	27.0	10.1
Contract or estimated rent of all reported dwelling units	35,938,118	21,239,794	7,890,202	6,808,122
Rent less than $10	9,131,929	1,727,691	2,897,568	4,343,204
Percent of reporting units	25.4	8.1	36.7	63.8
Rent $50 or more	3,577,291	2,950,103	490,473	136,715
Percent of reporting units	10.0	13.9	6.2	2.0
Average monthly rent:				
All dwelling units (incl. vacant)	$24.15	$30.83	$18.35	$10.00
Owner-occupied units	$27.47	$36.69	$20.88	$13.69
Tenant-occupied units	$21.17	$27.01	$12.36	$6.45
Average value of owner-occupied units	$3,073	$4,131	$2,408	$1,419

Included in these housing characteristics are type of structure, year built, number of rooms in the dwelling unit, whether or not the residential structure was converted from a nonresidential structure or a structure containing a different number of dwelling units, persons per room, mortgage status of owner-occupied nonfarm dwelling units, and whether or not furniture was included in the rental of the tenant-occupied nonfarm units. The significant uses of these data in fields other than housing are somewhat less obvious. These Housing reports contain the only description of families of areas smaller than states and cities of 100,000 or more. (See Chapter 12.) In addition to a measure of the number of families in each area, and the color or race of the family head, Volume II of the report on Housing presents the distribution by size of household and the relation of rooms to persons for the household.

While wage or salary income of individuals and families was obtained on the 1940 population schedule, these data were not tabulated for areas smaller than states and cities of 100,000 or more. The distribution of dwelling units by value and by monthly rental serves as a general measure of the economic level or buying power of the families in an area. As indicated above, average rental of nonfarm units is presented in *Housing*, Volume I. Volume II also shows the number of dwelling units with rental of various amounts and thus permits a study of the relative number of units with rents of $30 or more, or $50 or more, or more than any designated amount. Volume II also indicates the number of dwellings having specified types of plumbing, lighting, refrigeration, cooking facilities, heating, and radio equipment. These data indicate the number of units deficient in various items of equipment, which may therefore point to a potential market; and the data also indicate the number of dwelling units that have the equipment and that may therefore represent the replacement market for the items. Less directly the dwelling units with electric lighting or with electric refrigeration or radio may serve as an indication of the potential market for vacuum cleaners, or food mixers, or other appliances.

Some of the more important types of data are presented separately in Volume II for owner-occupied, tenant-occupied, and vacant units, for the cities of 50,000 inhabitants or more, the metropolitan districts, and the states. A few selected items are presented separately for dwelling units occupied by white and nonwhite households. Thus Volume II of the Housing reports presents a relatively complete description of the housing in the United States as a whole and in the counties, urban places, and other major areas throughout the United States.

It is well known that the quality and equipment of homes vary in general with the monthly rental or rental value of the homes. The extent to which the different elements vary with rental is not so well known but this is revealed by the statistics presented in Volume III of the reports on Housing for 1940. Certain of the more significant summary figures for the nonfarm dwelling units of the United States are presented in Table 3. Similar data are presented for nonfarm dwelling units of each state, each city with 50,000 inhabitants or more, and each of the 85 principal metropolitan districts. Similar data are presented by value groups for owner-occupied rural-farm units of each state and by estimated rent groups for the tenant-occupied rural-farm units of states. An analysis of these data will indicate the type of equipment that may be found in the dwelling units of an area. Such data should be invaluable in indicating rental groups at which an effective market for various types of commodities exists.

A special series of census reports for 1940 presents statistics on the characteristics of families and on the relationship of the families to the houses that they occupy. These reports are described in the section on Families in Chapter 12. Special mention in connection with housing statistics is required for three of the reports. The report on the general characteristics of families [2] presents data on the characteristics of owner and tenant families in urban and rural areas of states, regions, and the United States and in cities of 100,000 or more and metropolitan districts of 200,000 or more.

The contract or estimated monthly rent of owner and tenant families is presented in relation to various family characteristics in another report in this series.[3] It will be found that different types of families predominate at the different rent levels and that rental varies with type of family. Such relationships will aid in determining markets for various products.

The relationship of rent to family income is not the same for small families as for large ones. It is not the same for families in small dwelling units as for those in large ones. The relationship to estimated rental value of owner-occupied units is not the same as relationship to contract rent of tenant-occupied units. The relation of various family and housing characteristics to the rent-income relationship is revealed in the report on income and rent.[4] The extensive tables of this report

[2] *Sixteenth Census of the United States, 1940, Population and Housing, Families: General Characteristics.* Government Printing Office, 1943.

[3] *Sixteenth Census of the United States, 1940, Population and Housing, Families: Tenure and Rent,* Government Printing Office, 1943.

[4] *Sixteenth Census of the United States, 1940, Population and Housing, Families: Income and Rent,* Government Printing Office, 1943.

TABLE 3. CHARACTERISTICS OF URBAN AND RURAL-NONFARM HOUSING BY CONTRACT OR ESTIMATED MONTHLY RENT IN THE UNITED STATES, 1940, AS PRESENTED IN VOLUME III OF THE HOUSING REPORTS OF THE SIXTEENTH DECENNIAL CENSUS

Item	Total Units	Under $10	$10 to $19	$20 to $29	$30 to $39	$40 to $49	$50 to $74	$75 to $99	$100 and Over
All dwelling units	29,683,189	4,625,259	7,074,917	6,630,995	4,686,646	2,671,603	2,345,381	553,949	541,246
In 1-family structures	17,510,847	3,429,588	4,107,099	3,567,246	2,436,212	1,415,526	1,442,382	380,663	400,936
Percent of all dwelling units	59.0	11.6	13.8	12.0	8.2	4.8	4.9	1.3	1.4
Median age (years)	24.6	26.0	32.2	28.7	21.5	17.1	15.0	14.3	14.7
Median number of rooms	4.4	3.1	4.2	4.9	5.1	5.3	5.8	6.5	7.8
Needing major repair or no private bath	5,069,394	1,782,600	1,911,511	799,933	269,343	99,838	75,291	17,270	17,884
Percent of reporting units	18.3	40.7	28.7	12.9	6.2	4.0	3.5	3.4	3.6
Needing major repairs	3,935,381	1,613,549	1,269,530	582,982	219,700	83,967	61,705	12,168	11,842
Percent of reporting units	14.2	36.8	19.3	9.4	5.0	3.4	2.8	2.4	2.4
No private bath	1,463,829	238,686	842,748	260,982	55,907	17,589	15,061	5,417	6,834
Percent of reporting units	5.3	5.4	12.6	4.2	1.3	0.7	1.1	1.1	1.4
Occupied dwelling units	27,747,973	4,364,946	6,625,831	6,247,149	4,445,257	2,518,652	2,170,318	492,543	442,502
Median size of household	3.18	3.00	3.12	3.21	3.18	3.21	3.32	3.47	3.77
With 1.51 or more persons per room	1,957,488	958,306	567,629	236,884	94,991	38,187	23,855	2,962	1,422
Percent of reporting units	7.1	22.2	8.7	3.8	2.2	1.5	1.1	0.6	0.3
With mechanical refrigeration	14,058,433	433,918	1,997,578	3,279,136	3,224,119	2,126,490	1,936,977	452,962	410,938
Percent of reporting units	51.6	10.2	30.6	53.2	73.5	85.7	90.6	93.4	94.6
With radio	23,888,851	2,281,312	5,704,891	5,883,857	4,265,299	2,429,468	2,094,021	475,511	426,618
Percent of reporting units	88.5	54.0	88.4	96.6	98.3	98.8	96.9	99.1	99.2
With central heating	13,642,789	143,289	1,414,104	3,404,859	3,501,519	2,192,396	1,935,718	448,555	405,012
Percent of reporting units	50.2	3.4	21.7	55.4	80.0	88.6	90.8	92.8	93.5
Median value of owner-occupied units	$2,938	$582	$1,289	$2,577	$3,642	$4,726	$6,225	$9,142	$14,846
Mortgaged owner-occupied units	4,804,778	243,251	697,313	1,029,221	972,854	689,547	745,214	191,388	158,207
Percent of reporting owner-occupied units	45.3	18.2	35.0	45.2	52.8	58.8	61.0	61.0	51.7

relate rent, family income, and tenure to various family characteristics and to the number of rooms and major repair and plumbing equipment of the dwelling unit. Data are shown separately for the urban and rural-nonfarm areas of the four major regions and the United States, and for the eleven metropolitan districts of 1,000,000 or more.

Further data for rural-farm families on relation of the characteristics of families to the characteristics of the dwelling units that they occupy are presented in the report on characteristics of rural-farm families.[5] Data are presented separately for the rural-farm owner and tenant families of which the heads are farmers and farm managers, farm laborers and farm foremen, employed persons at nonfarm occupations, persons seeking work or on emergency work, and families with heads not in the labor force. Some of these are presented by rent or value groups of the home, and data are shown separately for the four major regions and for the nine divisions of the United States. In addition, the employment and farm occupation status of the family head are related to characteristics of the dwelling unit, including number of rooms, water supply, toilet facilities, state of repair and plumbing equipment, lighting equipment, and persons per room.

Housing data obtained in the 1940 census were much more comprehensive than from any previous census of the United States. Nevertheless certain housing items have been included in previous decennial censuses. The number of "occupied dwelling units" in 1940 is roughly comparable with the number of "private families" shown in the 1930 census report on Families.[6] The number of families on a slightly broader basis but still reasonably comparable has been presented for each census since 1850. The classification of homes by tenure has been shown for each decennial census since 1890. The number of owned homes that were encumbered was included in the censuses from 1890 to 1920. The value or monthly rent of nonfarm homes and the number of families having a radio were included in the 1930 report on Families.

The reports of the Census of Agriculture for 1920 and 1930 indicate the number of farm operator's dwellings that were lighted by electricity, the number with water piped into the dwelling, and (for 1930 only) the number with water piped into a bathroom. These statistics are only roughly comparable with statistics for corresponding items as presented for rural-farm dwelling units in 1940 because the data from the Census of Agriculture represents the homes of farm operators only,

[5] *Sixteenth Census of the United States, 1940, Population and Housing, Families: Characteristics of Rural-Farm Families.* Government Printing Office, 1943.

[6] *Fifteenth Census of the United States 1930, Population, Volume VI, Families,* Government Printing Office, 1933.

whereas the 1940 figures include all dwelling units on farms. On the other hand, the statistics obtained in the Census of Agriculture include urban-farm dwelling units, whereas the 1940 farm data are limited to rural-farm units.

The most comprehensive housing inventory data other than those included in the decennial census reports are those obtained in the Real Property Inventories that were conducted as work projects during the period 1934 to 1939. The first of these inventories was conducted early in 1934 as a Civil Works Administration project sponsored by the Bureau of Foreign and Domestic Commerce. This project covered 64 cities throughout the 48 states. Data obtained in these inventories were in general similar to those obtained in the Housing Census and these data will be found useful in comparison with the 1940 Housing Census data.

After the inventory of the 64 cities was completed, many other cities clamored for similar surveys of their local housing conditions. Suitable techniques were developed and local communities were encouraged to sponsor Real Property Inventories as local Work Projects Administration projects. Such locally sponsored surveys were conducted in more than 150 communities during the period 1934–1939. Because of the local sponsorship, the results of these surveys vary widely in quality, coverage, and extensiveness of results that were published. A brief summary of results of the 203 surveys conducted through 1936 was prepared by Peyton Stapp, Works Progress Administration, and is presented in *Urban Housing, A Summary of Real Property Inventories Conducted as Work Projects, 1934–1936* (available from the Government Printing Office, Washington, 1938). The most complete file of results of all these inventories is that maintained by the Division of Research and Statistics of the Federal Housing Administration, Washington, D. C. Farm housing data also were obtained in the Farm Housing Survey that was conducted in January 1934.[7] This survey covered nearly 600,000 farmhouses in 308 counties of 46 states. The counties were selected as representative agricultural areas of the United States. The results are presented for each county and for states, with regional totals of the data for the selected counties. Subjects covered by the survey include color of head, number of occupants, tenure, age of house, material of house, number of stories; number of rooms,

---

[7] The survey was a project of the Civil Works Administration, directed by the Bureau of Home Economics, with the advice and cooperation of other bureaus and personnel of the U. S. Department of Agriculture. The results are presented in the Department of Agriculture Miscellaneous Publication 323, *The Farm-Housing Survey*, Government Printing Office, Washington, 1939.

bedrooms, and clothes closets; type of plumbing, lighting, heating, refrigeration, and cooking equipment, and presence of power washing machine; condition (reported as good, fair, or poor) of foundations, roofs, chimneys, doors and windows, screens, exterior and interior walls, ceilings, floors, and stairs. Information obtained in the survey also indicated that 22 percent of householders were interested in borrowing an average of $464 for home improvements.

Mortgage Finance. Two-fifths of the nonfarm dwelling units of the United States are occupied by the owners of the units, and 45 percent of the owner-occupied units are owned subject to a mortgage. Even more than 45 percent of the owner-occupied homes were purchased with the financial assistance of a mortgage loan. It is necessary to know the nature and character of this mortgage debt in order to understand conditions of home tenure in this country. The most extensive series of data on home mortgage finance are those presented in Volume IV of the reports of the 1940 Housing Census. Data presented in these reports are limited to owner-occupied nonfarm one- to four-family properties. The mortgage data presented in the Housing Census do not include properties that are entirely tenant occupied nor multifamily properties containing five or more dwelling units. These data relate to value of the mortgage properties, amount of outstanding indebtedness, type of holder of first mortgage and the interest rate, and type and frequency of required payments on the first mortgage. The most extensive data are presented for the United States, regions, states, cities of 100,000 inhabitants or more, and the principal metropolitan districts. Limited data also are presented for counties and smaller urban places.[8] The mortgage characteristics of owner-occupied nonfarm homes was the subject of inquiries in the censuses of 1890[9] and 1920,[10] and the data obtained in those inquiries are useful as bases of comparison for the 1940 data. Some information relating to the finances of farms may be found in the reports of the Census of Agriculture. These farm mortgage data refer to the farm as a whole and include the farmhouse. A sample survey of home mortgage characteristics was conducted under the direction of the Bureau of Foreign and Domestic Commerce in 1934. While the results of this survey are limited to the 52 cities in which field canvasses were completed,

[8] *Sixteenth Census of the United States, Housing, Volume IV, Mortgages on Owner-Occupied Nonfarm Homes,* Government Printing Office, Washington, 1943.

[9] *Eleventh Census of the United States, Volume XXI, Report on Farms and Homes: Proprietorship and Indebtedness in the United States: 1890,* Government Printing Office, Washington, 1896.

[10] *Fourteenth Census of the United States, Mortgages on Homes in the United States: 1920* (census monograph), Government Printing Office, Washington, 1923.

the survey includes tenant-occupied as well as owner-occupied properties.[11]

The Construction Industry and the Manufacture and Distribution of Building Material and Home Equipment. Additional knowledge of the housing situation can be obtained from the statistics of the construction industry which assembles houses and other buildings at their site and from the statistics of the industries that manufacture and distribute the building materials and home equipment that are used in houses. Statistics on these subjects may be obtained from the results of the various censuses that have been conducted by the Bureau of the Census. The most recent census of construction was conducted in 1940.[12] There are, unfortunately, several limitations in these data that arise because of the nature of the home building and construction industry. Construction work done by public agencies, establishments, or persons with their own forces on structures for their own use or occupancy is not included in the census. The reports from all concerns reporting less than a $500 volume of work performed during the year also were omitted.

Residential building is an activity, not a type of business concern. A construction establishment may work on residential building, nonresidential building, and on projects other than buildings. It may engage in the construction of new buildings and in repairs and alterations to existing buildings. A building contractor may operate outside the city in which his home office is located and even outside his home state. All of these factors limit the usefulness of the results of the 1939 Census of Construction in measuring the extent and type of residential building activities in relation to the contractors that do the building and the location of the establishment.

The census does present an extensive series of data on the number of establishments, value of work performed, number of employees, total payroll, and value of materials used and equipment installed for each of the various kinds of contractors, such as builders, general contractors and various types of special trade contractors, including heating and plumbing, tile and masonry contractors. Certain of the data are classified by value of work performed, location of work (as in home city, in home state, or outside home state), type of construction (as new buildings and additions to existing buildings, repairs and alterations to existing buildings, and work other than on buildings), and

---

[11] *Financial Survey of Urban Housing,* Government Printing Office, Washington, 1937. Detailed data are presented in this report for 22 of the cities.

[12] See *Sixteenth Census of the United States, Business, Volume IV, Construction: 1939,* Government Printing Office, Washington, 1943.

legal form of organization (as corporate, noncorporate). The number of paid employees on the payroll each month during 1939 also is presented. Data are shown for geographic divisions, states, and cities of 100,000 or more. Similar censuses of the construction industry were conducted in 1929 and 1934 [13] but the coverage was less complete than in 1939.

The Census of Manufactures of 1939 covers all manufacturing industries in the United States.[14] For most manufacturing concerns the reported information includes the number of wage earners, wages, cost of materials and supplies, kind, quantity, and value of products, and value added by manufacture. All of the component parts of houses that are produced in manufacturing establishments are included in this census. Unfortunately, a house is a composite of the products of a broad list of different types of manufacturing plants. There is no "house-producing" industry that starts with trees, clay pits, and iron ore mines and produces a complete house or even all of the constituent parts of a house. In 1939 the lumber and timber industry produced 25 billion board feet of lumber, 135 million doors, 35 million window sashes, and a billion square feet of plywood. Most of these lumber products were used in the construction industry.

Diligent search is required to find all of the other industries that produce the constitutent parts of houses. The paint, varnish, and lacquer industry is part of the "chemicals and allied products" group. Asphalt shingles and roll roofing are found among the "products of petroleum and coal" group. Window glass, brick, hollow tile, wall tile, vitreous china plumbing fixtures, porcelain electrical supplies, cement, mineral wool, wallboard, and plaster are in the "stone, clay, and glass products" group. Plumbing and heating equipment, including oil burners and supplies, and structural iron are included in the "iron and steel and their products" group. "Nonferrous metals and their products" group includes lighting fixtures; and mechanical stokers are in the "machinery" group.

The quantity and value of principal items are shown by states in the reports of the Census of Manufactures. A Census of Manufactures was conducted in alternate years from 1929 to 1939, but no census has been conducted since 1939; a Census of Manufactures for 1946 is now being planned.

[13] *Fifteenth Census of the United States: 1930, Construction Industry*, Government Printing Office, Washington, 1933; and *U. S. Census of Business: 1935, Construction Industry*, Government Printing Office, Washington, 1937.

[14] *Sixteenth Census of the United States: 1940, Manufactures, 1939, Volumes I to III*, Government Printing Office, Washington, 1942. See also Chapter 3.

These Census of Manufactures' statistics are the best indication of the quantity of various types of material that are utilized in producing and maintaining the houses of the United States. Such data serve as a guide to the size of the market for any new product that will be used in producing houses.

Most of the various parts of new houses and the replacement parts needed for existing houses pass through the normal channels of distribution in moving from the manufacturing industry to the construction industry which assembles these parts into complete houses and uses them in maintaining existing houses. The lumber and building group of retail outlets is primarily concerned with the distribution of building materials. In 1939 the retail sales of the 40,000 stores in this group totaled one and three-quarter billion dollars. (See also Chapter 6.) This group comprises lumber yards, building material dealers, heating and plumbing equipment dealers, paint, glass and wallpaper stores, and electrical supplies stores. A substantial portion of the products distributed by hardware stores is also utilized in the construction industry.

The retail trade reports of the Census of Business of 1939 show the number of retail stores and total sales of the stores in the lumber and building group and the number and sales of hardware stores in each incorporated place with 2,500 inhabitants or more and in each county of the United States.[15] Further detail with regard to type of store, number of employees, and total payroll are shown for cities with more than 10,000 inhabitants, for states, regions, and the United States total.

Data regarding wholesale establishments by type of operation and kind of business are available in the reports on wholesale trade of the Census of Business of 1939.[16] The number of establishments, sales, operating expenses, number of employees, payroll, and inventory are shown for wholesalers of plumbing and heating equipment and supplies, lumber and construction materials, and electrical wiring supplies, in the United States, states, and larger cities. Somewhat less complete data are shown for the remaining cities with 50,000 inhabitants or more.

CURRENT DATA

Various series of benchmark data in the field of housing and construction are described above. These data present a comprehensive picture of the type, condition, and location of housing in the United States and of the characteristics of the construction and related in-

[15] *Sixteenth Census of the United States, Business, Retail Trade: 1939 Volume I* (part 3), Government Printing Office, Washington, 1941.

[16] *Sixteenth Census of the United States, Business, Wholesale Trade: 1939 Volume II*, Government Printing Office, Washington, 1942.

dustries. Because of the cost of assembling the complete data the materials are obtained only at infrequent intervals; because of the extensiveness of the data a considerable period of time must elapse between collection and publication of the data. Practically all of the benchmark data outlined above relate to 1940 or earlier. Changes have occurred since 1940 and we cannot hope to obtain equally complete statistics at any time in the immediate future. Therefore, we must rely on less comprehensive but more current data to reveal trends since the date of the benchmark information. Furthermore, a knowledge of the trend as revealed by the series of monthly data is useful in determining required action in any situation.

Many of the current series discussed below are presented in the *Survey of Current Business*.[17] Each issue contains data for 14 months; special supplements contain monthly data for four years, monthly averages for longer periods, and also descriptions of the source and composition of each series.

Construction Activity. The most extensive and most widely used measure of the extent of construction activity is a by-product of the enforcement of local building regulations. Practically every city and village has a building ordinance which contains restrictions regarding building in the area. Ordinarily, the restrictions prohibit the building of apartment and commercial buildings in certain portions of the community; they specify minimum construction standards to safeguard the health and welfare of the occupants of the buildings. In order to enforce these restrictions the owner is required to obtain a permit from the building inspector before construction of a new building is started so that the inspector may review the plans and inspect the building during construction. Records of the type and value of new buildings and additions and alterations for which these permits are issued are assembled for each month by the Bureau of Labor Statistics. Data may be obtained on the number of projects and estimated cost of residential and nonresidential buildings for which permits are issued, also on the number of dwelling units in new one-family, two-family, and three-family or larger residential structures. These data are assembled for practically every urban place, and estimates have been made for the nonfarm total of each state and for the United States. Data on building activity in rural-farm areas cannot be obtained from building permit records since very few rural-farm areas have building ordinances. Therefore the records based on these permit data are limited to the nonfarm areas.

[17] Published monthly by the Bureau of Foreign and Domestic Commerce, U. S Department of Commerce.

Because a building permit must be obtained before any work may be started on a new building, the fluctuation in building permit volume precedes the fluctuation in construction employment and building activity and also precedes the time at which new or additional dwelling units become available for occupancy. A limited number of building permits are allowed to lapse because of change in the plans of the owner. On a few occasions in the past, the building permit records for certain cities have been seriously distorted by changes in the building ordinances and the resulting rush of owners to secure permits considerably in advance of intended use. Fortunately, disturbances of this type are extremely rare. Various releases, bulletins, and reports are issued by the Bureau of Labor Statistics; many of them may be obtained on request.[18]

Another source of data on construction activity is the records of the volume and type of construction contracts awarded, which are assembled by several local and nation-wide private organizations.[19] Many of the less expensive residential buildings are omitted from these compilations. The series are particularly useful, however, as measures of the type and value of nonresidential buildings and of nonbuilding construction.

The Bureau of Labor Statistics compiles monthly reports on employment, average weekly earnings, average weekly hours of work, and average hourly earnings for many of the manufacturing industries related to building and construction for which production data may be obtained from the Census of Manufactures. The principal manufacturing industry group related to construction is the "lumber and timber basic products" group. Employment and payroll data also are presented for the construction industry as a whole and for construction activities on privately and publicly financed projects. Similar monthly employment and payroll data are presented for establishments engaged in retail trade in the lumber and building materials group.[20]

[18] Because of the varied nature of individual requirements it is suggested that persons interested in these building permit data write to the Division of Construction and Public Employment, Bureau of Labor Statistics, U. S. Department of Labor, Washington 25, D. C., stating the type of data wanted, the area, and the period of months or years for which the series is needed.

[19] The principal ones are the F. W. Dodge Corporation and the *Engineering News-Record*, both of New York City.

[20] Most of these employment and payroll data are presented in the *Monthly Labor Review*, Bureau of Labor Statistics, U. S. Department of Labor, Government Printing Office, Washington. Somewhat greater detail is shown in the monthly pamphlet *Employment and Payroll*, which contains more current data than the *Review* and may be obtained on request from the Bureau of Labor Statistics.

A monthly series on employment by states in the construction and maintenance of Federal and state highways is compiled by the Public Roads Administration. This Administration also compiles monthly data on average hourly wage rates paid to common laborers engaged in road building. The rates are published separately for each of the nine regions and the United States as a whole.

Current Data on Manufacture and Distribution of Building Materials. Data relating to production in various manufacturing industries are compiled by the Industry Division of the Bureau of the Census.[21] Most of these data are on a monthly basis. Some of the information relates to shipments and stocks in addition to production. The principal building materials that are included in these production series are lumber; softwood plywood; hardwood plywood; red cedar shingles; warm-air furnaces and winter air conditioning units; oil burners; mechanical stokers; blowers, fans, and unit heaters; domestic pumps, water systems, and windmills; porcelain enameled products; paint; brick; hollow tile; structural clay products; wallboard; asphalt and tar roofing and siding products; power material handling equipment including graders, cranes, shovels, and concrete mixers.

Production of portland cement and various gypsum products is covered by statistics compiled by the Bureau of Mines of the Department of the Interior. Gypsum products for which data are shown separately include base coat plaster, Keene's cement, lath, and tile.

Sales by retail establishments of various types are compiled on a monthly basis by the Department of Commerce. (See Chapter 6.) The data are published for various types of retail establishments, and separate figures are shown for building material dealers and hardware dealers.

Prices, Cost, and Rent. Several series of price data relating to housing and the construction industry are now available. A weekly series and a monthly series of wholesale prices are compiled by the Bureau of Labor Statistics. One of the components of the over-all price index is the building material group.[22] Only the total for this group is shown in the weekly series, but data also are shown separately for seven subgroups in the monthly series. In addition, plumbing and heating materials are presented as one of the subgroups of the metals and metal products group. A special monthly release presents average wholesale

---

[21] See Chapter 3. The data relating to the various products are presented in separate series of current releases which may be obtained on request from the Bureau of the Census, Washington 25, D. C.

[22] The series are published in releases by the Bureau of Labor Statistics and in the *Monthly Labor Review.* See also Chapter 11.

prices in dollars and cents and an index of prices of individual commodities including 120 different commodities in the building material group and the plumbing and heating subgroup. The general fluctuations in wholesale prices of building materials are reflected by this series. The data are subject to the usual criticism of orthodox price indexes, since they do not reflect the increased costs resulting from the necessary substitution of inferior but higher priced materials; neither do they reflect the decline in costs resulting from the introduction of new and improved materials.

An index of the cost of construction of a new six-room house is compiled for 75 cities by the Federal Home Loan Bank Administration.[23] The index is intended to reflect changes in labor as well as material costs of the houses. It is probable, however, that some portions of these changes are not fully represented. Especially during the period of wartime price ceilings, it was difficult to obtain from retailers reports which indicated that higher prices were being obtained through changes in selling practices, even though these changes were not strictly illegal. As in the case of wholesale prices, it is difficult to measure changes in price resulting from improvement in materials or from the substitution of inferior materials without a corresponding reduction in price. The cost of labor on the site is an important component of the cost. It is difficult to reflect in this component the changes in cost resulting from changes in the relative importance of the nonunion groups with their lower hourly rates or the changes resulting from increased or decreased efficiency of the available labor supply. The index of cost is available quarterly for each of the 75 cities. The 75 cities have been separated into three groups of approximately 25 cities each, and the index relates to a different month in the quarter for the cities in each of the three groups. Monthly series of cost indexes of materials and labor for the United States have been developed by averaging these quarterly data for the various cities.

The Bureau of Labor Statistics is developing a monthly index of material prices paid by contractors. The new index will be presented in the *Monthly Labor Review* when it is available and may be the subject of special monthly releases.[24]

Rent is one of the major elements in the index of cost of living that is published by the Bureau of Labor Statistics. The rent index is available by quarters for each of the 34 larger cities that are included

[23] Published in the monthly publication *Federal Home Loan Bank Review*, Government Printing Office, Washington.

[24] Further information may be obtained from the Division of Construction and Public Employment of the Bureau of Labor Statistics.

in the consumers' price index and for the total of these cities. Because of rent restrictions in war centers, the index of rent does not reflect changes in demand for rental residential property in these areas. When these restrictions are removed rentals are expected once more to fluctuate with the changes in demand and will serve as an indicator of the probable profitability of any contemplated new rental project.

Current data on housing and construction are of greatly increased value if they can be obtained for individual cities or urban centers. The national series does not indicate the local situation. To meet this need for local data, the Bureau of Labor Statistics is planning to present several price and employment series for each of 50 local areas. Monthly data on employment and payroll in the construction industry, on wholesale prices of building materials, and on material prices paid by contractors will be given for each of the areas.

Home Mortgage Finance. Practically every loan secured by real estate is covered by a mortgage and almost every mortgage is recorded with the local recorder of deeds and mortgages. Changes in activity in real estate and changes in financing activity are reflected in the totals of mortgage recordings. The Federal Home Loan Bank Administration has compiled a monthly series on the estimated number and amount of nonfarm home mortgages recorded in each state and in the United States. The basic mortgage records cover farms, nonfarm homes, and nonresidential properties. The local cooperating institution is able to eliminate farms from the series by examination of size, location, and description of the property. Nonresidential properties are eliminated by excluding all mortgages with an amount of $20,000 or more. The $20,000 limit was chosen on an arbitrary basis. It excludes a few larger residential properties, especially apartment buildings, and it includes smaller nonresidential properties. Detailed inspection of the data indicates, however, that most nonfarm mortgages of less than $20,000 are residential, most larger mortgages are nonresidential, and the total of mortgages less than $20,000 is an excellent approximation of residential mortgages. These mortgage data are presented separately by states for each of the leading types of mortgage lenders—savings and loan associations, insurance companies, bank and trust companies, mutual savings banks, individuals, and other mortgagees.

It should be noted that recorded mortgages include not only purchase mortgages used to finance acquisition of houses, but also the full amount of any refinancing mortgages resulting from minor or major changes in the amount or term of the mortgage, refinancing by a different mortgage lender, with or without change in amount or term of the mortgage, and change in mortgage borrower because of change in ownership resulting from death of the owner or from voluntary sale of the property. Thus the one and one-quarter billion dollars in nonfarm residential mortgages recorded in 1943 does not indicate that mortgage debt has been increased by a like amount.

A monthly series of data on new home mortgage loans made by all savings and loan associations is also compiled by the Federal Home Loan Bank Administration.[25] This series is based on reports from cooperating savings and loan associations whose assets represent about three-fourths of the assets of all associations. Savings and loan associations account for approximately one-third of all mortgage loans. In contrast to the mortgages-recorded series discussed above, this series for savings and loan associations represents new loans only. In mortgage refinancing, the series includes only the increase over the previous mortgage. The new home-mortgage loans are summarized separately by purpose of loan as: construction, home purchase, refinancing, reconditioning, and other. They are also summarized by class of savings and loan association as: Federal, state member, and state nonmember, and by Federal Home Loan Bank district.

Nonfarm Real Estate Foreclosures. When a home owner is unable to meet the terms of the mortgage on his home, the mortgage lender may resort to legal means to recover his money by forcing the sale of the property at a foreclosure sale. The fluctuation in the number of foreclosure sales gives an indication of the condition of the real estate market. The number of nonfarm foreclosures in 1943 was only slightly more than one-tenth as great as the number at the bottom of the depression in 1934. A monthly series on number of nonfarm mortgage foreclosures is compiled and published by the Federal Home Loan Bank Administration.[26]

Occupancy and Vacancy Surveys. During the period of the war severe restrictions were imposed on the total number of dwelling units to be built because of the critical materials needed for each unit. The National Housing Agency was assigned the task of determining the areas to which this limited number of houses should be allocated. In order to perform this Federal "programming" of housing, the National Housing Agency required additional data on the housing need of the various war centers. It called on the Special Surveys Division of the

[25] The series is published currently in the *Federal Home Loan Bank Review*. A summary for the period 1939 to 1943 is presented in the March 1944 *Statistical Supplement to the Review.*

[26] *Federal Home Loan Bank Review* and *Statistical Supplement to the Review* for March 1944.

Bureau of the Census to conduct local dwelling unit vacancy surveys on a sample basis in several areas. There was no regular program of areas or frequency with which these surveys were conducted. In 1943 the Bureau of the Census made 142 surveys in 123 areas; some areas were surveyed more than once during the year. Results of the surveys are published in a series of reports.[27] Additional surveys of the same nature were made also by the Bureau of Labor Statistics. The information obtained in the typical survey indicates whether or not each dwelling unit was occupied or unoccupied and for unoccupied dwelling units whether the dwelling unit was habitable; whether it was for rent, for sale but not for rent, or neither for rent nor for sale; whether it was equipped with all the "standard" facilities, i.e., installed heating, gas or electric lights, running water, flush toilet and bathing unit; the number of rooms in the dwelling unit; and the monthly rental asked for the unit if it was for rent. For occupied dwelling units information was obtained on the number of rooms that were available for rent to roomers (if any) and the number of roomers these rooms were expected to accommodate. All types of residential structures except public housing developments were covered by the surveys. When significant, data were secured and tabulated separately for white and nonwhite dwelling units. The results of these surveys give an excellent picture of the local vacancy situation.

In some of the surveys (50 surveys in 49 areas in 1943) the information obtained from occupied dwelling units was expanded to include total number of rooms, total number of persons, and the number of subfamilies in the dwelling unit. A subfamily consists of a married couple, with or without children, in addition to the head of the household. The data were tabulated to show relationship between number of persons and number of rooms in the various units; and the number of units that were overcrowded (having more than one and one-half persons per room); the number that were occupied to capacity (having from three-fourths to one and one-half persons per room); and the number that were not occupied to capacity (having less than three-fourths persons per room). This supplementary information threw light on the unused capacity in existing homes in the area. It would be desirable if these vacancy and occupancy surveys were continued on a regular basis in the various urban centers, but at the time of this writing, no plans have been formulated for such a continuing program.

[27] A list of the areas surveyed and copies of reports for specific areas may be obtained from Special Surveys Division, Bureau of the Census, Washington 25 D. C.

Surveys of Housing Requirements of War Workers. The Bureau of Labor Statistics has conducted surveys of housing requirements of war workers in 15 of the centers of war production throughout the United States. Data were obtained by interviewing a selected sample of the employees in war industries and in other establishments. The results of each survey show whether the worker is a member of a family group or is an unattached person, his eligibility for war housing under the regulations of the National Housing Agency, whether he wishes to bring dependents into the area, type of living quarters now occupied and the degree of satisfaction with present housing accommodations, and the interrelationship of these elements. These results indicated the need and demand for additional war housing in each of the following areas:[28] Akron, Baltimore, Chester (Pa.), Denver, Harrisburg (Pa.), Lancaster (Pa.), Macon, Memphis, Milwaukee, Mobile, New Orleans, Omaha, San Antonio, San Diego, and Tampa. Although these reports relate primarily to the specific problem of war housing, they also throw some light on the postwar housing needs of the area.

Nongovernmental Sources of Current Data. A considerable volume of statistics are compiled and published by trade associations, publishers of magazines, and other nongovernmental concerns and organizations. Such data are quite extensive in the field of construction cost. Among the more widely known of these data are the cost indexes relating to general building construction that are prepared monthly for the United States as a whole by the American Appraisal Company, the Associated General Contractors of America, and the *Engineering News-Record.* The American Appraisal Company also publishes separate indexes for the 30 cities included in their United States total. The Aberthaw Construction Company prepares a monthly index of the cost of industrial building in the United States. E. H. Boeckh and Associates publish monthly indexes of construction costs in each of 20 areas throughout the United States. Data are shown separately for several types of commercial and residential buildings. All of these indexes include the cost of both material and labor.

Statistical data relating to construction and real estate also are available as follows:

1. A statement of assets of the leading life insurance companies is published each month by the Association of Life Insurance Presidents. The statement shows separately the outstanding amount on mortgage loans on farms and on other real estate, and the amount of real estate owned by the companies.

[28] A copy of the report for any area may be obtained on request from the Bureau of Labor Statistics.

2. Dun and Bradstreet compiles and publishes a monthly series on the number of commercial failures and total liabilities of such failures. Concerns in the construction industry are shown separately.

3. The Car Service Division of the Association of American Railroads compiles a weekly series of freight carloadings. The loadings of forest products (primarily lumber) are shown as a separate group.

4. Stevenson, Jordan, and Harrison publish monthly figures on production of window glass which they compile for the window glass manufacturers.

Local Sources. Sources of current data outlined above relate primarily to the Federal agencies and publications of Federal agencies. Local sources of data must not be overlooked in any study or use of housing and construction data. Quite often significant series of data are available for a city or county even though corresponding data are not available on a nation-wide basis. The Cleveland Health Council, under Howard Whipple Green, has compiled and published many reports containing significant data for the Cleveland area in total, and by cities, census tracts, and blocks within the area. The Bureau of Labor Statistics does an excellent job of collecting building permit data from the local building inspectors and compiling and publishing the results. But they must wait until the last of the laggards has completed and mailed his report before they can complete their summaries. Furthermore, because of space limitations in the reports the published summaries do not contain as complete detail for a city as can be obtained from the local source of the data.

Both primary and secondary local sources of data should be considered. Secondary sources that compile the data for publication or for their own use include the local Chamber of Commerce, real estate board, housing authority, and the local offices of such Federal agencies as the National Housing Agency or its constituent agencies, including the Federal Housing Administration, the Federal Public Housing Authority, and the Federal Home Loan Bank Administration. In many cities a special daily periodical (often called the Daily Court Reporter) contains statistical data in addition to information concerning number and characteristics of building permits issued, real estate deeds recorded, mortgages recorded, foreclosure actions instituted, and sheriffs' sales of real estate.

The primary local sources of data include the building inspector, the county recorder or other official who has custody over the recording of deeds and mortgages, and the sheriff or other official who is in charge of public sales of real estate. It is often possible to obtain from the local offices the statistics on local operations of the Federal agencies in the field of housing. The local housing authority usually retains excellent records of operations of the local public housing projects. Of course, all price, rent, and employment series are based on reports from local concerns, but it is seldom feasible to duplicate the coverage of these services. The Federal agencies are most useful as the source of such data and of figures that facilitate comparison of activity in one area with that in other areas and in the United States.

CURRENT SERIES BASED ON OPERATIONS OF FEDERAL AGENCIES

The Federal Government has broad interests in the field of housing, home mortgage finance, and construction. Most of the Federal agencies retain excellent current records, and trends in housing and mortgage finance may be determined by an examination of the published summaries of these records.

The activity of a Federal agency is related to the statutes and regulations under which it operates. Any change in these regulations may cause a sudden change in the activity of the agency which is not representative of the activity of the market as a whole. As an example, the required down payment on the purchase of a new home under the Federal Housing Administration plan was reduced from 20 percent to 10 percent in 1939. Federal Housing Administration activity increased tremendously. Part of this increase represented the production of houses which would not otherwise have been built but also a part represented houses that would have been built but would not have been financed under the Federal Housing Administration plan. Thus, a sudden change in a series of data based on activity of a Federal agency must be reviewed carefully before it is accepted as indicative of a similar change in the industry as a whole. The more significant series of data of the various Federal agencies are outlined below.

Federal Housing Administration. The Federal Housing Administration insures mortgages on houses. The terms of such mortgages are extremely favorable, especially on new owner-occupied homes. Therefore, a major portion of such houses are financed under this plan. Statistics of Federal Housing Administration operations are available [29] on a monthly basis showing separately the number of properties, the number of dwelling units, and amount of mortgage loan for modernization, for purchase, or for construction of nonfarm residential structures. Data are shown separately for loans on new houses and on existing houses. Separate series show applications for mortgage insurance, the

[29] *Insured Mortgage Portfolio*, published by Federal Housing Administration, Washington, D. C. Additional data may be obtained from the Division of Economics and Statistics, of the Federal Housing Administration.

applications on which commitments to insure have been issued, the new houses on which construction has started, and those on which construction has been completed and the mortgages insured. Activity under war housing regulations is shown separately from the normal activity of the Federal Housing Administration. Certain of these data are summarized for each of the approximately 60 insuring offices of the Federal Housing Administration. Special summaries of the Federal Housing Administration records show the type of originating mortgagee on these mortgages (insurance companies, savings and loan associations, etc.) and the total number and amount of mortgages insured in each county of the United States. Additional tabulations have been prepared showing the distribution by value of property, annual income of borrower, and amount of mortgage loan.

When the purchaser of a property under the Federal Housing Administration plan fails to keep up his payments, the lender may foreclose, obtain title to the property, and submit this title to the Federal Housing Administration in exchange for repayment of the outstanding debt. The number of such properties turned over to the Federal Housing Administration gives some measure of the current status of local mortgage loan markets. Further indication of current status may be obtained from information on the ease with which the Federal Housing Administration disposes of such properties and the amount of losses suffered in such transactions. Data of this type are published by the Federal Housing Administration.

Home Owners' Loan Corporation. During the period 1933 to 1936 the Home Owners' Loan Corporation refinanced the mortgage obligations on more than a million properties that were in imminent danger of foreclosures. In order to protect its interests in the properties it was necessary for the Home Owners' Loan Corporation to acquire nearly 200,000 of these properties. It has resold most of these properties but the series on foreclosure activity and properties held reveals the condition of the home mortgage market. Data on Home Owners' Loan Corporation activity are published at approximately three-month intervals in the *Federal Home Loan Bank Review.* Other information concerning the Home Owners' Loan Corporation may be obtained from the Division of Economics and Statistics of the Federal Home Loan Bank Administration.

Federal Public Housing Authority. The Federal Public Housing Authority is the Federal agency concerned with the construction and operation of most of the housing projects that are built, financed, or operated by the Federal Government. This agency prepares monthly reports and summaries of the housing projects under its direction

These reports show the number of projects, number of dwelling units in the projects, and development costs of the new projects which have been assigned to cities, are under construction, or on which construction is completed. The projects are classified by type as dormitories or family dwelling units and as permanent, demountable, temporary, or converted structures. The summaries also show the occupancy rate of all projects and of projects that have been completed for three months or more. Data are available [30] monthly for each separate project and are summarized by regions and for the United States as a whole.

In December 1942, special studies were conducted of the characteristics of tenants of projects that were occupied at that time, and in June 1943 of projects occupied since December 1942. These special studies indicate where occupants come from, duration in the community, why they needed housing, number of persons, family income, and current and former rental rate.

Residential Building with Priority Assistance. The restrictions of new residential building during the wartime period resulted in the development of an additional series of data on building activity. It was necessary to obtain a priority in order to purchase the essential materials needed to build a new house during the war. Records of priorities that were issued to prospective builders serve as an excellent measure of building activity. These records are available by months for the period since 1942 for each war housing locality (which is usually a city and its environs) and for each state. They show for each locality the number of dwelling units in each of the following categories: Priority assistance granted, construction to be started, construction started, construction completed, available for occupancy, occupied by owners, and occupied by tenants. All records are limited to privately built nonfarm homes and exclude public housing projects and all farm houses.

A limited number of so-called hardship cases located outside the war housing localities also are excluded from the statistics. This series of data should represent an accurate measure of nonfarm building activity during the war.[31]

Other Pertinent Data on Federal Agencies. There are a number of other series of data compiled by Federal agencies that may be of interest

[30] Division of Operating Statistics, Federal Public Housing Authority, Washington 25, D. C.

[31] National data may be obtained from the Division of Research and Statistics, Federal Housing Administration; local data from the local Federal Housing Administration office.

in any study of current trends in housing and construction. Two of the more important of these are the monthly totals of farm mortgage loans outstanding by Federal land banks and land bank commissions, compiled by the Farm Credit Administration; and the weekly and monthly totals of loans secured by mortgages on real estate shown as a separate item in the statements of reporting member banks of the Federal Reserve System.

CHAPTER 14

LABOR

CHARLES D. STEWART
Bureau of Labor Statistics
Department of Labor

The importance of labor as a human and economic factor in our industrial and business life accounts for the widespread and varied use of labor statistics by business management, government, and union organizations. To a considerable extent, labor statistics simply bring together in systematic form the essential facts as to the numbers and characteristics of the labor force such as are collected and analyzed in the operations of a single firm. Whether for economic analysis or for other purposes, summarized records for the nation as a whole which are a counterpart of a firm's labor statistics are of obvious usefulness to the business analyst—so much so that a large part of the labor statistics currently available are the result of voluntary reporting by business establishments. How essential labor statistics are as raw material for economic description and analysis has been indicated in previous chapters in connection with their use in constructing general measures of industrial production and national income. In short, because labor and its use is a primary factor in economic life, employment and labor force data constitute a significant measure of current and historical changes in the economy.

For business purposes, the most intensive use of labor data is perhaps not so much for general economic analysis as for dealing with plant manpower problems, for public hearings, or for collective bargaining purposes. At this level of analysis, the data are most useful when summarized by specific industry groups and geographic areas to show change and variation with respect to number employed, wage rates, hours, turnover, absenteeism, strikes, accidents, etc. Labor statistics of this kind have great potential value to individual firms as a background for what may be called "management statistics." Such data are regularly examined by officials in many companies in order to appraise the relative position of the firm, with respect to these factors, as against the experience of other firms in the same industry. Management may determine whether its position is relatively favorable or so unfavorable that there is need for corrective action.

Except for periodic census data, comprehensive and detailed statistics dealing with the labor force are of relatively recent origin. If we look back to World War I we discover an almost complete absence of systematic statistics on employment and working conditions. Much guesswork was necessary in compiling certain statistics of utmost importance for a nation at war. Little progress was made during World War I in developing either general or detailed manpower information such as we now regard as essential for the handling of wartime manpower problems.[1] The paucity of statistical information in that period can be seen from the fact that it remains impossible to reconstruct an adequate measure of the impact of the first war on the American labor force. The various state and national estimates of manufacturing employment then published were quite frankly reports covering a relatively small number of identical establishments reporting to state or national labor departments; none of the resulting indexes could be assumed to represent actual developments.

During the 1920's there was a growing demand for state and national employment series and related labor data, perhaps chiefly as a measure of business activity by state and by industry. In the 30's the need for some gauge of unemployment resulted in substantial improvement in current employment series. Improved current employment figures, however, were not sufficient for a complete knowledge of what was happening in the labor market. Something must be known of the total labor force—the size of which is affected markedly by business cycle movements. Because of this, the depression efforts to construct an adequate unemployment series failed despite the gains made in the measurement of employment. This shortcoming was corrected in large part with the beginning of the *Monthly Report on the Labor Force* in April 1940 which, by a scientific cross section survey, provides a current estimate of unemployment together with a simultaneous measurement of changes in the civilian labor force and the agricultural and nonagricultural components of employment.

Timeliness perhaps more than anything else gives monthly series a value that is lacking in data compiled at less frequent intervals. Their value is enhanced if they are tied to periodic counts such as are given

---

[1] Cf. Myers and Ober, "Statistics for Wage Stabilization," *Journal of the American Statistical Association*, December 1943, pp. 425–426. For example: "The most ambitious study of occupational wages in World War I, undertaken at the request of the War Industries Board, was not started until the summer of 1918 and did not result in a preliminary report until the spring of 1920."

by a complete Census. Generally monthly series based upon sample data must be periodically adjusted to benchmark data obtained from Census enumerations or from the data available as a by-product of the administration of the Social Security Act. Aside from periodic corrections for level, the tie-in to Census data permits the analyst to relate the specific current series to a wider complex of economic data as provided, for example, in the Census of Manufactures. The periodic censuses also provide a longer historical series than is possible on the basis of recently developed monthly series. Major attention in this article, however, is directed to the various statistical series now available to business analysts on a recurring basis, for these are the series of greatest value to business organizations engaged in hearings or collective bargaining, or to business analysts engaged in current analysis of the business situation.

For convenience the field of labor statistics may be considered in three parts: (1) the group of series which provide totals for large segments of the labor force with only broad classifications by industry, sex, geographic area, or other characteristics; (2) series which give more detailed information by industries and for special and related characteristics; and (3) series derived from operating statistics of agencies with responsibility in manpower or social security fields. The *Monthly Report on the Labor Force*, designed to give national totals by age and sex for the labor force, for employment in agriculture and nonagriculture, and unemployment, is the best example of the first. The Bureau of Labor Statistics sample series on employment, hours, and earnings, with emphasis on totals and interrelations of data for detailed industry groups, is the most familiar illustration of the second. The third type is illustrated by the statistics derived from operating data of such agencies as the Social Security Board, the United States Employment Service, the Interstate Commerce Commission, and the Civil Service Commission.

The various series may also be distinguished on the basis of the method of collection or estimating. The global-type estimates may be derived, as in the case of the *Monthly Report on the Labor Force*, by sampling on a household enumeration basis, similar to the Census of Population except that the monthly estimates are obtained from a small sample rather than a complete enumeration. A total figure for a broad component of employment may, however, be estimated by a second method, as in the Bureau of Labor Statistics series, by weighting and adding figures for specific industries obtained by a sample of establishment reports for specific industries, grouped according to a scheme of industrial classification. The special merit of the establishment approach is the industry detail and the possibility of internal analysis of wages, hours, earnings, and the like rather than the aggregate summary, which is of the character of a by-product.

THE LABOR FORCE AND ITS MAJOR SEGMENTS

For general analysis in the field of manpower, there is an obvious need for an over-all statistical framework into which the details can be fitted. The total population within certain age groups is the ultimate measure of the labor resources of a country, but it is the labor force, however defined,[2] that at any given time is the base figure to which employment and unemployment data must be related. The decennial Census of Population provides a labor force benchmark as of a given period in the Census year—a given week in 1940. While subject to a normal growth which may be forecast over a considerable period of time, the actual labor force at any given moment is subject not only to seasonal fluctuations but also to business cycle conditions and, more recently, to abnormal wartime factors. The assumption underlying the unemployment estimates of the 30's, namely, that the size of the labor force could be forecast merely by projecting a smooth curve, was partly responsible for the inadequacy of the various unemployment estimates in that period.

The keystone in the field of labor statistics is, then, a current estimate of the number of men and women at work or seeking work—a monthly figure which reflects the influence of the dynamic factors constantly at work upon the population of working age. The *Monthly Report on the Labor Force*, originated by the Statistics and Research Division of the Works Progress Administration in April 1940 and since September 1942 conducted currently by the Bureau of the Census, meets this essential requirement.[3] One advantage of the population-sampling

[2] The labor force as now commonly defined includes persons 14 years of age and over in the noninstitutional civilian population who are working or seeking work during the census week. The previous concept of "gainful workers" differed in that it included all civilians 10 years of age and over who reported a gainful occupation regardless of whether they were working or seeking work in the census week, and excluded most new workers without job experience. See *Comparative Occupation Statistics for the United States, 1870 to 1940*, Sixteenth Census of Population, pp. 7–8.

[3] A revised sampling procedure was introduced in October 1943, embodying a number of significant features designed to correct deficiencies in the old sample which became serious with the large shifts in population from rural to urban areas during the war. The sample is selected, among other things, to represent degree of urbanization, geographic location, migration since 1940, industrial composition for urban areas, and type of farming for rural areas. Included in the sample are 68

method used in obtaining the monthly census estimates is that it provides not only a total labor force figure but also unduplicated totals of the numbers employed in agriculture and nonagriculture, and the number unemployed, classified by age and sex. (See Exhibit 1.) In addition, this approach provides figures as to various broad groups of nonworkers over 14 years of age, such as homemakers and students, and

EXHIBIT 1. ESTIMATES OF CIVILIAN LABOR FORCE, BY EMPLOYMENT STATUS AND BY SEX, APRIL AND MAY, 1940 TO 1945.[2]

Item	Estimated number (in thousands) of persons 14 years of age and over [2]											
	1945		1944		1943		1942		1941		1940	
	May	April	May	April	May	April	May	April	May	April	May	April
Total civilian labor force	52,030	51,930	52,840	52,060	53,550	52,540	54,340	53,850	53,880	53,090	53,890	53,310
Unemployment [3]	730	770	880	770	920	950	2,310	2,740	5,120	5,810	7,490	7,800
Employment	51,300	51,160	51,960	51,290	52,630	51,590	52,030	51,110	48,760	47,280	46,400	45,510
Nonagricultural	43,350	43,410	43,360	43,790	43,720	43,720	42,980	42,690	39,550	38,870	36,480	36,530
Agricultural	7,950	7,750	8,600	7,500	8,910	7,870	9,050	8,420	9,210	8,410	9,920	8,980
Males												
Civilian labor force	33,790	33,840	34,910	34,880	36,260	35,990	39,820	39,710	40,270	40,230	40,640	40,220
Unemployment [3]	430	430	420	440	530	520	1,460	1,890	3,700	4,310	5,550	5,970
Employment	33,360	33,410	34,490	34,440	35,730	35,470	38,360	37,820	36,570	35,920	35,090	34,250
Nonagricultural	26,910	26,940	27,400	27,750	28,520	28,680	30,740	30,330	28,610	28,180	26,220	25,960
Agricultural	6,450	6,470	7,090	6,690	7,210	6,790	7,620	7,490	7,960	7,740	8,870	8,290
Females												
Civilian labor force	18,240	18,090	17,930	17,180	17,290	16,550	14,520	14,140	13,610	12,860	13,250	13,090
Unemployment [3]	300	340	460	330	390	430	850	850	1,420	1,500	1,940	1,830
Employment	17,940	17,750	17,470	16,850	16,900	16,120	13,670	13,290	12,190	11,360	11,310	11,260
Nonagricultural	16,440	16,470	15,960	16,040	15,200	15,040	12,240	12,360	10,940	10,690	10,260	10,570
Agricultural	1,500	1,280	1,510	810	1,700	1,080	1,430	930	1,250	670	1,050	690

1 Estimates for period prior to November 1943 revised Apr. 24, 1944.
2 All data exclude persons in institutions.
3 Includes persons on public emergency projects prior to July 1943.

the monthly movements in and out of the labor force, which proved of great value in the analysis of manpower problems during the war years. Because of the necessarily small sample used in the monthly surveys, the *Monthly Report on the Labor Force* is not designed to provide estimates of employment by specific industry groups within nonagriculture, for example, nor is it designed to yield estimates for geographic

counties or combinations of adjoining counties selected from the 2,000 primary sampling units into which the country was divided. Instead of establishing fixed quotas for primary sampling units, the modification adopted establishes a fixed ratio of dwelling units from selected subareas, with the aim of automatically adjusting the sample for population movements. Further description of the sampling procedures may be obtained from the Special Surveys Section of the Bureau of the Census. The revision of the monthly estimates for 1940–1943, with a technical note on methods by which the old series was tied to the 1940 decennial Census of Population and to the results of the new sampling procedure, is presented in the *Monthly Report on the Labor Force*, No. 22, for April 26, 1944 (Bureau of the Census).

areas. The technique permits special purpose surveys and special tabulations for administrative use by Government agencies. Special analyses are published from time to time—for example, on hours of work or the composition of the unemployed—but much of what may be called by-product data is not generally available to the public.[4]

As distinguished from the monthly Census labor force estimates, the monthly employment series published as a summary of the BLS specific industry estimates refers only to employees in nonagricultural

EXHIBIT 2.   ESTIMATED NUMBER OF EMPLOYEES IN NONAGRICULTURAL ESTABLISHMENTS, BY INDUSTRY DIVISION.

Industry division	Estimated number of employees (in thousands)			
	April 1945	March 1945	February 1945	April 1944
Total estimated employment [1]	37,804	38,062	37,968	38,689
Manufacturing [2]	15,102	15,368	15,517	16,309
Mining	761	796	798	844
Contract construction and Federal force-account construction	690	636	599	683
Transportation and public utilities	3,795	3,788	3,771	3,744
Trade	6,995	7,084	6,985	6,968
Finance, service, and miscellaneous	4,458	4,394	4,360	4,236
Federal, State, and local Government, excluding Federal force-account construction	6,003	5,996	5,938	5,905

[1] Estimates include all full- and part-time wage and salary workers in nonagricultural establishments who are employed during the pay period ending nearest the 15th of the month. Proprietors, self-employed persons, domestic servants, and personnel of the armed forces are excluded.
[2] Estimates for manufacturing have been adjusted to levels indicated by final 1942 data made available by the Bureau of Employment Security of the Federal Security Agency. Since the estimates of production workers in manufacturing industries have been further adjusted to preliminary 1943 data, subsequent to December 1942, the two sets of estimates are not comparable.

establishments.[5]   (See Exhibit 2.)   The establishment reporting technique underlying most of the BLS employment data is not suited to measuring changes in the number of workers in all nonagricultural activities since it excludes domestic servants, unpaid family workers, proprietors of unincorporated businesses, and other self-employed per-

[4] Published reports based upon the *Monthly Report on the Labor Force* are available from the Special Surveys Section of the Bureau of the Census. Monthly data are republished in the *Monthly Labor Review* and the *Survey of Current Business*.

[5] Published monthly in mimeographed form in the "Employment and Payrolls" release and republished regularly in the *Monthly Labor Review, Survey of Current. Business*, and the *Federal Reserve Bulletin*. The series is available since January 1929. Revised estimates for the seven major industrial divisions covering the period January 1939 to March 1944 are available in a mimeographed release, "Revised Estimates of Employment in Nonagricultural Establishments in the United States, 1939–1944." Comparable data on an annual basis from 1929 to 1938 were published in the *Monthly Labor Review*, September 1944, p. 655, but are available in more detail in a memorandum, *Revision of BLS Employment Estimates*, obtainable upon request to the Bureau of Labor Statistics.

sons, which are included in the Census figure. Prior to the publication of the *Monthly Report on the Labor Force*, the nonagricultural employees series were the only governmental estimates available as a general measure of change in the level of employment. But for current analysis of factors in nonagricultural employment, most interest probably has always attached to the subclassification of the total by seven broad nonagricultural industries, used for an endless variety of purposes by business economists concerned with general economic developments.

The two nonagricultural series differ in respects other than coverage. The population approach of the Census series counts any individual in only one job and thus results in an unduplicated total; the establishment approach of the BLS aims to estimate for each specific industry·within the broad groups the total number of employees in the industry, with corresponding hours and earnings data wherever possible, without regard to the individual's employment in more than one establishment or in other industries. For many purposes this feature of the latter series is obviously desirable, particularly with respect to hours and earnings data, and is naturally inherent in an approach which reflects the actual record-keeping practices of reporting employers. Fluctuations in the employment estimates may therefore represent to some extent changes in the rate of turnover and dual job-holding as well as changes in the volume of employment.[6]

Similarly in agriculture there are two different measures of current farm employment—the Census series derived as part of the *Monthly Report on the Labor Force* and the agricultural employment series estimated since 1909 by the Bureau of Agricultural Economics of the Department of Agriculture.[7] The BAE estimate is obtained by means of mailed returns from crop reporters and is designed to measure the number of persons at work on farms in a given week. Hence it includes workers who may work, for example, four days in nonagriculture and only two days on a farm; and it may count twice any worker employed on two farms, provided he works at least two days a week on each.

[6] If an attempt is made to reconcile the two series, an adjustment can be made for the factors already mentioned, and estimates can be obtained from unpublished Census tabulations with respect to the segments of employment excluded from the BLS series. There would remain certain differences between the two series which are less susceptible of ready analysis: under-reporting of part-time workers in the Census series, differences in the date of the month to which the estimates refer, seasonal fluctuations with respect to what may be termed casual types of employed not fully reflected by the payrolls of the establishments in the reporting sample, and similar factors.

[7] See Chapter 5 for further discussion of the BAE agricultural employment series and related farm labor data.

The Census series, as already indicated, gives an unduplicated agricultural employment total but is by no means a substitute for the BAE type of series. The BAE reporting procedure, for example, makes it possible to estimate employment by geographic division and to relate other farm labor data, such as wage information, to the employment figures. The Census series also differs from the BAE series in that it excludes children under 14 years of age; includes workers in certain agricultural processing and servicing establishments; and does not set two days of work per week as the definition of employment. Differences in the seasonal pattern of the two series may be explained in part by the fact that the two series do not refer to the same week of the month.[8]

LABOR DATA FOR SPECIFIC INDUSTRIES

Employment and Payrolls. The detailed report on employment and payrolls published monthly by the Bureau of Labor Statistics for 154 manufacturing industries and 20 selected nonmanufacturing industries is based upon voluntary reports from about 40,000 employers in manufacturing and 160,000 employers in nonmanufacturing. (See Exhibit 3.) A large proportion of the reports are obtained jointly by the BLS and agencies of 17 states. For Government and certain other segments of employment, these reports are supplemented by data from the Interstate Commerce Commission, the Maritime Commission, the Civil Service Commission, the Bureau of the Census, and other agencies. The questionnaire calls for monthly payroll data for the pay period ending nearest the 15th of the month for the wage earners (i.e., production workers) working any part of the period, the amount of wages paid (excluding special bonuses but including vacation pay), and number of hours actually worked, including vacation hours. In addition to wage earners, the schedule also calls for the total number of employees (wage earners and salaried workers) classified by sex, and other information required for interpretation of the data. The coverage of the reporting sample ranges from approximately 25 percent of total employment for wholesale and retail trade to approximately 80 percent for public utilities and 90 percent for mining. For the 154 specific manufacturing industries, the monthly sample includes reports from establishments employing about 80 percent of the total wage earners. To obtain estimates for 20 broad groups within manufacturing, as well as totals for durable and nondurable manufacturing,

[8] See "Note on Revisions," in *Monthly Report on Labor Force*, No. 22, for April 26, 1944, for further discussion of the Census series.

EXHIBIT 3. ESTIMATED NUMBER OF WAGE EARNERS IN MANUFACTURING INDUSTRIES.

(Excerpt from published table)

Industry	Estimated number of production workers (in thousands)			
	April 1945	March 1945	February 1945	April 1944
All manufacturing	12,678	12,940	13,081	13,814
Durable goods	7,471	7,661	7,770	8,421
Nondurable goods	5,207	5,279	5,311	5,393
Durable goods				
Iron and steel and their products	1,631	1,658	1,666	1,680
Blast furnaces, steel works, and rolling mills	475.8	478.5	478.4	485.5
Gray-iron and semisteel castings	72.5	74.6	75.3	74.6
Malleable-iron castings	24.1	25.4	26.0	25.0
Steel castings	70.9	71.8	72.4	76.9
Cast-iron pipe and fittings	16.1	15.7	15.7	15.0
Tin cans and other tinware	41.7	41.9	41.1	36.2
Wire drawn from purchased rods	32.0	32.7	32.6	33.7
Wirework	33.9	34.7	35.1	33.9
Cutlery and edge tools	23.9	24.4	24.2	22.6
Tools (except edge tools, machine tools, files, and saws)	26.8	27.5	27.4	28.1
Hardware	46.0	46.8	46.7	46.6
Plumbers' supplies	22.8	23.2	22.7	23.4
Stoves, oil burners, and heating equipment, not elsewhere classified	62.0	63.6	64.0	61.2
Steam and hot-water heating apparatus and steam fittings	54.3	55.2	55.6	56.9
Stamped and enameled ware and galvanizing	86.0	86.9	87.9	89.1
Fabricated structural and ornamental metalwork	67.5	70.0	73.2	75.4
Metal doors, sash, frames, molding, and trim	10.3	10.7	10.9	13.0
Bolts, nuts, washers, and rivets	23.6	23.9	24.0	27.9
Forgings, iron and steel	34.4	35.4	35.7	38.4
Wrought pipe, welded and heavy riveted	24.1	24.4	23.6	26.3
Screw-machine products and wood screws	42.4	43.0	43.0	46.8
Steel barrels, kegs, and drums [2]	8.4	8.4	8.3	7.1
Firearms	29.8	30.7	32.3	53.3
Electrical machinery	682	693	696	755
Electrical equipment	419.7	426.4	429.0	459.1
Radios and phonographs	114.5	116.7	117.5	130.4
Communication equipment	103.7	105.0	104.5	116.8
Machinery, except electrical	1,130	1,152	1,165	1,227
Machinery and machine-shop products	441.4	449.9	454.2	475.6
Engines and turbines	65.2	66.7	67.7	71.4
Tractors [2]	55.6	57.2	58.0	59.9
Agricultural machinery, excluding tractors	42.7	43.9	44.8	45.6
Machine tools	73.6	74.6	74.8	80.4
Machine-tool accessories	63.9	64.4	65.2	71.0
Textile machinery	25.9	26.4	26.4	27.8
Pumps and pumping equipment	68.9	71.5	72.6	82.4
Typewriters	13.0	13.1	13.0	11.5
Cash registers, adding and calculating machines	29.2	29.8	30.4	33.4
Washing machines, wringers and driers, domestic	12.8	12.8	12.6	13.7
Sewing machines, domestic and industrial	10.8	11.1	11.2	9.3
Refrigerators and refrigeration equipment	49.9	51.1	52.4	52.9
Transportation equipment, except automobiles	1,874	1,970	2,042	2,442
Locomotives	33.5	34.0	34.1	36.3
Cars, electric- and steam-railroad	57.9	58.6	59.2	59.1
Aircraft and parts, excluding aircraft engines [3]	619.1	637.6	646.4	763.8
Aircraft engines [3]	203.5	210.6	213.7	259.0
Shipbuilding and boatbuilding	853.2	917.1	973.0	1,192.7
Motorcycles, bicycles, and parts	9.6	9.5	9.6	9.1
Automobiles	659	668	680	724

certain uncovered components for which periodic benchmark data are available are estimated according to current changes in related industries. Altogether, the coverage in manufacturing represents more than 65 percent of the total factory workers in the country.

The *Detailed Report on Employment and Payrolls* is released in mimeographed form on about the 10th of each month. Preliminary data for the 7 major nonagricultural divisions and the 20 broad manufacturing industrial groups for the preceding month are available at that time. In addition, the release contains estimates for one month earlier for about 175 selected manufacturing and other industries, and state and regional estimates of the total employees in nonagricultural establishments and for manufacturing. A separate mimeographed release, *Indexes of Wage-Earner Employment in Manufacturing Industries, by Metropolitan Area,* is published about ten days later, covering 102 metropolitan areas or cities.[9] Special industry tabulations, by area, are made in response to specific needs, as in the case of aircraft, shipbuilding, other ordnance items, cotton goods, etc.[10]

The estimates of employment by states now included in the detailed report referred to in the preceding paragraph consist of two series, employment in all manufacturing establishments and employment in all nonagricultural establishments. Upon the completion of a program now being conducted through the regional offices of the Bureau of Labor Statistics, estimates will be available for many industries within each state on the same regular monthly basis as the national statistics.

Hours and Earnings. The same basic report provides the data for computing hours and earnings data for a similar group of manufacturing and nonmanufacturing industries; these are published in the mimeographed release on *Hours and Earnings* two weeks after the *Employment and Payrolls* release. (See Exhibit 4.) Because not all reporting establishments supply information on man-hours, the average weekly hours and hourly earnings series are based on a smaller sample of reporting firms than the employment and payrolls series. For industry groups and all manufacturing, the average weekly hours are weighted by the current number of wage earners in each industry, and the average hourly earnings for each industry are weighted by the actual hours worked. If large interindustry shifts in employment occur, or changes in overtime hours, as during the war, the average hourly earnings figure cannot be construed as a measure of wage rate changes. The average weekly earnings data are computed from a

[9] These releases are available from the Bureau of Labor Statistics.

[10] See the *Cotton Goods Industry* reports, covering employment, hours, earnings, and turnover rates, for 66 local areas, from January 1942 to date.

EXHIBIT 4. HOURS AND EARNINGS IN MANUFACTURING AND NONMANUFACTURING INDUSTRIES.

(Excerpt from published table)

Industry	Average weekly earnings [1]			Average weekly hours [1]			Average hourly earnings [1]		
	Apr. 1945	Mar. 1945	Feb. 1945	Apr. 1945	Mar. 1945	Feb. 1945	Apr. 1945	Mar. 1945	Feb. 1945
							Cents	Cents	Cents
All manufacturing	$47.16	$47.43	$47.37	45.2	45.4	45.4	104.5	104.4	104.3
Durable goods	52.99	53.25	53.30	46.5	46.7	46.8	113.9	114.0	113.9
Nondurable goods	38.81	38.95	38.69	43.2	43.5	43.4	89.9	89.6	89.2
Durable goods									
Iron and steel and their products	52.07	52.09	51.56	47.0	47.1	46.9	110.8	110.7	109.8
Blast furnaces, steel works, and rolling mills	56.64	56.10	54.58	47.1	47.0	46.3	120.3	119.5	118.1
Gray-iron and semisteel castings	53.13	54.00	53.16	48.0	48.4	48.1	110.8	111.6	110.6
Malleable-iron castings [2]	52.37	52.72	52.79	47.5	47.4	47.7	111.2	111.3	110.5
Steel castings	53.81	53.84	52.96	46.8	46.9	46.5	114.9	114.7	113.8
Cast-iron pipe and fittings	41.82	42.35	43.79	47.2	46.7	47.6	88.9	91.0	91.9
Tin cans and other tinware	41.19	41.73	41.87	45.1	45.6	45.8	91.2	91.5	91.5
Wirework	50.78	51.90	51.41	47.2	48.1	47.7	107.7	108.1	107.9
Cutlery and edge tools	44.66	44.94	45.37	45.9	46.2	46.6	97.7	97.5	97.4
Tools (except edge tools, machine tools, files, and saws)	47.36	47.35	47.58	47.4	47.3	47.4	100.4	100.1	100.3
Hardware	47.87	47.61	47.23	47.2	47.6	47.6	100.5	100.1	99.2
Plumbers' supplies	50.07	49.97	50.06	46.6	46.6	47.2	107.5	107.2	106.1
Stoves, oil burners, and heating equipment, not elsewhere classified	49.09	48.76	49.27	46.5	46.6	47.1	105.5	104.7	104.5
Steam and hot-water heating apparatus and steam fittings	49.87	49.32	49.70	47.4	47.2	47.7	105.1	104.5	104.3
Stamped and enameled ware and galvanizing	47.93	48.71	49.18	45.7	46.2	46.6	104.8	105.4	105.6
Fabricated structural and ornamental metalwork	53.43	52.29	53.58	47.3	46.5	47.6	112.9	112.5	112.4
Metal doors, sash, frames, molding and trim [2]	53.27	53.76	53.54	47.4	48.2	48.1	112.4	111.6	111.3
Bolts, nuts, washers, and rivets	51.13	52.21	50.49	48.1	48.5	47.7	106.8	107.3	105.9
Forgings, iron and steel	61.71	61.62	62.73	48.1	48.0	48.7	128.4	128.5	128.9
Screw-machine products and wood screws	51.73	52.44	52.38	48.4	49.0	49.2	106.8	106.9	106.4
Steel barrels, kegs, and drums [3]	46.13	41.90	43.36	45.6	41.9	43.7	101.5	99.9	99.0
Firearms	57.56	59.96	59.26	44.7	46.6	46.4	128.7	128.7	127.8
Electrical machinery	$49.84	$50.02	$49.85	46.7	46.6	46.7	106.8	107.3	106.7
Electrical equipment	51.91	52.51	52.31	46.9	47.1	47.0	111.1	112.0	111.3
Radios and phonographs	43.22	43.04	43.05	46.1	45.9	46.3	93.5	93.4	93.1
Communication equipment	48.04	47.18	47.31	46.1	45.7	45.9	103.8	103.0	102.8
Machinery, except electrical	55.51	56.07	56.13	48.1	48.6	48.8	115.3	115.3	115.1
Machinery and machine-shop products	54.82	55.06	55.02	48.2	48.7	48.7	113.5	113.0	112.9
Engines and turbines [2]	58.28	59.91	60.70	47.4	48.0	48.4	123.3	125.1	125.5
Tractors [3]	52.86	52.98	53.11	45.6	45.9	46.2	115.8	115.5	114.9
Agricultural machinery, excluding tractors	54.18	54.68	54.12	47.0	47.5	47.3	115.3	115.1	114.4
Machine tools [2]	59.53	60.49	60.34	50.2	50.9	51.0	118.7	118.8	118.3
Machine-tool accessories	60.86	61.70	61.82	49.4	49.8	50.5	123.3	123.2	122.7
Textile machinery	50.33	51.03	50.68	49.3	49.9	49.4	102.6	102.8	102.7
Typewriters	49.40	49.56	49.52	48.6	49.0	49.1	101.7	101.1	100.8
Cash registers, adding and calculating machines	58.70	59.91	59.12	48.0	48.7	48.3	122.9	123.7	123.0
Washing machines, wringers and driers, domestic	50.45	48.49	49.23	46.8	45.5	46.8	108.3	106.6	105.1
Sewing machines, domestic and industrial	57.44	57.99	57.89	51.0	51.4	51.6	113.2	113.6	113.2
Refrigerators and refrigeration equipment	52.66	52.58	52.76	46.1	46.1	46.6	114.2	113.9	113.3

[1] These figures are based on reports from coöperating establishments covering both full- and part-time employees who worked during any part of one pay period ending nearest the 15th of the month. As not all reporting firms furnish man-hour data, average hours and average hourly earnings for individual industries are based on a slightly smaller sample than are weekly earnings. Data for the current and immediately preceding months are subject to revision.

[2] Effective January 1945 the term "production worker" has been substituted for "wage earner." Since there is only a slight difference in their definitions there is no appreciable effect on the employment and pay-roll data; however, noticeable differences in averages of hours and earnings occurred in a few industries.

larger sample including firms not providing hours data, with the result that for individual industries the weekly earnings estimates will not in general be equal to the product of average weekly hours and hourly earnings.

With the wartime emphasis on extending the work week, the individual employer attached more interest to comparative hours data than previously. Relative differences in hours among industries, areas, and establishments in the same labor market area have proved a factor in causing workers to shift from one job to another. As hours were lengthened in an effort to step up war production quickly, industry analysts as well as others began to examine the relation of hours of work to safety, health, absenteeism, turnover, costs, and optimum conditions of production. Information on average weekly hours became increasingly important as the War Manpower Commission extended the application of the 48-hour standard work week to more and more industries and areas. While data by area are not regularly published, such information can be tabulated from the schedule discussed above, and has been, for the use of Government agencies, private companies, trade associations, and unions—provided the data do not disclose individual establishment data.[11]

The average hourly and weekly earnings data are of manifest interest in connection with wage stabilization, comparative costs, and wartime changes in workers' incomes. For purposes of determining changes in straight-time hourly earnings, the above data on average hourly earnings require two major adjustments. First, the average hourly earnings need to be corrected for overtime premium pay.[12] A second refinement is also necessary, if the straight-time hourly earnings figures are to be used as a measure of changes in basic wage rates. The wartime increase in average gross hourly earnings or straight-time hourly earnings for all manufacturing reflects the weight of numbers in the rapidly growing war industries as well as any real changes in basic wage rates. The influence of changes in composition can be adjusted by weighting the industry averages by employment in a base period (say January 1939) rather than by the current volume of employment. This gives a better approximation of changes in basic wage rates, though necessarily overstating wage rate changes because of the failure to take account of changes in occupational and employment composition within individual

[11] Similar information was available from statistics collected by the War Manpower Commission and the War Production Board in connection with their operating statistics.

[12] See "Elimination of Overtime Payments from Gross Hourly Earnings," *Monthly Labor Review*, November 1942, pp. 1053–1056.

firms and industries. The resulting estimates of straight-time average hourly earnings for total manufacturing, and for the durable and nondurable components, as shown in Exhibit 5, are published monthly in the *Monthly Labor Review*, and are available for selected industry groups in mimeographed form. More specific data with respect to changes in

EXHIBIT 5. EARNINGS OF FACTORY WORKERS, SELECTED MONTHS, 1939 TO 1945.

Month and year	Average weekly earnings			Average hourly earnings			Estimated straight-time average hourly earnings [1]			Estimated straight-time average hourly earnings weighted by January 1939 employment [2]		
	All manufacturing	Durable goods	Non-durable goods	All manufacturing	Durable goods	Non-durable goods	All manufacturing	Durable goods	Non-durable goods	All manufacturing	Durable goods	Non-durable goods
	(1)	(2)	(3)	(4)	(5)	(6)	(7)	(8)	(9)	(10)	(11)	(12)
1939: Jan	$23.19	$25.33	$21.57	$0.632	$0.696	$0.583	$0.623	$0.688	$0.574	$0.623	$0.688	$0.574
1940: Jan	24.56	27.39	22.01	.655	.717	.598	.644	.703	.589	.635	.697	.589
1941: Jan	26.64	30.48	22.75	.683	.749	.610	.664	.722	.601	.648	.711	.600
1942: Jan	33.40	38.98	26.97	.801	.890	.688	.762	.835	.670	.729	.810	.667
July	36.43	42.51	28.94	.856	.949	.725	.809	.885	.701	.759	.846	.694
Oct	38.89	45.31	30.66	.893	.990	.751	.839	.919	.723	.782	.869	.716
1943: Jan	40.62	46.68	32.10	.919	1.017	.768	.859	.941	.733	.794	.886	.724
Apr	42.48	48.67	33.58	.944	1.040	.790	.878	.959	.751	.808	.897	.741
July	42.76	48.76	34.01	.963	1.060	.806	.899	.981	.766	.823	.919	.750
Oct	44.86	51.26	35.18	.988	1.086	.824	.916	.997	.781	.836	.929	.765
Dec	44.58	50.50	35.61	.995	1.093	.832	.927	1.011	.788	.846	.942	.773
1944: Jan	45.29	51.21	36.03	1.002	1.099	.838	.931	1.013	.793	.850	.945	.778
Apr	45.55	51.67	36.16	1.013	1.110	.850	.942	1.023	.806	.862	.955	.792
July	45.43	51.07	37.05	1.018	1.116	.862	.950	1.035	.815	.874	.973	.799
Oct	46.94	53.18	37.97	1.031	1.129	.878	.956	1.038	.829	.881	.969	.815
Dec	47.44	53.68	38.39	1.040	1.140	.883	.963	1.046	.832	.886	.975	.818
1945: Jan	47.50	53.54	38.66	1.046	1.144	.891	.970	1.053	.840	.894	.984	.825
Feb	47.37	53.30	38.69	1.043	1.139	.892	.968	1.048	.842	.892	.978	.827
Mar.[3]	47.43	53.25	38.95	1.044	1.140	.896	.969	1.048	.846	.896	.981	.831
Apr.[3]	47.16	52.99	38.81	1.045	1.139	.899	.971	1.050	.850	.899	.985	.834

[1] Average hourly earnings, excluding the effect of premium pay for overtime.
[2] Average hourly earnings, excluding premium pay for overtime, weighted by man-hours of employment. In the major divisions of the manufacturing industry for January 1939.
[3] Preliminary.

wage rates by occupation, industry, and area are available from the occupational wage rate surveys discussed below.

Occupational Wage Rates. In consequence of the growing tendency to use factual information in collective bargaining, wage administration, and Government labor regulation, the demand for wage statistics has increased enormously in recent years. A large part of this demand relates to current wage rates by occupation, locality, and industry.

The collection and publication of occupational wage rate statistics received a tremendous impetus with the advent of wage stabilization as part of wartime labor policy. During the first six months of the collection of occupational wage rates for wage stabilization (April-October 1943) wage rate information was collected from about 60,000 establishments, representing major manufacturing and selected nonmanufacturing industries in localities of 25,000 population or more.

In order to make it possible to provide the necessary detail in a reasonably short time it was necessary to limit the collection and analysis of the wage data to the barest essentials. Key jobs were selected and defined to represent each industry. Only the characteristic industries or those that were determinative of the local wage pattern were studied. Typically this involved all manufacturing industries with three or more establishments in a locality. In the early stages of the occupational wage rate program, the studies were also confined to industries that are typically concentrated in urban areas; industries in which wage determination has been typically on a national or broad regional basis (iron and steel, railroad transportation) were not covered under this program, but were reserved for nationwide studies.

The occupational wage rate data collected in 1943 and in 1944 provided one of the most important sources of information for the administration of wage stabilization by the War Labor Board. Soon after transmittal to the Regional Boards the data were also made available to other governmental agencies, employers, trade unions, and the public generally, in a variety of forms. Local mimeographed releases were made by each Regional Office of the Bureau whenever the demand for the data required quantity distribution. A number of bulletins and printed articles in the *Monthly Labor Review* summarized comparable wage data from a large selection of urban centers. In addition, a special service was established by the Bureau under which unpublished information available in the files was transcribed and transmitted to unions or employers on request. (See Exhibit 6.) The identity of individual reporting establishments was, of course, not revealed.

The Bureau's current program for the collection of occupational wage rates is designed primarily to facilitate orderly reconversion and to promote collective bargaining and settlement of labor disputes. A considerable amount of detail by locality is consequently still required. Many State and Federal agencies concerned with wage regulation, however, require industry wage information for broader areas or on a Nation-wide basis. Minimum wage regulation, for example, is concerned with wages of workers below specific wage rate levels, and frequency distributions of rates are of importance in this connection. The current program, therefore, provides for the publication of occupational wage information for key jobs for all localities of 100,000 population or more and, in addition, for Nation-wide and broad regional summaries representing localities of all sizes. In addition to average

EXHIBIT 6. STRAIGHT-TIME AVERAGE HOURLY EARNINGS * FOR SELECTED OCCUPATIONS

> The Bureau of Labor Statistics desires to make its information available to all parties on an impartial basis. If the wage material transmitted herewith is to be used in wage negotiations or in proceedings leading to official action on a wage determination, you are respectfully requested to convey to us the names and addresses of other persons directly involved at least 1 week before the material is used. If this is impossible, we should be advised of the names and addresses of the interested parties by wire at the time this report is received.

Industry or group ___ Electric light and power † ___ S. I. C. Code No. ___ 8211

Wage area ___ State of xxxxxx ___ Number of establishments studied ___ 37 ___ Period covered ___ July, 194 3

Occupation, Class, and Sex	Number of Establishments Reporting Occupation	Number of Workers on All Shifts	Straight-Time Hourly Earnings		
			General Average	Lowest Establishment Average	Highest Establishment Average
Male:					
Draftsmen	3	8	$0.97	$0.94	$1.10
Electricians, maintenance, Class A	7	12	1.10	0.98	1.15
Electricians, maintenance, Class B	2	6	0.99	(‡)	(‡)
Engineers, power house, public utilities	10	48	0.85	0.64	1.09
Firemen, stationary boiler	13	53	0.86	0.60	0.99
Generators, switchboard operators	2	6	1.09	(‡)	(‡)
Groundmen	5	12	0.68	0.58	0.73
Guards	6	29	0.75	0.41	0.83
Janitors	9	32	0.63	0.43	0.75
Linemen	21	83	1.06	0.79	1.12
Machinists, maintenance, Class A	7	17	1.05	0.96	1.12
Mechanics, maintenance, Class B	4	4	1.17	1.04	1.32
Meter readers	12	66	0.80	0.54	0.92
Meter repairmen	5	20	0.97	0.73	1.00
Stock clerks	10	22	0.83	0.63	0.98
Substation operators	18	93	0.84	0.54	1.01
System operators	5	15	1.03	0.78	1.27
Trouble men	21	64	0.97	0.58	1.11
Truck drivers	4	8	0.74	0.65	0.84
Turbine operators	3	11	1.06	1.01	1.14
Watchmen	4	9	0.64	0.30	0.74
Water tenders	2	10	1.09	(‡)	(‡)
Working foremen, operating departments	27	57	1.06	0.63	1.29
Female:					
Meter readers	4	31	0.67	0.43	0.71

* Exclusive of premium payments for overtime and night work.

SPECIAL COMMENTS:

† Based on information obtained from 37 establishments employing the great majority of the workers in the electric light and power utilities in this area.

‡ Averages not shown to avoid disclosure of plant identity.

[Source: U. S. Department of Labor, Bureau of Labor Statistics.]

hourly rates, distributions of rates are provided for all key jobs and for each industry as a whole. Separate occupational rates are shown for union and nonunion establishments, large and small establishments, time and incentive workers, etc. The wage data are supplemented by additional detail regarding overtime payments, vacations with pay, and other labor practices. In all stages of planning its wage studies the Bureau has taken advantage of the counsel of unions, trade associations, and individual employers.

This program has necessitated a somewhat more modest selection of industries to be studied each year. Representative industries were selected from all major industry groups on the basis of the following criteria: importance of the industry in terms of number of employees; prevalence of collective bargaining; and importance as a source of new postwar jobs. In all, this program involves the collection of occupational wage rate information from 30,000 establishments annually. Some 20,000 to 25,000 of these are included in Nation-wide industry studies, with provision for separate tabulations for all cities of 100,000 population or more. The remainder will be covered in strictly local studies of importance in a particular city, state, or region.

Trend of Urban Wage Rates. A useful statistical tool of fairly recent origin exists in the BLS indexes of urban wage rates. These indexes measure changes in actual hourly rates and are relatively free from the influence of overtime and extra shift pay, changes in industrial or occupational structure, changes in the composition of the labor force, and similar factors. The base is October 1943. The series proper dates from April 1943, although general trends of manufacturing wage rates have been computed (partly on an estimated basis) for the period between January 1941 and April 1943. Changes in wage rates are computed semiannually. The results are published promptly in the *Monthly Labor Review* as well as in separate pamphlets which are available on request.

The series are based on observations in about 7,000 establishments in 69 urban areas, selected and carefully weighted to represent all geographic regions and a great variety of urban industry. The basic data are collected semiannually by trained Bureau representatives from the payrolls of a constant group of representative employers, for selected and carefully defined occupations. The indexes not only measure general trends in wage rates but permit separate study of wage movements in major cities and in the several geographical regions of the Nation. As presently maintained, the series have fairly broad representation in the manufacturing industries, and more limited representation in nonmanufacturing industries. Plans are now being made to introduce one or more new nonmanufacturing series.

Labor Turnover Rates. Originated by the Metropolitan Life Insurance Company in the 20's, the labor turnover series has been greatly expanded since its transfer to the Bureau of Labor Statistics in 1929. From a single-figure tabulation (for each class of turnover) based upon reports from 600 firms, the turnover estimates now comprise a monthly series for 76 industries in 20 major divisions in manufacturing and selected nonmanufacturing industries, based upon voluntary reports from 9,000 firms. There are several significant differences between the turnover data and the BLS employment and payrolls reports. The former now relate to total employees, whereas the employment and payroll estimates for detailed industry groups refer generally to wage earners only. In the turnover series the establishments are classified according to current major product as against the prewar industrial classification, which has been maintained in the employment and payrolls statistics. For these reasons, month-to-month changes in employment as indicated by the turnover rates are not generally comparable to those shown by the Bureau's basic employment statistics.

As shown by the material in Exhibit 7, turnover rates are published for five classes of turnover: separations classified by quits, discharges, layoffs, military and miscellaneous separations, and accessions. For each of these classes the turnover rate (per 100 employees) is published monthly for all manufacturing and for each of 76 industries, including all the important war manufacturing industries, and for 5 nonmanufacturing industries. The data are further classified by sex in more than 25 selected industries engaged extensively in war production. During the war, special tabulations of quit rates classified by industry and area, showing an employer his own plant experience contrasted with that of other companies, proved particularly useful to companies in dealing with their own personnel problems. In general, the detailed classification of separations by cause is extremely valuable in disclosing changes occurring in the labor market which are not revealed by a single figure summarizing the net change in employment from month to month.

Absenteeism. The wartime importance of absenteeism gave rise to a demand for accurate information on the subject in order to understand its extent and to throw light on its causes. Plant managements needed comparative data in order to assess their own positions and gauge the necessity for corrective action. By means of a special questionnaire to a sample of plants in important war industries, the BLS was able to provide such information, classified by industry, with little delay at a time when the problem of absenteeism was assuming large

EXHIBIT 7. MONTHLY LABOR TURNOVER RATES (PER 100 EMPLOYEES) IN SELECTED GROUPS AND INDUSTRIES.

(Excerpt from published table)

Group and industry	Total separation		Quit		Discharge		Lay-off		Military and miscellaneous		Total accession	
	Apr.	Mar.	Apr.	Mar.	Apr.	Mar.	Apr.	Mar.	Apr.	Mar.	Apr.	Mar.
Manufacturing												
Munitions[3]	6.4	6.5	4.1	4.3	0.8	0.9	1.1	0.9	0.4	0.4	4.1	4.4
Nonmunitions[3]	6.8	7.3	5.7	6.1	.4	.4	.4	.5	.3	.3	5.5	5.7
Ordnance	8.0	8.3	5.5	5.9	1.1	1.2	1.0	.8	.4	.4	6.1	6.5
Guns, howitzers, mortars, and related equipment	6.8	6.0	3.5	3.6	.8	.8	2.0	1.2	.5	.4	4.6	5.5
Ammunition, except for small arms	9.0	9.2	6.4	6 8	1.2	1.4	1.0	.6	.4	.4	6.8	7.0
Tanks	6.7	8.2	4.8	5.3	1.1	1.2	.5	1.3	.3	.4	6.3	8.3
Sighting and fire-control equipment	3.5	3.6	2.1	2.2	.5	.4	.6	.7	.3	.3	2.6	2.6
Iron and steel and their products	4.4	4.7	3.3	3.4	.4	.5	.3	.4	.4	.4	3.5	3.7
Blast furnaces, steel works, and rolling mills	2.9	3.2	2.3	2.4	.2	.2	.1	.2	.3	.4	2.6	2.7
Gray-iron castings	6.8	6.9	5.4	5.5	.7	.6	.3	.3	.4	.5	4.9	5.4
Malleable-iron castings	5.7	6.7	4.9	5.5	.4	.6	.1	.1	.3	.5	4.2	4.1
Steel castings	6.3	6.6	5.0	5.2	.8	.8	.1	.2	.4	.4	5.2	5.3
Cast-iron pipe and fittings	8.4	7.9	6.0	6.1	1.6	1.0	.4	.3	.4	.5	6.3	6.6
Tin cans and other tinware	9.6	10.9	6.7	7.6	2.3	2.7	.2	.2	.4	.4	9.8	10.3
Wire products	2.8	3.6	2.0	2.6	.2	.3	.1	.2	.5	.5	2.5	2.9
Cutlery and edge tools	5.4	5.1	4.4	4.1	.5	.8	.1	.1	.4	.1	5.3	4.0
Textile-mill products	6.4	6.6	5.5	5.7	0.3	0.4	0.3	0.2	0.3	0.3	5.0	5.1
Cotton	7.6	7.9	6.7	6.9	.4	.5	.2	.2	.3	.3	5.9	6.2
Silk and rayon goods	6.4	6.8	5.4	5.7	.4	.5	.3	.2	.3	.4	5.2	5.4
Woolen and worsted, except dyeing and finishing	4.1	4.2	2.9	3.4	.2	.2	.7	.4	.3	.2	3.2	3.2
Hosiery, full fashioned	4.2	4.8	3.6	4.2	.2	.2	.2	.2	.2	.2	2.7	2.9
Hosiery, seamless	6.3	6.1	5.8	5.4	.2	.3	.1	.3	.2	.1	4.8	4.9
Knitted underwear	5.6	5.6	4.4	5.1	.2	.2	.9	.2	.1	.1	4.1	4.5
Dyeing and finishing textiles, including woolen and worsted	4.1	4.2	3.1	3.1	.4	.5	.2	.2	.4	.4	3.0	3.6
Apparel and other finished textile products	5.4	5.7	4.7	5.1	.2	.2	.4	.3	.1	.1	4.2	4.6
Men's and boys' suits, coats, and overcoats	4.1	4.3	3.8	3.9	.1	.1	.1	.2	.1	.1	3.1	3.5
Men's and boys' furnishings, work clothing, and allied garments	5.3	5.6	4.8	5.2	.2	.2	.2	.1	.1	.1	4.4	4.4
Leather and leather products	5.5	5.7	5.0	4.9	.2	.3	.1	.2	.2	.3	4.7	5.1
Leather	4.2	4.7	3.7	3.7	.2	.5	(4)	.3	.4	.3	3.8	3.5
Boots and shoes	5.8	5.9	5.3	5.1	.2	.3	.1	.2	.2	.3	5.0	5.4
Food and kindred products	8.7	9.6	7.3	8.0	.5	.5	.5	.7	.4	.4	6.7	6.5
Meat products	8.0	10.1	6.7	8.0	.4	.5	.5	1.1	.4	.5	4.6	4.4
Grain-mill products	10.8	11.5	9.5	10.2	.7	.9	(4)	.1	.6	.3	9.8	8.7
Tobacco manufactures	8.2	9.1	7.5	7.9	.4	.4	.2	.6	.1	.2	7.2	7.3
Paper and allied products	6.0	7.1	5.1	5.9	.4	.5	.1	.2	.4	.5	5.3	5.9
Paper and pulp	5.8	6.6	4.7	5.5	.4	.4	.2	.2	.5	.5	4.7	5.5
Paper boxes	7.3	8.0	6.4	6.8	.4	.6	.1	.2	.4	.4	7.0	7.0

[1] Since January 1943 manufacturing firms reporting labor turnover have been assigned industry codes on the basis of current products. Most plants in the employment and pay-roll sample, comprising those which were in operation in 1939, are classified according to their major activity at that time, regardless of any subsequent change in major products.
[2] Preliminary figures.
[3] The munitions division which replaces the Selected War Industries group, include thes following major industry groups: ordnance; iron and steel; electrical machinery; machinery, except electrical; automobiles; transportation equipment, except automobiles; nonferrous metals; chemicals; products of petroleum and coal; rubber. The nonmunitions division includes lumber; furniture and finished lumber products; stone, clay, and glass; textile-mill products; apparel and finished textile products; leather; food and kindred products; tobacco; paper and pulp; miscellaneous industries. Comparable data for 1943 and 1944 appear on p. 143 of this issue of the Review. [4] Less than 0.05.

proportions in the current discussion of manpower problems. The series was discontinued in 1945.

Strikes. Statistical data on strikes cannot be collected in the same fashion as other labor information since strikes are sporadic and cannot be covered by a routine periodic reporting service. The basic measures in strike statistics as now compiled by the BLS are the number of strikes, the number of persons, the number of man-days of idleness, and the ratio of idleness to total available working time. Following the issuance of preliminary estimates based largely on newspaper clipping services, the Bureau sends schedules to all parties concerned in each strike (employers, unions, as well as any outside agent, such as a conciliator) to obtain detailed and authentic information. From the data given on the schedules, the Bureau prepares annual reports (published in the May *Monthly Labor Review* and later in bulletin form) which give not only the complete and verified total figures for each month of the year but also analyzes strikes by industry, state, and city and by causes, results, labor organizations involved, and other pertinent classifications. In this annual report the larger strikes are described in detail; also special analyses are included on current matters of special interest, such as strikes under the War Labor Disputes Act and strikes in which the National War Labor Board intervened.

Industrial Injuries. Since January 1943, monthly estimates of industrial injury frequency rates have been made currently by the BLS for selected manufacturing industries based on a sample of about 10,000 manufacturing establishments. The frequency rate represents the average number of disabling industrial injuries for each million employee-hours worked and is therefore a clear-cut measure of the rate independent of the volume of employment or man-hours. This series supplements the annual data previously published showing frequency rates in selected manufacturing industries.[13] In addition, annual data are published on the number of disabling injuries, classified by degree, for nine broad industrial groups, based upon employer reports to the Bureau and other sources of accident data.[14] Special articles dealing with the problems in individual industries appear regularly in the pages of the *Monthly Labor Review*. Noteworthy is the series of studies on shipbuilding accident experience conducted as part of the Navy and Maritime Commission's industry-wide safety program. Other statistical data in the field of industrial injuries are regularly pub-

[13] See "Changes in Injury Frequency Rates and Employment in Manufacturing, 1936–41," *Monthly Labor Review*, May 1943, pp. 949–954.

[14] See "Industrial Injuries in 1943," ibid., February 1944. pp. 242–243.

lished in the annual reports of the Bureau of Mines and Interstate Commerce Commission.

Productivity Studies. The BLS publishes from time to time series on labor productivity in selected industries for which consistent data on output and man-hours are available. For manufacturing, annual productivity indexes for 45 industries covering the period 1919–1940 were published in 1942. Indexes representing 29 of these industries are shown for 1939–1944 in the most recent study.[15] Wartime changes in the character of production in many industries make it impossible to continue all the original series. Studies for nonmanufacturing industries include various segments of mining, railroad transportation, electric power generation, and agriculture. Special studies have been made from time to time for industries particularly important in the war production program. In these industries, particular interest attaches to monthly or successive changes in productivity as experience is gained in producing a single item, such as Liberty ships. Articles are published in the *Monthly Labor Review* for individual industries which present statistical data on productivity as well as analysis of the factors affecting productivity. The BLS issues a monthly *Summary of Current Technological Developments* based upon information in trade and technical publications.[16]

Collective Bargaining and Union Agreement Studies. The BLS maintains a file of approximately 12,000 current employer-union agreements. On the basis of these agreements, supplemented by field visits to various plants and unions, studies are published from time to time showing the extent of collective bargaining throughout industry as well as for particular industries.[17] Reports are also prepared from time to time on provisions in union agreements such as type of union recognition, seniority rules, vacation policies, grievance procedures, and provision for arbitration. These studies appear in the *Monthly Labor Review* and are reprinted in separate form.

Since 1907 the BLS has made an annual survey of union wages and hours in certain important time work trades, such as building, printing, street railways, bakery, and bus and truck driving. The indexes computed from these studies provide the longest trend series of wage data in existence. The annual reports, in addition to the indexes,

[15] *Productivity and Unit Labor Costs in Selected Manufacturing Industries, 1939–1944*, available in mimeographed form from the BLS.

[16] See *Wartime Technological Developments*, a study made for the Subcommittee on War Mobilization of the Senate Committee on Military Affairs, Subcommittee Monograph No. 2, May 1945.

[17] See "Extent of Collective Bargaining and Union Status, January 1944," *Monthly Labor Review*, April 1944, pp. 697–705.

show the proportion of union members working under the various wage and hour classifications and the number receiving increases or decreases from year to year, together with occupational and city averages.

ADMINISTRATIVE OR OPERATING STATISTICS

Social Security Data. The unemployment compensation and the old age and survivors insurance programs provide labor information derived directly from operating statistics or indirectly by means of studies undertaken by the Board in fulfilling its responsibility to Congress for "making recommendations as to the most effective methods of providing economic security through social insurance." Several statistical series of importance in the field of labor data appear regularly in the *Social Security Bulletin* and in the *Social Security Yearbook,* an annual supplement to the *Bulletin.*[18] In addition, articles presenting the results of special analyses undertaken for administrative purposes are published from time to time in the *Bulletin.*

Under the unemployment compensation program the state agencies are required to submit quarterly reports by major industry groups and annual reports by detailed industry groups showing the monthly employment and quarterly wages of covered employees.[19] Preliminary quarterly estimates for seven broad industry groups, based on a sample including approximately 90 percent of all covered employment, are published in multilithed form within six months following the end of the quarter.[20] The coverage of small firms varies from state to state because of differences in statutory size-of-firm inclusion, varying from employers of one or more in some states to eight or more in others; and employers in highly seasonal industries may not be subject to state unemployment compensation laws because their operations are not of sufficient duration. The preliminary estimates are also subject to a small bias inherent in series based on a sample of establishments. The annual reports, published or available about one year after the close of the calendar year, avoid this limita-

[18] Available from the Superintendent of Documents.

[19] Unemployment compensation reports cover all persons whose "wages are subject to taxation for unemployment compensation purposes and no distinction in reporting is made to separate wage earners from corporate officials, executives, supervisory, and clerical personnel." To the extent that employers report the number of wage items during a given month, instead of the number of employees on the payroll for the last pay period ending in the month, double counting occurs which tends to inflate the level of employment.

[20] *Estimated Employment and Wages of Workers Covered by State Unemployment Compensation Laws,* Bureau of Employment Security, Social Security Board.

tion.[21] In the absence of manufacturing and business censuses since 1939 these annual reports provide indispensable data for benchmark and other purposes. The data are limited, however, by the coverage of the unemployment compensation program, which excludes government, railroads, and nonprofit institutions, as well as agriculture and the self-employed. Because the establishment reports are classified on a current product basis, instead of on a prewar industry basis, there arise certain problems with respect to comparability with other series.

Most of the other monthly series derived from the operating statistics of the unemployment compensation program are of indirect rather than direct relevance to labor statistics in so far as they are financial in character. However, the state data covering benefit claims, number of beneficiaries, weeks of unemployment compensated, and amount of benefits paid, by months, and collections by quarters represent significant contributions to currently available labor market information. The claim and benefit statistics are the only current state information on unemployment trends; they are limited, however, to the measurement of unemployment for the groups covered by State unemployment compensation programs and they are frequently affected by administrative action as well as by economic causes.

The statistics derived from the wage and employees records of the old age and survivors insurance program provide supplementary benchmark data and labor information not otherwise available. Quarterly and annual data on the number of applicants for employee account numbers, classified by age, sex, and race, by region and state afford detailed facts bearing upon the dynamics of employment and the labor market. Illustrative of the research possibilities in the field of old age and survivors insurance data is the development, during the past four years, of a continuous work history sample, some of the results of which are presented in the February 1944 issue of the *Social Security Bulletin*. The study was undertaken to obtain the type of information needed in the administration of the various existing social security programs and in evaluating proposals for broadening social insurance in this country. The sample covers 4 percent of the accounts of all living workers at any given time and is designed to provide data on the continuity of earnings and employment. The potentialities of

[21] Ibid., *Annual Summary*. For economy reasons, only summary data have been published for recent years. More detailed industry and state data are available upon request to the Bureau of Employment Security, Social Security Board. County data, by industry, are tabulated by most state agencies and are available generally on request.

the method, explored in the article referred to, give promise of a flow of valuable labor market information in usable statistical form. To date, the results available to the public are limited to tabulations showing the proportion of covered workers with taxable wages at some time during 1934–1941, classified by specified number of years with earnings, and by sex, with supplementary tabulations by amount of wage income in covered employment.

U. S. Employment Service. The regular employer visits by representatives of the local United States Employment Service office provide the basis for collection of labor market data needed for operating purposes. Periodically, the interviewers obtain detailed information from the employers and fill out a complete form (ES-270, Report of Current and Anticipated Employment) for each firm visited, showing the employer's current employment, anticipated requirements, number of persons employed by color and sex, data on accessions and separations, and narrative comments on employers' hiring practices, relations with the Employment Service, and training programs. These labor statistics differ from those collected by the BLS in a number of ways. Collected for operating purposes, the ES-270 (i.e., the *Employer Report*) does not purport to estimate total employment nor to cover the whole range of nonagricultural industries.[22] The underlying techniques of the ES-270 report is an essential tool of Employment Service administration and if continued in the postwar period will provide a valuable indicator as to short-range fluctuations in employment and economic conditions.

The *Labor Market* is a monthly publication of the U. S. Employment Service. It contains special studies on over-all developments in the labor market that are of current interest, in addition to analyses and data regarding U. S. Employment Service operations. Included are industry and area analyses based upon ES-270 data and other materials and a record of the changes that occur from month to month in the classification of more than 100 of the country's major labor market

[22] Generally the smaller establishments in manufacturing are not covered, and no attempt is made to cover all establishments in mining or in transportation, communication, and other public utilities; or establishments in trade and services. Establishments are currently reclassified on the basis of changes in major products, with the aim of showing employment by major current product, whereas the BLS data show employment by groups of establishments according to the prewar classification. Under the latter procedure, for example, the automobile industry is understood to mean the prewar establishments regardless of what their wartime product may have been, with new plants of automotive companies classified, however, in the aircraft or other appropriate industry group.

areas.[23] This classification system was extensively used during the war period in connection with contract letting and termination, and for similar purposes, wherever labor supply and demand considerations were of importance in the making of administrative decisions.

[23] Available from the Reports and Analysis Service, U. S. Employment Service, Washington, D. C. Additional statistical information, such as placements and other operating data of the Employment Service, is published in tabular form in the *Labor Market*, the *Manpower Review*, and the *Social Security Bulletin*.

SELECTED LIST OF PUBLICATIONS AND AUTHORS

INDEX